Faustian Bargains

The Great Game in Cuba: CIA and the Cuban Revolution

Our Man in Haiti: George de Mohrenschildt and the CIA in the Nightmare Republic

A Farewell to Justice: Jim Garrison, JFK's Assassination, and the Case That Should Have Changed History

Jim Garrison: His Life and Times, the Early Years

Hellman and Hammett: The Legendary Passion of Lillian Hellman and Dashiell Hammett

Kay Boyle: Author of Herself

Modern Times (BFI Film Classics)

In the Realm of the Senses (BFI Film Classics)

Seven Samurai (BFI Film Classics)

Literary Masterpieces: One Hundred Years of Solitude

Literary Masters: Gabriel García Márquez

Literary Topics: Magic Realism

Bob Knight: His Own Man

Natural Tendencies: A Novel

Privilege: The Enigma of Sasha Bruce

The World of Luis Buñuel: Essays in Criticism (Editor)

Big Bad Wolves: Masculinity in the American Film

The Waves at Genji's Door: Japan Through Its Cinema

Voices from the Japanese Cinema

Women and Their Sexuality in the New Film

Marilyn Monroe

Filmguide to The Battle of Algiers

FAUSTIAN BARGAINS

---

*Lyndon Johnson and Mac Wallace in
the Robber Baron Culture of Texas*

JOAN MELLEN

BLOOMSBURY

NEW YORK · LONDON · OXFORD · NEW DELHI · SYDNEY

Bloomsbury USA
An imprint of Bloomsbury Publishing Plc

1385 Broadway	50 Bedford Square
New York	London
NY 10018	WC1B 3DP
USA	UK

www.bloomsbury.com

BLOOMSBURY and the Diana logo are trademarks of Bloomsbury Publishing Plc

First published 2016

© Joan Mellen, 2016

ISBN: HB: 978-1-62040-806-3
        ePub: 978-1-62040-807-0

Library of Congress Cataloging-in-Publication Data

Names: Mellen, Joan, author.
Title: Faustian bargains: Lyndon Johnson and Mac Wallace in the robber baron
culture of Texas / Joan Mellen.
Description: New York: Bloomsbury USA, an imprint of Bloomsbury Publishing Plc, 2016.
| Includes bibliographical references.
Identifiers: LCCN 2016009706| ISBN 9781620408063 (hardback)
| ISBN 9781620408087 (paperback) | ISBN 9781620408070 (ePub)
Subjects: LCSH: Johnson, Lyndon B. (Lyndon Baines), 1908–1973—Friends and associates.
| Wallace, Mac, 1921–1971. | Legislators—United States—Biography. | United States.
Congress. Senate—Biography. | Presidents—United States—Biography. | Texas—Politics
and Government—20th century. | Political culture—Texas—History—20th century.
| Political corruption—Texas—History—20th century. | Texas—Biography.
| BISAC: BIOGRAPHY & AUTOBIOGRAPHY / Political.
Classification: LCC E847.2 .M45 2016 | DDC 328.73/092 [B]—dc23 LC record available at
https://lccn.loc.gov/2016009706

2 4 6 8 10 9 7 5 3 1

Typeset by RefineCatch Limited, Bungay, Suffolk
Printed and bound in the U.S.A. by Berryville Graphics Inc., Berryville, Virginia

For Ralph Schoenman and Mya Shone,
with gratitude, always

"Lieutenant, everyone knows what. Why don't you try to find out why?"
—DASHIELL HAMMETT, ADVICE TO
A YOUNG WRITER

"Take nothing on its looks. Take everything on evidence."
—MR. JAGGERS IN CHARLES DICKENS'
GREAT EXPECTATIONS

Contents

Timeline

August 27, 1908: Birth of Lyndon Baines Johnson in rural Stonewall, Texas, on the Pedernales River.

May 16, 1912: Birth of Josefa Johnson, younger sister of Lyndon Baines Johnson and future lover of Mac Wallace and John Douglas Kinser.

October 15, 1921: Birth of Malcolm Everett (Mac) Wallace in Mount Pleasant, Texas.

January 10, 1925: Birth of Billie Sol Estes in Abilene, Texas.

1925: The Wallace family moves to Dallas. Five surviving children are born between 1925 and 1938.

November 12, 1928: Birth of Robert Gene (Bobby) Baker in Pickens County, South Carolina.

1932: Lyndon Johnson moves to Washington, D.C., where he has been hired as secretary to newly elected U.S. congressman Richard M. Kleberg.

Fall 1934: Mac Wallace enters Woodrow Wilson High School in Dallas.

1937: Lyndon Baines Johnson is elected to serve the remainder of the term of Congressman James P. Buchanan.

April 1938: Mac Wallace injures his lumbar spine playing quarterback for Woodrow Wilson High School and requires spinal surgery.

June 2, 1939: Mac Wallace graduates from Woodrow Wilson High School.

November 3, 1939: Mac Wallace enlists in the U.S. Marine Corps at New Orleans as a private.

June 27, 1940: Stationed in Hawaii, Mac Wallace reinjures his back in a fall on the USS *Lexington*.

August 28, 1940: Mac Wallace is discharged from the Marine Corps. His medical discharge is dated September 25, 1940.

February 1, 1941: Mac Wallace enrolls at the University of Texas at Austin.

1941: Lyndon Johnson runs for the United States Senate but is defeated by Pappy "Pass the Biscuits" O'Daniel, despite the support of Herman and George Brown of Brown & Root.

December 13, 1941: Following the Japanese attack on Pearl Harbor, Mac Wallace attempts to re-enlist in the U.S. Marine Corps.

September 1943: Mac Wallace and Nora Ann Carroll meet at a University of Texas mixer.

1943–44: Mac Wallace at the University of Texas: bookkeeper of the *Cactus*, UT yearbook; member of the University Ex-Servicemen's Association; member of the Tejas Club, a non-Greek fraternity for students without financial resources; member of the Cowboys.

1943–44: Mac Wallace and Nora Ann Carroll an "item."

April 1944: Mac Wallace is elected president of the student body of the University of Texas and takes office on May 1, 1944.

July 26, 1944: Visit of Lyndon Johnson to the University of Texas campus. The event has been put together by Mac Wallace as student body president.

October 12, 1944: University of Texas President Homer Price Rainey enumerates sixteen attempts by the Board of Regents to limit academic freedom.

November 1, 1944: President Rainey is fired by the Board of Regents of the University of Texas.

November 2–4, 1944: Mac Wallace leads peaceful demonstrations in support of the reinstatement of Homer Rainey. The FBI field office at San Antonio conducts an investigation of Wallace's political beliefs and loyalty to the United States.

December 1944: Nora Ann Carroll chooses future neurologist Ted Cary over Mac Wallace to be her husband.

1944: With Lyndon Johnson's surreptitious assistance, Richard M. Kleberg is defeated in his bid for re-election by Lyndon Johnson friend John E. Lyle.

1944: Courtesy of the good offices of the president of the student body, Mac Wallace, Lyndon Johnson addresses the students.

February 1945: Nora Ann Carroll graduates from the University of Texas at Austin.

March 8, 1945: Mac Wallace resigns as president of the student body of the University of Texas and moves to New York City without graduating.

September 1945–January 1946: Mac Wallace studies for a master's degree at the New School for Social Research. October 1945: Mac Wallace takes a job as a research assistant at the National City Bank.

January 1946: Mac Wallace resigns from the National City Bank and returns to Texas to work on Homer Raincy's gubernatorial campaign.

September 1946: Mac Wallace enters the University of Texas master's program in economics, having been awarded a graduate assistantship.

1947: On June 2, 1947, Mac Wallace graduates from the University of Texas with a bachelor's degree in business administration and a major in economics.

Mid-June 1947: Mac Wallace meets Mary Andre Dubose Barton.

July 4, 1947: Mac Wallace marries Mary Andre.

August 1947: Mac Wallace is awarded a master's degree in economics from the University of Texas.

September 1947: Mac Wallace enters the Ph.D. program at Columbia University in New York while teaching philosophy at the downtown Brooklyn campus of Long Island University.

October 1947: Mary Andre becomes pregnant.

1948: Lyndon Baines Johnson steals the Texas election to the United States Senate defeating former governor Coke Stevenson.

Spring 1948: Mac Wallace withdraws from Columbia University but teaches as a part-time tutor at City College. He signs on nights as an itinerant longshoreman on the New York docks to earn extra money. Mac Wallace and Nora Ann Carroll are reunited in New York City.

June 26, 1948: Birth of Michael Alvin Wallace.

June 29, 1948: Mary Andre files for divorce from Mac Wallace.

August 24, 1948: Mary Andre withdraws her divorce petition.

Academic Year 1948–49: Mac Wallace is an assistant professor at North Carolina State College at Raleigh.

September 19, 1949: With the assistance of Lyndon Johnson and Cliff Carter, Mac Wallace is employed at the U.S. Department of Agriculture, Finance Department, as an agricultural economist. He lives in Alexandria, Virginia, with his wife, Andre, and toddler son, Michael.

November 1949: The FBI begins its second security check on Mac Wallace.

November 1, 1949: Alice Meredithe Wallace is conceived.

1950: Mac Wallace has an affair with Josefa Johnson, who is the lover of Austin golf pro and would-be actor John Douglas Kinser.

April 4, 1950: Mac Wallace passes the FBI's scrutiny and is declared "Eligible on Loyalty."

August 1, 1950: Birth of Alice Meredithe Wallace.

August 10, 1950: Andre Wallace files for divorce in Travis County, Texas. Michael is two years old, Meredithe one week old.

1950–51: During this period, Andre Wallace has an affair with John Douglas Kinser.

October 11, 1951: Mac Wallace returns to Austin having received the promise of a job with the State Department. He is taking his paid leave.

October 22, 1951: Mac Wallace shoots John Douglas Kinser. An hour later, Wallace is arrested at the Marshall Ford Dam.

October 23, 1951: *Habeas corpus* hearing organized by Mac Wallace's friend William E. Carroll, younger brother of Nora Ann. Released, Wallace is immediately rearrested and charged with murder.

October 25, 1951: Mac Wallace is released from Travis County jail under bond posted by M. E. Ruby and J. E. Greenhaw, both of Hays County, Texas, and friends of Mac's father, Alvin J. Wallace.

October 1951: The Office of Naval Intelligence does its first security investigation of Mac Wallace.

November 2, 1951: Mac Wallace is indicted for the murder of John Douglas Kinser.

January 31, 1952: Mac Wallace writes to FBI Director J. Edgar Hoover requesting FBI assistance at his trial.

January 31, 1952: Mac Wallace's mother, Alice Marie Riddle Wallace, is committed to the Terrell State Hospital for the mentally incompetent.

February 1, 1952: In Washington, D.C., Mac Wallace resigns from his job at the Department of Agriculture.

February 6, 1952: J. Edgar Hoover replies to Mac Wallace's letter and request.

February 18, 1952: Trial of Mac Wallace for the murder of John Douglas Kinser begins.

February 28, 1952: Mac Wallace is convicted of murder with malice aforethought for the murder of John Douglas Kinser yet is awarded a suspended sentence.

April 29, 1952: Mary Andre Wallace separates again from Mac Wallace.

May 1, 1952: Mac Wallace is hired by Jonco Aircraft in Oklahoma and files for divorce from Mary Andre.

June 6, 1952: Mac Wallace is granted a divorce from Mary Andre Wallace and is awarded custody of their two children, Michael and Meredithe.

September 22, 1952: Mac Wallace's arrest record is sent by the Austin Police Department to Luscombe Airplane Corporation, a wholly owned subsidiary of Texas Engineering and Manufacturing Company (TEMCO) owned by Lyndon Johnson supporter D. H. Byrd.

November 15, 1952: Mac Wallace is charged with being "drunk in a judge's office" in Georgetown, Williamson County, Texas.

December 21, 1952: Mac and Andre Wallace remarry in Dallas.

1952–54: Mac Wallace is employed by the Jonco Aircraft Corporation in Shawnee, Oklahoma.

1953: Mac Wallace is a lecturer at Oklahoma Baptist University at Shawnee, Oklahoma.

1954–1961: Mac Wallace is employed by TEMCO Electronics and Missiles Division, Garland, Texas, with a SECRET security clearance.

1955: Lyndon Johnson becomes majority leader of the United States Senate.

February 28, 1957: Mac Wallace appears with his lawyer, Polk Shelton, in court in Austin and his record is wiped clean, his murder conviction erased.

July 12, 1957: The first full Office of Naval Intelligence report on Mac Wallace and the first attempt by the Navy to "revoke and deny" his SECRET security clearance.

December 10, 1958: Mac and Andre Wallace are divorced again.

July 10, 1959: The Office of Naval Intelligence releases its report on Mac Wallace.

December 31, 1959: Mac and Andre Wallace remarry and buy a house at 2817 Crest Ridge Drive, Dallas.

February 8, 1960: Another Office of Naval Intelligence report is filed. Supplements will be submitted on April 25, 1960, and December 28, 1960.

November 17, 1960, Mary Andre files for divorce from Mac Wallace, which is granted on January 30, 1961. This will be their final divorce.

January 17, 1961: Agriculture official Henry Marshall announces he will no longer approve specious schemes for the purchase of cotton allotments by Billie Sol Estes, a Pecos, Texas, farmer.

February 2, 1961: Mac Wallace is arrested in Dallas on charges of drunk and disorderly conduct.

February 19, 1961: Mac Wallace quits his job at TEMCO and is hired by Ling Electronics in Anaheim, California.

June 3, 1961: Murder of Henry Marshall in Robertson County, Texas.

July 20, 1961: The Office of Naval Intelligence requests another investigation of Mac Wallace and a nineteen-page report is subsequently issued.

December 25, 1961: Sudden death of Josefa Johnson.

1962: The Office of Naval Intelligence sends the FBI to interview Andre Wallace in Timpson, Texas.

January 1962: Mac Wallace meets Virginia Ledgerwood, a student majoring in education at Fullerton State College.

March 29, 1962: Billie Sol Estes is arrested by a U.S. Marshal and begins a series of trials that culminate in his incarceration on federal charges.

May 1962: A Robertson County grand jury inquires into the "suicide" of Henry Marshall.

September 1962: The Office of Naval Intelligence orders another investigation of Mac Wallace. The report is issued on December 27, 1962.

January 24, 1963: Billie Sol Estes is sentenced to eight years in the state penitentiary and on April 15, 1963, to fifteen years in federal prison.

January 1963: Virginia Ledgerwood, working at Ling Electronics, becomes pregnant.

April 20, 1963: Mac Wallace and Virginia Ledgerwood are married in Baja California, Mexico.

May 31, 1963: Mac Wallace is arrested for driving under the influence in Rusk County, Texas; he pleads guilty and spends three days in jail.

June 1963: Michael Wallace moves to California to live with his father.

July–August 1963: Nora Ann Carroll visits Mac Wallace in California.

October 17, 1963: Elizabeth Elaine Wallace is born to Mac Wallace and Virginia Ledgerwood Wallace.

November 1, 1963: Virginia Ledgerwood Wallace leaves Mac Wallace and moves back to her parents' home two weeks after Elaine is born.

November 22, 1963: Assassination of President John F. Kennedy. Lyndon Johnson takes office as President of the United States.

September 18, 1964: Mac Wallace's security clearance is lowered from SECRET to CONFIDENTIAL as the result of thirteen years of effort by the Office of Naval Intelligence.

January 9, 1967: Trial of Bobby Baker in Washington, D.C., on nine criminal counts ranging from income tax evasion to larceny and fraud in his business operations and conspiracy.

June 8, 1967: Unprovoked and premeditated Israeli attack on the USS *Liberty*, a noncombatant surveillance ship flying the American flag.

March 31, 1968: Lyndon Baines Johnson announces that he will not run for re-election.

1969: Mac Wallace is asked by Ling Electronics to take three months off to solve his drinking problem.

August 1, 1969: Mac Wallace separates from Virginia Wallace for good and leaves Placentia, California, to return to Texas.

1965–71: Billie Sol Estes in prison, serving the first of two separate terms.

1969: Mac Wallace drives back to Texas, where he works as an assistant manager at the Robinson-Wallace Insurance Agency in Dallas and teaches part time at the Texas A&M, Arlington campus.

1970: Bobby Baker goes to federal prison on fraud and other charges.

February 16, 1970: Divorce of Mac and Virginia Wallace is final.

April 27, 1970: Mac Wallace writes his will.

January 7, 1971: Death of Mac Wallace after visiting his daughter Meredithe and meeting his first grandchild when his car hits a bridge abutment south of Pittsburg, Texas, on a clear night.

July 1971: Billie Sol Estes is released from prison after serving six years.

January 22, 1973: Death of Lyndon Baines Johnson.

July 11, 1979: Estes is convicted on two felony counts of conspiring to defraud investors and concealing assets from the Internal Revenue Service.

August 7, 1979: Estes is sentenced to another ten years for fraud.

March 1984: Billie Sol Estes testifies before a Robertson County, Texas, grand jury under immunity and accuses Lyndon Johnson, Cliff Carter, and Mac Wallace of having conspired in the murder of Henry Marshall.

June 23, 1992: Death of former Texas Ranger and U.S. Marshal Clint Peoples.

1998: Press conference is held in Dallas by John Fraser (J) Harrison to announce that an unidentified fingerprint taken from a carton on the sixth floor of the Texas School Book Depository on November 22, 1963, belongs to Mac Wallace.

May 25, 2005: Death of J Harrison.

May 14, 2013: Death of Billie Sol Estes.

Introduction

It may be that no president has suffered more of the slings and arrows of an ambiguous reputation than Lyndon Johnson. By 1968, when he decided not to run for re-election, Johnson was excoriated as the architect of the catastrophic acceleration of the Vietnam War that John F. Kennedy had unceasingly resisted. Many noticed that Johnson was patently guilty of the very "extremism" for which his propaganda machine had blamed his 1964 opponent, Arizona senator Barry Goldwater.

In that campaign, Johnson had had himself painted as a tireless devotee of peace. This mythology was symbolized in a campaign advertisement depicting a child plucking the petals from a daisy, followed by the image of a nuclear explosion, with a voiceover by Lyndon Johnson declaring that "we must love each other" or die. Famously, fifty-eight thousand Americans died in Vietnam, along with more than two million Vietnamese. Recent evidence has emerged that it was Johnson who in 1965 began the full-scale bombing of Cambodia, an outrage that many have believed should be laid at the door of Richard Nixon and Henry Kissinger.

In the years following his death in 1973, his biographers have sought to paint Lyndon Johnson as a master of "statesmanship," the majority leader—and then President—who knew better than anyone else how to maneuver bills into law, who could create a constituency of senators as no one had before him. As President, Johnson was lauded for assuming the mantle of Franklin Roosevelt and struggling to eradicate poverty and injustice through a series of policies known as the "Great Society." If Johnson was sometimes intemperate, and given to such vulgarities as exposing a surgical scar across his belly that he claimed assumed the shape of the country of Vietnam, he was to be praised for his unrelenting efforts to address the needs of the poor.

This is a chronicle of the dark side of Lyndon Johnson and of the collateral damage wrought by his actions. It relocates Johnson as a man who virtually began in national politics by selling government contracts, not only to the most powerful of his Texas friends, Herman and George Brown, proprietors of the Brown & Root construction company, but to a whole troop of Texas contractors who prospered under the umbrella of Johnson's largesse. Johnson emerged from government service with a fortune of twenty-five million dollars, according to information uncovered by *LIFE* magazine researcher Holland McCombs working on an exposé of Johnson in 1963–65. Johnson elevated himself into being the wealthiest man to occupy the nation's highest office up to that time. That many of the realities of his service had to be suppressed, and that the memoir of his presidency was studded with false-hoods, were small enough price to pay.

Yet dissenters on the subject of Lyndon Johnson's sincerity and effectiveness have made their views known over the years. One was Dr. Martin Luther King Jr., who, in disgust at how little Johnson's policies were actually delivering, declined Johnson's invitation to visit the White House on the occasion of the 1965 passage of the Voting Rights Act. Dr. King traveled to Selma, Alabama, instead. The surviving sailors of the USS *Liberty*, few and dwindling in numbers, have over the years since 1967, when their ship was attacked by a foreign power, lamented the political durability of a Lyndon Johnson whose insincerity and callousness have largely been kept secret from the general public by the zealous guardians of Johnson's good name. Their story will be told here.

Among Johnson's victims was a farmer named Billie Sol Estes, whose story has been all but ignored by Johnson's biographers. For Estes, Johnson was a man who sponsored acts of murder when his reputation was threatened by the presence of inconvenient witnesses. Like Estes, another Johnson acolyte, secretary to the Senate majority leader Robert Gene (Bobby) Baker, was aban-doned by Johnson when testimony about their close relationship threatened to expose Johnson's participation in Baker's scams.

Another casualty of involvement with Lyndon Johnson was a young Texan named Malcolm Everett (Mac) Wallace, whose connection to Johnson led to his being reborn after his premature death as a murderous urban legend ranging over the Texas countryside. It was claimed by a troop of authors with no credible evidence that Wallace, on orders from Johnson, had even partici-pated in the assassination of John F. Kennedy.

Mac Wallace was but one case in point of what happened to those who fell under Lyndon Johnson's sway. *Faustian Bargains* becomes Mac Wallace's story as well as Johnson's, a cautionary tale as Wallace comes to represent the many young men whose lives were diminished by their association with Lyndon Johnson. An intriguing figure, Wallace provides a lens through which to view Lyndon Johnson's dark side. Although their lives rarely intersected, they were united in death. Wallace opens a window onto a side of Johnson's life few have dared explore.

The year 2014 inaugurated a full-court press designed to restore Lyndon Johnson's credibility. "Nobody wanted that war less than Lyndon Johnson," his daughter Luci Baines Johnson declared on the front page of the *New York Times*. "He was struggling to fulfill our commitment to these people," added her older sister, Lynda Bird Johnson Robb, referring to the Vietnamese people, although in reality the "commitment" was to the leaders of South Vietnam whom the U.S. government had thrust into power and who enjoyed scant popular support.

The *Washington Post* concluded a five-part series on May 22, 2014, with the contention that Johnson was not even truly a Texan. Rather, he was to be viewed as a resident of Washington, D.C. So, despite the thousands of pages already chronicling in minute detail the comings and goings of Lyndon Johnson, we might reassess the man and reexamine the assertion that "LBJ's unprecedented and ambitious domestic vision changed the nation." It may be time to reevaluate whether Lyndon Johnson was a figure deserving of respect and credibility as the mainstream press and Johnson's biographers (with the exception of Ronnie Dugger) and family would have us believe.

Much has been written about Lyndon Johnson, by those who worked for him and by independent biographers, particularly Robert A. Caro. To date, Caro has produced four substantial volumes; and I was encouraged in pursuing this project by the surprising absence in Caro's work covering the time period in question, of two significant figures in Johnson's life.

Billie Sol Estes is entirely absent, even as Estes formed a necessary spoke to Johnson's wheel during the years of his government service as he amassed his considerable fortune. Mac Wallace, whom Estes accused of committing acts of murder on Johnson's instructions, likewise never appears. Yet Estes and Wallace, and Estes in particular, played a considerable role in providing history with a portrait of Lyndon Baines Johnson.

Biography, of course, is inevitably selective, as it must be. This chronicle of the hidden nooks and crannies of Lyndon Johnson's life in the shadows may yield some surprising realities.

CHAPTER 1

Texans

"Who is to give Texas character?"
—SAM HOUSTON

Lyndon Johnson was born on August 27, 1908, in Stonewall, Texas, on the Pedernales River. Only a little more than fifty years earlier Texas had been a territory that quickly devolved into a commonwealth, a country in its own right. "Tecas" had been settled by renegades, people in flight from the law, from creditors and law enforcement, who scrawled "GTT," "Gone to Texas," defiantly on their doors. Safely in the new republic, out of the reach of the law, a law unto themselves, they bred a culture with no small addiction to lying, thieving, slandering, and betrayal.

Foreign travelers, appalled, chronicled the Texas of the mid-nineteenth century with dismay. One noted, in horror, "a country filled with habitual liars, drunkards, blasphemers and slanderers; sanguinary gamesters and cold-blooded assassins." Another visitor found those who had settled Texas to be "quarrelsome, rude, boastful and vulgar, men with the bark on." Nor did only foreigners take exception to the absence of moral restraint and civilized social life in Texas. In the first volume of his *History of Texas from 1685 to 1892*, Texas historian John Henry Brown conceded that the republic was plagued by "the avarice of selfish and dishonest men and unscrupulous swindlers and forgers."

Anarchy prevailed as a distinct Texan character emerged in the period of the republic. Violence lurked in the very air and the ubiquity of guns—and Bowie knives—was a signature of social life. In the years to come, Texans would enlist in the U.S. military more profusely than people from any other part of the country.

The exaggerating and bragging gave way to the creation of legends, among them the heroism of Davy Crockett, who in reality did not perish as any sort of hero of the Alamo. The supposedly noble last stand at the Alamo had been opposed by General Sam Houston, who did his best to save those stubbornly determined on their martyrdom.

It was from this culture that Lyndon Johnson emerged. For a time, he claimed that he had been born in a log cabin, a legatee of Abraham Lincoln. It was not so. The log cabin in question was a campsite that had been headquarters for a cattle driving operation in the 1870s and '80s. No one had been born there despite Johnson's claims to the local Texas press. When Holland McCombs did his research into Johnson's background for *LIFE* magazine in 1964, he discovered that Lyndon Johnson was born in a "small shack" with a slanting roof and a sagging porch perched on a slope leading up from a muddy river of no consequence in the Texas Hill Country.

Johnson's mother, Rebekah, was a college graduate with ambitions for her clever son, who from his early childhood she was either unwilling or unable to restrain. Robert A. Caro describes the restlessness of Lyndon Johnson's early childhood in the first volume of his multivolume chronicle of Johnson's life, *The Years of Lyndon Johnson: The Path to Power.* Constantly running away, Lyndon, Caro quotes one of Johnson's childhood friends, "was overpowering if he didn't get his own way." Yet her heritage marked her, and her son, as legatees of Texas history with a background of consequence. Rebekah Johnson's grandfather, George Washington Baines, a leading Baptist clergyman, had baptized General Sam Houston himself. There is an extant letter from that singular hero of Texas history to "Brother Baines," which closes: "Mrs. Houston joins in affectionate regards to Sister Baines, yourself and family."

Lyndon Johnson's maternal grandfather, Captain Joseph Wilson Baines, served with honor in the Confederate cavalry, and later as Secretary of State of Texas. The progressive example of Sam Houston, who as governor of Texas was to refuse to sign the Ordinance of Secession preceding the Civil War, was opposed to Texas remaining a slave state. Houston was to sacrifice his political career for his principles. But such a notion did not take root among Lyndon Johnson's forebears.

His father, Sam Johnson, was a state legislator and a severe alcoholic, who Rebekah married in spite of herself. He was physically attractive and charming, as Robert Caro notes, a populist who was no friend to the banks, railroads, and oil companies, and who never lost an election. Sam Johnson was also a man with a gift for friendships, which is how Sam Rayburn came to be Lyndon Johnson's mentor and supporter. Sam took his eldest son to sessions of the legislature from the time he was about ten years old.

At their first meeting Rebekah interviewed Sam Johnson for an article being written by her father, Joseph Wilson Baines, a lawyer and editor of the McKinney, Texas, *Advocate.* (For a time Baines occupied the same seat in the Texas legislature that his son-in-law Sam Johnson came to hold.)

"I asked him lots of questions," Rebekah would remember, "but he was pretty cagey and I couldn't pin him down. I was awfully provoked with that man." She married him anyway, a loud cursing man with a fierce temper.

Lyndon Johnson was one of five children. A contrary child, he refused to do his homework or his chores, so that neighbors believed that his mother needed advice on how to control her older son. He "played pranks" like flipping the hat off a friend's head with his fishing pole and catapulting it into the river. He spat at a teacher, and she locked him into an icebox, an anecdote of Johnson's childhood ferreted out by Holland McCombs. This teacher suggested that Mrs. Johnson tie Lyndon to the bedpost, advice his overindulgent mother preferred not to take. Johnson's childhood cruelties are recounted in the chapter "A Born Manic-Depressive" in D. Jablow Hershman's *Power Beyond Reason: The Mental Collapse of Lyndon Johnson.*

Having disdained the restrictions of higher education for as long as he could, Lyndon Johnson went to San Marcos College, a school freshly accredited. Here he stole his first election, manipulating elections to the student council, as in later years he freely admitted. Johnson termed the political operation he created at San Marcos "Hitlerized" and "a pretty vicious operation." He had no interest in his course work, but learned early how power worked, creating a group loyal to himself.

He was already a man to be feared. One professor at the University of Texas explained his unwillingness that his name be used to Johnson's biographer, Robert Caro. "They could punish me, you know."

Having graduated from San Marcos, with few prospects, Johnson became a Houston high school teacher. He taught public speaking and was adviser to the debating club. Fiercely competitive, he was single-minded in his persistence. Winning was already everything.

With energy to spare, Johnson contributed his efforts to local political campaigns, where he came to the notice of one of the scions of the legendary King Ranch. The ranch was run by Robert J. (Bob) Kleberg Jr., the younger son of founder Richard King's daughter Alice Gertrudis King Kleberg and her husband, R. J. Kleberg. Bob Kleberg's older brother, Richard, had not been suited for managing the ranch: He lacked the vision, the dedication to hard work, and the persistence. "Mr. Dick," as Richard Kleberg was known, was handsome, witty, and a playboy.

"Mr. Dick" dabbled in many subjects, from genetics to Latin America. He was an expert rifle and pistol shot and a dashing horseman. He was rugged and yet loveable, a man, as his son-in-law told Holland McCombs, "with a heart as big as the open spaces of the [sic] King Ranch." Descendant of a line of patrons, born into privilege, with what passed for an aristocratic lineage in Texas, Dick Kleberg was naive about other people and their motives.

Kleberg had studied law at the University of Texas at Austin. With no appetite for the actual practice of law, he decided at the turn of the 1930s to run for the U.S. Congress for the Fourteenth District. His campaign manager was Roy Miller, a lobbyist for the Texas Gulf Sulphur Corporation. Whether Dick Kleberg was encouraged to seek national office by his brother Bob—who preferred to run King Ranch unimpeded—or by Miller, or by a local politician named Welly K. Hopkins, he aimed to fill a vacancy left upon the death of Republican Harry McLeary Wurzbach. That Kleberg was a Democrat was a reflex of his being a son of the South rather than by the force of his convictions.

When twenty-two-year-old Lyndon Johnson was recommended to Kleberg to serve as his assistant, Kleberg invited him to Corpus Christi for an interview. Dick Kleberg's mother, Alice Gertrudis King Kleberg, took an instant dislike to Lyndon Johnson, who was already obsequious and adept at flattery. Emphatically, according to Robert J. Kleberg Jr.'s daughter, Helenita, she advised her son not to hire him. Dick Kleberg ignored her advice.

South Texas rancher J. Evetts Haley in his polemical biography of Lyndon Johnson tells the story of how Johnson intersected with a San Antonio political group called the Citizens' League, a "whale of a good local machine." As Haley recounts the incident, the Citizens' League offered their support to both Kleberg and his opponent, Carl Wright Johnson of San Antonio. Whoever would contribute four thousand dollars to the Citizens' League, along with the promise that the league could choose who was appointed postmaster, would gain its support. Carl Wright Johnson turned them down. Carl Johnson enjoyed the favor of the Bexar County political organization, which included San Antonio, and was confident of victory. Kleberg, after all, had never held public office of any kind.

Kleberg agreed to pay the four thousand dollars, which Lyndon Johnson delivered to the Citizens' League. The league kept its promise and supported Kleberg, who won the election. The post office appointment duly went to one of its leaders, who held the post for many years. Loose with the facts and short on accuracy, Haley places this incident at the time of Richard Kleberg's first campaign. In fact, it is true, but, according to Helenita Kleberg, it occurred during a later campaign. None of Lyndon Johnson's biographers mentions the incident.

In 1931, having defeated Carl Wright Johnson, Richard Kleberg went to Washington in the company of his lanky new secretary, Lyndon Baines Johnson. They traveled together by train and even for one night shared a room at the Mayflower Hotel. Kleberg encouraged his friends to "help Lyndon get to know his way around." Among them was John Nance Garner, the speaker of the House. Later Kleberg remembered how he would "scare poor Lyndon with some of my butt-headed stubbornness, and refusal to play the game," by which Kleberg apparently meant his intransigence when it came to New Deal legislation.

Lyndon Johnson ran Richard Kleberg's office as if he were the congressman. "Kleberg didn't do anything," said Luther Jones, in charge of Kleberg's Corpus Christi office. Johnson mailed letters "signed" by Kleberg without first showing them to the congressman. He even wrote letters to Alice Kleberg, signing her son Dick's name without his knowledge. Johnson later acknowledged that Kleberg "was not very smart, and his interests were not in any drudgery."

"This is Dick Kleberg," Johnson said to whoever telephoned. He was a talented mimic. Dick Kleberg was more often than not on the golf course while Johnson chose a good number of his political positions. Franklin Delano Roosevelt was inaugurated on March 4, 1933, and almost immediately Johnson hitched his wagon to Roosevelt's star.

On New Deal–related legislation, Johnson immediately attempted to offer Richard Kleberg's support. Kleberg, however, took sufficient interest in some of these matters to speak for himself. Scion of the greatest landowner in the United States, he opposed several Roosevelt programs as "socialism, very dangerous." Kleberg announced that he would be voting against the Agricultural Adjustment Act because it was "socialistic." He planned to vote against the Social Security Act, which was also "socialistic" and a law that would "destroy the country." Fiercely ambitious, with an eye toward gaining Roosevelt's favor, Johnson threatened to quit. Reluctant to lose the services of his energetic assistant, Kleberg voted "aye" on both the agriculture bill in 1933 and social security in 1934. Johnson soon obtained the conservative Kleberg's permission to campaign for liberal Texan Maury Maverick, who was running for a seat in the U.S. House of Representatives in 1934 as Johnson continued to build alliances.

In 1935, Johnson left Kleberg's office and, on Sam Rayburn's recommendation, was appointed to head the National Youth Administration (NYA) for Texas. He persuaded Kleberg to hire his feckless younger brother, Sam Houston Johnson, who misused funds, even as Kleberg placed him on the King Ranch payroll as a "public relations consultant." Sam Houston Johnson threw Kleberg's bills into the trash, with the result that a school board back in Kleberg County, Texas, filed suit to force the congressman to pay school taxes that were in arrears. Kleberg was obliged to pay a tailor's bill for two hundred dollars for one of Sam Houston Johnson's suits. And there was a "sexual liaison" in the office that Robert Caro writes "infuriated Kleberg's wife."

Back in Texas, people were whispering about Lyndon Johnson: "Don't get in his way. He'll climb over you." Running the National Youth Administration for Texas, Johnson commandeered Works Progress Administration furniture. A local called him an "overbearing big shot" on his way up.

In 1937, Texas congressman James P. Buchanan died suddenly. Eleven candidates declared for the primary, among them Lyndon Johnson. Johnson had befriended former state senator and lawyer Alvin J. Wirtz and on the strength of that alliance, Johnson was elected to the U.S. Congress. Johnson at once set forth on a course of treating public office as a commodity for his personal profit, as if elected office were a financial asset.

Almost immediately, Johnson was appointed to the House Naval Affairs Committee, on the recommendation of President Roosevelt, who argued that Johnson would "be a great help on naval affairs." He told Chairman Carl Vinson that he wanted to see Lyndon put on the committee. Johnson began having regular breakfasts at the White House.

Toward the dispensing of government contracts, Johnson took a free-wheeling approach. A Texas architect named Arthur Fehr was appalled when Johnson urged him to break the law by filing for a project with more than one federal agency. Fehr protested that this was dishonest. Johnson then advised him to "go get yourself another architect and go file it with the other agency." Fehr refused to participate in this double-dealing scheme.

Finally, Fehr was eliminated from the project entirely. "As cold a cutter as you ever saw" was Fehr's judgment of Lyndon Johnson. Years later when Fehr revealed this story to Holland McCombs he requested that he not be quoted by name.

Johnson's most significant action as a congressman was his shepherding of the second contract for the massive Marshall Ford Dam through Congress on behalf of Herman and George Brown, the proprietors of Texas construction company Brown & Root. Later George Brown would spin the half-true story that the contract had been done before Lyndon Johnson entered Congress. Brown had neglected to mention that the contract had proceeded in two stages; Lyndon Johnson had been instrumental in the second stage, which involved overcoming the obstacle that the federal government could finance a project only on government land. The government owned no land in Texas because under the 1845 annexation agreement the Republic of Texas, unlike every other territory, refused to cede any public lands to the United States. At once, Lyndon Johnson gained the (almost) lifelong support of Herman and George Brown.

R. M. Dixon, head of the Texas Board of Water Engineers, and a consulting engineer, recalled, "Most everyone in those days considered that Lyndon was the same as a major stockholder in the Brown and Root organization. His crime was the overseeing of taxpayers' money into the coffers of government contractors." Dixon added: "Though it's hard to prove by signed and sealed contracts, everywhere Brown & Root's money went, there was Lyndon also . . . Lyndon is supposed to have got his first big money from some of the extras that Brown & Root got from the government on the Marshall Ford Dam project . . . He's got money all around, but you never find his name anywhere. How do you manage that?"

Lyndon Johnson and Herman and George Brown entered into a symbiotic relationship, the most lucrative of the Faustian bargains of this story. "Remember that I am for you, right or wrong," George Brown wrote to Johnson on October 27, 1939, flush with the victory of the Marshall Ford Dam, "and it makes no difference whether I think you are right or wrong. If you want it, I am for it 100%."

In a letter that could not have been authored by tough-minded Herman Brown, George added, "In the past I have not been very timid about asking you to do favors for me and hope you will not get any timidity if you have anything at all that you think I can or should do." According to Brown crony, and Lyndon Johnson supporter, Ambassador George C. McGhee, Lyndon Johnson called George Brown every day of his life.

The Marshall Ford Dam contract was followed by an even juicier plum. In 1940, the Browns received the lion's share of the federal contract for the building of a Corpus Christi Naval Air Training Center. As a member of the House Naval Affairs Committee, Johnson arranged the contract, while Congressman Richard Kleberg helped secure the assignment for Brown & Root. Kleberg "actively collaborated," according to the *Corpus Christi Caller*. Brown & Root had never built a military installation. "We always took the attitude that we could do anything in the world," said Brown & Root's chief designer, Albert Sheppard. "It just took a little longer when it was impossible."

The Navy was skeptical and insisted that the government include Henry Kaiser in the deal. Kaiser had entered the construction business in the same year as Herman Brown, 1914. After a decade, he had diversified into pipeline construction and dam building. In the 1930s, Kaiser, sometimes on his own, or as part of the so-called Six Companies, helped build the Hoover (Boulder), Bonneville, and Grand Coulee dams. Kaiser had greater notoriety and respectability than Brown & Root, and it was Kaiser's participation on the Corpus Christi Naval Air Station that persuaded the Navy to go ahead.

In a story told in *Builders: The Story of Herman and George R. Brown*, the biography of the Brown brothers by Joseph A. Pratt and Christopher J. Castaneda, the Navy instructed George Brown to forge the agreement with Kaiser participating at 50 percent. Instead Brown negotiated with Kaiser, offering him 25 percent with the incentive that Kaiser need not provide men or materials, just his name. Kaiser in turn asked for 75 percent. Affecting outrage, George Brown gathered up his papers and prepared to leave. Kaiser then agreed to Brown's terms, and Kaiser took 25 percent. Kaiser's participation was listed under the name of the Columbia Construction Company. The Navy had preferred that Kaiser build the naval base, but Brown & Root became the chief contractor.

The bluff was Brown & Root standard operating procedure. To retain Brown & Root's seven percent investment tax credit, Armco Steel, on whose board Herman Brown sat, did the direct lobbying with Lyndon Johnson. Construction began in 1940. It would become the largest naval air training center in the world. At the ceremony celebrating the contract, Lyndon Johnson was pictured, Holland McCombs was told, with his arm around one of the Brown brothers. When McCombs searched, he discovered that all the photographs taken on that occasion had been destroyed.

The Navy allocated thirty million dollars for the Corpus Christi construction. With auxiliary installations and outlying fields, the "cost plus" that forever after would grace Brown & Root's government contracts, the final figure topped one hundred million dollars. Out of the Corpus Christi naval station emerged Brown Shipbuilding Company, which would come away after World War Two with having completed $357,100,000 worth of work for the Navy. As for the quality of the work of Brown & Root, so long as Herman Brown remained at the helm, it was nonpareil, exemplary.

Already restless in Congress, Lyndon Johnson decided in 1941 to run for the United States Senate. Herman Brown contributed more than one hundred thousand dollars. Brown & Root executives received "bonuses" that they dutifully dispensed to the Johnson campaign. On the Brown & Root books, these were listed as "business expenses," "attorneys' fees," and "company bonuses." The checks were written to employees at a Brown & Root subsidiary, Victoria Gravel, then delivered in cash to the Johnson people.

A five-thousand-dollar check was made out to J. O. Corwin Jr. of Victoria Gravel. Under oath, during the ensuing Internal Revenue Service investigation, Corwin admitted he had mailed half of it to the Johnson campaign headquarters. Another check went to the "Lyndon Johnson Club." A Brown & Root Vice President received a bonus for thirty thousand dollars that went to the Johnson campaign.

Johnson's supporters fanned out all over Texas using blackmail and intimidation. In a pattern Lyndon Johnson would adopt for the rest of his career, he hid behind intermediaries. To secure local Texas press support, in a rare example that came to light, Johnson sent his uncle, Clarence Martin, a judge, to call on John Sliney, the editor of the *Odessa American* newspaper. They retired to the editor's private office where Martin made his pitch. Odessa was competing with Midland over the installation of an air base. Midland had the advantage since it already had housing available for both officers and enlisted men. Odessa had requested federal funding to build similar housing, the better for the town to compete for the air base on a level playing field.

"If you support Lyndon, you will get the housing project," Judge Martin told Sliney, and the newspaper would prosper. If the paper didn't endorse Lyndon Johnson, Martin made clear, Odessa would not get the housing funds. Editor Sliney's response appeared on June 25, 1941, in a column titled "Kicking Around the Basin."

"If we ever want any federal money out here, he's a good man to have on our side," Sliney wrote. "Personally, I feel like that federal money is part mine, just as much as it is Mr. Johnson's or Mr. Roosevelt's . . . I'm hanged if I'll be bamboozled into voting their way to get my hands on a little of our money."

Sliney added: "Rugged individualism has always been a Texas trait. We're loyal to the administration in every respect, but we do reserve the right to do our own thinking and voting." The *Odessa American* endorsed Johnson's opponent. "You vote for whomever you please for your own reasons," John Sliney told his readers. The Odessa housing project received no federal support. Later, Johnson encountered Sliney at a barbecue he was hosting. Recognizing Sliney, Johnson's face "hardened," as if to say, "What the hell are YOU doing here?"

In the 1941 election to the U.S. Senate, Johnson presented himself as a Roosevelt supporter, while his opponent, W. Lee "Pappy" O'Daniel, campaigned with a hillbilly band and posed as a populist, a friend of the people. O'Daniel had replied to the question of what he would do when he got to Washington with the same answer he had given in 1938 when asked what he would do when he got to the governor's mansion in Austin: "I guess I'll just pass the biscuits." Their political positions were similar. Lyndon Johnson spent some $750,000, and he lost to O'Daniel by 1,311 votes.

The illegality of Brown & Root's contributions to Johnson's 1941 campaign came to light when the collector of internal revenue for the First District of Texas, Frank Scofield, scrutinized Brown & Root's tax returns. What happened next was injustice, Texas style. Soon after, Scofield was framed for soliciting political contributions from members of his staff. Although acquitted of the charge, Scofield was so sickened by the experience that he resigned from government service. His more cooperative successor, Robert W. (Bob) Phinney, who was later to serve Lyndon Johnson in other capacities, moved the Brown & Root files from their fireproof home to a Quonset hut, which caught fire on June 5, 1953, destroying the incriminating records.

In Washington, Brown & Root lawyer and Johnson ally former Undersecretary of the Interior (a position he resigned in May 1944) Alvin Wirtz accompanied Lyndon Johnson to visit President Franklin Roosevelt, whose 1940 campaign Herman Brown had financed in Texas—although Brown despised every New Deal policy and hated Roosevelt for helping "unions and Negroes." Their purpose was to decrease the penalties assessed to Brown & Root for the illegal campaign contributions. The next day, Roosevelt called in Assistant Secretary of the Treasury Elmer Irey.

In 1944, when the matter of the illegal contributions was finally settled, the penalty assessed to Brown & Root had shrunk from $1,593,272 to a trim $372,000. Brown & Root continued to march to its own drumbeat, ignoring the restrictions on campaign contributions; they contributed an unreported $25,000 to Texas governor Ben Ramsey's campaign for the Texas State Senate and also financed Johnson's 1941 campaign for Congress.

During World War Two, the symbiotic relationship between Lyndon Johnson and Herman and George Brown flourished. When Johnson sought to secure newsprint scarce in wartime for the *Dallas Times Herald,* which had endorsed him, he went to Southland Paper Mills, a Brown & Root subsidiary. Don MacIver, a one-time business editor for the rival *Dallas Morning News,* later revealed that the *Times Herald* had supported Johnson and so had gained access to more newsprint than anybody else. The *Dallas Morning News* was "being beaten because we did not support him all the time."

Gossip about Johnson had begun to swirl in Texas by the time of World War Two. Two incidents are worthy of note. In his losing campaign for the Senate in 1941, as Robert Caro points out, Johnson's frequent theme was that "if the United States went to war, he would go to the trenches." Eventually the Hill Country newspaper, the *Fredericksburg Standard,* called upon him to live up to his promise, something he had no intention of doing. He had enrolled in the naval reserves three years earlier, managing an appointment as a lieutenant commander, a rank for which he apparently held contempt, in part, as Caro suggests, because it entailed his having to salute superior officers when he was in uniform.

There were no trenches at sea, and Johnson, known from boyhood as a physical coward, faced no enemy gunfire. Avoiding combat, he requested a job in Washington but maneuvered himself into a junket touring the west coast in the company of his assistant John Connally. Meanwhile he pursued his affair with Alice Glass, who had been his mistress dating from the time of his marriage to Claudia Alta "Lady Bird" Taylor in 1934.

Lyndon Johnson's war service amounted to his being present on one flight out of Australia while accompanying men under fire on an another airplane. He was never in any danger. The flier who shot down the enemy plane did not receive a medal, but General Douglas MacArthur reluctantly awarded Johnson a Silver Star. Back home, having declared that he would not accept the decoration, Johnson wore it prominently on his lapel. He gave himself the nickname "Raider" Johnson. A reporter, Caro remarks, said that he got the Silver Star for a "flight," not a "fight." Johnson's final remark on the matter was that the Silver Star wasn't sufficient honor for what he had done (which was in fact nothing but chat up the enlisted men). Johnson came to believe that the Silver Star, as Caro put it, "was not a sufficiently high honor for such heroism as his."

During the war, Johnson also began to accumulate a sizable personal fortune. It was in Lady Bird's name that in 1942 he purchased KTBC radio in

Austin for $17,500. It was said in Texas that Lady Bird Johnson had financed both Lyndon Johnson's 1941 campaign and his 1942 purchase of KTBC radio out of her inheritance from her mother. Actually, Claudia Taylor enjoyed no such inheritance from her mother, not ten thousand dollars as was claimed, not anything. It was also said that the Johnsons repaid a ten-thousand-dollar loan from Lady Bird's father at a rate of five hundred dollars a month. Yet at that time Lyndon Johnson's income was eight hundred dollars, which was his congressional salary.

Details of the circumstances of the sale of KTBC emerged because J. Evetts Haley, author of *A Texan Looks at Lyndon*, was the general ranch manager for J. M. West, who had purchased the station in 1939. When the FCC delayed in finalizing the contract, West appointed Haley to investigate. Suddenly the owner, whose name was Dr. James G. Ulmer, found his rights to his radio stations revoked by the FCC. Ulmer turned to now influential lawyer Alvin Wirtz, who by this time was a state senator, for assistance in retaining the rights to his stations from the FCC so he could finalize the sale to West. When Ulmer arrived at Wirtz's office to pay him his retainer, Wirtz was nowhere to be found, although Ulmer did note a signed photograph of Lyndon Johnson prominently displayed.

In 1942, West died, nullifying the sale of KTBC. That same year, Lady Bird Johnson applied to purchase the station, a sale quickly granted by the FCC. She paid, according to Haley, $15,500, although it was worth a million dollars, according to Ulmer. The inhibitions of the Clayton Antitrust Act did not slow the Johnsons down as their media interests in Texas expanded. The jewel in their crown would be a monopoly on television broadcasting in Austin.

CHAPTER 2

A Man of Good Character

*"Sometimes we find our true and inherent
selves during youth."*
—MICHAEL ONDAATJE, *THE CAT'S TABLE*

Beginning in the late 1930s when he was a congressman, Lyndon Johnson
cultivated the habit of recruiting bright young Texans to serve as his aides and
speechwriters, intermediaries and confidants. With shrewdness and perspicacity, he chose people of high intelligence so that many, like John Connally,
went on to achieve power and fortune in their own right. The first was Walter
Jenkins, who was recommended by a University of Texas dean in 1939 when
he was a student. Jenkins would go on to serve Johnson for twenty-five years.

John Connally became governor of Texas. Barefoot Sanders rose from U.S.
attorney to a judgeship. Both Connally and Sanders had been presidents of
the University of Texas student body. Horace Busby, once editor of the *Daily
Texan*, the college newspaper, would serve Lyndon Johnson as a speechwriter
and all-around troubleshooter on and off for a lifetime. Howard Burris advised
Johnson on national security matters and created a bridge between Johnson
and the Central Intelligence Agency. Bill Moyers became a highly respected
journalist and public intellectual as well as a servant to Johnson's ambitions.

Intellectual independence was not tolerated. When Ronnie Dugger, who
also had been an editor of the *Daily Texan*, applied for a job on Johnson's senatorial staff, he was rejected. "Ronnie's not our kind of guy," Horace Busby
warned Johnson. Dugger went on to found the *Texas Observer*, a landmark of
progressive journalism in Texas, and would write the only critical biography
of Lyndon Johnson, published in 1982. Johnson had let Dugger know that
he expected a "friendly" book. When Dugger sent back the message that he
planned to "write a fair and accurate book of interest to serious people,"
he was never again granted another interview with Lyndon Johnson.

These relationships, Ronnie Dugger's excepted, might be seen as Faustian bargains. A tireless power broker, Johnson had much to offer. The young people supplied their best energies, their loyalty, and their willingness to ignore Johnson's malfeasances. When Princeton professor of history Eric Goldman briefly endured the experience of serving Johnson, he observed Johnson's relationships with his young acolytes at close range.

All of these people, Goldman concluded, had "staked their careers and a good deal of their inner selves on Lyndon Johnson." Yet Johnson was "destroying everybody around him." Many became "not only Johnson's protégés, but also his victims." Special assistant to President John F. Kennedy, Ralph Dungan, speaking of how Johnson corrupted those who served him, said that "he really took the substance, the psychological and spiritual substance of people and sucked it right out like a vampire."

Goldman noted that Horace Busby suddenly began to sound conservative because "that was the way his leader, Lyndon Johnson, talked most of the time." Johnson Press Secretary George Reedy amplified this view in his memoir. People who served Lyndon Johnson, Reedy wrote, "were required to drop everything to wait upon him and were expected to forget their private lives in his interests."

Mac Wallace is a case in point, his history with Lyndon Johnson a window into Johnson's methods. Wallace's story is so intriguing because, unlike other of Johnson's acolytes, it is difficult to prove what he did for Lyndon Johnson, and what Lyndon Johnson, in turn, did for him. More than any other of Johnson's protégés and acolytes, Wallace's connection to him remains cloaked in secrecy.

In the major events of Mac Wallace's life, Lyndon Johnson remains invisible. Yet one truth is irrefutable. Everything that was positive and promising in Wallace's life came to him before he made the acquaintance of Lyndon Baines Johnson and joined Johnson's circle.

Thirteen years Lyndon Johnson's junior, Malcolm Everett Wallace was born in Mount Pleasant on October 15, 1921, into a similar hardscrabble and culturally barren backwater in east Texas. His father, Alvin Wallace, having served in World War One, returned to a land without opportunity. To earn cash, he signed on to road crews, when he could. He farmed. Mac Wallace's mother, Alice Marie Riddle, was half Cherokee, so that Mac had high cheekbones, glossy black hair, and a toothy smile.

Late in 1924, when Mac Wallace was three years old, the Wallaces moved to Dallas, one hundred miles to the west. One of Alvin's cousins had forty dollars and they purchased a cement mixer, beginning a contracting business by paving curbs. It was a similar career trajectory to another poor Texan, Herman Brown. Herman began humbly in 1914 by paving roads with the friendly assistance of his mules, while he lived in a tent with his schoolteacher bride, Margaret, surname Root.

The Wallace family multiplied, so that Mac had four brothers and a sister. Neither parent had gone to college. Yet Mac had a kindly father in fair-haired Alvin, known as A. J., who took an active interest in raising the children, teaching them dominoes, a favorite Wallace family pastime.

Mac Wallace enjoyed a Texas boyhood as he imbibed Texas values. You played football. You defended yourself from the class bully. It was Mac Wallace who, along with his best friend, faced down the thug who stole their lunch money.

"We're going to fight this guy until he agrees to leave us alone," Mac said. At their next encounter, his friend ran home, leaving Mac to confront the bully by himself. He was already physically strong, and no coward. Yet he was a solid student drawn to books and learning. The family called him "Mikey."

In the fall of 1934, Mac Wallace entered Woodrow Wilson, a new Dallas high school quickly lauded for its attention to scholarship. Mac joined everything from student government to the Pan American Student Forum to the Spanish Club. He was elected to the student council and twice to the office of Vice President of his class, including as a senior. He played quarterback on the football team.

Mac Wallace was not alone in his ambition among his classmates. Joining him on the football team, playing guard on the offensive line, was Ralph N. Geb, later to become a Strategic Air Command pilot and a member of U.S. Air Force intelligence. Geb's brother, Frederick August Geb, joined CIA, under cover as a lieutenant colonel in U.S. Army intelligence. Years later, a Woodrow Wilson classmate named Eugene Noblitt became convinced that Ralph Geb was the man photographed at the Russian consulate in Mexico City as "Lee Harvey Oswald," although he was short, heavyset, and in no manner resembled Oswald. Eugene Noblitt remembered Mac Wallace on the football field as "tough as nails." Another Wallace classmate was a bona fide criminal type. Russell Douglas (R.D.) Matthews supposedly "used to work for LBJ" and was a stalker and a hit man.

Mac Wallace stood at five feet eleven inches in height. He was slim, with black hair, flashing dark eyes, and a dimpled chin. "Tall, dark, and handsome" pronounced a girlfriend of his youth. He wore glasses, which did nothing to diminish his swagger, and masked his class insecurity with a full-blown ego. He grew up to be a man solicitous of the well-being of his younger siblings.

During a football game in April 1938, when he was seventeen years old, Mac Wallace was tackled on a running play so violently that he fractured a lumbar vertebra. Spinal fusion surgery led to his being confined to his bed in a body cast for three months, after which he wore a spinal brace for another three and a half months. A seven-inch scar now snaked down his spine. He lost an entire school year.

Mac graduated "with honor," the locution of the day, from Woodrow Wilson High School on June 2, 1939, with a 90.2 grade point average. He shared with Lyndon Johnson a poverty that made attending university doubtful. Tuition at the University of Texas at Austin was free, but even the incidental costs of college were too expensive for the Wallace family. November 3, 1939, found Mac Wallace on St. Charles Avenue in New Orleans, headquarters of the Southern Recruiting Division of the U.S. Marine Corps. He enlisted as a private.

At his recruiting interview, he swore that he had never been convicted of a crime by a judge or a jury; never been arrested; never been an inmate of a reformatory or a correctional institution for juveniles. He was not a fugitive from justice. His fingerprints were recorded with the precision that was standard Navy practice. (The Marines, then as now, were part of the Navy.)

On November 6, Mac Wallace was sent for sea training at San Diego. His character, the Marines determined, was "excellent." On November 10, his photograph was taken: a sober young man with thick black eyebrows and dark hair. His complexion was described as "ruddy." He seems older than his eighteen years.

The Wallaces did not own guns and did not hunt. Mac's weapons training was new to him as he proceeded through a Rifle Qualifications Course and bayonet training. He learned how to use an automatic rifle, and achieved a score of 3/0, SS, which was no more than satisfactory. He practiced with a Thompson submachine gun. At the Pistol Qualifications Course, his grade was a mediocre 55 percent.

On January 6, 1940, Mac Wallace was assigned to the USS Lexington, an aircraft carrier belonging to the Pacific fleet, residing at Pearl Harbor. His time in the Marine Corps was antiheroic. He came down with a sore throat a week into his service and went off to the sick bay. Carrying an electric deck polisher, he smashed his hand against the "hatch coming," a two-inch lip encircling a hatch, and fractured his finger. He tripped on a paint scraper and slid down a ladder that had been standing in an open hatch, falling ten or twelve feet, "bumping his back repeatedly." The doctors discovered considerable scar tissue around his spine.

He was already a man with an abundant appetite for life, and a wicked sense of humor. He decided to take advantage of his sojourn at the Navy hospital to ask his doctor to circumcise him. This would make him "a real man."

Soon after the procedure, an attractive nurse entered the room and he experienced an erection. "It hurt like hell!" he later confided to his girlfriend. He was a man able to laugh at himself, except when his pride was injured. Then his spirit would deflate rapidly.

"This man may eventually need another spinal fusion," the Navy doctor concluded as Mac Wallace left the Navy with a medical discharge. The Marines asked him to sign a statement testifying that his back condition "was not aggravated by service conditions," and he acquiesced. He left the service on September 4, 1940, having served ten months. His discharge papers record that the Marines assessed his character over the duration of his service as "excellent."

Mac Wallace returned to Texas, where he enrolled at North Texas Agricultural College in Arlington, part of the Texas A & M University system. Bypassing the courses in livestock and farming, he chose a standard academic program: history, Texas history, algebra, and Spanish. On February 1, 1941, he enrolled at the University of Texas at Austin with sixteen transfer credit hours in tow.

On December 13, 1941, a week after the Japanese attack on Pearl Harbor, Wallace applied for re-enlistment in the Marines. A "real man" was patriotic and fought for his country. It was what a Texan did. He included with his application "an opinion from a civilian doctor," the man who had performed his original spinal fusion, that his back was "as good as ever."

Major W. E. Burke denied Wallace's plea that he be permitted to fight in the war. "It is a policy of the Marine Corps not to accept any man for re-enlistment who was last discharged by reason of a medical survey," Burke wrote. Wallace appealed and again Burke, who had been promoted to lieutenant colonel, turned him down.

Deeply disappointed, Mac Wallace immersed himself in life at the University of Texas, seizing upon opportunities to distinguish himself, large and small. Poverty stalked him in these days before the GI Bill was enacted.

Too poor to pledge for a Greek fraternity, he joined the Tejas Club, which affected the culture of a fraternity and was designed for those who couldn't afford the real thing. Responding to the exigencies of the Great Depression, the University of Texas had opened co-op residences in the fall of 1936. When he was a junior, Wallace resided at the co-op Shangri-La House, where his roommate was future FBI special agent Joseph Louis Schott. Crowded conditions meant that for two years they spent their nights out on a sleeping porch.

Mac Wallace seemed always to be planning to run for campus office. Schott, however, had no interest in politics, and they drifted apart. In May 1943, Schott went off to military service with the U.S. Army. Meanwhile there wasn't a student activity for which Wallace did not volunteer as he searched for opportunities to gain recognition. He became bookkeeper for the *Cactus*, the college yearbook. He joined the Hogg Debate Club. In 1942 and 1943, he was a member of the students' assembly for the Arts and Sciences College, a legislative group that handled apportioning how student taxes were to be utilized, and supervised student publications.

He was invited to join the Cowboys, an honorary service organization for men. Those initiated as Cowboys were branded on their chest with the letters TU. Wallace suffered some apprehension, but he would never have declined or done anything that might label him a coward. Then, just before his initiation, fortune smiled and the branding ritual was prohibited by the university.

Mac Wallace was also "social chairman" of the Men's Inter-Community Association, whose purpose was "to give the unorganized students of the campus a chance to develop leadership ability and to make friends." In 1943, he was MICA's Secretary-Treasurer, following Joseph Schott, who had been a member of the MICA executive council.

Wallace also joined the Ex-Servicemen's Association, which had been founded on Pearl Harbor Day. He had not gone to war, but he was proud that he had served. Later the *Cactus* could not keep up with his activities so that the 1944–45 edition described him as "a junior at the law school," which he had never been. He was aggressive, ambitious, and strove to rise above the ordinary, traits he shared with the young Lyndon Johnson.

All the while, as his college years stretched from 1941 to 1945, he held down one job after another: "shop fitter," ironworker, general laborer. From 1939 to 1945, he worked for his father's construction firm, now constituted as Wallace and Bowden, General Contractors. Alvin Wallace's older sister, Nellie Arlene, had married L. R. Bowden, who entered into a partnership with his brother-in-law. Still, in the fall of 1943, Mac had to withdraw from school to accumulate enough money to continue. In 1944 he worked as a night watchman on the midnight shift at a gas plant.

The University of Texas was on a wartime trimester system as students were anxious to complete their studies before they went off to war. In a given year, Mac Wallace might be taking as many as twenty-eight semester hours. Wallace's grades fluctuated. He received A's in Modern Literature and Introduction to Visual Arts, but a D in Intermediate Accounting. To keep up, he attended summer school in 1942, 1944, and again in 1947. He earned a B in each of the four economics courses he took in the summer and fall of 1944.

In 1943, Mac Wallace met Nora Ann Carroll, the woman who would turn out to be the love of his life. Her father was a prominent Beaumont attorney and a confirmed conservative. Nora Ann, however, was iconoclastic and feisty; her family nickname was Sas, for Sassy. She was a concert violinist, viola player, and pianist who played Vivaldi at a state conference of the Daughters of the American Revolution when she was in high school. She presented her parents one year with a Christmas list that included Leon Trotsky's biography of V. I. Lenin. Although her father and his cronies thoroughly disapproved of Franklin Roosevelt and his New Deal, Nora Ann presented Mrs. Roosevelt with a bouquet of bluebonnets on the first lady's visit to Texas.

When Nora Ann arrived at the University of Texas in the autumn of 1941, her baggage contained a full wardrobe for sorority rush week, including a fur coat (rabbit) and a matching heart-shaped hat. She joined the best sorority, Pi Beta Phi, and was elected to the board of directors of the student union. She came armed with a boyfriend, Edward T. Cary, a medical student at Tulane, whom she had known since they were children.

Among her admirers at the University of Texas would be future congressman and Lyndon Johnson ally Jack Brooks, who would be present on Air Force One on November 22, 1963. Brooks is pictured in the rear of the plane as Lyndon Johnson is being sworn in as President of the United States. Brooks, who was also from Beaumont, hoped to marry Nora Ann Carroll, but his rivals were many.

Nora Ann lost her virginity to Ted Cary in March 1943 on the Carys' living room couch. Two months later, by registered mail, Cary sent her his fraternity pin. Nora Ann invariably left the pin at home, or she wore it on her underwear. When Ted Cary requested that she join his church, Nora Ann had a ready answer: "I don't wish to perjure myself so young!" One of her sorority sisters called her "the leader of the revolutionary socialistic movement."

Nora Ann Carroll was admitted into an accelerated wartime academic program, Plan 2, that allowed you to complete the requirements for graduation in two years. As her elective, Nora Ann chose second year Latin.

She and Mac Wallace met at a university mixer on September 25, 1943. Forming a wide circle, the women joined hands and moved in a clockwise direction. In an outer circle, the men moved counterclockwise. When the music stopped, you danced with the person directly opposite. Nora Ann and Mac slowed their pace so as to be certain to wind up together. Nora Ann then wiggled into the right position and they faced each other. The music resumed. He took her into his arms.

"I should have worn a jockstrap!" Mac Wallace said shortly after that mixer. Nora Ann laughed. She decided that Wallace was a gentleman, if rather free in his speech, as he certainly was for the early 1940s. In a letter to her mother, Nora Ann described herself as "confused over a new face: Mac Wallace—a successful campus politician last year—a handsome brunette with whom I went to the pep rally tonight." It was at once serious for them both. "Nothing may come of it," she added, "but if he finds out I am pinned & really cares and decides to steer clear, I'll kick myself! Oh, damn!"

"We just clicked!" Nora Ann remembered seventy years later. She sympathized with Mac's financial plight and sometimes, according to her brother William E. (Bill) Carroll, helped him out with money from her generous allowance. Mac was two years older than most of the male students and more self-possessed and self-confident. Nora Ann was appalled when some men bragged that they had gone out with her when they hadn't. Some even claimed to have seduced her.

Nora Ann Carroll majored in economics as did Mac Wallace. A photograph shows the two of them listening to their favorite professor, Clarence Ayres. As his future student Ronnie Dugger would describe him, Ayres was "the intellectual senior in the economics department." In his lectures he drew "improvisationally, from music, technology, history, politics, art, science, any field that gave him, as he stood in class, a light for his thought." Nora Ann became Ayres' research assistant and lifelong admirer.

Together Mac and Nora Ann studied the historical origins of the Bible although Nora Ann was a member of the Christian Association and Mac was not. At six o'clock on Friday evenings "Hazen suppers" were held at the YMCA. Twenty-five or thirty students gathered to ponder such issues as "what would Jesus have said about 'cultural lag'?" "How does Christianity relate to block voting on campus?" "What was the relative influence of heredity and environment?" "How were they to address the class struggle?" Eating chop suey, shrimp salad, and chocolate pie, they debated the historic approach of Jesus.

At twenty-three, Mac Wallace was something of an atheist. He embraced the disenchantment of his generation staring into the eye of the Holocaust. In a letter to Nora Ann, Mac expressed his religious ambivalence:

> For there is no God.
> How can I prove it? How can you disprove it?
> Where is your evidence? Where are your facts?
> Where, you ask, are mine? I will show you in the acts of men.
> If there be a God, why is there—war?
> If there be a God, why is there disease and pain?
> If there be a God, why is there want?
> But Man is evil, you say. And he must be punished.
> Ah, but do only the evil die on battlefields? Do only the evil fall ill
>   and suffer? Are only the evil in want?
> Or, better yet, if man is evil why did God create him? In order to gain
>   a sadistic pleasure from torturing and punishing him?

Mac reflected on the historical Jesus: "His influence, indeed! What did he preach? The brotherhood of men? Then what of Jim Crowism? What of anti-Semitism? And the Mexicans in Texas and California? Hell, what of our poor *white* trash? Do we treat these as brothers?"

Mac Wallace matured into a man with a strong social conscience, and the courage of his convictions. Nora Ann knew him "for all his faults," but believed that his strengths overcame his weaknesses. At college he did not drink more than anyone else. His temper could be volatile; when a young frat boy bragged that he had seduced Nora Ann, Mac took off for his frat house threatening to "kill A. Y. Olds if he didn't show proper respect." Yet no violence erupted.

Mac Wallace still played football, for the Tejas Club team if not for the Longhorns, and the *Daily Texan* reported his touchdown passes and touchdown runs. In December 1943, the Tejas team clinched a tie for first place in their intramural league. Sometimes Nora Ann sat on the sidelines and watched Mac play.

Christmas of 1943 found Mac Wallace purchasing books as Christmas presents for his siblings: *Cortez and the Conquest of Mexico*; *He Wouldn't Be*

King (about Simón Bolívar), *The Heroes* (Greek myths); H. G. Wells's *Outline of History*; Louisa May Alcott's *Jo's Boys*; *Bambi*; *Decisive Battles in U.S. History*; *The First Christmas*; and *Rip Van Winkle*.

Mac confided that he intended "to put 'em in the bookcase with a card giving them to all the children jointly." He knew that his brother David, who was very interested in biography and history, would read most of them. Martha Jean, who currently liked fairy tales and romantic tales, would read *Bambi*, *Rip Van Winkle*, *The Heroes*, and *The First Christmas*. "Jim won't be there to read, Jerry won't read anything not prefaced by a dollar mark," and "Bruce is too young to read." Mac was still persuaded that "it was a good idea—giving them books."

That Christmas he purchased a wedding ring. He ribbed Nora Ann: "Don't get excited now, lady, no one's putting any pressure on you; it's A. J.'s gift to mother," a replacement for a ring that was now too small for his mother.

Mac described the wedding ring: a platinum band with five small diamonds that would replace a ring that his mother could no longer wear because it had grown "a little tight on her finger." Mac was presenting his mother with a set of dishes: "tea glasses, water glasses, sherbet dishes and salad plates with a flower design."

The only person outside the family for whom he bought a present was Nora Ann. He was already in love with Nora Ann and she with him, although from this exchange it seems clear that she was holding back. Nora Ann would tell Mac periodically, "I certainly am in love with you today!" adding an ironic bite worthy of the nickname "Sas." He assumed that one day they would be married. All that he was, all that he believed, were connected to his love for Nora Ann Carroll.

He wrote her such long letters, Mac explained, because "writing to you makes nearly as pleasant a sensation as *being with* you." He complained about her not replying to his many letters—"I ain't getting no responses"—blaming himself, not realizing that in not writing back to him, Nora Ann was observing a personal code that would allow her to remain loyal to Ted Cary.

Nora Ann considered this 1943 Christmas letter the most "touching" of all the many Mac Wallace sent her. Mac closed with an endearment in Spanish: "*Vives en mi Corazon.*" You live in my heart. Mac Wallace would remain in love with Nora Ann for the rest of his life.

In May 1944, he sent her a love poem that reflects the affection as well as the conflict lurking between them, his desire to capture her loyalty and her evasive and staunch hold on her independence. Between the lines is Mac's perception of Nora Ann's ambivalence over cutting her ties to Ted Cary, a future doctor who came from a prominent family and promised a conventional future, a person of whom her father would approve:

> A lovely little dark-eyed nymph
> Merrily skips across my mind
> Tilting my thoughts and slanting plans
> Till wild disorder is left behind.
>
> Running barefoot around my brain
> She gaily laughs and shakes her head
> Shunning each proffered compromise
> Preferring to taunt and tease.
>
> Carefree and reckless—she'd best take heed
> That I have a plan to stop her play
> For I will imprison her in my heart
> And condemn her always there to stay . . .

Mac assumed that he was better than the men who were his rivals for Nora Ann's affection. With his ambition and his many talents, with Nora Ann by his side, he imagined a future of consequence.

CHAPTER 3

"He Must Be a Real Leader"

"It might be said that this was an early
manifestation of the student protest concept."
—HOMER P. RAINEY, PRESIDENT OF
THE UNIVERSITY OF TEXAS

In the spring of 1944, Mac Wallace, now a member of the senior class, decided to run for student body president, the highest office to which a UT undergraduate might aspire. John Hill, his opponent, enjoyed the support of the Greek fraternities. As a high school student, Hill had been elected president of a student government convention in Tyler, Texas. The fact that he had never lost an election in his life fired Mac Wallace's healthy competitive instincts.

Nora Ann Carroll joined a parade of classmates marching to the Tejas Club to "draft" Mac Wallace to run for student body president. Soon she would be lobbying among her Pi Phi sorority sisters to secure votes for him.

In the ensuing campaign, Mac Wallace presented himself as devoted to the rights of students. He promised greater academic freedom. High on the list of causes he supported was the "state-wide movement for suffrage extension, extending the vote to eighteen, nineteen and twenty-year-old citizens of Texas." Granting eighteen-year-olds the right to vote would extend "democracy's borders." If young men of eighteen were risking their lives for their country, he argued, they should be eligible to vote.

As part of his campaign, though not a member, Mac Wallace attended a meeting of the Common Sense Club, a group of students concerned about social issues. They had been organized to study the writings of Thomas Paine, taking their name from Paine's Revolutionary era pamphlet.

Scenting Communism, the FBI investigated the club. The Bureau concluded that although "some Communist Party members have joined the group, Communism was not an issue in Common Sense in 1944 and

Communists had no control in [the] organization." At Common Sense, economic regulation was discussed as the means of addressing the endemic evil of poverty.

Mac Wallace was never a Communist. He was someone who looked out for the underdog. He and Nora Ann Carroll were "liberals" who supported the cause of labor and of unions. Nora Ann owned a copy of the Industrial Workers of the World (IWW) songbook and occasionally sang their songs. Mac and Nora Ann subscribed to Keynesian economics.

When Nora Ann did attend a left-wing discussion group and express her views, she was scorned as "bourgeois." Years later, Mac's brother Jerry Neal Wallace remembered him as "one of the first people in Texas, one of the first Southern-bred people, to associate with blacks." A fraternity brother named John O. Markward later told the FBI that Mac Wallace had the reputation of being an individual "holding liberal views on labor and the racial question."

As McCarthyism took hold, guilt by association became a reflexive means of smearing people. Mac Wallace did have a Communist friend, an editor at the *Daily Texan* named Elgin Williams. No activist, Williams was, rather, an eccentric who provided comic relief for his friends; they were amused when Elgin's girlfriend had an abortion and they put the fetus in a bottle and pickled it. Meanwhile Nora Ann pondered what to do with her life. "What shall I do when I get my degree in March?" she wrote her father in September 1943.

Mac Wallace was elected president of the University of Texas student body on April 4, 1944, without his having solicited the support of any Texas politician. His continuing poverty was reflected in his cheap ill-fitting tweed suit. Despite his lower social status, Nora Ann's mother preferred him now to Ted Cary.

Among his first acts as president of the student body was to write a letter to Governor Coke Stevenson. Being president of the University of Texas student body was as much a state political position and a calling card to one's future as it was a campus office. Mac Wallace's letter to the governor had the tone of one political leader addressing another. He requested a "personal conference" with the governor so that they might discuss issues affecting the students in "future University plans and proposals."

The tone of his letter to Dr. O. D. Weeks, the faculty adviser for the Students' Association, is humble, respectful, and tactful. "I am sure there are several things you could tell me concerning my duties and responsibilities and I would draw on your experience," Mac Wallace wrote to Weeks on May 1.

After Governor Stevenson invited Mac Wallace for a "personal discussion," leaving an appointment time vague, Mac wrote back with a suggested time, four days thence. Then he sent a personal letter to each member of the Board of Regents, all conservatives, all Stevenson appointees. He urged that their meeting be open to the public, an idea for which he "received universal acclaim from the students."

Mac Wallace's interactions with authorities and with the students were open and frank. He was forthright; he fought for democratic governance of the university with the students enjoying significant influence.

The response from regent D. F. (Frank) Strickland set the tone for Wallace's coming relationship with the Regents. "The University to me is just another great state agency which spends many million dollars of the peoples [sic] money each year," Strickland wrote as he opposed opening board meetings to the students. Mac Wallace kept his cool. When another intransigent regent, Orville Bullington, invited him and his "entire official staff" to attend some, if not all, board meetings, invoking their mutual goal of creating "a great University," Mac Wallace replied that he would attend the very next board meeting.

U.S. Vice President Henry Wallace visited the University of Texas campus, and he and Mac Wallace got along famously. A photograph of the two was published in the *Daily Texan* with the caption "President and Vice President Wallace."

"I detest hero worship," Mac wrote to Nora Ann, who was attending summer school in Middlebury, Vermont. "But I sure as hell admire Wallace." When, pressured by party bosses, President Roosevelt bumped Henry Wallace from his 1944 presidential ticket, Mac Wallace was indignant. "I stuck by the radio during the convention and devoured newspaper reports," he wrote Nora Ann. "I thought he fought like a tiger; it was magnificent. Moreover, he would have won out except that Roosevelt took the thirty pieces of silver—security for No. 1—and gave him the kiss of death." Mac urged Nora Ann to obtain a copy of Wallace's speech, which announced "the birth of a Liberal party—which it seems will not be the Democratic Party."

"Damn the old line bastards," Mac added. "They have achieved their main objective—destroying the possibility of a continuing liberalism in the White House." He opposed the influence of "corporate interests on the university . . . the Sealy and Smith Foundation is a beautiful skin stretched around a framework of secure private practices, private clinics where student labor is exploited. He raised the issue of who wielded "the power in deciding how the med school will be run and for whose gain." He was a populist as he tackled the issue of university control of its own medical school.

Mac Wallace was a young man who admitted to preferring people who have "the guts to take sides" over "wishy-washy individuals." He was generous in acknowledging the accomplishments of his friends.

In July 1944, Mac Wallace recorded his first awareness of Congressman Lyndon Johnson. Charged with creating a political culture for the student body, in the same spirit that he had invited Henry Wallace, Mac had written a letter to Johnson's lawyer, Edward Clark, about Johnson "speaking to a gathering of our campus citizens." Clark had drawn close to LBJ even before Johnson ran for Congress. "I didn't know what office he was going to run for," Clark remarked, "but I knew he was going to run for some office, and I knew he was going to run for a big office. And I was willing to buy a ticket on him." Clark had gone from being Texas Secretary of State to working on retainer for Herman Brown at Brown & Root. He went on to become Johnson's principal attorney and, as Robert Caro puts it, "principal operative in Texas."

Johnson contributed a title to Mac Wallace for his presentation, "Current Trends in Government and Politics." Mac Wallace suggested that a more felicitous approach would be the "significance of the happenings rather than the happenings themselves."

"We would like to know what we may expect to see happening in the future," Mac added. He suggested that "Mr. Johnson send us a supply of his campaign literature so that we may distribute it around the audience before the speech." Johnson's views in writing, Mac explained, would "furnish fuel for the questions during the forum period following the speech."

Outspoken in his liberal views, views that Lyndon Johnson did not publicly share, then or later, Wallace wrote a resolution "against any economic or military intervention on the part of the United States in any foreign war." The politics swirling around the University of Texas earned his disapproval. "You are attending a University that is controlled by politics," he told his fellow students. "Our appropriation must come through the state legislature. Our Regents are appointed by the Governor!" Having spoken on August 2, 1944, at a meeting in an open-air theater attended by two hundred students, he was praised in the *Daily Texan* for a talk that was "inspirational."

"Diogenes with his lantern might find an honest man in our present society," Wallace said. "But it would take a strong searchlight to find a free man." Mac Wallace's conduct at the University of Texas offers an alternative approach to the politics practiced by Lyndon Johnson.

* * *

The issue that defined Mac Wallace's presidency of the student body centered on the president of the University of Texas, Homer P. Rainey, whose liberal views, whose admiration of John Dewey, set him on a collision course with the Regents of the University of Texas and with the McCarthyist views that were gaining credibility over the political culture of the state. John Dewey, born on October 20, 1859, was the leading American philosopher and public intellectual of the first half of the twentieth century; his most influential book was *Democracy and Education* published in 1916. This was followed by *How We Think, Experience and Education*, and *Art as Experience*. Dewey was considered a progressive and social reformer, a pragmatist and logician, an expert in theory of knowledge, and a Darwinian. He was a Ph.D. and a professor first at Michigan and Chicago and then at Columbia University, where he spent most of his career. Dewey's views resided in the premise that education was the road to a citizenry with the capacity to participate actively in a democratic society.

A native of Clarksville, Texas, Homer P. Rainey, born January 19, 1896, had been ordained as a Baptist minister at the age of nineteen. A man of many parts, in his youth he was a pitcher in the Texas League. He received his master's degree (1923) and his doctorate (1924) from the University of Chicago. Before his arrival as president of the University of Texas in 1939, he had been president of Bucknell University in Pennsylvania (1931–35).

Rainey's inaugural address had been populist in spirit. Under the influence of John Dewey, he invoked "democratically sponsored education and freedom" and called attention to an inherent conflict between "reactionary nouveau riche capitalism and the concepts of a liberal democracy." His goal, Rainey declared, was "to preserve the autonomy and educational integrity of the university" against the "politico-economic control of the Board of Regents and reactionary governors." Rainey had two governors in particular in mind: Pappy "Pass the Biscuits" O'Daniel and Coke Stevenson. O'Daniel was a conservative who had become a household name on the strength of his populist radio program that featured a hillbilly band. He served as governor of Texas from 1939 to 1941, when he resigned to run for the U.S. Senate. His opponent was Lyndon Johnson, whom he defeated in the only election Johnson ever lost. The official tally was 175,590 to 174,279.

At Texas, Homer Rainey increased the size of the faculty and added a Latin American Institute. He expanded the building construction program for the College of Fine Arts, advocated a liberal education, and allocated an increase of funds for library holdings. He organized the management of the Hogg Foundation for Mental Health, focusing on the well-being of "the individual," a view he derived from the thinking of John Dewey.

Homer Rainey's first major confrontation with the Board of Regents came when they ordered him not to renew the contracts of three liberal economics instructors, W. N. Peach; Wendell Gordon, a disciple of Clarence Ayres; and J. Fagg Foster. On March 22, 1942, these three untenured faculty members had attended an anti-union meeting in Dallas. Their hope was to gain an opportunity to oppose from the floor the anti-labor views of the meeting organizers. Sponsored by the *Dallas Morning News*, this "mass meeting" focused on the Fair Labor Standards Act.

Chairing the meeting was Karl Hoblitzelle, proprietor of a chain of theaters and a power in Texas politics. Later, Hoblitzelle would become a CIA asset and the agency would administer his foundation after his death. At issue now was whether during wartime unions should suspend activity in the face of the needs of military production.

The instructors defended the minimum wage and supported work stoppages at defense plants, views conservatives believed amounted to heresy during wartime. They believed that the Fair Labor Standards Act required the payment of overtime wages for work in excess of forty hours a week, whether or not the country was at war. Since defense contractors were profiting, so should workers.

They had requested a place on the program, only to be turned down, and had remained silent during the meeting. Afterward, two of the professors granted an interview to the *Dallas Morning News* that appeared in the paper the next day. They pointed out that at the meeting "organized labor was the object of particular and consistent condemnation by the speakers." They termed the meeting "undemocratic and unrepresentative."

After reading the *Dallas Morning News* article, a federal district judge named T. W. Davidson wrote to the Regents urging that "changes be made in the economics faculty" at the University of Texas. In Texas in particular, unions faced persistent opposition. The open shop was favored and Lyndon Johnson's chief supporter, Herman Brown, employed three lobbyists planted at the state legislature to ensure that any pro-union bill would be defeated and right-to-work laws be upheld. Brown also planted spies within Brown & Root to guard against the slightest murmur of union organizing. At his Austin radio station, Lyndon Johnson did not hire union labor and there was no union organizing.

At the next meeting of the university's board, regent Frank Strickland removed a small card from his coat pocket and passed it across the table to

Homer Rainey. Written on the card were the names of the economics instructors.

"We want you to fire these men," Strickland said.

"Why?" Rainey said.

"Well, we just don't like what they're teaching," Strickland said.

"What's that got to do with anything?" Rainey said. "Aren't they honorable men? Four members of our staff acted strictly in accordance with their rights and privileges as citizens." When Rainey refused to dismiss the instructors, the Regents did not renew their appointments. (The fourth instructor had chosen to leave the university.)

The Regents also eyed Clarence Ayres with suspicion, but he was more difficult to dislodge. Ayres was a fierce anti-Communist. He believed that Communists should not serve on the faculty since they were not free to pursue the truth. Still, perceiving that Ayres was independent-minded, the Regents viewed him as a threat. They placed spies in his classroom to write down what he said. Another target of the Regents was Robert Montgomery, one of Mac Wallace's teachers and a longtime friend of Lyndon Johnson.

Although the term "McCarthyism" would await the arrival of the senator from Wisconsin, by the summer of 1942 Congressman Martin Dies of the 2nd district of Texas was already enacting the views he would further as founder of the House Committee on Un-American Activities. Dies served as its chair from 1937 to 1944. By the summer of 1942, the Regents were charging that "there were a great many unpatriotic attitudes held and activities undertaken" by faculty members. Even as the war in Europe against fascism was at its height, there were those who behaved as if the true enemy of the United States was the Soviet Union and were breathing life into a "Cold War" that had not yet been named.

That summer of 1942 Congressman Dies, in the company of an investigator, visited the campus for two weeks. They were unable to unearth a single Communist. A regent suggested that a "patriotism test" (to be known during the McCaerthyist period as a loyalty oath) be administered to all faculty members and university staff, a test Homer Rainy opposed.

Now, in 1944, Mac Wallace perceived that "U.T. and Rainey" would "be punished for an 'open' fight." He determined on a strategy of not getting "down on the mat at once" but to "suspend judgement [sic] till I get all the possible facts in hand." The Regents and "Jesse," Mac Wallace believed, were "men of vested interests" whose views were antithetical to those of Homer Rainey and himself. Jesse was Jesse Jones, the owner of the *Houston Chronicle*, the leading newspaper in Texas. Jones was a habitué of Suite 8F at the Lamar Hotel in Houston, Herman Brown's two-bedroom redoubt for his powerful cronies: defense contractors, politicians, judges, bankers, insurance moguls and businessmen, the power elite of Texas.

The institutions of higher learning in Texas, Mac Wallace warned, were in danger of being controlled by a "small wealthy clique," the same clique that brought Lyndon Johnson to power. Mac Wallace used words like "solidarity." He talked of "a spirit of sympathy for our fellow man, a spirit of loyalty to the ideals fostered by the University of Texas." He acted quietly as mentor for the head of the student body of nearby Huston-Tillotson University, a black school that had recently been accredited.

Members of the Common Sense Club were attacked as "fellow travelers," secret supporters of the Communist Party. In fact, they were not Communists, but liberals; they fought for a sixty-five-cent minimum wage, opposed racism, and supported a campus building program so that returning veterans would find housing. They also continued to support the eighteen-year-old vote.

During the year of Mac Wallace's presidency of the student body, the Regents rejected Homer Rainey's plan for a school of social work. They denied funding for a study of criminal law "in need of reform." They refused to fund the *Texas Law Review*. They would not approve a study of war booms in three Texas towns and scuttled a study of air transportation in Latin America. Professors applying for funding to attend professional meetings were denied travel expenses. A furor raged over moving the medical school from Galveston to Austin, where it would come under the university's control. The common denominator for all these actions was the Regents' attempt to eradicate dissent before it surfaced.

The Regents demanded the firing of a professor who supposedly assigned *The Big Money*, volume three of John Dos Passos's masterpiece, *U.S.A.*, to sophomore engineering students. The selection had in fact been a committee decision. The Regents claimed that *U.S.A.* was "indecent, vulgar and filthy and unfit to be made a required course [sic] in English for boys and girls." One regent proposed that "ministers and mothers of Texas examine this book!" A novel is not a course, "required" or otherwise.

English professor Henry Nash Smith argued that *The Big Money* was an entirely appropriate text for that historical moment. It opens with the return of a veteran from World War One, and was "a timely [choice] for the boys who would face a post-war era also," and upon whose shoulders rested "the task of saving, in that world, the ideals for which many would have died in a war."

The Regents went on to cancel a $150 grant for a study of the influence of the Sacco and Vanzetti case on American literature. Regent Orville Bullington termed the beleaguered anarchists "Communist murderers, among whose champions was none other than the author of the novel *U.S.A.*" The Regents also attacked the principle of tenure, declaring that they had the power to fire any professor by declaring an "emergency." Teachers' salaries and promotions were to be under their control.

Homer Rainey opposed all these policies. He described himself as fighting for freedom from "undue political interference." Pressured by the Regents, he refused to resign. "One must attach himself to a cause much bigger than himself and lose himself working for it," Rainey said. The faculty rewarded him with a unanimous vote of confidence. His views landed him on the anti-Communist Minute Women's list of two hundred Texas subversives.

On October 20, 1944, Mac Wallace issued a resolution allying himself with Homer Rainey. "Rainey has by his example as a fine Christian gentleman and by his public speeches urged this student body to assume the responsibilities of its potential role as moral and intellectual leaders in the post-war world," he wrote. His ambition for his own future is apparent as he pictured Homer Rainey as "inspiring us continually to strive to become able leaders in our communities in the future."

Coke Stevenson distanced himself from the conflict and refused to discuss changing the method of how Regents were appointed. It was now that he claimed he was "too experienced a rancher to burn his lips on a hot coffee pot." Mac Wallace decided to hitchhike to Houston, where the Regents were meeting far from the eyes of the students and their supporters.

"I know I am not too dignified for it if Henry Wallace isn't," he said. He debated with Nora Ann about the wide gulf in their social status. He wrote her that he prayed "a little Thanksgiving" for his parents being "as they are." They were "neither 1) snobs nor 2) meddlers." He was reading Spinoza, who, he noted, is "dialing some heavy blows against the established order."

The Regents met for more than twelve hours in Houston. Only at the penultimate moment was Mac Wallace admitted to the room as the student representative. "I am speaking for the seven thousand students," Mac Wallace said, as he began a speech that went on for forty-five minutes. "We are afraid of two things. That someone would forget us and that drastic action will be taken."

Nevertheless, on November 1, 1944, Homer P. Rainey was fired by the Board of Regents by a vote of six to two. The next morning's *Austin American* carried the headline MULTI-MILLIONAIRE REGENTS FIRE RAINEY. The

National Association of Manufacturers, at war with the minimum wage, and anti-union, publicly opposed the students.

Arriving back in Austin early Thursday morning November 2, Wallace encountered several thousand undergraduates waiting for him in front of the administration building. Some carried copies of the *Daily Texan*, whose banner headline read RAINEY FIRED. The state flag of Texas was hanging at half-mast.

At once he began to organize a mass movement. Its purpose was to persuade the Regents and the governor to reinstate Homer Rainey. As a class-mate later told the FBI, "Wallace had not been particularly interested in the specific question of what could or could not be taught at the University of Texas. Wallace had sided with the president of the university because he believed in the principle of being free to choose whatever you might wish in a course of study."

"We have to be orderly, not weak," Mac told the crowd. "They made the decision, but we will fall or stand on the wisdom of the decision. They did the planting, but we will harvest the crop . . . you might say they did the gambling and we are the stakes."

Then he led a march to the capitol to demand that Governor Stevenson request that the Regents meet with the students on the coming Saturday morning, November 4. While four thousand students massed in front of his office, Coke Stevenson received Mac Wallace, along with two other student leaders.

Had Dr. Chauncey D. Leake, dean of the medical school, been brought to Austin from Galveston to assume the presidency of the university? Mac Wallace asked Stevenson. The governor professed not to know anything about this rumor.

Mac Wallace asked the governor whether he had conferred with the ex-student (alumni) or faculty committees on possible appointments to replace the three Regents who had resigned. Stevenson admitted that he had not and wanted to know if a "Scratch Stevenson" campaign of 35,000 letters had been circulated among the students, as had been rumored. Stevenson promised to consider the students' request that the Regents meet with them on Saturday. Later Mac Wallace reported to the students that he had had a "man-to-man talk" with Stevenson.

That evening, the Reverend Blake Smith, pastor of the University Baptist Church, told a packed Gregory Gymnasium that the Regents "had tried to intimidate Dr. Rainey, who was fighting the same kind of battle as the men overseas are fighting." At the University of Texas, they were struggling with the same issues "for which young men are dying today." If Coke Stevenson were a friend of the university, Smith added, he would appoint new Regents committed to reinstating Homer Rainey.

The issues consuming Mac Wallace and his student constituency were very different from Lyndon Johnson's preoccupations: Lyndon Johnson took no interest in the growing warfare between labor and business; freedom to dissent; a growing "McCarthyism" after McCarthy himself had come on the scene; and even, as World War Two drew to a close, opposition to foreign wars.

When Reverend Smith had finished, the crowd rose to its feet in a standing ovation. At this tumultuous moment, Mac Wallace walked out onto the stage to announce that Governor Stevenson had refused to send the telegram requesting that the Regents meet with the students. "Jim Fogartie [the student judiciary chairman] and I will send it ourselves," he said.

"Isn't that what you wanted?" he asked the crowd.

A roar of approval was his reply. Then he read a Western Union telegram from Homer Rainey. "Please convey to the entire student body my deep appreciation for their love, their loyalty and their support." He thanked Mac Wallace "for your fine leadership." When Mac Wallace proposed an open meeting with the Regents, "right here," he was drowned out by cheers. He urged the students to cut their classes until they received a commitment from one of the Regents to attend the Saturday morning meeting.

"I want to hear what Mr. Bullington has to say," Mac added, referring to the conservative Republican regent who characterized the New Deal as being run by "gutter reds and parlor pinks."

"Don't forget Strickland!" a student yelled out. Frank Strickland was a legislative lobbyist for Karl Hoblitzelle, who had chaired the anti-union, anti-labor meeting in Dallas two years earlier that had resulted in the termination of the three economics instructors, Peach, Gordon, and Foster.

Mac Wallace strategized out loud. "We're in bad trouble up here," he acknowledged. "But I think we can get some help from over the state." He proposed another student march to the door of Governor Stevenson the following day. Their demand would be that the Regents come to the gymnasium on Saturday morning and "explain to the students the basis of their Houston decision."

Friday, November 3, dawned cloudy, dark, and cool. Having painted posters at the campus YMCA, the students massed in front of the university tower.

By eleven thirty A.M., Mac Wallace stood at the head of some eight thousand students wearing black armbands. Behind a banner reading FUNERAL PROCESSION FOR ACADEMIC FREEDOM, they began to walk, six abreast, in silence, up Congress Street to the capitol building.

At the front, students carried two flags, those of the United States of America and of the Republic of Texas. The city of Austin had declared the procession to be a legitimate funeral and had cleared all traffic from the streets. It was a fine hour for Mac Wallace, for Texas, and for the United States at a time when dissent was respected, an early pushback against what was later termed "McCarthyism," but for which credit belongs to Texas congressman Martin Dies, who chaired the House Committee Investigating Un-American Activities (the Dies Committee) beginning in 1938.

Through their banners and posters, the students connected their struggle at the University of Texas to the war against fascism in Europe. One banner read: WE WANT RAINEY, SHALL WE BE GOVERNED BY 卐? The ex-servicemen's group reminded onlookers that many students had seen combat: WE FOUGHT FOR FREEDOM. ARE WE LOSING IT TO HOMEGROWN FASCISM?

At the time, the University of Texas at Austin was among the most prestigious educational institutions in the country. The demonstration reflected a well-educated student body. The students placed their struggle in a historical context. One carried a poster bearing a likeness of Abraham Lincoln. It read: WE TOO NEED A GREAT EMANCIPATOR. Another invoked Commodore John Paul Jones: WE HAVE JUST BEGUN TO FIGHT. Yet another pointed out, YOUTH FIGHTS THE WAR. THE REGENTS FIGHT YOUTH.

Some signs were literary: WILL STEVENSON FIDDLE WHILE U.T. BURNS? RATS AND REGENTS LEAVE A SINKING SHIP. Others were whimsical: NO RAINEY/NO CLASSES/VOTE THE LADS/AND THE LASSIES. Some were spiritual: RESISTANCE TO TYRANTS IS OBEDIENCE TO GOD. The Latin American student contingent composed its message in Spanish: COMPAÑEROS LATINO-AMERICANOS, NUESTRO AMIGO EL DR. RAINEY HA SIDO CESADO POR LOS ENEMIGOS DE LA LIBERTAD.

Mac Wallace marched alone at the head of the mile-long funeral procession of students, just behind a solitary police officer on a motorcycle. The officer was present more for show than need as all the events on behalf of Homer Rainey were entirely nonviolent. Mac's black Cherokee hair was glossy and combed back; his eyeglasses were rimless, his square jaw set. In his ubiquitous ill-fitting tweed suit he was not an elegant figure, yet in his white shirt and dotted tie, he was dignified. His shoulders were thrust back. His arms swung at his sides.

Behind Mac Wallace was a line of four or five black automobiles, behind which the students marched. A sign stretched horizontally across Congress Street. It read: ACADEMIC FREEDOM IS DEAD. Some students carried a black-draped coffin with the legend affixed: ACADEMIC FREEDOM. By the count of the San Antonio field office of the FBI, there were between five thousand and eight thousand demonstrators, about 97 percent of the student body.

Marching with the students, the University of Texas Longhorn band played Chopin's "Funeral March." Otherwise, all that could be heard for blocks was the shuffling of feet. Then the students began to sing "The Eyes of Texas" in funereal cadences.

As they approached the state capitol grounds, the sun burst through the clouds. At this, the students erupted into a more spirited rendition of "The Eyes of Texas." "WE WANT RAINEY!" some shouted. The black-draped coffin mourning the death of academic freedom at the University of Texas was deposited in the rotunda of the state capitol.

Mac Wallace addressed the sea of students, men and women in equal numbers, surrounding him on three sides. Behind him on a balcony, two students held up a banner: WE FIGHT HITLERISM ABROAD/WE'LL FIGHT IT AT HOME. In his speech, Mac Wallace demanded of Governor Stevenson the name of the person with whom he intended to replace Homer Rainey. "The students won't return to class until the Regents agree to meet with them," he said.

At a pep rally that night in Gregory Gymnasium from the podium, Mac Wallace addressed Nora Ann: "Tonight there's a girl in the audience whose father has signed a petition not to reinstate President Homer Rainey. I now ask that girl to talk to her father and get his support!"

"I'll do it, Mac!" Nora Ann shouted from her seat. As the conflict at the university had extended its tentacles all over the state of Texas, Nora Ann Carroll's corporate lawyer father in Beaumont had signed two petitions. One urged Governor Coke Stevenson not to rehire the economics instructors. The other endorsed the Regents' decision to fire Homer Rainey.

That night the faculty, by resolution, voted that Dr. Homer P. Rainey be reinstated as president of the university. The faculty commended the students for their orderly behavior during the demonstrations.

Gregory Gymnasium was packed with ten thousand people on the morning of Saturday, November 4. Nine empty chairs stood in a line awaiting the Regents. Not a single regent showed up. The students debated whether to boycott classes through Christmas. They agreed that at every class and lab on Monday and Tuesday a student should rise and announce to the professor that "we are in class under protest." There was no point in their losing credit for the entire semester.

Mac closed the meeting by thanking the students for "a University of Texas spirit that cannot lose." As they filed out of the gym, the students contributed to a fund to carry their message on the radio throughout the state of Texas, beginning the next day. Some stations would donate time to the students' message as a public service, offering the same courtesy to the Regents.

That day, the University of Texas faced Southern Methodist University in football at home. Mac and Nora Ann attended the game together. Homer Rainey was also present. At halftime, Mac suddenly stood up and removed his overcoat.

"Hold my coat," he said to Nora Ann. "I have to go to the speaker's stand." He had not told her that he had prepared a speech.

Over Texas Memorial Stadium's loudspeakers, at this, his finest hour, Mac Wallace addressed the crowd. Describing his remarks as a "eulogy" for the presidency of Homer Rainey, he quoted John Dewey on democracy and freedom. Rainey and Clarence Ayres were admirers of Dewey as were their disciples Mac Wallace and Nora Ann Carroll. They all subscribed to Dewey's view that a primary purpose of a university was to help define social goals for society.

Mac described Homer Rainey as "a living biography of [the] principles espoused by John Dewey." He said that the student body was fighting for those same principles in university life. You could hear a pin drop, so silent was the stadium.

Those in military service were restricted from participating in political demonstrations. Mac requested that the civilian students rise and stand with bared heads for one minute of silence "in honor of a great man, HOMER PRICE RAINEY." SMU students and townspeople might participate, if they wished, he said.

Every student at that football game, as well as the majority of the fans, rose to their feet and remained standing. Tears rolled down Homer Rainey's cheeks. Tears stood in Nora Ann Carroll's eyes as, proudly, she held Mac Wallace's coat. The moment of silence seemed to last forever.

Mac had led and no one else could have led the students so well, Nora Ann thought. His address to the crowd seemed to her to be "absolute perfection." It was the defining moment of Mac Wallace's life.

The silence was broken only when the crowd burst into the theme song of the student struggle, "The Eyes of Texas."

Texas beat Southern Methodist that day, thirty-four to seven.

The Austin community's response to Mac Wallace's leadership in the movement to reinstate Homer Rainey was respectful and grateful. The *Austin American* wrote that the demonstration at the SMU game "was in accord with other orderly mass movements led by Wallace in the past three days, starting with the march on the capitol Thursday and the downtown funeral parade Friday." City manager Walter Seaholm termed the student parade "one of the most orderly I have ever seen. Those of us in city administration appreciate the way they conducted themselves."

When he was told that Mac Wallace had organized the parade, Seaholm remarked, "He must be a real leader."

The ensuing national debate was widespread. Professor J. Frank Dobie termed the politicians who closed in on Rainey "native fascists." A *Chicago Sun* editorial was titled "CAN TEXAS SAVE ITS UNIVERSITY?" In *Harper's* magazine, literary critic Bernard DeVoto noted that Homer Rainey had alienated the powers in Texas by being an integrationist "associated with a Negro-white group." Rainey was accused of friendliness to Negroes.

Congressman Lyndon Johnson kept his distance from the upheaval.

Nora Ann Carroll's birthday fell on November 18. To celebrate with her, Edward Cary traveled to Austin from New Orleans. Meanwhile in Nora Ann's honor, Mac threw a costume party at his humble garage apartment.

In the flush of the struggle, Nora Ann had considered marrying Mac Wallace. "Have toyed with idea of marrying Mac & spending Christmas with him in Mexico," she wrote to her father on November 9. "We could live comfortably on what we both made & would continue here for 2 or 3 years while he gets a law degree during which time I could start on my Ph.D. in Eco."

Nora Ann admitted to her mother that "I don't like Ted when I don't see him." She preferred to "go my own way—no doubt in direction of economics after the grueling course I am following now of calculus, physics and 3 chem courses. And of course there's Ayres' influence." That Clarence Ayres had evinced confidence in her abilities bolstered her self-confidence. Her women friends were more conventional. "How is Mac?" one wrote. "Are you still going with him? Do you ever wear your pin?"

The costume birthday party at Mac's apartment featured considerable consumption of alcoholic beverages. Mac abstained because later in the evening he was to go to his job as a night watchman at the gas plant. Mac— Nora Ann assumed it was Mac—seemed constantly to be refilling her glass and Nora Ann seemed not to notice it as she kept on drinking.

She was barely conscious at the moment that she and Mac Wallace had sexual relations for the first time. Nora Ann remembered herself feeling like an inert "sack of potatoes." "One does not seduce a rag doll," she would say later, with some indignation. There was never any doubt that she was attracted to Mac Wallace, more than to any man, previously or later.

Afterward, Nora Ann fell asleep on the floor of Mac's loft-like apartment. When he went off to the gas plant, he made her promise to return later, and she agreed. Once he was gone, guilt washed over her. Since Ted Cary was in town, she decided she had better tell Ted what had happened before he heard about it from someone else. Mac was volatile. There might be a nasty confrontation.

When she confessed to Ted, he did not lose his temper. Instead, he burst into tears. "Let's forget this," he said when he came to himself. "We'll have a good life together." Ted Cary rested on the confidence of his social class, and no less on Nora Ann's sense of the class divide between her and Mac Wallace. ("I was a snob," Nora Ann later admitted.)

Then Ted Cary went off to confront Mac Wallace at the gas plant. Ted seemed to want to know everything about Mac Wallace, his history and his accomplishments. He affected to find Mac a person of enormous interest. For an hour, Mac bragged about all he had done. It seemed as if he would go on forever.

"What about you?" Mac finally addressed Ted.

"There's not much to tell," Ted Cary said. Ted had bested Mac Wallace, as Nora Ann Carroll described the incident. He had lured Mac into talking about himself while Ted himself revealed nothing. He had dominated the conversation and so his rival, revealing Mac to be the weaker of the two. In the machismo culture of the day, this meant that Ted was the victor. Now Ted faded into the night, his mission accomplished.

Nora Ann returned to Mac's apartment as she had promised. No one was at home. On the ground outside the door was her birthday present, a forty-dollar bottle of Jolie Madame perfume, a magnificent gift from someone as poor as

Mac Wallace. There was also a letter. He was sorry things had ended on a sour note, Mac wrote. He knew he had made a fool of himself and that he had lost the woman he loved. So in November 1944 Mac Wallace suffered two profound defeats. Homer Rainey would not return to the University of Texas and he had lost Nora Ann.

Nora Ann was so disturbed by that sexual moment with Mac Wallace that she persuaded herself that she must be pregnant. She decided that as soon as she graduated in February, she would move to Chicago and become an undergraduate again; she would study French and German to prepare for her Ph.D. while she waited for the birth of the baby. When she realized she was not pregnant, she adjusted her thinking. Marriage "seems highly unlikely for a number of years," she reasoned. She thought she might "run around Paris and Heidelberg . . . depending also on whether I get a husband." It is apparent that she was not in love with Ted Cary.

For a time, Mac Wallace persisted in his support of Homer Rainey. "They couldn't get a man to walk into that office over the dead body of academic freedom and be a good man," he said. "We don't want a Quisling. We want Rainey." But he had lost, and Coke Stevenson refused to reinstate Rainey. An army colonel named Orr charged that the academic freedom endorsed by a pacifist professor named Arthur Goldwyn Billings, who had been imprisoned as a conscientious objector, amounted to "socialism."

Mac Wallace replied to the colonel. "Freedom of expression, of thought, and freedom of research and investigations are essential to the well-being of a democratic body," he wrote. "A man can talk all he wants to about pacifism or socialism or racial equality, or any subject, that is a liberty guaranteed by the Bill of Rights." He qualified his statement by adding that "he must stop short of that area in which 'talking' becomes detrimental to the public welfare."

Then he invoked Socrates, Jesus, and Copernicus, historical figures who had been "ridiculed, condemned, imprisoned, even killed" for "teaching revolutionary ideas." He pointed out that there were classes at the University of Texas discussing "the effects and ills of capitalism; the theories of socialism, communism and fascism; the biological equality of races." Education, he believed, "is bearing an open mind and tolerant attitude when confronted with the different aspects of a question."

When later in the month he testified before the Texas State Senate committee on education investigating the Rainey firing, Mac Wallace reassured the senators that no professor had written any of the speeches delivered by the students. The "so-called sit-down strike, the march on the Capitol and the funeral procession" had been the fruit of "a concerted effort of the entire student body . . . no one had dictated their movements or demonstrations." He took no personal credit.

For his part in the student movement, Mac Wallace was investigated by the FBI, but the Bureau could not discover from its multiplicity of informants that he was a Communist. If he was "identified with a Communist or front organization during his school life," one informant said, it would have been "without realizing the true aims or purposes of the group."

On November 28, 1944, with tears in his eyes, Homer Rainey told the Senate Education Committee that the peril the United States faced was not Communism, "but the dangers that are going to arise in the world because of great power that the United States will have after the war." In March 1945, he lectured before the American Council of the American Federation for Civil Liberties. Texas is being run by "oil, utility and motion picture interests," Rainey said, the last a reference to Karl Hoblitzelle. "There are two ways we can lose our liberty," he added, "by military invasion and by the action of socially disintegrating forces such as are now at work in Texas."

"Brother, we will ruin you and see that you never hold another job in American education," a regent told Rainey. This turned out to be an empty threat. Homer Rainey became president of Stephens College in Columbia, Missouri, and went on to a professorship at the University of Colorado.

The University of Texas was censured by the American Association of University Professors, a stigma that endured for nine years. In July 1945, the Southern Association of Colleges and Secondary Schools, the accrediting agency for the University of Texas, placed the university on indefinite probation.

Before long, Ted Cary talked Nora Ann Carroll into applying to Tulane University in biochemistry. He opposed her pursuing her studies in economics since that would have represented a tie to Mac Wallace. Ted was persuasive, but there was also pressure from her roommate, psychology student Pat Elliot, who herself had dated Mac and would manage to remain in contact with him for the next two decades.

"Mac is flawed," Pat argued. He had a "massive ego" and was at the very least an "occasional boozer." Nora Ann then convinced herself that she was "keeping her head" by casting her lot with Ted Cary.

Mac Wallace did not give up. He knew Nora Ann was the love of his life and he hoped he might yet prevail. So he underestimated his rival, a short, dumpy fellow, cross-eyed and homely. Nora Ann was in love with Mac, but still she would not sacrifice the security and class privilege that attached to being a doctor's wife. Mac Wallace had been wooed by many as president of the student body. That counted for something, Nora Ann thought. But "on my score pad it didn't count for as much as he believed." She began to think in terms of preparing herself to help Ted with his research.

At Christmas in Beaumont, Nora Ann instructed her mother: "It is imperative that Mr. Cary spend every second of his Xmas with us. I have given up Mac completely and need Mr. Cary to strengthen my resolve, so resign yourself."

As for Mac Wallace, he was not accustomed to losing and he took the loss of Nora Ann hard.

Nora Ann Carroll graduated from the University of Texas in February 1945. Seated together in an automobile outside the law school, she and Mac said their final good-byes. Nora Ann sobbed uncontrollably, clearly not as certain of her decision as she pretended to be. Then she went home to Beaumont. Two days later, her father died suddenly of peritonitis. On March 7, Mac wrote to her as "Nora Ann, darling," offering consolation as if things were not over between them.

The following day he resigned as president of the students' association. Without having graduated, he announced that he was leaving the University of Texas to pursue his studies "elsewhere." He might return in 1946, he told people, if he could assist Homer Rainey in a bid to become governor of Texas. Then Mac headed for New York.

Three weeks later, "unable to bear life with Mother," unwilling to remain in Beaumont, Nora Ann Carroll left for New Orleans, where she enrolled at Tulane University as a graduate student in zoology. She described her move to New Orleans as "I leave Mac Wallace."

CHAPTER 4

Lyndon Johnson Betrays Richard M. Kleberg and George Parr Works His Magic

*"People who keep their mouths shut live
longer . . . down this way."*
—ANONYMOUS, AS RECORDED BY
HOLLAND McCOMBS

By 1944, Richard M. Kleberg had served seven terms in Congress. On several occasions he ran unopposed. He had broken conclusively with "Rooseveltism" over Roosevelt's failed court-packing scheme announced on February 5, 1937. In 1944, Kleberg faced a Democratic Party primary campaign. The person who manipulated the election, and engineered his defeat, was his former secretary, Lyndon Baines Johnson.

The genesis of Johnson's betrayal of Richard M. Kleberg was a meeting between Kleberg's brother, Bob, and the boss of South Texas, the "Duke of Duval [County]," George Parr. Present as well was Parr's father, Archer, a figure every bit as corrupt as the Duke. George Parr controlled three Texas counties, Duval, Jim Wells, and Zapata. There was no election he did not control, no scam he could not infiltrate. Under the Parrs, the county treasury existed as a personal political slush fund. Holland McCombs provides a succinct description of Parr:

> When the major oil companies started drilling in Duval and neigh-
> boring counties, they were at George's mercy. And he showed no
> mercy. He ruled the heavy Mexican population as a benevolent
> despot. And trimmed anybody who opposed him down to size. If oil
> companies did not lease through him (with enormous cuts), they
> might find their leases no good, or erased. The oil companies
> complained. George got tough—physically and otherwise. The state

sent the Rangers. George hired them away from the state—and put some of them in charge of the rackets he let run (from gambling to prostitution). George Parr became so powerful he virtually ruled politics in several South Texas counties, delivered votes en masse to his favorite candidates for local, state and national office . . . On the surface he seemed to be a dashing, polo-playing, rich South Texas rancher. Actually, he was a ruthless and crooked political despot, who brooked no opposition.

George Parr was convicted of tax evasion in 1932 and had served nine months in prison, but his power continued unabated. Parr would be suspected of having done "everything in political bossmanship from burning down the Duval County Courthouse to destroying incriminating records, to murder for political motives." According to *The Handbook of Texas*, under the leadership of Archer Parr and his son George "corruption and paternalism flourished in Duval County." It was George Parr, more than any other single individual, who would be responsible for Lyndon Johnson's rise to power.

Early in 1934, Archer Parr was campaigning for re-election to the state senate. One day the Parrs, father and son, knocked at the door of King Ranch. Bob Kleberg did not suffer fools gladly. His remarkable self-confidence had been nurtured by his having managed with aplomb the huge King Ranch enterprise since his early twenties. Now he saw no reason to offend his moral sense by granting any favors to either Archer or George Parr.

Archer Parr was on the ropes. In 1933, he had been accused of receiving one hundred thousand dollars from a Houston road contractor named W. L. Pearson, payment for Parr's assistance in Pearson's being awarded the road contracts in Duval County. The federal government had filed income tax liens of $101,407.31 against Archer Parr, and $25,344.97 against his wife. In the 1934 election for the Texas state senate, Archer Parr was opposed by a rancher named Jim Neal. Neal ran on the slogan, "Archer can't make it over the hill with that last $100,000."

Then Archer Parr had a brainstorm. In the southernmost part of his district, there was a concrete road designated Texas-US 77. It ran from Raymondville north to the barbed-wire fence of King Ranch. All efforts to extend the highway through King Ranch to Kingsville had proven futile.

If he could persuade Bob to extend the highway to Kingsville, Archer Parr believed, he might still be re-elected to the legislature. Taking his son George along, Archer paid a call at King Ranch and explained his plight to Kleberg:

The construction of the extension of Highway 77 would have to run fifteen miles through the Norias division of King Ranch.

"I don't want a road through my pasture," Kleberg said. That should have settled the matter. For Kleberg, the subject was closed. Archer Parr turned away, tears of frustration in his eyes.

"You're crucifying my father!" George Parr erupted in anger as he headed for the door. "I'll gut you if it's the last thing I do!"

The newspapers sided with the Duke of Duval on the matter of the road. Kleberg quietly contacted his friend Nelson Rockefeller, who consulted city planner Robert Moses, an expert in the construction of highways, roads, bridges, and more. Moses devised an alternate route for Highway 77, but it didn't prove practical. Archer Parr lost his election.

George Parr was indicted by a federal grand jury in San Antonio for income tax evasion. On May 21, 1934, he pleaded guilty and was sentenced to two years and a five-thousand-dollar fine, sentence suspended. Parr's probation was revoked on June 3, 1936, and he was committed to El Reno, an Oklahoma reformatory where he served until April 9, 1937, and where Lyndon Johnson supporter Billie Sol Estes would later be incarcerated.

Some six years later, on August 7, 1943, Parr applied for a pardon. Congressman Richard M. Kleberg was less than enthusiastic about George Parr's pardon. As Kleberg's son-in-law, Dick Reynolds, would later observe, Kleberg was an "honest and fearless man," even if his work ethic left something to be desired. George Parr had exhibited no evidence of character redemption, and so "Kleberg declined to sign the petition for his pardon." Parr had not only not improved in character during his parole, but he had grown more corrupt. From then on, Reynolds said, George Parr was bent on doing Dick Kleberg in, "and with the help of those South Texas politicians who were mighty friendly with Lyndon (and depending on him) DID DO HIM IN."

The request for George Parr's pardon was denied on January 22, 1944.

Kleberg's opponent in the 1944 primary was John E. Lyle, a South Texas lawyer who had been elected to the Texas state legislature in 1941. In 1942, Lyle had gone off to serve in the U.S. Army in Europe so that he never actually took his seat. He was an intimate of Lyndon Johnson.

Lyle had met Lyndon Johnson and they had become friends in late 1934 or early 1935. Lyle had been practicing law in Corpus Christi when Johnson went to work for Kleberg. Lyle was an active supporter of Johnson in his 1941 losing campaign for the U.S. Senate. Based as he was in Corpus Christi, it was inevitable that Lyle would seek the favor of Archer and George Parr. Lyle and Johnson became such "close personal friends" that when Johnson wanted to talk confidentially to George Parr, he enlisted Lyle as his intermediary.

In his absence, Lyle's name was entered in the primary for U.S. representative for the Fourteenth Congressional District to run against Richard Kleberg. While Lyle remained in Europe, his wife campaigned on his behalf. Lyndon Johnson affected to be indifferent to the outcome of this election. A spokesman explained that he "did not feel that it was proper for a U.S. representative from one district to campaign or use his influence in another district."

Meanwhile Johnson lobbied with Sam Rayburn, speaker of the House, to arrange to have John Lyle discharged from the Army. Rayburn did not know John Lyle, but he pulled the requisite strings and before long Lyle was campaigning in Texas—with the assistance of George Parr. As Johnson's future antagonist, Billie Sol Estes, put it to the author, who asked him about the Lyle-Kleberg campaign, "if Lyndon Johnson didn't want you to be elected, you would not be elected." Lyle defeated Kleberg 29,152 to 17,608.

A local reporter remarked with only slight exaggeration that Lyle won "without making a speech or shaking a hand." Once Dick Reynolds asked his father-in-law, "Mr. Kleberg," as he referred to him, about Lyndon Johnson, the better for Reynolds to know how to approach this man. "Mr. Kleberg, who was never one to say bad things about anyone if he could help it," Reynolds recounted to Holland McCombs, "said soberly and simply that he could not say that Lyndon did anything against him. But he never did anything FOR HIM either." Lyndon Johnson "had practiced devices to succeed," Reynolds added.

John Lyle accounted for his victory over longtime congressman Richard Kleberg in his oral history for the LBJ library: "Several people had come to the conclusion that Mr. Kleberg was not the kind of representative that they wanted and proceeded to ask quite a number of prominent people who had always supported me if they would support me as a candidate for Congress." Lyle acknowledged that these people were all "supporters of Lyndon."

One observer, who insisted even twenty years later on remaining anonymous, summed up John Lyle's defeat of Richard Kleberg in this way: "If Johnson did not help defeat Kleberg—and this while Kleberg was having personal and health troubles—he certainly stood by and saw such a crooked and brutal thug as Parr cut the throat of the good and honest man who started him on his way up . . . that's just about as low as you can get. And Lyndon got that low."

On February 20, 1946, President Harry Truman granted George Parr a full and unconditional pardon, with the enthusiastic support of John Lyle. The response of the Klebergs to these events may be discerned in the reply of Kleberg's widow to an inquiry from Johnson biographer Ronnie Dugger. "I don't think you'd be interested in my opinion of Mr. Johnson," Mamie Kleberg said, "with bitterness."

A typical Johnson–Brown & Root maneuver in these last years of Lyndon Johnson's tenure as a congressman involved the sale of Fort Clark in 1946. Built in 1857, on 3,800 acres on the Rio Grande, Fort Clark guarded the Mexican border and defended against Native American depredations. It had been a World War Two training base. Now it was put up for surplus sale by the government. The property was dotted with locked-up warehouses, but no one bidding was permitted to view what was stored in those buildings. Attorney Josh Groce prepared a bid for Henry and John Catto, San Antonio ranchers and real estate operators.

Nine bids were submitted. The Catto brothers bid $130,000. Only two bids were higher than the Catto's, including one for $135,000. The winning bid was $325,000, almost three times higher, submitted by Texas Railway Equipment Company. This turned out to be a front company for Brown & Root.

"Now, just how do you think Brown & Root found out what was in the warehouses?" Groce asked Holland McCombs years later. Although his name was nowhere to be found on the matter, once more Lyndon Johnson's role emerged. As a member of the Naval Affairs Committee, Johnson knew about the sales of government-owned properties after the war. He knew that on the Fort Clark property resided equipment for construction and road building and other machines.

There was a witness to all this. Bart Moore, a San Antonio contractor, had once been friendly with Herman Brown. Moore's source was Hal "Boss" Peterson, a local rancher and contractor. One night, Peterson confided to Moore: "Brown & Root and I have bought old Fort Clark." Peterson revealed that one of the barracks buildings was going to be moved to Kerrville for veterans' housing. In one of the warehouses alone, Peterson had observed "piles of air conditioning equipment, electric stoves and all sorts of electrical equipment." Moore himself was angry because Herman Brown had pushed him and Peterson out of the project. Now Moore was talking.

Moore was indignant. Brown & Root had obtained inside information "from Lyndon, or through Lyndon, or through Lyndon's influence as to the approximate value of the equipment in the warehouses ... this was not only the obvious, but the ONLY reason that Brown & Root bid more than twice the amount of the next highest bidder." Brown & Root sold the contents of the warehouses for more than a million dollars. Then they sold the old barracks. Then they sold the land.

Once more there was nothing on paper. No one could prove that Lyndon Johnson had been involved. In 1957, Senator Lyndon Johnson visited Fort Clark. "I want to go on record that last week at Fort Clark was one of the most enjoyable weeks I have ever spent in my life," he wrote to Herman and Margaret Brown. He exhibited no self-consciousness about any shady or dishonest aspects attached to the sale of Fort Clark to Brown & Root.

Among Lyndon Johnson's final efforts as a congressman was his vote in favor of passage of the Taft-Hartley Act. Taft-Hartley reserved the right of the states to pass open shop laws, and forbade the requirement of union membership as a condition of employment. It insisted upon the "right to work" without belonging to a union. Herman Brown might well have been the staunchest opponent of unions not only in Texas, but in the United States. In keeping with his symbiotic relationship with Herman Brown and Brown & Root, Lyndon Johnson opposed unions and the right of workers to organize in unions as long as Herman was alive.

It is impossible to penetrate the byways of the 1948 election to the United States Senate in Texas without assessing the role of George Parr. More than any other single individual, Parr was instrumental in the outcome that placed Lyndon Johnson at the forefront of political power and so colored American history for the next twenty years. When Lyndon Johnson in 1948 embarked upon his second campaign for the United States Senate, the first person to whom he turned was George Parr. This was not a matter for the telephone, or even for intermediaries, as was Johnson's wont. Rather, Johnson decided to make a personal trip to South Texas for the purpose of calling on Parr. Johnson was accompanied by John Connally, one of the bright young men firmly under his sway.

Connally had been a student body president at the University of Texas (1938–1939) and had been elected to the exclusive "Friar's", the best and the brightest eight men of each senior class. In 1939, Connally became a legislative assistant to Johnson; to help Connally finance his education, Johnson got him a job with the National Youth Administration. In 1941, Connally earned a law degree from the University of Texas. Connally managed Johnson's losing 1941 campaign for the United States Senate as well as his re-election campaign to the House of Representatives in 1946. By now, John Connally had demonstrated his loyalty. He was Johnson's campaign manager in his campaign for the United States Senate in 1948. (Connally had also been managing the Johnson radio station KTBC in Austin.)

Johnson's opponent would be rancher Coke Stevenson, who had resigned as governor on January 1, 1947. Stevenson was deeply conservative, and cautious. He remained notorious for the statement he had made when he refused to discuss changing his method of appointing Regents at the University of Texas, that he was "too experienced a rancher to burn his lips on a hot coffee pot." That figure of speech became attached to his persona like a burr. Yet Stevenson was a formidable opponent, having been a banker, county attorney, judge, speaker of the Texas House for several terms, lieutenant governor, and then governor, resigning that office of his own volition. Johnson hesitated, and his supporters said they would run John Connally. The next day, Johnson announced his own candidacy.

Johnson demanded to know where his opponent stood on Taft-Hartley. He accused Stevenson of making a deal with the "big labor leaders," while he, Johnson, was anti-union and for the open shop. His adoration of Franklin Roosevelt had long been forgotten.

In the Democratic Party primary, Stevenson led Johnson 39.7 percent to 33.7 percent.

As Lyndon Johnson was about to come calling, George Parr had no conflict with supporting him over Coke Stevenson. The governor had refused to appoint as District Attorney of Webb County a candidate whom Parr had favored. That was all it took. Parr broke with Stevenson.

The chronology is murky, but apparently Stevenson was unaware of alliances Lyndon Johnson had developed in the years that he had served in the House of Representatives. As Stevenson now sought support, he called on oilman, rancher, and all-around entrepreneur Sid Richardson, and on Arch Underwood, both of whom had been his supporters in earlier campaigns. Underwood, of Lubbock, Texas, was the owner of cotton compresses and warehouses and had been a confidant of Franklin Roosevelt, terming himself "a crackpot New Dealer." He was a major figure in the cotton business, owning eight of the businesses storing government-owned cotton.

Oilman Clint Murchison Sr., Sid Richardson, and Arch Underwood had grown up together in the hamlet of Athens, Texas, and might be expected to form a united front now. Each chose to abandon Coke Stevenson because Lyndon Johnson "had done them some money-saving favor that required political repayment."

Lyndon Johnson and Coke Stevenson shared conservative campaign rhetoric. If you went by their espoused political views, it would be difficult to tell them apart. The outcome would be decided on who wielded the most power. According to Robert Caro, George Parr gave Johnson "full credit" for his pardon being granted. George Brown added that "we helped him [Johnson] down there through Wirtz" so that before the campaign began, "Johnson had a 25,000-vote head start."

In 1948, Lyndon Johnson, with John Connally in tow, went to visit George Parr before Johnson even decided to make the 1948 race for the Senate. Arriving in South Texas for this pre-campaign visit, the exact date unrecorded for history, Lyndon Johnson had a particular question for George Parr. He wanted to know how many votes were required to ensure victory.

Parr marshaled his forces to accomplish this calculation. He was assisted by a lawyer named Polk Shelton, who had run against Johnson in 1937 for the seat in Congress vacated by James Buchanan. Johnson had run as a supporter of FDR; Shelton was against Roosevelt's court-packing scheme, a 1937 effort to expand the U.S. Supreme Court to as many as fifteen justices and so dilute the Court of people hostile to New Deal programs (the Senate struck the reorganization plan down, 70 to 22). Shelton had won most of the "Negro" vote on the strength of his father's longtime opposition to the Ku Klux Klan, an issue in which Johnson had taken little interest. But after the election, Johnson made overtures to both Polk and his brother Emmett. The Sheltons were "strong for him ever since then," Emmett Shelton said in his oral history interview for the LBJ Presidential Library. Later the Sheltons worked as lawyers for George Parr.

George Parr was already notorious in Texas for delivering landslide election totals to candidates he supported, not only in his home county of Duval, but also in neighboring Jim Wells, Zapata, and Nueces (Corpus Christi) counties. Often he would arrange to have totals withheld until it was clear how many votes his candidate required to win. The number of votes cast and the majorities varied with the closeness of the election.

It was not unheard of for a Parr candidate to win by one, two, or three hundred votes to one in a locale. Over the years, too, the ballot lists he influenced contained the names of people who had taken up residence in a cemetery, were absent, underage—or never had lived at all. In Coke Stevenson's three gubernatorial races, in which he had enjoyed the support of George Parr, the Duval County vote totals had been 3,643 for Stevenson to 141 for his two opponents, combined; 2,936 for Stevenson to 77 distributed among five opponents; and 3,310 for Stevenson to 17 votes divided among eight opponents.

In the first primary held in July 1948, Coke Stevenson received 477,077 votes to Lyndon Johnson's 405,617. Neither received a majority vote, forcing a runoff election. The runoff was scheduled for August 28.

On Election Day, the Texas Election Bureau, averring that all eligible votes had been cast, declared that Coke Stevenson had won election to the United States Senate by more than one hundred votes. The Duval County total of votes cast was 4,622 with Stevenson receiving only 40 of those votes. What, people wondered, had become of all those people who had been so solidly for Coke Stevenson in his races for governor?

On Thursday, September 2, Lyndon Johnson went on the radio and declared victory; at that moment Coke Stevenson was leading by 113 votes. The following day there was an announcement that there had been a "recanvass" and a "correction" in Jim Wells County, precinct 13 in particular.

Eight hundred eligible voters were registered in Jim Wells County. Six hundred ballots had been issued in Precinct 13 by presiding judge Luis Salas. Yet the first returns from precinct 13 awarded Lyndon Johnson 765 votes to Coke Stevenson's 60. A week later, "corrected" returns awarded Johnson 967 votes and Stevenson 61. In all, 1,028 votes emerged from the 600 ballots issued. Of the 203 votes added in the "correction," 202 went to Johnson and one to Stevenson. Yet when the last voter to turn up on Election Day had cast his ballot, just a few minutes before the seven P.M. cutoff time, no one was waiting to vote.

The first 841 names of people who had cast their votes before seven P.M. were in black ink. The handwritings varied. The 203 new voters, who, someone joked, must have emerged out of the mesquite, lined up in alphabetical order. All these names were written in a uniform bluish-green ink, in identical handwriting.

Some of the irregularities were penetrated immediately. "Hector Serda," whose name was in green ink, was away at school in Kingsville on Election Day. A housewife named Enriqueta Acres swore that she was not registered to vote because she had not paid her poll tax; she had not voted.

One South Texas wag remarked, "That was just TOO raw—even for George." Nearly thirty years later, Luis (nickname "Indio") Salas confessed to Associated Press reporter James W. Mangan, who broke the story, how George

Parr had summoned him three days after the election to add two hundred more votes for Lyndon Johnson. Salas had produced a quasi-memoir, which he said he had written to "show the corruption in politics."

Coke Stevenson fought back. He hired two former FBI agents named Kellis Dibrell and Jim Gardner, who knocked on George Parr's door in an attempt to question him. Parr affected indignation that they should be coming to see him about election results not in Duval, but across the line in Jim Wells County!

Rushing to Lyndon Johnson's aid was Congressman John Lyle, who affected to be convinced that "somebody was trying to steal the election from Lyndon." Lyle at once joined forces with George Parr. Lyle's responsibility was to figure out "how many votes were out, how many boxes were out, how many of the uncounted votes we might expect, and what the tabulation might be." There was some question about how many ballot boxes there were, and then one turned out to be empty.

"As far as I know," Lyle said in 1986 in an oral history interview he did for the LBJ Library from his office, "Johnson did not meet with George Parr" and there was "never any suggestion by anybody to illegally change any votes." Apart from the obvious falsehood that Johnson had not met with George Parr, Lyle's statement is misleading. The issue was not that votes were "changed," but that fraudulent ballots had been added.

Johnson's people were bent on discovering exactly how many votes it would take to win the close count. They were aided by the fact that the poll list was in the custody of B. F. Donald, cashier of the Texas State bank of Alice, of which George Parr was president. Lyle claims also that Lyndon Johnson did nothing to assist him in his candidacy for Richard Kleberg's seat in Congress; in fact Johnson intervened with Sam Rayburn to arrange that the Army release Lyle from his wartime service so that he could campaign, as Lyle acknowledges himself in his oral history interview for the LBJ Library.

Lyle claimed that Lyndon Johnson and George Parr "were not close at all." In fact, during the entire period that the Jim Wells County ballots were under scrutiny Lyndon Johnson telephoned George Parr every single day. Johnson's first calls arrived while Coke Stevenson was in the lead. Parr insisted that he had done all he could in Duval County. He promised to go over to Jim Wells County to see what he could do there.

In September, in the midst of the turmoil over the election, there was a meeting of the Democratic Executive Committee at which a vote would be taken as to who should represent Texas at the party convention, the Truman Democrats (known as the Loyalists) versus the States' Rights Party. The meeting was held in Fort Worth in the ballroom of the Blackstone Hotel on September 13, 1948. Before it began Herman Brown took two members of the committee, who were committed to voting for Coke Stevenson, aside for a short and earnest conversation.

Both Coke Stevenson and Lyndon Johnson were present as the Democratic Executive Committee debated whether Box 13 from Jim Wells County should simply be thrown out in its entirety. When it came to a vote, the two members of the committee who had been buttonholed by Herman Brown voted for Lyndon Johnson. The vote was 29 to 28 in Johnson's favor. One woman changed her vote, so there was a tie. The issue that remained was whether the results of the primary election would be certified.

It seemed that Herman Brown was almost as nervous as Lyndon Johnson. Some said that Brown had invested half a million dollars in Johnson's campaign. Herman himself told San Antonio attorney Josh Groce that "when all that Box 13 stuff came up they *had to* win that race, or maybe they could not pay off." Groce had served as one of Coke Stevenson's attorneys as he fought to be certified. On behalf of Stevenson, he filed suit against the State Democratic election officials charging that Stevenson had been deprived of his civil rights. All the while Lyndon Johnson affected indifference and maintained that whatever was being done, was being done by his supporters.

A federal judge named T. Whitfield Davidson issued a restraining order against putting Lyndon Johnson's name on the ballot. The person appointed to implement the matter was William Robert (Bob) Smith, the U.S. Attorney who had sent George Parr to prison. Smith was a man known for his rectitude. Judge Davidson ruled, in sum, cutting through the stifling rhetoric: "In cases of fraud, the rule is—throw open the doors and let the light in." The boxes would be opened.

The victory for Coke Stevenson that Box 13 be opened was short-lived. When the surviving Box 13 was opened, it was empty. Judge Davidson ordered the hearing closed. The court case that ensued focused, as Caro writes, on whether a single precinct could elect a United States senator with dubious votes. Offering the opening argument for the Johnson side was Austin lawyer John Cofer. Robert Caro describes Cofer as "the most renowned of the stem-winding, arm-waving school of courthouse lawyers," someone who "roared" and "bellowed" to make himself heard. John Cofer was a hulking man, "gaunt, six foot four inches tall and cadaverous." He was a connoisseur of sophistry, and his efforts would weave for many years through Lyndon Johnson's political career and through the fates of those with whom Johnson forged his Faustian bargains.

Cofer attempted to intimidate the members of the Democratic Executive Committee with ferocity and histrionics: "You are here to count the votes," he shouted, according to Caro. "You may or may not be able to understand law, but by the Holy Writ, you can count!" But despite Cofer's histrionics, the judge ruled that the complainant (Stevenson) "has had a seat in the Senate of the United States taken away from him."

In 1964, researching his *LIFE* magazine article on LBJ, Holland McCombs discovered a witness to Lyndon Johnson's frequent calls to George Parr. His name was J. B. Donohoe, and he requested that his name be kept "completely out of the report." McCombs noted that Donohoe feared "possible reprisals by both George Parr and LBJ."

J. B. Donohoe was uniquely placed to witness the close contact between George Parr and Lyndon Johnson because of his relationship with J. Campbell King, chairman of the Democratic Executive Committee of Duval County. King was also sales manager for a Chevrolet Sales and Service Agency, which was operated in a fifty-fifty partnership by Donohoe and George Parr. King talked freely to Donohoe, knowing that Donohoe was a friend of Archer Parr, and that Donohoe was considered by both Parrs to be safe and loyal. Although Donohoe wanted no part of local politics, he knew in minute detail how the Parrs, father and son, had built their crooked political machine. Archer Parr had known Donohoe since he was a boy and trusted him entirely.

When Donohoe read and heard about Lyndon's "detachment," he laughed and said, in effect: If he was so aloof and out of it all, why was he putting in all those calls to George? Donohoe said that he had been sitting in Parr's office when many calls from Lyndon Johnson had come in. According to Donohoe, Parr also received calls from Johnson supporters all over the state. Always they asked: How many votes do you have? How many would it take? They emphasized the importance of their being told the exact vote count. How many votes would it take to win the election was what they wanted to know.

Campbell King revealed to Donohoe that 2,500 votes had been cast in Duval County in the 1948 primary. Yet some 4,711 votes had been reported. As Parr took Lyndon Johnson's calls, he was oblivious of his partner Campbell King's presence or of Donohoe's.

King told Donohoe that Johnson sometimes telephoned George Parr "several times a day, saying Coke was ahead again." Parr visited the Chevrolet dealership often during this time, and afterward King and Parr talked about how they had stolen the election for Lyndon. In one conversation with Donohoe, Parr used the phrase, "after I stole the election." More than once Donohoe heard King and Parr refer to how they had "stolen the election for Lyndon."

The ensuing legal battle over the 1948 election returns attracted national attention. The U.S. Senate prepared to dispatch investigators to South Texas in an effort to determine whether Lyndon Johnson should be seated. In panic, Johnson called George Parr yet again. He had heard a rumor that the Duval County ballots were going to be burned up.

"Don't let them burn up those ballots. It will make me look bad!" Johnson said.

"To hell with you!" Parr exploded. "I'm not going to let my men go to prison just to make you look good!" By the time the Senate investigators arrived, a janitor had burned the ballots.

Recounting this story to Holland McCombs, Donohoe chortled. "Yes," he said, "Lyndon was very worried about what George did AFTER he had stolen the election for him. But when the election was in doubt, it was obvious he didn't care HOW George got the votes, just so he GOT THEM!" Listening to Donohoe, McCombs wrote down: "What about crime doesn't pay?"

After three separate investigations and five court actions, Lyndon Johnson played his final card to be seated in the United States Senate. If his name was not on the ballot by October 3, he had no hope of success. Abe Fortas had been a lawyer both for Johnson and for George Parr, and it was Fortas who came up with the solution, to stay Judge Davidson's ruling by approaching a single Supreme Court justice.

In the company of a Texas delegation headed by James V. Allred, a former two-term Texas governor and federal judge, Fortas approached only Justice Hugo Black, a former Klan supporter, at the U.S. Supreme Court. Black ruled that were Coke Stevenson's charges against Johnson accurate, Johnson had committed a criminal offense and the matter should be handled by the Texas courts. Hugo Black's ruling for Johnson stood. Time had run out and the matter was never returned to the Texas courts.

For good measure, the clerk of the Supreme Court denied that Josh Groce had filed a motion on Coke Stevenson's behalf to vacate Black's decision. He had. On October 5, Black's order was endorsed by the full Supreme Court so that Johnson's name could appear on the November ballot in Texas. Johnson easily defeated his Republican adversary by 702,985 to 349,665. The Stevenson people petitioned the U.S. Senate to prevent the seating of Johnson. Investigators were sent into Duval and Jim Wells counties. But when the investigators arrived, they discovered that the ballots of the Democratic primary of 1948 had been "burned by a janitor," as George Parr had decreed.

As president, Johnson was to pay his debt and appoint Fortas to the U.S. Supreme Court. Fortas lasted only four years before he was obliged to resign amid charges of corruption and conflicts of interest.

Duval County continued in its anarchic ways so similar to the wild days of the Republic. On September 9, 1952, the son of an Alice lawyer named Jake Floyd, who had been effective in his efforts against George Parr, was shot down, having been mistaken for his father. One gunman went to jail after a lengthy trial. "It was and still is," Emmett Shelton told Holland McCombs, "generally suspected that George Parr was behind it all."

In George Parr's domain there resided a deputy sheriff named Sam Smithwick. In July 1949, eight months after the election, a South Texas radio personality named William H. (Bill) Mason talked about the irregularities connected with Box 13. Mason had declared that Lyndon Johnson had stolen the election of 1948. Deputy Smithwick then claimed that Mason had slandered him by calling him the owner of a dime-a-dance palace and on July 29, 1949, Smithwick shot Mason to death. Smithwick was duly sentenced to life in prison.

On March 23, 1952, serving his life sentence at the Huntsville, Texas, state penitentiary, Smithwick wrote a remarkable letter to Coke Stevenson. He had "recovered" the missing Box 13 from the Parr people who had been in the process of disposing of it, Smithwick said. He invited Coke Stevenson to visit him at Huntsville to discuss "this matter in detail."

> Dear Sir:
>   You probably do not remember who I am but I am the fellow who got in trouble in Alice over killing Mr. Mason, something that I regret very much and I am now serving a life sentence in the Texas Penitentiary.
>   I am writing you in regard to the 1949 [sic] Election in Jim Wells county when you were running against Lindon [sic] Johnson as you recall the election box with all the votes disappeared and that is the main cause of my trouble with Mr. Mason as he was on one side and I was on the other.
>   On June 24, 1949, five days before I got in trouble I arrested Gonzalo Loera, the son of Maria Loera, and Lupe Garcia, the son of Melario Garcia, and from them learned that Louis [sic] Salas who

was the depot agent at that time, and a bossom [sic] friend of Mr. Mason's, had stolen the box and give it to them to dispose of, but I recovered the box from them and am quite sure that I can produce it if you are interested. I could never get in touch with you because I didn't have a chance or anyone to trust to send to you and was never allowed to make bond after that. I intended to get in touch with you, but after recovering the box and getting it put safely away, on my way to contact you I met up with Mr. Mason and as you know what the result was now.

If it would be possible for you to come to Huntsville Prison to visit with me at your earliest convenience, I would like to go into this matter in detail with you.

I trust that I will hear from you in the very near future.

Respectfully yours,

Sam Smithwick

Sam Smithwick, #118236

Coke Stevenson wasted no time and set out for Huntsville, but before he arrived, Sam Smithwick was dead. Stevenson was told that Smithwick had strangled himself in his cell by tying a towel around his neck, attaching it to the window bars, and then, as Caro writes, "slipping off his bed." Smithwick's death was ruled a suicide. His "burning his lips on the coffee pot" remark notwithstanding, Coke Stevenson was not so naïve as to believe that Sam Smithwick's death was a suicide. Stevenson later remarked that he believed there was a line from George Parr to Chicago and back to Dallas and the Kennedy assassination.

In 1967, being interviewed for his biography by Ronnie Dugger, Johnson accused Texas governor Allan Shivers of having made a speech in 1956 accusing him of Sam Smithwick's murder. "Shivers charged me with *murder!*" Johnson told Dugger. "Shivers said I was a *murderer!*" Johnson repeated. Dugger could discover no newspaper account of Shivers saying any such thing. Dugger tried to confirm Johnson's story with Shivers himself, but Shivers declined to respond.

Johnson seemed then to be a man who courted his own exposure. He showed Dugger a photograph of four men sitting on the front fender of an automobile. One balanced a ballot box marked "Precinct 13." Later Luis Salas told Dugger that the photograph had been taken on the day of the 1948 runoff.

CHAPTER 5

Senator Lyndon Johnson

"We know just about the worst about Lyndon,
whether we can prove it or not."
—HOLLAND McCOMBS, EXPRESSING HIS
FRUSTRATION TO WILLIAM LAMBERT, HIS
EDITOR AT *LIFE* MAGAZINE

Right after he became a U.S. senator, Lyndon Johnson had a meeting with oilman Clint Murchison Sr. to pay his respects, setting the tone for his years as "Master of the Senate."

In the summer of 1949, Johnson requested of Interstate Commerce Committee chairman Ed Johnson that he, Johnson himself, chair the subcommittee that would explore the renomination of Leland Olds, the chairman of the Federal Power Commission. Shortly after he entered the U.S. Senate, Lyndon Johnson had taken on the role of organizing the political demise of Olds. In those times, in which the Dies Committee continued in its red-baiting ways, the task was relatively simple.

Olds was an old-fashioned liberal who believed that federal price controls should properly be imposed on the sale of natural gas. This placed Olds in direct opposition to George Brown, who ran the Brown & Root subsidiary Texas Eastern natural gas company. Texas Eastern had been constituted after World War Two when Brown & Root purchased the government pipelines known as Big Inch and Little Inch.

Enlisting McCarthyist tactics, Lyndon Johnson placed John Lyle, the old friend who owed him his seat in Congress, in charge of the research necessary to smear Olds as a Communist. Lyle pored over Olds's youthful political essays. Before it was over, Lyle had declared that Olds was not only a "Communist," but a supporter of V. I. Lenin. "He has reserved his applause for Lenin and Lenin's system," Lyle charged. Olds was not re-nominated to chair the Federal

Power Commission. Johnson had effectively drummed Olds out of government for good.

Safely in the U.S. Senate, Lyndon Johnson dedicated himself to furthering the interests of his Texas cronies while feathering his own nest. High on the list, of course, was Brown & Root, which garnered contracts to build military bases all over the world, from Guam, to Spain, to France, so that they functioned as an institution of the U.S. government. Often Brown & Root worked alongside the U.S. Navy. George Brown had declared that Brown & Root would support Lyndon Johnson "in everything he did." George also falsely claimed that Brown & Root had been the "lower bidder on everything that they got from the government" so that "there was no way for him [Lyndon Johnson] to help us." It wasn't so.

Holland McCombs penetrated deeply into Lyndon Johnson's manipulation of government contracts, which accelerated rapidly when he became a U.S. senator. It seemed to McCombs as if from the moment Lyndon Johnson entered the Senate ("I almost said 'was elected,'" McCombs corrected himself sardonically), Johnson had found means to enrich himself.

McCombs located Melvin Winters, of Johnson City, Texas, with whom Johnson had done business in the past. Winters had been a boyhood friend of Johnson's who had gotten rich out of his contracting business. Winters had left the contracting business, but when Lyndon Johnson went to the Senate, McCombs learned, "Here comes Melvin rushing back into the contracting business. And he did well, mighty well." Johnson arranged for government contracts without his friends having to bid on them at all, not only for Herman and George Brown, but for many others.

Another Johnson friend named Larry Blackman came away with "half a million in a tax deficiency case. And only one man can do that," McCombs was told. Earl Clements in Kentucky was implicated in a $182,000 fraud case that suddenly went away. Tax fraud cases against Johnson friends vanished once he placed his friend Bob Phinney in charge of the South Texas office of the Internal Revenue Service.

Phinney's chief qualification as a tax man was that he was "one of Lyndon's men." Phinney, according to Holland McCombs' interview with Emmett Shelton, "was in the old WPA and worked for Lyndon's radio station for a while." Then, after Lyndon was elected to Congress, he got the Austin, Texas, postmastership for Phinney. "Bob had no qualifications for the job, but Lyndon put him in over several qualified men." (It was said that you couldn't get a job at the Austin post office without a letter of approval from Johnson's office.) "Today," Shelton added, "Bob Phinney is director of Internal Revenue here. Lyndon put him there also. And he had no qualifications for that job either, and still doesn't . . . He's really a good-hearted man, belongs to my church, and wouldn't do anything crooked—*unless* Lyndon *told* him to."

Emmett Shelton was among McCombs' most forthcoming sources. If you wanted to open a national bank in Texas now, Shelton added, you had to see Lyndon Johnson's man, Jake Jacobson. Johnson's Austin lawyer, Ed Clark, handled the licenses for state banks. On the ground in Texas, representing Johnson was Clifton Crawford (Cliff) Carter, a highly decorated World War Two veteran, who owned the 7-Up Bottling Company in Bryan, Texas, and did Johnson's "work and dirty work for many years." In his conversations with Holland McCombs, R. M. Dixon called Carter "one of Lyndon's key Ganymedes and errand boys."

Another bank over which Johnson gained influence was the Moore State Bank in Llano, a Hill Country town. Emmett Shelton observed that Johnson placed A. W. Moursund as chairman of the board at a salary of about twenty thousand. The bank had been paying dividends to stockholders, and suddenly they were no longer paying dividends. The matter came to light because the stockholders complained.

One way of penetrating how Johnson enriched himself, and how he could afford such investments, McCombs concluded, was to "get a rundown of KTBC advertisers." To obtain contracts through Lyndon Johnson, "you got to do business with KTBC. If you'd advertise on the station, Lyndon would sign your recommendation letter."

At the Capital National Bank in Austin, the chairman of the board was Ed Clark and the president was Howard T. Cox; the officers included Walter Jenkins and Johnson's "all-over holding man," A. W. Moursund. Jesse Kellam was there too, but, Shelton pointed out in the political tutorial he gave Holland McCombs, "it's his, lock, stock and barrel. His name doesn't show. But it's his just the same."

Another beneficiary of Johnson's largesse was John Mecom, an oilman who owned Warrior Constructors, which won the contract to build the new post office and federal building in Austin. Mecom's operations were international. Among those he employed was Lee Harvey Oswald's "friend," George de Mohrenschildt, whom J. Walton Moore, running the CIA field office in Dallas, dispatched to look in on Oswald. (Mecom's private foundation would later be exposed by Texas congressman Wright Patman as a CIA proprietary front. (A "proprietary" was a corporation organized or utilized by CIA as a cover to conceal its illegal domestic operations.)

Yet another of Johnson's Texas contractor friends was Henry Bartell (Pat) Zachry, who, like Billie Sol Estes, went into business at the age of eight selling milk and eggs from his own livestock. Zachry started out by building county roads, like Herman Brown—with whom he later did business and against whom he sometimes bid. He moved on to levees and buildings. Zachry grew up to be an engineer, contractor, rancher, and business leader. He began to contribute to Johnson's campaigns during the 1941 senatorial campaign; the executives at the Zachry firm complained that Johnson should have helped more considering the faithful support Johnson had received from Zachry.

When Johnson entered the U.S. Senate, things changed. Zachry Construction, based in San Antonio, received these government contracts: the Reese Air Force Base at Lubbock; the Walker Air Force Base at Roswell, New Mexico; Biggs Field in El Paso; Bergstrom Air Force Base at Austin (the paving and utilities); and Air Force bases at Abilene, Wichita Falls, and other places. Zachry also received a thirty-million-dollar contract to build the Twin Buttes Dam on the Concho River near San Angelo, Texas.

On this dam project, Zachry used substandard materials, rocks that did not meet government standards. There was a long-distance call from Zachry to Lyndon Johnson. Johnson then telephoned the Secretary of the Interior. There was not a word in writing on any of these developments. Despite the fact that Zachry's use of below-specification rock had been exposed, the government paid off on the project without a word of complaint. (The dam was finally approved in February 1963 when Lyndon Johnson was Vice President).

The Transport Company of Texas was headed by Edgar Linkenhoger of Corpus Christi and numbered among its employees Sam Houston Johnson. Sam Houston worked also as a sixteen-thousand-dollar-a year clerk of the U.S. Senate for the Conference of Democratic Senators, of which his brother Lyndon was the head. His duties, he himself said, included "appearing at conferences" with "big, gruff, tough Ed Linkenhoger."

Along with George Parr and John Lyle, R. M. Dixon thought, as he told Holland McCombs, Linkenhoger was recognized as among Johnson's leading political operatives. Linkenhoger received material allocations during the war that other people couldn't get as he built up his fortune. The Transport Company of Texas soon received a major Navy contract for "housekeeping" for a missile firing range and radar base on Kwajalein Atoll in the Marshall Islands in the Pacific. (Another participant in the Kwajalein Atoll project was Pat Zachry.)

John Lyle, who had resigned from Congress, was the lobbyist for Transport and its second largest stockholder. (Lyle's clients also included the Bechtel

Corporation.) The third largest Transport stockholder was the estate of Sid Richardson, which was managed by John Connally.

Edgar Linkenhoger had been the subject of a federal tax fraud complaint that was settled for two hundred thousand dollars. He had been fined for violating International Commerce Commision trucking regulations. But Linkenhoger had been a longtime supporter of Lyndon Johnson and was close to George Parr. Transport was awarded the Kwajalein contract over Lockheed, Pan American, and Chance Vought.

The details of how the contract was awarded at once expose a scam. Transport was selected, it was said, because of its familiarity with Kwajalein. But this supposed advantage was based on a single government-financed visit by two Transport executives. A member of the panel that recommended Transport had resigned from the Navy only to go to work for Texas Transport. An admiral declared that the project was urgent; there was no time for competitive bidding. The missile firing range on Kwajalein Atoll would be Transport's first overseas contract.

The angry competitors threatened not to bid on any future Navy projects. In 1958, Transport of Texas moved in with its mandate, as a military base facilitator, to operate schools, a hospital, a dental clinic, supply, transportation, and public works. In an article by Herbert Solow, "How Not to Award a Navy Contract," published in *Fortune* magazine in December 1960, Lyndon Johnson is mentioned only to be exonerated for any involvement in the irregularities: "The name of Lyndon B. Johnson keeps popping up in the case—though his role seems to have been that of an innocent bystander," Solow wrote.

What began as a three-million-dollar contract mushroomed, with cost plus dimensions (government agreement to cover overruns, with the contract cost determined only at completion on the ground that contingency costs were undetermined on signing) to seventy-three million dollars.

Charles Luckman, a builder, designer, and architect, a "boy wonder" who made the cover of *Time* magazine on June 10, 1946, was yet another fortunate recipient of Lyndon Johnson's favor. Government contracts came his way. In 1952, Luckman had a contract for an Air Force missile test center in Florida and would go on to the 1958 redesign of Los Angeles International Airport. The NASA Manned Spacecraft Center in Houston, which Charles Luckman designed, was another example of how Senator Lyndon Johnson rewarded his friends. Among Luckman's favorite aphorisms was "Success is that old ABC—Ability, Breaks, and Courage."

For those "breaks," Luckman did not rely on chance. Johnson's choice of Luckman parallels his relationship with Herman and George Brown, whose outstanding professionalism and expertise nonetheless required Lyndon Johnson as facilitator. Charles Luckman was to give the Kennedy-Johnson campaign one hundred thousand dollars off the top of a government contract procured for him by Lyndon Johnson.

If you did not support Lyndon Johnson, you were excluded from participating in the big projects. James D. Fowler, who admitted that he had not voted for Lyndon Johnson in 1941, was removed from engineering work on Bergstrom Air Force Base. This had been in 1942 or 1943, as Fowler recalled, and he was excluded from working on any aspect of building Bergstrom. The word was out, as Holland McCombs put it: "Lyndon feeds his friends and beats his enemies." On Bergstrom, Fowler would have partnered with architect Max Brooks, who went on to receive big federal jobs like the ten-million-dollar Federal Center in Austin, NASA's Manned Spacecraft Center in Houston, the U.S. Embassy in Mexico City, a job in Puerto Rico, and more.

Johnson held a controlling interest in a Houston grain storage house, the Mahone Grain Company. For this information, McCombs' source was one Fred Sublette, a close friend of Robert H. Mahone Jr., the president of the company. Yet try hard as McCombs did, he could not document "any Lyndon Johnson ownership." As always, there was nothing on paper implicating Lyndon Johnson, even as his personal wealth grew.

So it should not be surprising that Congressman Lyndon Johnson would confer favors upon his contractor father-in-law, Thomas Jefferson Taylor. A defense plant had originally been scheduled during the war to be located near Gladwater or Longview, Texas. Then the U.S. Army Corps of Engineers changed its mind. The federal ordnance and ammunition plant was relocated to Taylor's home territory of Karnack, driving up land values. Taylor was paid $77,000 for his land.

Uncovering all this, Holland McCombs was incredulous. "Why in the cornbread hell would the little East Texas Piney Wood town of Karnack be picked out as the site for the government ordnance plant—unless it was because Lyndon Johnson's father-in-law and his properties had something to do with it?" McCombs wondered. The project was, officially, the Longhorn Army Ammunition Plant and the deed was transferred from T. J. Taylor to "United States of America." This project was completed during World War Two, while Lyndon Johnson was a congressman.

Taylor Construction went on to build nineteen rural electrification systems in the Austin area, receiving subcontracts from Brown & Root. Lady Bird's father's net worth climbed to over a million dollars as Taylor Construction was awarded contracts at Camp Swift, Camp Hood, and other government military installations. Taylor's penchant was for getting "Negroes" into debt to him, debts from which they could never extricate themselves. Taylor took their land in payment for the debt, refusing to allow them to work out the loans. When he died in 1960, Taylor owned 13,400 acres of prime real estate.

During his time as a U.S. senator, Johnson's Austin radio station, KTBC, was another source of personal profit. From the original investment of $17,500, in 1956 Johnson earned $1,029,531. Those who advertised on KTBC received healthy government contracts. One such firm was the Jaques Power Saw Company of Sherman and Austin. They made a light and good power saw, and the Jaques Saw people went to the government to get some contracts. They got them, Emmett Shelton told McCombs, but they also had to run a program on KTBC. "One of their guys griped about it at the time."

Jaques sponsored a religious program comprised of prayers and hymns. Before long, Jaques was "selling enough power saws to defense and military agencies to make him the largest manufacturer of tree-felling machinery in the country." Jaques insisted to Holland McCombs that he was never forced to advertise on either KTBC or the Johnson television station, KVET. As Robert Caro writes, "they were buying—and Lyndon Johnson was selling."

Similarly sized venues like Amarillo had three television stations and Midland and Odessa had two. Austin for years had only KVET, owned by Johnson. On its board of directors sat the Johnson cohort: his lawyer, Ed Clark; John Connally's brother, Merrill L. Connally; the IRS man, Bob Phinney; Jake Pickle, a Johnson PR man; and Jesse Kellam, who was useful for such mundane tasks as purchasing ten thousand dollars' worth of stock of the Lamar Savings and Loan for Lyndon Johnson. Holland McCombs uncovered that the stocks were purchased in the name of KTBC. Other investments were sheltered under the Brazos-Tenth Corporation, which evolved into the LBJ Company.

In March 1964, the LBJ Company owned 29 percent of KWTX-TV in Waco, Texas, which in turn owned 50 percent of Brazos Broadcasting Company, owner of KBTX-TV in Bryan, Texas; a 75 percent stock interest in Texoma Broadcasters, Inc., owner of KXII in Ardmore, Texas; and a 79 percent interest in Victoria Broadcasters, Inc., licensee of KMAL, a radio station in Victoria, Texas. The LBJ Company was also holder of the Muzak franchise in Austin.

*   *   *

By the time he began his investigation of Lyndon Johnson in 1963, Holland McCombs had worked for more than two decades for Time/Life and was an experienced researcher. During that period he also served as the principal researcher for Tom Lea's biography of King Ranch and had been an intimate of the Kleberg family. He was a Texan and had scoured the state of Texas for people willing to talk about the details of Lyndon Johnson's relationships with his increasingly rich contractor friends. Many of those who talked to McCombs, from J. B. Donohoe to Emmett Shelton to R. M. Dixon to Josh Groce, insisted that their names not be used. Engineer James D. Fowler wavered, but finally allowed his name to be mentioned. McCombs turned to the strategy of following the money to document Johnson's rise to great wealth.

The Johnson people had suggested that the Johnson money, including the funds they used to purchase the first radio station, had originated from Claudia Taylor (Lady Bird)'s inheritance. McCombs found that this was patently false. There was no inheritance to speak of, nor had there ever been.

On stock transactions and deals, Lyndon Johnson's name never appeared. There was only one area of economic gain that could not entirely be hidden and that was real estate, in particular the many ranches that Johnson had been buying up. In April 1964, McCombs was already asking: "From his early days of acquiring real estate around Austin, from time to time, LBJ enterprises have come up with a lot of buying money. Where did it come from then and now? . . . We can develop that Lyndon had one product to sell: political influence . . . since 1931 his business has been politics—Lady Bird notwithstanding."

In 1951, Johnson bought one of the old family ranches, belonging to his aunt and uncle, Judge and Mrs. Clarence Martin. It consisted of 415 acres; Johnson had been born on an adjoining piece of the old ranch owned by a neighbor. It was rumored that Johnson bought one ranch, or most of it, from his cousin Tom Martin's widow under something like forced-sale conditions and at forced-sale prices. It was said that Johnson put in a million dollars in cash, and people wondered how he could have accumulated so much money.

A partial list of Johnson ownership "included 9,295 acres, which included Lyndon's and Lady Bird's half ownership in the Haywood Ranch of 4,561 acres, 831 acres of the Lewis place, 415 acres of LBJ Ranch, and KTBC ownership of 1,719 acres of the Voyless Ranch. They also owned 1,800 acres of another ranch, probably the Schornhorst Ranch."

McCombs despaired that all of this information was unusable. "Only one man could fix it" wasn't evidence of concealing a crime. All R. M. Dixon, the

water engineer and shrewd Johnson observer, could offer was a generaliza-
tion. Johnson's crime "was the overseeing of taxpayers' money finding its way
into the coffers of government contractors." Brown & Root were known recip-
ients of Johnson's manipulation of government money into the hands of his
friends. But it was no small group that profited from Johnson's wielding of
economic power through the awarding of government contracts. There were,
Dixon said, "government contractors, lawyers, bureaucrats, politicos, and
their associates who grew to be big and powerful and rich by virtue of political
preferential treatment and the pouring of the taxpayers' money into the
coffers of government contractors and the enriching distribution thereof."

Dixon was among the frankest of McCombs' sources. He added: "The
American General Insurance Company (which has become so big that it's
aiming at gaining control of the Maryland Casualty Company) is a Brown
property, Houston based and with some two billion dollars insurance in force.
And that's the one run by Gus Wortham and is the one from which LBJ
borrows money." Dixon summed up Johnson: "He feeds his friends and bites
his enemies; he learned it from FDR and Rayburn."

Holland McCombs attempted to provide a balanced description of Lyndon
Johnson, whom he found "full of paradoxes." McCombs noted that "both his
mother and father were kind and compassionate people. So is Lyndon. His
personal kindness to family, friends, employees and plain people is legion
and legend. But in the hard game of government, politics and profit, he has
been as ruthless and power-pushing as the financial robber barons of U.S.
economic history. In their fields, Carnegie, Hill, Gould, Vanderbilt, and others
of that ilk, played for keeps. So has Lyndon . . ."

McCombs, troubled, added: "We have a great journalistic opportunity, and
a careful responsibility." Looking forward to publication, he told his editor,
William Lambert, "when the time comes, we must caucus with our conscience
and consider all facts, with pro and con, and then lay it out like it is without
fear or favor." McCombs hoped he would be able to "speak out with the truth."

During his time as a United States senator, Johnson drew close not only to
J. Edgar Hoover, but also to CIA. Serving on a subcommittee of the Senate
Armed Services Committee, the first Joint Committee on Foreign Intelligence,
Johnson appointed his ally Senator Richard Russell to the subcommittee to
serve with him. Together the two saw to it that CIA operations would remain
exempt from congressional oversight, which had been granted to the Senate

Armed Services Committee. CIA's freedom from oversight, nurtured by Lyndon Johnson, would continue into the next millennium.

It should by now not be surprising that among CIA's Texas assets were numbered Herman and George Brown. According to a document released by CIA, George Brown was granted a covert security clearance on October 23, 1953, and a provisional covert security approval on April 22, 1965, which became security approval on June 18. Herman Brown received his first clearance in 1953. Nine lesser employees of Brown & Root were named on the same document as being CIA contact sources. Herman and George Brown were not only assets of the Domestic Contact Service of CIA, as might be expected for businessmen customarily debriefed by the Agency, but also of the clandestine services as well, which focused on covert operations and "dirty tricks" abroad. The document outlining all of this emanated from CIA's powerful Office of Security, and remains partially redacted.

CHAPTER 6

Mac Wallace Goes to Washington Under the Auspices of Lyndon Johnson

Shall he go, or come? —How guide him?
Prompt decision is denied him;
Midway on the trodden highway
Halting, he attempts a by-way;
Ever more astray, bemisted,
Everything beholding twisted . . .
—JOHANN WOLFGANG VON GOETHE,
FAUST: PART TWO, (ACT V, SCENE 5)

In New York in the spring of 1945, Mac Wallace rented an apartment on Riverside Drive and signed up for courses at Columbia University. His mood reflected presciently the coming postwar confusion among a generation in search of how they might find a place for themselves in the world. Mac wrote to Nora Ann that he doubted the existence of God in the light of endemic injustice: "Do we treat others as we would have them do unto us? Or do we lie, cheat, steal, rob, swindle, rape, torture, maim and kill? Do we make war? Oh so callous a God he would have been had he been."

He visited Grant's tomb and noted that General Ulysses S. Grant had "lost nearly twice as many men as Lee. The butcher! He drove his men into slaughter by the tens of thousands because he wasn't General enough to win except by attrition—the most inhuman way possible, the most bestial." Mac was an idealistic young man who longed for "progress and peace, a small gleam of light in a world almost completely dark, the last great hope of the human race."

Nora Ann Carroll had not yet married Ted Cary. In his long letter to her, and believing that she still loved him, Mac tried one final time to persuade her to reverse her decision:

"I want to tell you how deeply, how profoundly, I resented your psudo [sic] deision [sic] of last winter. Nothing ever rankled me so, nothing ever offended me so, nothing ever made me so angry."

Writing under the influence of alcohol, as he would admit, he laid down an ultimatum, demanding that she join him, and a friend and "his woman," for a trip to New England and Canada. "The only way you can atone for last winter is to be here on April 14. Otherwise it is 'kits' between us—finally, and irrevocably," he wrote. There would be "no strings attached." He took a swipe at Ted Cary and "his two by four morals," and promised "a week to remember and cherish."

His reference to the "boo-hooing in the auto" at their last meeting allowed Nora Ann to seize the high ground. Such a term trivialized the strong feelings that she had, and the anguish she felt at having had to break with him. She did not reply and a week later, in a missive dated March 23, 1945, Mac offered his "sincerest apologies" for the tone of his previous letter.

The loss of Nora Ann unnerved him. Having left the safe haven of the University of Texas, where he was a student leader whose prospects seemed measureless, he lost focus. He no longer had a clear idea of what he wanted to do with his life. He wrote Nora Ann that he now aspired to be a fiction writer and included in his letter a largely autobiographical short story. At a bar, the hero encounters a "Marine, a quiet fellow [who] wore three campaign ribbons and one of them had four stars on it. That meant quite a bit of fighting. Maybe he'd have a few stories to tell."

To this Marine, the narrator invokes his own brief service, protesting, "I'm glad it wasn't longer." He reveals that he had traded on his having served in the Marines at the University of Texas, adding that the "story had just grown up of its own volition" or that of his "political compadres." This semifictional Mac Wallace insists on his good fortune: "Better a fractured back and a medical discharge than to have stayed in and had his number come up . . ." He adds that war is "no good for anyone. Best thing is to let it slide off into the abyss of the unconscious and the unfeeling." He does not include that he had attempted to re-enlist after Pearl Harbor only to be rejected.

In his apology, Mac solicited Nora Ann's forgiveness. "Accept this as the real Mac, not the other letter," he wrote. Still, he could not resist renewing the offer that they meet again. "If you can make it up, the *invitation* still stands." Mac admitted that he was taking the loss of Nora Ann "very badly."

As an intellectual, he explored the fate of society at this transitional moment. He foresaw the repression of the Cold War looming, an insight born of his experience with the University of Texas Board of Regents. "Where do we go from here?" he wrote Nora Ann. "Into the Hearst-Howard-McCormick war, the anti-Russian war?" He perceived the role of the reactionary press in fostering pretexts for a renewed military buildup and a "Cold War."

While Mac Wallace believed that "the postwar world" was "shaping up terribly," the economy boomed. Alvin Wallace prospered and was listed in the census records as a "bridge builder." The principal supplier of his raw concrete was the Centex Concrete Company, owned by Lyndon Johnson supporter Clint Murchison Sr. Wallace's firm became a major Centex customer. A recipient of government contracts, Alvin Wallace did well enough to move his family in 1945 to a five-bedroom house with a three-car garage, tile fireplaces, French doors leading to a garden, and an impressive entrance hall staircase.

Uninspired by the graduate courses he was taking, in May, Mac joined the Newtex Steamship Corporation. He bragged to Nora Ann that his job was "extremely interesting and fairly remunerative" and claimed that he was being groomed to replace his boss, who was "on his way out" because of excessive drinking. To draw Nora Ann back into the circle of their common interests, he invoked John Dewey in the full flower of his pragmatist thinking: "Prof. Dewey would be the first to say: for a habitual drunkard to say, 'I don't believe in drinking' is for him to say nothing, since as a matter of real fact he *does* believe in drinking."

He applied to law school, which he planned to enter on June 11, professing himself impatient to "get at the law books." Recognizing that he was faltering on his path to an adult life, he declared, "I must hurry, hurry, hurry." On an emotional treadmill, he changed direction frequently. Working full-time, he enrolled in three night classes at the Marxist-oriented Jefferson School of Social Science: Contemporary Philosophers, History of Political Thought, and Economic Analysis of the Civil War Period.

"I think he should stay out of politics and revolutions," he wrote to Nora Ann of their friend Elgin Williams, who was sympathetic to the Communist Party. "I know he will stay out—especially of revolutions." With no clear direction himself, he was contemptuous of Williams' reluctant activism. He rejected "Elgin's views," along with those of the "CP," he said. In Elgin Williams, he saw not a belief in revolutionary change, but "cynicism." Yet Elgin Williams had already settled on a dissertation topic—Sam Houston and land speculation in the Republic of Texas during the period of annexation—and was headed for a future in academe.

On June 11, 1945, Mac Wallace enrolled at the School of Law at Columbia. Two weeks later, he dropped out "for reasons of ill health." He had contracted a nasty skin infection that required expensive injections that he could not afford. He never went back. Instead, he registered for the fall semester beginning in September 1945 at the New School for Social Research as a candidate for a master's degree in economics. He took courses in "money and credit (essentially Keynesian)" and "trade policies and tariff construction." His course with Keynesian professor Abba P. Lerner was Economics of Control and offered "a very clear marginal analysis approach to economics." He did not "accept much of his [Lerner's] theory," but preferred, he claimed, "knowledge of what such men are talking about" to "the simple sneer with which UT arms us." He spoke with grandiosity about "a dichotomy between the technological and the institutional as a tool for analysis" and boasted that he won as many converts to his views as the professor, whom he dismissed as a "cultural relativist."

Mac Wallace was not promoted at the Newtex Steamship Company. He left Newtex to take a job as a research assistant in the credit department of the National City Bank at 55 Wall Street. From his perch at the bank, he said, he learned a lot about General Motors "or the soap and candle monopoly agreement in Venice" and "what industry's outlook is."

Wallace dropped out of the New School without receiving a degree. At the turn of the new year 1946, he quit his job at the National City Bank to "work on a campaign" and returned to Texas. Homer Rainey was seeking the Democratic Party nomination to be governor of Texas and Wallace would be his Dallas city campaign manager. He would also be the state director of College Students for Rainey. To complete his undergraduate degree, he enrolled in classes at the University of Texas and commuted between Dallas and Austin.

Homer Rainey survived the primary only to face railroad commissioner Beauford H. Jester. No candidate having won a majority, there would be a runoff. Horace Busby, a former editor of the *Daily Texan*, graduated in 1946 and immediately joined the Rainey campaign. (In 1948, Busby would embrace a lifetime of service to Lyndon Johnson.) Busby and Mac Wallace had never been friends and did not become friends now.

A black supporter was promised money by the Rainey campaign "to keep blacks from showing up at Rainey's speeches." There was a threat that if he didn't receive the payoff, "there might be some blacks to show up." Even liberal Rainey feared that should it become known that he had black support, the whites would shun him. Black support in those times, no less for liberals, was something to be kept secret.

"They're going to have to find themselves another boy to do this," Busby said. He refused to hand over the money. Defiantly, Jester bussed in three or four busloads of blacks to attend his own events. Busby later remarked that "it didn't worry him [Beauford Jester] at all and here we were, the big liberals, passing out money telling them to keep blacks out of sight."

Perhaps aware that his participation was not valued, Mac Wallace worked on the Rainey campaign halfheartedly. One day he abandoned his campaign duties and headed for the library to "browse through some Auden." The politicians who turned up at his door repelled him. "The work we are doing for Rainey," he wrote Nora Ann in July 1946 "has caused all sorts of debris to wash up on the shores of my office . . . you meet some of the most heartwarming people (generally, though, incompetent) and yet meet some of the real political dregs—old, broken-down speakers, letter-to-the-editor writers, bums, pompous young 'bosses,' etc." He afforded the postwar world fourteen years before there would be a collapse. "Now is the time for the correction of error," he added. It may have been during this time that he began to "date" Josefa Johnson, as Horace Busby has suggested.

Finally he came to the point of this letter, news that he wanted to share with Nora Ann. Once the Rainey campaign was over, he was getting married. In the fall, he would move back to Austin and earn a master's degree and "maybe my Ph.D." His wife would teach in the English department. He declined to reveal her name to Nora Ann, as it had "political connotations—which is a clue, if you remember your U.T. friends & their backgrounds." All her life, Nora Ann Carroll would ponder the identity of this woman whom Mac had said he was planning to marry, even as she doubted that there had been a marriage in the offing at all.

Homer Rainey was defeated handily. He had at his disposal a scant $130,000 to Beauford Jester's two million dollars.

Nora Ann Carroll married Edward Cary on August 17, 1946, in New Orleans. Her mother had her heart set on Nora Ann's being married in Beaumont in a long white satin wedding gown, accompanied by at least six attendants. Instead Nora Ann wore a short white dress and a perky white straw hat she purchased at a children's shop.

At the University of Texas that fall, Wallace was awarded a graduate assistantship ("part-time assistant") in the economics department. His former roommate, Joseph Louis Schott, had returned from his war service. Schott brought with him a .25 caliber Schmeisser automatic pistol. He had captured a German officer, who had concealed the pistol on his person. The ammunition had been loose in his pocket. Schott had stripped him of it all.

On a bright sunny day, a group of friends were gathered on the grass at the University of Texas campus. The just-married Nora Ann was present, visiting her brother, Bill, who was now a UT student, and so witnessed the moment when Joe Schott presented Mac with the Schmeisser pistol and the ammunition as a gift. Schott had observed Mac's dark mood. He attributed Mac's low spirits to his frustration that he hadn't served his country in the war.

I've had my gut full of the war, Joe later recalled thinking. Tired of carrying the pistol around, having tested it and discovered that upon firing it tore a slit of skin from your index finger—Joe and his father both had this same result—Joe presented the Schmeisser to his old friend Mac Wallace. He believed that Mac might enjoy having the pistol as a souvenir.

As a senior, Wallace was now eligible to be elected to the Friar's Society. The 1946–47 Friar's group of eight included not only Wallace, but Horace Busby; Dolph Briscoe Jr., a future governor of Texas; and future congressman Jack B. Brooks.

In June 1947, Wallace graduated from the University of Texas with a bachelor's degree in business administration and a major in economics. Then he focused on the master's degree that he had already begun so that for a time he was both completing his undergraduate degree and pursuing graduate work.

Among his advisers was Dr. Bob Montgomery. "Dr. Bob" had known Lyndon Johnson since Johnson was a student at Southwest Texas State Teachers College at San Marcos. Admiring this clever, ambitious young man, Montgomery had followed Lyndon Johnson's career from the time when he was Congressman Richard Kleberg's secretary. When Johnson served as National Youth Administration director for Texas, he had resided for a time at Montgomery's home.

That summer of 1947 Mac took up with a pretty, sexually adventurous young woman named Mary Andre Dubose Barton. "Andre," as she preferred to be known, and her sister Ruth had been adopted by Kostromey Palestrina Barton, a Methodist minister known as "KP," who taught at the University of Texas, and his wife, Roberta, a former English instructor at UT. Roberta had been a reporter at the San Angelo *Standard Times*.

Andre had been born Mary Alice, only at the age of thirteen to change her name to Mary Andre. Born in Nashville, Tennessee, on February 28, 1924, she was three years younger than Mac Wallace. Andre was a woman of many talents; she could play Mozart by ear, sang in the choir, learned to fly an airplane, and was accomplished at drawing and painting. As a student at the University of Texas, she had dated the son of Dr. Clarence Ayres.

After less than two weeks of acquaintance, Mac and Andre were talking about marriage. Just before the wedding, Andre confessed that she had enjoyed sexual encounters with women, sometimes even in public at Austin's Zilker Park. Mac decided to go ahead with the marriage anyway. It was as if a demon had lodged in his heart.

Mac Wallace and Mary Andre Dubose Barton were married on July 4, 1947, at the First Methodist Church in Austin. Among those attending the wedding were Joseph Louis Schott and Elgin Williams. Schott had been so surprised when Mac told him that he was getting married that he was at a loss for words. He had never heard of Andre. But Schott had been estranged from Mac for some time now, preferring to spend his time with the ex-GI's with whom he had served in the Army, and Mac had been offended. No story marked this wedding on the society pages of the *Austin American*. That night, Schott presented the young couple with two bottles of scotch. He knew this would be a welcome gift. They were both drinking heavily.

When they returned from a brief honeymoon in Houston and Galveston, Mac sent Andre to Dr. D. R. White, a University of Texas psychologist, to cure her of what was then termed "sex perversion," her lesbian proclivities.

"I've reached a time when I want to settle down," Mac wrote to Nora Ann, informing her of his marriage. He couldn't have been dumber than to marry virtually minutes after I did, Nora Ann recalled she thought at the time. (It had in fact been a year, but these events were more than sixty years in the past.) He was "a damn fool in his emotional life and he suffered for it the rest of his life."

In August, Mac received his Master's degree in economics, and in September he returned to New York, where he enrolled in the Ph.D. program at Columbia University, joining Elgin Williams. Andre soon moved to New York, where they lived at 311 West 100th Street. The neighbors found them a "nice young couple," and Mac "an honest and substantial person." He seemed to be an "introspective man" who "stayed to himself." In September, Andre became pregnant. Mac worked part-time as an interviewer for an organization called Radio Research to make ends meet.

Now began Mac Wallace's career as an itinerant academic moving from school to school, his employment never ensured. He never assumed a tenure-track position. During the academic year 1947–48, he taught philosophy as a part-time instructor at Long Island University's downtown Brooklyn campus. One of his LIU students would later tell the FBI that Wallace was "one of the best instructors I ever had," and "a fine man." For one semester in 1948, Mac worked as a part-time tutor in the economics department at the City College of New York. A colleague reported him to be "a person of excellent habits and character." That spring he withdrew from the Ph.D. program at Columbia.

On February 1, 1948, Andre returned to Austin to live with her mother and await the birth of the baby. The marriage was already in trouble. Later Andre would claim that Mac had sent her home, that her return to Texas had not been her idea. She contended that Mac had tried to persuade her to have an abortion.

Having received a master of science degree in biological chemistry from the University of Michigan, where Dr. Ted Cary had alighted, Nora Ann decided to treat herself to a week of theater in New York. "You know, Mac is here," her former roommate, Pat Elliot—now living in New York—told Nora Ann. She gave Nora Ann his address.

Mac and Nora Ann made a date to attend a performance of Euripides' *Medea*. When Mac called up from the desk to Nora Ann's room at the Piccadilly Hotel and asked to use her bathroom to "wash up," she was disconcerted. At the door, she gave him what she termed "a cool, restrained embrace." Nora Ann was determined not to be unfaithful to her husband; neither she nor Mac dared relax. As Nora Ann remembered, "the fire was contained but undiminished."

Medea was a "gruesome, morbid play," Nora Ann thought, and this added a macabre atmosphere to an already disturbing situation. By the end of this revenge tragedy, Medea has killed her children. "We behaved ourselves," Nora Ann was to recall, "but the evening gave neither of us comfort."

Mac had to rise at three A.M. and head for the docks. To earn extra money to support Andre in Austin and himself in New York, he was "shaping," working as a longshoreman unloading ships in New York Harbor before heading for his regular day job. He did not inform Nora Ann that Andre was pregnant.

Michael Alvin Wallace was born in Austin on June 26, 1948. Three days later, on June 29, Andre filed a petition for divorce. She charged that almost immediately upon their marriage, Mac had begun "a course of conduct that made the marriage insupportable." The judge hearing the action was Charles O. Betts.

On August 24, two days short of the divorce being final by default, since Mac Wallace had not returned to answer, Andre withdrew her petition. Mac had been hired as an assistant professor at North Carolina State University, where he taught economics and industrial management. Andre joined him in Raleigh, only after three months to return to Texas. She took a job with the Texas Highway Department doing drafting work while Mac remained in Raleigh.

Mac Wallace impressed his North Carolina State colleagues with his "extraordinary keen mind." He enjoyed talking politics, although to some of his acquaintances he seemed to be a "lover of argument." His views were liberal, but not radical. He advocated a more equitable distribution of wealth and generous government spending, the perspective of someone who had grown up in poverty and had embraced the programs of the New Deal. In the general election in 1948, Mac and Nora Ann would vote for Progressive Party candidate Henry Wallace. (Ted Cary voted for Harry Truman.)

Mac led "a very quiet and retiring life" in North Carolina and seemed to have "no actual associates outside the college staff." However, the conservative political atmosphere was stifling. After one academic year, Mac Wallace resigned. Unemployed, at loose ends, and with his academic prospects having run their course, he returned to Texas.

Although no witnesses or documents acknowledge their meeting, somehow Mac Wallace and Cliff Carter, Lyndon Johnson's right-hand man in Texas, found each other. Carter met Johnson in 1937 when he was a volunteer in Johnson's congressional campaign. He served in World War II under Captain Edward Clark, and went on to take part in Johnson's 1948 campaign for the U.S. Senate. On the ground in Texas, he collected campaign contributions for Johnson, and was a lifelong member of Johnson's inner circle. Unflinching, he was the intermediary of intermediaries. Unlike Horace Busby or Lloyd Hand, or John Connally, Mac Wallace did not join Johnson's staff. According to the Holland McCombs files, Wallace had done some favors for Johnson in his 1948 campaign for the Senate. Johnson now returned the favor. Wallace became an employee of the U.S. Department of Agriculture. That he was hired by Cliff Carter leaves no doubt that it was Lyndon Johnson who gained him the job. As usual with Johnson there was nothing in writing.

On September 19, 1949, Wallace reported for work at the Department of Agriculture's finance department as an "agricultural economist" or "research economist." He had been required to provide references. One came from FBI Special Agent Joseph Louis Schott, at the Newark, New Jersey, FBI field office.

Mac was paid $71 a week, in today's money more than $700. He rented an apartment in Arlington, Virginia, at 516 North Payne Street, where Andre and their toddler son, Michael, joined him. He purchased a dark blue 1939 Pontiac. All his life, he would drive old, used cars. One winter day in 1949 Nora Ann Carroll met up with Mac Wallace again in New York. He talked about having spent time with Lyndon Johnson, and seemed to be bragging about the "bigwigs" he had met. He made his life and I made mine, Nora Ann thought then.

To qualify for federal employment, you were subjected to a security check. The FBI consulted its November 8, 1944, investigation of Wallace, a file titled "Communist Political Association, District #20, San Antonio Field Division, Internal Security—C." The prevailing view among the many informants approached by the Bureau was that Wallace was "a man of good character and reputation as well as a loyal American citizen."

The chairman of the economics department at North Carolina State reported that Wallace was "a very capable economist and a man with an extraordinarily keen mind." One colleague noted that "Wallace had a tendency to present to his classes labor's side of any controversy more favorably than he did that of management," separating his views from those of Lyndon Johnson.

A woman colleague said that Mac Wallace was a person with religious principles, a member of the Episcopal faith. When one day she had remarked that Communism "denied all of the generally accepted moral, ethical and Christian principles, Wallace had agreed with her." A former classmate concurred: Wallace was "strongly anti-Communist in his feelings."

Others were not so sure. Henry Scarborough, a fellow member of the Tejas Club, told the FBI that Mac was "very liberal," and in conversation showed an admiration for Communist Russia. The most damaging appraisal came from Horace Busby, now employed "in the office of Senator Lyndon Johnson." Busby's comments were nothing short of defamatory.

In a signed statement, Busby told the FBI that he thought Wallace was an opportunist. "We were not good friends, or even 'friends,'" Busby wrote, "a fact understood by both of us." In early 1944, Busby recounted, he was invited to be the publicist for the Common Sense Club. After attending a few meetings, he concluded "that Wallace's effort to secure the vote for eighteen-year-olds was simply a publicity device for Wallace's efforts to become student body president." Busby told the Bureau that "Wallace was consumed with great political ambition," and in the service of that aspiration "sought leadership of the pro-Rainey or liberal side." Busby added that Wallace's organization of the mass demonstrations in support of Homer Rainey were designed for his personal aggrandizement."

Joseph McCarthy had won election to the U.S. Senate in 1946; at a speech on February 9, 1950, he declared that he was aware of "205 card-carrying members of the Communist Party who worked for the United States Department of State." Martin Dies had paved the way. Writing in 1950, Busby declared that "Wallace's methods and views seem to be Marxist, to say the least." He wrote that during the Rainey campaign the leaders "kept Wallace out of public view and public activity because he had damaged his reputation and impaired his usefulness, having been branded as a 'Red.'" Busby's statement was clearly designed to influence the FBI not to clear Wallace on the matter of his loyalty. He called him a man with "great ambition fired with bitterness and ruthlessness, which sometimes handicaps his judgment about associates." He had heard Wallace "defend Communism, as a political and economic theory." Busby declared that he "would not entrust Wallace to positions of great responsibility, especially if the position afforded him opportunity for personal advancement at the expense of the security of his country."

By 1950, Busby had begun his lifetime of service to Lyndon Johnson. Had Mac Wallace been close to or important to Lyndon Johnson at that time, it is doubtful that Busby would have spoken so strongly against him. The Busby written statement, which followed a postponement of Busby's interview with the FBI, is important because, since Busby had only relatively recently entered Lyndon Johnson's service, it reflects that Johnson did not influence Busby to speak in Wallace's favor.

Despite Horace Busby's best efforts, which on the basis of the tone of his statement seem to reflect nothing so much as personal animosity, the FBI declared Mac Wallace officially "eligible on loyalty" for the position with the Agriculture Department that he had already taken up. When Wallace's FBI file was released in the 1990s, the entire Busby statement was redacted.

Emmett Shelton recounted to Holland McCombs how "Lyndon's people are supposed to help others get loans for small businesses if they can arrange to buy or get a piece of it. I understand a man named Mack [sic] Wallace was sent down here from the Agriculture Department to work out some things like this." It is a rare example of someone in Texas taking note of Mac Wallace's connection to Lyndon Johnson. In McCombs' handwritten notes, the words *hatchet man* are appended, after "work out some things like this."

Whatever his political ambitions were or had been, Wallace was leading a diminished life as a government worker. Still, his colleagues were impressed by his "scholastic background and teaching record" and considered him a "New Deal type," a "liberal, but a liberal in the honest sense of the term." Among the topics debated at the office was industrial pension plans. Wallace contended that if a business failed and the government had to take over its pension plan, corresponding government control would invariably follow, not a good thing. He talked about limiting the scope of pension plans and termed his own position one of "enlightened conservatism." He supported social and economic reforms, he said, but was repelled by "extreme statements and proposals by short-sighted people."

His co-workers, with whom he got along, found him "a stable young man" with "his feet on the ground." His writing style remained exceptional; an article he wrote, "Survey of Virginia Agriculture," appeared in the *Agricultural Finance Review* in 1950. Two coauthored articles were to appear in 1951 and 1952. Otherwise, he continued to lead a quiet life. He played golf with an Agriculture Department colleague named Edward Collins, whom he had known at North Carolina State and with whom he had "participated in numerous panel discussions."

Mac Wallace was invited socially to the Johnson home in Washington, D.C. Many years later he would remark to his wife, Virginia, that he had been closer to Lady Bird Johnson than to Lyndon. Otherwise there is no documentation of the specific occasions when he was hosted by the Johnsons. Between 1949 when he began work in Washington and the autumn of 1950 he engaged in a dalliance with Johnson's younger sister, Josefa. The source is Horace Busby, who has stated matter-of-factly that Johnson assigned him to deal with "the Josefa situation."

In 1949, Josefa Johnson, tall, beautiful, and wild, was thirty-seven years old to Wallace's twenty-eight. She was divorced from a man named Willard White, who had been a lieutenant colonel in the U.S. Army during the war and was notorious for having sent home a cartload of Adolf Hitler's linen and silver. At loose ends, alcoholic and promiscuous, Josefa was an embarrassment to her brother as she roamed between Austin and Washington, D.C.

It was rumored in Austin that Josefa Johnson was one among a clique of "blondes," although she was not a blonde herself, who entertained Texas lobbyists and legislators at Madam Hattie Valdes's private club on South Congress Street. Hattie's "girls" were often impoverished University of Texas co-eds, or bored married women, *belles de jour*. It was "a stable of high-class prostitutes."

Josefa's history included a string of rescues by her brother from compromising situations. Following one drunken party, she wound up in a sheriff's office. Other rescues were from hospital wards for alcoholics.

Having worked on Johnson's 1948 senatorial campaign, although no details have emerged as to what her duties were, Josefa knew too much about her brother's business. This was alarming because she had no compunction about talking about her brother's practices. Horace Busby concluded that Josefa had a "frighteningly low opinion of herself, so much so that if there was a man to be picked up, Josefa picked him up." The assignment to rein in Josefa passed to Mac Wallace, briefly, according to Horace Busby.

During the short period when he worked at the Department of Agriculture, from September 1949 to October 1951, Mac Wallace traveled to Texas doing odd jobs for Senator Lyndon Johnson, according to Holland McCombs in the one reference he makes in his copious files to Mac Wallace. McCombs was a journalist and his research about Lyndon Johnson, based on his 1963–64 investigation, which continued into 1965, never saw the light of publication. Once Johnson became president that became impossible. That McCombs' research is available is owing to his decision to deposit it at the University of Tennessee at Martin, which was constructed at the site of his family home. This detail of Mac Wallace's life is, strictly speaking, hearsay. One might add that in a certain sense all journalism is hearsay. One might also note that Lyndon Johnson's business practices, as Holland McCombs discovered, were never documented, and, again, his name appeared nowhere.

As he devoted himself to building a personal fortune, Lyndon Johnson manipulated the granting of small business loans to fellow Texans. His people fanned out to help needy Texans; the price was that Johnson was to receive a piece of any enterprise that received federal support.

Wallace was assigned to strong-arm businessmen into rewarding Johnson for the small business loans that Johnson had bestowed upon them. Mac Wallace's role was to facilitate the Faustian bargains low-level Texas contractors and businessmen had made with Lyndon Johnson, to collect payment.

For these forays to Texas, Mac Wallace later earned the melodramatic sobriquet of Johnson's "hatchet man." The term was first attached to Wallace at the time he was an employee at the Department of Agriculture and seems not to have involved violence. Johnson sent Mac Wallace back to Texas to "arrange to buy or get a piece of" the businesses of those to whom Johnson had awarded the favor of those loans.

In Holland McCombs' copious records of his investigation of Lyndon Johnson for *LIFE* magazine, there are few references to Mac Wallace. One appears in McCombs' notes for his essay "Politics and the Power Structure of Texas." His name is misspelled as "Mack," suggesting that a McCombs source, in addition to Emmett Shelton, was Billie Sol Estes, by then a Johnson adversary, who for decades misspelled Mac Wallace's name that way. So McCombs writes: "I understand a man named Mack [sic] Wallace was sent down here from the Agriculture Department to work out some things like this." The reference is to business arrangements for concerns based in Austin. A typical example involved KRGV-TV in the small town of Weslaco but in this case the emissary was not Wallace, but a much closer Johnson associate named Jesse Kellam, who was also referred to, according to J. Evetts Haley, as Johnson's "hatchet man."

According to McCombs, and J. Evetts Haley, Lady Bird Johnson had asked the owner of Weslaco how interested he was in renewing his license. He could have it if he would let the Johnsons have half of the station, he was told. The sobriquet "hatchet man" would attach to the urban legend of Mac Wallace decades after Wallace's death. In another notebook, in McCombs' illegible handwriting, is a reference to a "piece on Dallas boy [or 'bag'] Wallace."

McCombs discovered that one of those small businessmen to whom Johnson sold a loan in exchange for a piece of his enterprise was "now head of one of the leading accounting firms of the state, has worked for, with, and [was] close to some of the cast of characters in the Johnson story." McCombs compiled a list of twenty-nine people whom he hoped to interview for his *LIFE* magazine research into the crimes and malfeasances of Lyndon Johnson. "Mack" Wallace's name does not appear on that list. He was not important enough.

Andre went to live with Mac Wallace in Virginia. Almost immediately the two again found it impossible to reside under the same roof. Andre reported a physical altercation to the police. Her husband had beaten her, she said. She was taken to a local hospital for treatment. On March 1, 1950, four months pregnant with their second child, Andre returned to Austin, where once more she and Michael moved in with her mother, Roberta Barton. Mac remained in Virginia.

Earlier in 1949, Josefa Johnson had begun a relationship with a new lover. His name was John Douglas Kinser. Unimpressed by Josefa's charms, his objective was to use her to solicit from her brother one of those small busi-ness loans Johnson wielded. An aspiring, though unsuccessful, actor and a golf professional, Kinser hoped to finance a nine-hole golf course called Pitch & Putt.

A married man, Kinser had been drafted into the U.S. Army as a private. Discharged in 1946 with the rank of captain, Kinser headed for New York, where he tried his luck on the stage. When he couldn't pay his bill at the Beaux Arts hotel, his wife, Shirley Prosser, rushed to New York from Austin and bailed him out and together they returned to Austin. They were divorced on June 25, 1949, and had a daughter, Diana Lynn Douglas, known as Penny Kinser, born on December 23, 1941. Kinser enrolled at the University of Texas. His majors were "dramatics" and anthropology.

On October 29, 1949, Kinser had escorted Josefa Johnson to a party at the Maximillian Room of the Driskill Hotel in Austin. The guest of honor was the new senator from Texas, Lyndon Baines Johnson. Kinser and Josefa appeared in public as a couple, although neither was faithful to the other. Rumor had it that he liked to "spank and be spanked." She was addicted to gossiping about her senator brother.

Alice Meredithe Wallace was born in Austin on August 1, 1950. Ten days later, Andre filed another divorce action against Mac Wallace. She claimed that her husband had subjected her to three years of cruelty. He had become an "obsessive drinker," and that had affected her own health. She charged Mac with "excesses, cruel treatment and outrages," and requested biweekly support of thirty dollars.

On August 25, Mac Wallace returned to Austin from Virginia. He did not contest the divorce, but signed a "no contest waiver." On October 10, Mac received official confirmation of his employment by the U.S. Department of Agriculture, which had been suspended pending the FBI's completion of his security clearance. Ten days later, on October 20, Andre withdrew her divorce action. It was dismissed on November 1. Mac returned to Virginia without her.

Left to her own devices in Austin, Andre joined a dramatic club. One day, her friend Grace Hewitt introduced her to a fellow member, John Douglas Kinser. When he opened the Pitch & Putt, Andre took to spending her after-noons there. During the summer of 1951, Andre and Kinser engaged in a sexual liaison.

Josefa continued to meet Kinser at noisy, smoky roadhouses, the Broken Spoke or the Wagon Wheel. Pitch & Putt was underfinanced, and it was now that Kinser made his move. He invited Josefa to a barbecue, a family party at his parents' house near Lake Austin. On this occasion, Kinser told Josefa what was on his mind. Perhaps she might use her influence with her brother to help him secure one of those government-backed small business loans.

Breezy and casual, Josefa was not particularly offended or resentful that Kinser was trying to use her to get to her brother. Matter-of-factly she turned down his request. "Lyndon wouldn't listen to me anyway," she remarked later, speaking of Kinser's solicitation.

That summer, Mac Wallace received a disquieting letter from Elgin Williams, informing him that behind his back there had been a sexual liaison between Andre and "a man." Elgin Williams himself was something of a sexual predator. He had attempted to seduce Nora Ann Carroll on a trip to New York in the summer of 1944, although he knew full well that she was Mac's girlfriend. Nora Ann had rebuffed him.

The chronology must be pieced together because there is little documentation of Wallace's comings and goings. In Austin during the summer of 1951, Mac made it his business to discover the name of Andre's lover. It was John Douglas Kinser. His pride outraged, he insisted that Andre escort him to the Pitch & Putt golf course, so that she could point Kinser out to him. "I'll bash his face in," Mac said.

They drove to the Pitch & Putt, where Mac removed his shoes and moved out onto the grass in search of Kinser. Kinser was nowhere to be found. Later Mac would claim that he had agreed to forget about the Kinser episode. Back in Virginia, already bored with his duties at the Department of Agriculture, he applied for a job with the State Department and was accepted. His employment would commence on January 1, 1952.

His plan now was to return to Texas in October for what he termed a "ten-day vacation." His movements seem erratic, his purpose undefined. He was exhibiting a restlessness that had taken hold of him the moment that he had lost Nora Ann Carroll. One might infer that he missed his children. Certainly it doesn't seem that the events that followed bore any relationship to what is meant by a "vacation."

In his old blue Pontiac, Mac drove to Austin, his first objective to visit his children, three-year-old Michael and one-year-old Meredithe. Then he would take the children to his parents' house in Dallas. From the moment of his arrival, he and Andre began to shout at each other. There was a witness, Roberta Barton, Mac's mother-in-law, who described Mac's behavior that day as "raving" at Andre.

Alone with his mother-in-law, Mac spoke frankly. "Andre doesn't know it," he said, "but I'm through with her. She has dragged my good name in the dust long enough." He called Andre "a homosexual and a whore" and accused her of having slept with both men and women since he married her.

A fragment of a letter from Andre to Mac, postmarked October 11, 1951, opens a window onto their fractured marriage. "Dear Mac," Andre writes, "the adjustment has been a thousand times harder than I had anticipated. Thank goodness 'old crutch' alcohol has been discarded . . . I am still 'on the wagon.' I had forgotten how much fun living could be." By Andre's own admission, her alcoholism had played a significant role in their relationship.

Mac packed up the children and drove them to Dallas, where he delivered them to his parents. On October 20, he visited Joseph Louis Schott at the FBI field office in Fort Worth. That night, Mac resumed his conversation with Schott at Schott's home. He planned to divorce Andre and gain custody of the two children, he said. He was reluctant to leave them in Andre's hands.

"It will not be easy," Schott said.

"I can do it," Mac said.

The following day, Mac returned the children to Andre in Austin. Again they argued about her affair with Kinser. Later Andre told the police that they drove to Zilker Park where, she claimed, Mac requested that she allow him to "go down on her," and she agreed. They were heard arguing at one of the local roadhouses.

Mac Wallace was locked in a sexual quadrangle. As a Texan male, he cultivated a proprietorial attitude toward his wife, and he treated his marriage as entirely apart from his sexual attraction to Josefa. Both Andre and Josefa had been pursuing sexual affairs with Kinser, who loved neither of them. Mac certainly does not seem to have loved either Andre or Josefa. His professional life had also taken a downward turn. From the apex of social approval as president of the student body of the University of Texas, having sacrificed his ambitions to be either a lawyer or an academic, he had contented himself with becoming a minor government official, sinking into anonymity.

CHAPTER 7

The Killing of John Douglas Kinser

"Now he looks like a man capable of anything."
—GABRIEL GARCÍA MÁRQUEZ, *ONE*
HUNDRED YEARS OF SOLITUDE

On the morning of October 22, 1951, Mac Wallace had yet another heated argument with his mother-in-law. His rage was focused on John Douglas Kinser, who he was convinced had taken advantage of Andre at a vulnerable moment. She had stopped drinking, she had seemed to be on the road to recovery. Kinser, Mac felt, had been the obstacle to her fulfilling her role as mother to his two small children.

On this steamy Austin morning, he told Roberta Barton that he wanted a divorce. He would turn over his life insurance to Andre. If anything happened to him, he wanted Andre to invest it in real estate. "I won't be around much longer," Mac said. It was the week after his thirtieth birthday.

"Nothing is going to happen to you," Roberta said.

"You never can tell," Mac said. Then he attempted to make a joke of his prediction that he would soon be gone, so that Roberta concluded that his doomsday remarks reflected nothing so much as his wallowing in self-pity over the wreckage of his marriage to Andre and his own diminished prospects.

In the blue Pontiac, Mac drove to the University Co-op. The manager, A. C. Rather, remembered him well from his time, seven years earlier, as student body president. Rather cashed his check without hesitation.

At three fifteen P.M. on this hot October afternoon, Mac headed for the Pitch & Putt golf course. He parked outside the squat white clubhouse, a primitive structure lacking hot water and air-conditioning. Kinser had sorely needed the loan that he had hoped Josefa would help him obtain through her influence with her brother.

Having just played the course, a federal employee named J. E. White was inside the clubhouse. "I shot a thirty today," White remarked to Kinser, who was standing behind the counter writing checks, juggling his various creditors.

"That's pretty good golf," Kinser said. White ambled outside, where he pulled up a metal folding chair and sat down. Mac opened the screen door and faced the man he would later tell people "ruined my family." He asked for a pack of cigarettes, and handed Kinser a dollar bill. Holding the dollar in his hand, Kinser punched a sale for thirty-three cents on the cash register. Mac then pulled out the .25 Schmeisser pistol, once the proud possession of a Nazi officer, stared straight at Kinser, and fired at point-blank range.

Kinser stumbled, knocking over a coffee Silex so that glass shattered all over the counter. Fleeing from his attacker, Kinser headed for the paneled pantry just beyond. Wallace rushed behind the counter in pursuit, continuing to fire the pistol. He shot Kinser in the left forehead, and twice in the groin.

Mac Wallace aimed carefully. His next bullet penetrated two arteries of Kinser's heart. Kinser fell, still clutching the dollar bill.

Mac emerged from the Pitch & Putt clubhouse with the Schmeisser pistol still in his hand. He glanced at J. E. White seated on his chair and gestured with the gun as if he were about to shoot White, too. White got up and ran for his life.

"Damn whistling I ran," White said later to investigators. "Valor in a thing like this is staying alive." White had the presence of mind to describe Kinser's assailant: five feet ten inches tall, about 180, a muscular build, dark hair, a ruddy or dark complexion. He was wearing tortoise-framed eyeglasses.

Bloodstains were found on the screen door of the clubhouse and a bloody trail led from the swinging door behind the counter to the door leading out. Blood was found on the metal folding chair outside the clubhouse, the chair that had been abandoned by J. E. White. Six gunshot wounds had been inflicted on the victim.

Mac walked away quickly, heading for the dark blue Pontiac, and set off "at a fast rate of speed." By then, White had summoned three golfers from the eighth tee. Ted Ungar jotted down the license number on his golf score card: 90766, which was close to the correct number: 2-90786. White ran into the clubhouse and called the police and an ambulance, although Kinser was already dead. Judge Travis Blakeslee ordered the body removed to the Hyltin-Manor Funeral Home to await an autopsy. When the police arrived at the Pitch & Putt, they retrieved three "hulls" or shell casings from a .25 caliber automatic pistol.

Mac headed north on Robert E. Lee Road. He stopped at the Trading Post, a café fourteen miles from the Pitch & Putt, and rushed into the toilet. Not having noticed him enter, the proprietor, Wiley Johnson, began to close up for the day.

"Don't lock me up!" a voice called out, a telling locution. The toilet door snapped open and Mac emerged. "I had to go to the restroom," he said. Pressing a handkerchief to his bleeding index finger, he purchased two cans of beer, rejecting the offer of a can opener. "I have one in my car," Mac said.

"I done had him," Wiley Johnson said later. He did not notice that Mac's index finger was bleeding. Andre was to tell the Rangers that the only gun she knew Mac to own was the one Joe Schott had given him.

Mac Wallace drove to the Hill Country, near Johnson City, where he claimed later to have deposited the gun in a tree stump. The weapon was never found.

Less than two hours after Kinser was shot, Mac Wallace's license number in hand, three highway patrol officers from the Weights and Measures Department pulled him over. They were at the Marshall Ford Dam, the site of Brown & Root's first government contract, procured for them by fledgling congressman Lyndon Johnson.

The officers searched the Pontiac with its Virginia tags. There was no weapon, but they did recover a live .25 Peters cartridge, a spent Peters cartridge, and two slugs from a .25 caliber weapon. The live shell turned out to be a match for shells found at the Pitch & Putt clubhouse. They also found a wrinkled, bloody shirt with the label and laundry marks torn out, and a blood-stained handkerchief, also missing its laundry mark, on the floorboard.

"The shirt and handkerchief are bloody because my left index finger is bleeding," Mac Wallace said. When the officer asked how he had gotten cut, Mac told him to mind his own business. The reason for his confidence emerged at the police station. After supplying his name and address, 2649 Woodley Place, NW, Washington, D.C., he indicated that he was in a hurry.

"I work for Johnson," Wallace told detective Marion Lee. "That's why I have to get back to Washington." It would take thirteen years before Marion Lee, no longer an Austin policeman, would reveal that Mac Wallace at that moment had invoked the name "Johnson." Wallace was not threatening, Lee remembered years later. He just said he had to get out of custody and get back to Washington because he was working "in some office that was connected to Mr. Johnson."

"Where have you been in the last hour?" another officer asked.

"No comment," Wallace said.

On the strength of the reports of the golfers at the Pitch & Putt, in those pre-Miranda times, the Austin police tossed Mac Wallace into jail and denied him the opportunity to contact anyone. Derwood Nollner, of the Department of Public Safety (Texas Rangers) lab, performed a paraffin test with Wallace's consent. There were fourteen nitrate particles on his right hand and seven on his left, leaving no doubt that he had recently fired a gun.

Asked to provide a blood sample, Mac Wallace refused. When a photographer attempted to take his picture, Mac stopped him.

"Let's don't have that," he said.

On the same page of the *Daily Texan* that reported the murder of John Douglas Kinser, an article described how the Longhorns, the University of Texas football team, presented Colonel David Harold Byrd, a leading Texas defense contractor and supporter of Lyndon Johnson, with leather chaps at a ceremony. Honorary president of the UT band, Byrd was among the team's most generous benefactors. The Longhorn Band played "The Eyes of Texas" in Byrd's honor. In a twist of fate, Byrd would figure in Mac Wallace's life before the close of the decade.

Mac refused to accompany District Attorney Robert J. (Bob) Long to a place where witnesses could identify him. Defying the Department of Public Safety, Sheriff Ernest Best supported him. "I'm afraid of what might happen to Mac Wallace," Sheriff Best said, not specifying the danger. By the time the four golfers who had been at the Pitch & Putt arrived to identify the suspect, the jail was dark. None would be certain that this was the man they had observed fleeing from the clubhouse after the shooting of John Douglas Kinser.

The prosecution enlisted a psychiatrist. Mac refused to talk to him. "We're going to take you if we have to put you in a straitjacket," Bob Long said.

"Go get your straitjacket!" Mac said. When Sheriff Best prevented them from bringing in the straitjacket, Long accused him of "obstructing justice." Mac was polite when the psychiatrist appeared. He "meant no offense to me, but he was playing this close to his vest and would not discuss anything without benefit of an attorney," Dr. Lee Freerborough said later.

Twenty-year-old William E. (Bill) Carroll, now a law student at the University of Texas and Nora Ann's brother, was listening to his car radio when he heard a news flash that his sister's former boyfriend was being held at the Austin city jail in connection with the murder of John Douglas Kinser. He had not seen Mac Wallace in years, and had never heard of Kinser.

On an impulse, Carroll drove to the jail to see if Mac needed anything. There he learned that Wallace had not been permitted to communicate with anyone. Captain Bill Sterzing, in charge of the city jail, refused to allow Bill to see Mac without authorization from the district attorney, Bob Long. Undaunted, Carroll drove to the courthouse, certain he would prevail as his mother and Long's wife were good friends. Long invited Carroll to chat with him—in the courthouse urinal.

"Have you ever hunted with Wallace?" Long asked. "Do you happen to know what kind of guns he owns?" Carroll did not reply.

"I have no power to get you in to see Mac Wallace," Long said.

Carroll then shook his finger in Bob Long's face. He had not planned to get involved in the Wallace matter, but now he was going to become involved. "Mr. Long," Carroll said, "you have just made the biggest mistake of your life."

Carroll headed for the chambers of Judge Charles O. Betts, the sponsor of his law school fraternity, and the judge who had heard Andre's divorce petition. Betts suggested that Carroll locate a lawyer who would swear out a writ of *habeas corpus* on Mac Wallace's behalf, to be served on the city jail. The Austin police would then have to bring Wallace before Judge Betts to show cause why he was being held incommunicado.

Judge Betts signed off on the writ. He changed the "return" provision to "instanter," so that Wallace would have to be produced immediately upon the authorities being served with the writ. The Austin police, Betts knew, were in the habit of moving prisoners out of the jail to Camp Mabry in North Austin, and then back to the jail, to avoid the writs. Sure enough, this maneuver was attempted by the district clerk, O. D. Martin. Carroll telephoned *American-Statesman* photographer Neal Douglass to take a picture of the Austin police in the act of contempt of court as they hustled Mac Wallace off to Camp Mabry to avoid Judge Betts' writ.

The lawyer Carroll enlisted, criminal defense attorney Polk Shelton, was among George Parr's lawyers and had been a stalwart worker for Lyndon Johnson in the 1948 election. As a congressman, Johnson had helped Polk Shelton's son-in-law move from the Army Reserves to the regular Army. "If he is your friend," Polk Shelton said of Lyndon Johnson later, "you feel like you can always go to him and ask him anything you want to ask him, if you want a favor . . . I guess if a man could love a man, I could love him."

Knowing none of this, Carroll was amazed when he saw that Shelton had already collected clippings on the Kinser murder. When Shelton left the office for home that afternoon, Carroll, C student that he was, represented Mac Wallace at the *habeas corpus* hearing.

The writ did not proceed unopposed. Bob Long's office argued that the laws of Texas permitted law enforcement to hold a suspect for thirty-six hours for investigation without either charging him or bringing him before a magistrate. In fact, there was no such law.

"You all have no more right to be holding Wallace than you have to hold me!" Judge Betts said as he ordered Wallace's release. Wallace had been incarcerated and held incommunicado for twenty-five hours. He enjoyed about a minute and a half of freedom, one local wag quipped, before the state produced a warrant for his arrest in the murder of John Douglas Kinser. While the *habeas corpus* hearing was in progress, murder charges had been filed. Bond was set at thirty thousand dollars.

Mac's father arranged for a personal surety bond. Alvin (A. J.) Wallace was frugal. This type of bond ensured that he wouldn't have to pay a fee of 5 percent of the face amount of the bond to a commercial bond company; rather, he could make a personal bond based on his property holdings in Fannin County. Then A. J. began to search for friends who might help.

On October 23, the day after the shooting, at ten thirty A.M., Mary Andre Wallace walked into Bob Long's office. There she was interviewed by Long's chief investigator, Onis Doherty. Andre admitted that she knew Kinser and had "done some work" for him at his golf course. Then Andre departed. She had an appointment with Mrs. Al Kinser, the victim's mother, she said.

On that same day, Mac wrote on the back of his brother James Eldon Wallace's business card: "Please release my 1939 Pontiac automobile and all contents therein to my brother, James E. Wallace." James Eldon was an industrial engineer who worked for the Lone Star Gas Company. For the rest of his life he would deny that his brother had murdered Kinser.

The next day, October 24, Mary Andre returned to Bob Long's office. She confided that she had married Malcolm Wallace after having known him "for about a week." Their married life had never been happy. After the wedding, Mac had sent her to Dr. D. R. White. During the early days of their marriage, "she and Mac had practiced sex perversion." There were few acts of "normal sexual intercourse."

Mac had opposed her first pregnancy and attempted to force her to go to a New York midwife for an abortion, Andre confided. She denied that she had ever been intimate with Kinser. Then she changed her story and admitted that she and Kinser had been lovers "the previous summer." She added that Mac was madder at Kinser for fooling around with Josefa Johnson than he was about her relationship with Kinser. Some of this can be confirmed. For the rest, we have only her word.

On October 25, Polk Shelton was hired officially as Mac Wallace's attorney. Shelton said he doubted that the state would be able to provide a motive and had only circumstantial evidence. Andre, by law, could not testify against her husband, rendering it impossible for the prosecution to invoke her affair with Kinser. Mac could shelter under the protection of the Fifth Amendment and need not testify. The Wallace family was so confident that A. J. told reporters that when it was all over, Mac would return to Washington, D.C., with his family.

The thirty-thousand-dollar bond was the highest court officials could remember, and Polk Shelton succeeded in getting it reduced to ten thousand dollars. Bond was posted by two contractor friends of Alvin Wallace. At eleven A.M. on the morning of October 25, 1951, Mac Wallace, out on bail, drove to Roberta Barton's house. For two hours, he unburdened himself yet again to his mother-in-law. He complained about Andre's homosexuality, and how she had been spotted in "homosexual joints." He seemed to have been rationalizing what had become the sordid soap opera of his life, culminating in an unspeakable act.

For the murder of John Douglas Kinser, he exhibited no remorse. He behaved, rather, as if he had not done anything wrong. He arranged for a journalism student to organize a press conference for him at the University of Texas Union Building, scene of some of the finest hours of his life.

He was overwhelmed by the number of friends who offered him assistance after his arrest, Mac told those assembled, mostly students. "Some things were grossly distorted," Mac said, although "not by the press and radio to whom I am grateful for getting my name on the air." He claimed to have come to Austin to visit his in-laws. Having himself committed the ultimate crime, he warned the people of Travis County that they "should not rest too easy about the observance of civil liberties in the county."

Those who knew Mac Wallace found the murder out of character. On October 26, Joseph Louis Schott was interviewed by FBI special agent R. W. Newby at the FBI academy at Quantico, Virginia, where Schott was undergoing training. He had known Wallace for ten years, Schott said, calling him "a very mild-mannered and stable individual, although he is outspoken." Mac was "very fond of the children."

On that same day, Mac Wallace himself telephoned FBI headquarters. His call was passed through to Alex Rosen, an agent high in the Bureau hierarchy. He could only have reached Rosen by invoking his friendship with Schott. If a subpoena were served upon the FBI, Wallace asked Rosen, would the Bureau provide testimony "as to whether paraffin tests were admissible as evidence generally?" Rosen told him that the FBI did not furnish expert testimony, except in cases in which evidence had been examined by the FBI. He asked whether the FBI had examined the evidence.

"I don't know," Wallace said.

"Are you the accused or are you inquiring on someone else's behalf?"

"I am the accused," Wallace said. "I'm out on bond pending the trial which is to come up on February eighteenth."

Describing Wallace's telephone call in a written memorandum months later, Rosen noted that Wallace had spoken "in a very intelligent manner and without any indication of any emotional disturbance." Wallace had confided that "he was at a loss to know where he could obtain assistance to refute the testimony," and whether "the Bureau in answer to a subpoena would be able to comment on whether such paraffin tests were conclusive or not." Rosen noted that Wallace was acquainted with Joe Schott (Schott's name is redacted, even in the reprocessed FBI file).

On October 30, a grand jury was convened in Austin. Among those subpoenaed was Joseph Louis Schott. Knowing that Mac Wallace "may have used a pistol acquired from SA Joseph Louis Schott," an FBI document reads, the Bureau decided that Schott would "appear as requested regarding matters about which the Bureau is aware." That October, the Office of Naval Intelligence conducted its first security investigation of Mac Wallace, the first of eight.

November 2 dawned, another Austin day thick with humidity. With cloudy skies spitting rain, the temperature already at eighty-four degrees, Andre, her hair newly cut short, entered a packed Travis County courtroom. She did not as much as glance at her husband. On this day, Mac Wallace was indicted for the murder of John Douglas Kinser. The murder indictment was signed by grand jury member Carl Bredt, assistant dean of student life at the University of Texas. Mac Wallace pleaded not guilty and was released on bail.

Mac Wallace now drove to Washington, D.C., not to return to work, but to solicit the support of the FBI. Whether he had maintained his residence, there is no record. He rented a room in northwest Washington, near where Schott was staying and which took Schott by surprise. Uppermost in his mind was the paraffin test that had implicated him in the Kinser murder. He wrote to Nora Ann, now Nora Ann Cary, who was living in Portsmouth, Virginia, where Ted Cary was serving as a doctor in the U.S. Navy. Mac knew that Nora Ann had a master's degree in biochemistry.

He needed a chemist who could supply him with information about what items might provide a positive reaction to the test for gunpowder, Mac wrote. Nora Ann replied with a terse letter. She knew nothing about this subject, she said, enclosing, pointedly from herself and her husband, a small book she had found on the subject. She thought now about Mac Wallace's "monumental ego" and that there had always been that side of him that was primitive.

On January 31, 1952, his trial date nearing, Mac Wallace wrote a long personal letter to FBI director J. Edgar Hoover. The letter is detailed and chatty, as if it were entirely normal for him to be confiding in the most powerful law enforcement officer in the country. He complained about Alex Rosen, who had not given him an answer to his paraffin inquiry. In fact, Rosen had been quite emphatic in explaining that the FBI would not be available to testify on his behalf at his trial.

Mac Wallace requested of Hoover that the FBI provide "expert testimony on the reliability of paraffin test procedures from a man from the FBI laboratory" or someone outside the laboratory who was "an authority on the subject." This testimony should apply "not in my particular case but in general."

Rambling on at length, he added, "It makes no difference what my attorney or I may know about such tests, for we are not even chemists, much less experts on the tests. Neither is it satisfactory to settle for what we can bring out by cross-examination of the chemist testifying for the prosecution, since he, as one paid by the Department of Public Safety, by the very fact of being involved in the case, and by reason of having read about the case in the local press, may be influenced in his testimony by factors other than the chemistry involved in the test procedure." The underlying assumption is that Hoover would be sympathetic to his cause.

Providing an Austin post office box, Mac concluded, "Your help in this matter will be much appreciated, and in trust that it will be given, I am Cordially, Malcolm E. Wallace."

It is not known whether Mac Wallace was aware of the now well-documented friendship between Lyndon Johnson and J. Edgar Hoover. Johnson and Hoover had met at the White House, according to author Burton Hersh, when Hoover stopped by to dish "the latest dirt" with Franklin Roosevelt in the late 1930s soon after Johnson became a congressman. Hoover had flown to Dallas to attend the victory party for Johnson at the Driskill Hotel in 1949.

On this same day, January 31, 1952, as Mac was writing Hoover, his mother, Alice Marie Riddle Wallace, departed from the family home for the Terrell State Hospital, an institution for the mentally incompetent. Her niece Connie Perdue claims she had been suffering from a brain tumor and had been increasingly unable to function. Her son's having been indicted for murder must have played a role in her breakdown. All the family stood in a circle in the entrance foyer of the Wallace home to bid her farewell.

On February 1, Mac Wallace resigned from his position with the Department of Agriculture. His transfer to the State Department was canceled. He returned to Austin in time to receive Hoover's February 6 reply to his letter. Joseph Schott believes that Hoover answered Mac Wallace's letter because Mac knew Joe. Hoover liked Joe Schott; after Joe graduated from Quantico, Hoover saw to it that he was assigned to his home city of Fort Worth. Schott is skeptical that Lyndon Johnson had anything to do with Hoover's answering the letter.

Hoover's reply to Mac Wallace was boilerplate. He echoed Alex Rosen's denial of Mac's request that the FBI participate openly in his case. Desperate, Mac called Schott. He needed the FBI to help defend him, Mac said.

"The FBI does not defend people," Schott said. "We work with prosecutors." Schott could not resist seizing an opportunity to express his indignation. "I gave you that gun as a souvenir," Schott said, "not to kill someone!"

"You better not do this to me!" Mac threatened. "I'll get you!"

"It's a federal crime to threaten a federal officer," Schott said coolly. "All I have to do is tell Hoover and you'll be interviewed by the FBI and they'll try you in federal court." Four days after Hoover's letter to Mac Wallace, the director instructed the San Antonio field office "without disclosing Bureau interest [to] obtain the results of the trial of this individual."

District Attorney Bob Long seemed to view the case as if the crime were not the murder of John Douglas Kinser, but the "perverse" sexual practices of Andre and Mac Wallace. Although he knew that Andre had had an affair with Kinser "the previous summer," it never came up at the trial. Long requested that Captain Clint Peoples of the Texas Rangers be assigned to the case as an investigator, the better to appear to have been thorough.

"It's a touchy case," Colonel Homer Garrison, who headed the Rangers, told Peoples. Peoples wondered whether "there was some hidden secret that made Wallace go off," perhaps that "Lyndon Johnson told Mac to go to Texas"? He pondered whether Mac Wallace might not have been more angry at Kinser because "he was fooling with this Johnson gal" than at Kinser's affair with Andre. Yet Josefa had become involved with Kinser at least two years before the murder and their relationship had long been known to Johnson and his circle.

Among those interviewed by Clint Peoples was Joseph Louis Schott. Schott did not think much of Clint Peoples, whose office in later years was in the same Fort Worth building. "He's a big talker," Schott thought, "a bullshit artist." He thought that Peoples was "way off base" in his speculation that Mac Wallace and Lyndon Johnson had conspired somehow in the Kinser murder.

From the files of the Internal Security Section of the Department of Public Safety, Peoples discerned that there was "no evidence of homosexuality of subject and/or Kinser," although there were "indications that Wallace's wife, Andre Barton, is a lesbian." The Austin police held in its files a report that Andre, clad only in her underwear, had been surprised by the Austin police in Zilker Park in the company of another woman. In "gay" places, Andre "danced only with women and did not pay attention to the men."

Peoples concluded that Mac Wallace had never met Kinser prior to the shooting. Motive bedeviled everyone looking into this case. Writing in the *Austin American*, Leonard Mohrmann, the most astute reporter covering the story, termed Mac Wallace's motive "the big question in the trial."

Contradictory explanations abounded. A college friend of Mac Wallace named Stuart Chamberlin was a fellow Homer Rainey supporter and an executive with the State of Texas Finance Department. Interviewed by Onis Doherty, Chamberlin "thought the shooting was over Andre." But as the trial neared, his outlook shifted. I have "no personal knowledge upon which to base my opinions and as a friend of Mac's I now want to retract those statements," Chamberlin said. Mac Wallace resided with Chamberlin during the trial.

At an Austin country club, Bob Long was approached by a local dentist, stationed at Bergstrom Air Force Base. This dentist had gone out with Josefa Johnson and even proposed marriage, only to be turned down. "You'd better look into Josefa Johnson," the dentist said. "She's deep into this thing."

Onis Doherty interviewed Josefa, who admitted that she had met Kinser at the Broken Spoke, a honky-tonk roadhouse on Barton Springs Road that claimed it served the best chicken fried steak in all of Texas. Josefa told Doherty that Pitch & Putt had been in financial trouble and Kinser had asked her to intervene with her brother about a loan.

With no stomach for this case, which was going nowhere, Long offered Mac Wallace a guarantee of outright release without prejudice should a lie detector confirm his innocence. Affecting indignation, Polk Shelton sputtered that Long's offer was a "grandstand play" and a "legal foul ball." There would be no polygraph.

CHAPTER 8

Texas Justice

*"And, in spite of the sense of struggle and
tragedy in the minds of many, with an electric
chair as the shadowy mental background to it
all, a sense of holiday or festival . . . And with
cries outside of 'Peanuts!' 'Popcorn!' 'Hot
dogs!' 'Get the story of Clyde Griffiths, with all
the letters of Roberta Alden' . . ."*

—THEODORE DREISER,
AN AMERICAN TRAGEDY

On February 18, 1952, the Austin courthouse was hot, noisy, and packed with
sweaty bodies. Spectators hung over the balcony. The circus atmosphere
recalled the pandemonium of the fictional trial of Clyde Griffiths, who
drowned his pregnant girlfriend in Theodore Dreiser's novel *An American
Tragedy*.

The first surprise was that Mac Wallace's attorney would not be Polk
Shelton after all, but another Lyndon Johnson intimate, John Cofer, the
leading criminal lawyer in Austin. Cofer's nickname was "The Wall," so
majestically did he tower over jurors. Polk Shelton claimed that he had hired
Cofer to handle the legal issues and any appeal that might be necessary. In
reality, Cofer served as the lead attorney for the defense.

On the surface, Shelton was warm and friendly, Cofer stuffy and pompous.
Seated beside him was Hume Cofer, assisting his father. Asked years later
how John Cofer became involved, Hume Cofer said that Lyndon Johnson had
"nothing to do with our firm being employed in the Wallace case." Yet, the
likelihood that so prestigious a figure as John Cofer was drawn to what was on
the surface a vulgar domestic murder based on sexual jealousy is slim. Rather,
Cofer's presence is more likely connected to Mac Wallace's having silenced a

man with whom Josefa Johnson may have shared details of Johnson's schemes, not least of how he had stolen the 1948 senatorial election in a campaign in which Josefa herself had been active.

Mac Wallace arrived, dressed in a dark blue suit. Since his days at the University of Texas he had grown pudgy, a bit ungainly, almost bloated. On the first day of the trial, he sat at the defense table reading a newspaper, as if the proceedings had no particular connection to him. When the time came, he rose and, clasping his hands behind his back, pleaded "not guilty" in a soft voice. During jury selection, Andre sat directly behind him. The *Austin American* newspaper described her as a "comely brunette."

Later Bill Carroll would speculate that had Mac pled guilty, he could have invoked the "paramour statute." Under Article 1220 of the Penal Code of the State of Texas, in a statute dating from the late nineteenth century, and representing a break with English common law, homicide was "justifiable when committed by the husband upon one taken in the act of adultery with the wife, provided the killing take place before the parties to the act have separated." The paramour statute dated back to the laws of Solon, an Athenian statesman and poet who reformed the legal system of Greece in 594 B.C., and had traveled into Roman civil law. It was part of Texas' own peculiar brand of justice.

The paramour defense was sometimes termed the "heat-of-passion defense." The sole circumstance in which it did not apply was if there had been the husband's "connivance in or assent to the adulterous connection," which was not the case with Mac Wallace. The paramour statute did not permit the man to kill his wife. Nor did it permit a wife to kill her husband's paramour. It was a law favoring the Texas patriarchy. You could go too far: In a case where a husband tied up his wife's lover and cut off his penis with a razor, his action was not deemed justifiable.

In practice, the paramour law was applied liberally. The husband did not actually have to burst in upon his wife and her lover in the act of sexual congress for him to be found not guilty of murdering the lover. In 1855, journalist Gideon K. "Legs" Lewis, a partner of Richard King, proprietor and founder of King Ranch, was shot and killed by the doctor husband of his lover. The doctor was not even tried for the murder, and he hadn't actually "caught" Legs and his wife in the act.

In the most frequently cited example of the paramour defense, in 1894 Anthony Price had caught his wife in a corn crib with one William Chandler. Price shot Chandler and was sentenced to two years in the penitentiary only for the conviction to be reversed on the ground that Price committed justifiable homicide. The appeals judge wrote: "We cannot believe that the law requires or restricts the right of the husband to the fact that he must be an eye-witness to physical coition of his wife with the other party . . . adultery can be proven by circumstances . . ."

By Texas standards, Mac Wallace had not committed a crime at all. Bill Carroll told the author Wallace almost certainly would have been acquitted had he pled guilty and mounted a "heat-of-passion" defense. Because he pled "not guilty" the paramour defense was unavailable to him.

All the jurors at the trial of Mac Wallace for the murder of John Douglas Kinser were middle-aged Caucasian men; there were no women, and for that era, of course, no African Americans. They were all lower-middle-class people: an electrician and a mechanic; a machinist and a post office employee; a body shop mechanic and a bookkeeper; a rancher/private investigator and a carpenter; a clerk for the Texas Employment Commission. Inappropriately, the wife of one juror, Bradford Boyd, was a distant cousin of the Kinser family.

"Juror Number One," Deckerd L. Johnson, who became the jury foreman, was a small man with a little mustache. He worked for the Texas Highway Department. In the *voir dire*, Johnson admitted that he was "acquainted slightly" with attorney Paul Holt, who was assisting the state. Deckerd Johnson hailed from a town in Leon County where Mac Wallace had relatives. Ruby Wallace, a sister of A. J., and Mac Wallace's aunt, was married to Harold Barrow, and "Uncle Harold" was from a small town called Centerville in Leon County, East Texas.

After the jury selection, Mac telephoned his Uncle Harold, who turned out to have a nephew named Gus Lanier, who was a lawyer and was Deckerd Johnson's first cousin. (Deckerd's middle initial, L, stood for "Lanier.") Uncle Harold promised Mac that he would get word through his nephew to Deckerd Johnson that the family expected Mac to "come clear."

Gus Lanier was dispatched by Uncle Harold to Austin. Bob Long later claimed that he had been reluctant to accept Deckerd Johnson on the jury, "but I was down to three challenges and let him on." Long's reasoning was specious. "I didn't like him because he had a little mustache," Long said.

On day two of the trial, Polk Shelton and the Cofers were joined at the defense table by Gus Lanier, who was introduced to the court as an attorney for the defense.

After a recess, Mac Wallace waited to return to the courtroom until the jury had been re-seated. Then, he and Gus Lanier greeted each other warmly and made a display of shaking hands. "They let this guy on the jury know," Long remarked later, "that Lanier was a friend of Wallace's." When reporters asked

Lanier about that handshake, he explained that he was a family friend. He claimed he had known Mac Wallace in school and was acquainted with the Wallace family.

Three days later, Gus Lanier disappeared from the defense table, never to be seen again.

At one point early in the trial, three-year-old Michael Wallace rushed into the courtroom, like an actor waiting in the wings, and hugged his father. Mac gave him a quick embrace and sent him on his way. Before long, Andre disappeared from the courtroom. Her seat was occupied by Bill Hodge, a member of the city of Austin's legal staff and a friend of Mac Wallace's at the University of Texas. Reporter Leonard Mohrmann termed the trial "rife with the unusual."

John Cofer challenged the admissibility of every piece of evidence obtained by Long's investigators. He demanded that the statements made by Mac Wallace during the period between his arrest and the *habeas corpus* hearing twenty-five hours later be considered inadmissible. This included the paraffin test, Mac Wallace's bloody clothing and handkerchief, and a photograph of his automobile.

Judge Betts overruled him. Polk Shelton then jumped up and submitted an application for a suspended sentence on the ground that Mac Wallace had no prior felony conviction. Shelton had made it his modus operandi in every one of his cases to request a suspended sentence in advance, just to have it on the record in case his client was convicted.

What characterized Long's prosecution was how determinedly he steered clear of any suggestion of a motive. His investigator, Onis Doherty, had researched the sexual dalliances of Andre Wallace, Josefa Johnson, Mac Wallace, and John Douglas Kinser. Yet on the stand Doherty testified only to such matters as his "plat" of the Pitch & Putt clubhouse. He presented photographs of the golf course. The name "Josefa Johnson" was kept out of the trial.

None of Long's twenty-three witnesses offered testimony that might have led to a conviction. Kinser's father testified that he had never observed Mac Wallace at his son's golf course, a statement that seems more useful to the defense than to the prosecution. Long asked Kinser what items were sold at the clubhouse costing thirty-three cents, and Al Kinser replied, "Cigarettes." Dr. Harold Williams, the county medical examiner who had performed the autopsy on John Douglas Kinser, testified that five bullets had entered the body, although there had been six. He offered no evidence that Mac Wallace had put them there.

Long's most useful witness was Joseph L. Schott, who explained that he had given his friend Mac Wallace a .25 caliber pistol he had taken from a Nazi officer. Schott explained how Mac Wallace's index finger had come to be bleeding. At this, John Cofer offered a loud, sonorous objection. The information about Schott's having given the pistol as a gift to Mac Wallace, and the fact that firing that pistol tore flesh from the index finger every time, Cofer contended, had been obtained illegally from Mac Wallace's wife; the law forbade her from testifying against her husband. The objection was sustained. Still, Cofer could not make disappear that two or three extra rounds of ammunition, of which Mac Wallace had not disposed, had been discovered in the pocket of his sweater.

When Schott stepped down, Mac Wallace jumped up and tried to embrace him. Schott wanted no part of his old friend now, and pushed him away. He never saw Mac Wallace again.

None of the eyewitnesses would swear that Mac Wallace was the man they had observed at the Pitch & Putt leaving the scene of Kinser's murder—not even J. E. White, who had seen him up close.

In his cross-examinations, Cofer humiliated as many of Long's witnesses as he could. Some of his histrionics aimed to prove that the witnesses had been wrong when they identified Mac Wallace's Pontiac at the scene. Placing a brown paper bag on the defense table, Cofer trapped a police officer into declaring that the license plates of only one state, Virginia, where Wallace's Pontiac was registered, used the color combination of silver and black. Mac Wallace's Pontiac, of course, bore Virginia tags.

"Are you sure about that?"

"Yes, sir."

Cofer then reached for the brown bag on the defense table and extracted a bundle of license plates that had been wired together and folded in accordion fashion. Cofer held the bundle under the eyes of the witness. Then he grasped the top plate, and allowed the other license plates, all silver and black, to fall toward the floor. Without a word, he displayed the plates to the jury. Then he read out the names of all the states besides Virginia that had silver and black license plates.

On the matter of the damaging paraffin test, Cofer engaged in similar sophistry. Among Mac Wallace's University of Texas acquaintances whom he enlisted to help him was Henry Scarborough, who by then had graduated with a B.S. in chemistry and was a graduate student in the Department of Botany. Scarborough had noticed that Mac had "foolishly" taken that paraffin test, remarking, "After all, he was incriminating himself."

Scarborough discovered a book in the University of Texas library called *Introduction to Criminalistics*. Its author was the man who had devised the paraffin test, and his book acknowledged that the test was not foolproof because many common everyday substances readily available for normal household use produced the same results as firing a gun.

In possession of a set of keys to the university chemistry lab, Scarborough had gathered a group that included Bill Carroll. They had tested some thirteen items mentioned in *Introduction to Criminalistics* to determine whether they would elicit the bluish-green color indicating a positive paraffin test. Among these items were fertilizers, urine, and manure.

As Scarborough later remembered, they "smeared their hands with several of these substances and then washed them. They put a hand into melted paraffin and when it formed a solid glove, it was peeled off." Scarborough added: "I treated it with a re-agent . . . a blue color indicated that nitrate was present, and I found that to be the case for these substances. I also ran tests on hands which had not been treated, and these did not show the presence of nitrate."

Henry Scarborough had been head of the Tejas Club. He did not much like Mac Wallace. Yet he had organized these paraffin tests on his behalf. Many of Wallace's acquaintances called upon to help in his defense obliged. All of them were puzzled that so intelligent a man could find himself in such a situation.

Mac asked Henry Scarborough to testify as an expert witness, but Scarborough declined. He had only a B.S. in chemistry, he pleaded, and there were dozens of Ph.D.s available in Austin. At one point, Mac admitted to Scarborough that he was resigned to going to prison. With his old bravado, Mac claimed that the only thing that bothered him would be the lack of access to women. But, he said, he had already discovered a way to surmount this obstacle.

On the day the district attorney's expert on the paraffin test, the man who had administered the test to Mac Wallace, was to take the stand, Mac insisted that Henry Scarborough attend the trial. He pointed to a seat at a table across the aisle from him. This was where Scarborough was to sit. Mac did not reveal that this was the prosecution table, and on the other side of this table sat Bob Long and an assistant. They kept eyeing Scarborough. Finally, they requested that he move to the other side of the aisle.

Henry got up, only to trip on a metal spittoon. A loud clatter ensued. The judge smiled and gave Scarborough a benevolent look. It was a farcical moment at a farcical trial. In the balcony, members of the Tejas Club could barely contain their laughter.

When Long put his expert witness on the stand to testify that Mac had failed the paraffin test, the expert argued that a specific pattern of blue spots had appeared on the paraffin. This was conclusive.

Rising to his full height, John Cofer produced a copy of *Introduction to Criminalistics*. He termed it "this authoritative book." Before Cofer was done, the state's chemist had to admit that not only was he acquainted with this text, but he had studied under the man who had written it.

Cofer's rebuttal witness, Dr. Cecil Hale of Southwestern Analytical Chemicals, then itemized a grab bag of substances that could result in a positive paraffin test on someone who had not fired a gun recently. Positive paraffin results, Hale testified, could come from "rusty razor blades; firecracker powder; an unburned kitchen match; used safety match folders; a cigarette stub; a drop of urine; and a beer can opener."

Up in the balcony, the members of the Tejas Club laughed uproariously. Later, FBI agents, reading Hale's testimony, also laughed at the idea that nitrate particles could be deposited by a drop of urine. With John Cofer at the helm, Mac Wallace had not, in the end, required the assistance of the FBI lab.

Long had subpoenaed Mac Wallace's mother-in-law, Roberta Barton, only for her to produce a doctor's note claiming that "it might be injurious for her if she underwent emotional strain." She would not testify. Then Long rested his case, to the consternation of many who had been waiting for the district attorney to point to some motive for the killing. A jury would be unlikely to convict Mac Wallace without one.

Refusing to acknowledge that the murder of John Douglas Kinser had anything whatsoever to do with his client, John Cofer produced ten character witnesses (out of twelve witnesses in all) who had no knowledge of the crime. Among them were Stuart Chamberlin and two UT economics professors, Clarence Wiley and Eustin Nelson. Others included Leslie Tiner, the St. Stephen's Episcopal School coach, and Blake Smith, pastor of the University Baptist Church.

Mac Wallace had confided to the press that he wanted to take the stand to deny the charge. "The jury would convict you sure as hell," Cofer told him. Certainly he could not have been compelled to testify; every defendant bears the right not to incriminate himself. And Cofer was too smart to allow even the appearance of his suborning perjury.

The trial drew to a close amid storms of outsized Texas rhetoric. "Our best witness is buried six feet under the ground," Bob Long declaimed. "That's why we can't tell you where their [Mac Wallace's and John Douglas Kinser's] paths crossed."

"You know he is guilty and you know he knows he's guilty," Assistant District Attorney Thomas Blackwell said to the jury.

In his summation, Polk Shelton spoke scornfully of the hesitant golf course witnesses. "If they won't swear Wallace was there, how can you?" he demanded of the jury, adding that the state had failed, except by "surmises and guesses," to make a case that the jury should "take Wallace's life and liberty." The state had put on a circumstantial case with shaky eyewitnesses, no murder weapon, and no confession.

As self-assured as the wiliest criminal defense attorney, Cofer intoned in his closing remarks that this was the first trial he had known where a man was charged without any indication of motive. "It is impossible," Cofer said, "as a matter of mental reasoning to overcome a reasonable doubt without a motive."

The trial had endured for ten days. On February 27, 1952, at four thirty P.M., the sequestered jury retired to the stifling room with its primitive amenities where they had been accommodated throughout the trial. Twelve beds were lined up side by side. Everyone had to get up at five A.M., so that they all could shave and finish breakfast by seven. After complaints, more hooks had been added to the few already there for clothes and more places provided for shaving, but the place remained miserably hot.

Deckerd Johnson, the foreman, told the jurors that if they couldn't come to a unanimous decision, and a hung jury resulted, Mac Wallace would not be tried again. At a single session, both questions were debated: Is the defendant guilty? If so, what should be the punishment? There was no separate punishment phase.

At eight P.M., the jury asked to examine Wallace's bloody shirt. Judge Betts had gone off to see a production of *Mr. Roberts* and was unavailable to grant the request. The substitute judge on call claimed that he was not familiar with the evidence and so was unable to rule on the matter of the shirt.

After two hours of deliberation, the jury reached a unanimous verdict. Eleven of the twelve jurors had not, in fact, been persuaded by John Cofer's histrionics and were ready to find Mac Wallace guilty of murder. Whether they were influenced by Mac Wallace's not taking the stand to assert his innocence, or Cofer's cleverness backfired, they found him guilty.

Deckerd Johnson acquiesced, only to exert his will in the punishment phase. Although the other jurors talked about sending Wallace to the state penitentiary for between fifteen and twenty years, Johnson demanded a suspended sentence, an issue that Polk Shelton had presciently placed on their agenda. Nor would he budge. Johnson insisted that were the others not to go along with him, there would be that hung jury. Johnson succeeded in winning one other juror over to his side to vote for the suspended sentence. Now there were two who ruled out any jail time. Unless the other jurors acquiesced, Mac Wallace would go free.

On the morning of February 28, at four minutes after nine, the jurors were ready to present their verdict. Mac Wallace stood inside the bar rail near the judge's bench. With him were his father, A. J. Wallace, and his brother James Eldon Wallace. Andre was not present in the courtroom. Leonard Mohrmann reported in the *Austin American* that Mac stared hard at each juror from behind his horn-rimmed glasses.

Before the verdict was read out, Bob Long raced for the exit. In a startling violation of legal etiquette, even for Texas, Long vanished into the humid Austin morning. Mac Wallace was found guilty of "murder with malice aforethought" and sentenced to five years in the state penitentiary. The jury's sentence recommendation was amended with the words *suspended sentence*. The time he would be in jail for the murder of John Douglas Kinser would be those twenty-five hours he had spent behind bars prior to the *habeas corpus* hearing.

At the words *suspended sentence*, Mac's impassive expression broke and "for a fleeting moment," one reporter wrote, a faint smile played about the corners of his mouth. Judge Betts' acceptance of the suspended sentence was mandatory. He remanded Mac Wallace to jail, and the sentence was conveyed, releasing him "on suspension with a personal recognizance bond of one thousand dollars." In five years, should he not commit another felony, the conviction would be expunged from his record.

Minutes after the verdict was read, Mac Wallace was set free on his own recognizance. He borrowed the money to pay Polk Shelton and John Cofer from his father and his brother James Eldon. According to James Eldon, it was "something over fifteen hundred dollars." For many years, he repaid them in monthly installments.

John Cofer requested that Mac Wallace thank the press and radio for their fair handling of his case. When reporters gathered to interview him after the trial, he said that he appreciated "the radio coverage." Cofer chimed in that he believed that the newspaper coverage had been "fair and accurate."

Mac would say no more. "I don't think any statement would be proper," he said. He volunteered that his "plans are rather fluid." Polk Shelton polled the jury. The consensus, he reported, was that "when a man like Wallace kills someone, he would have to have had a pretty good reason. They did not know what the reason was." Not knowing, they had acquiesced in the suspended sentence.

Nora Ann Cary had followed the trial avidly. The murder revealed cowardice, she thought, something Mac couldn't handle that led him to kill a man. Yet she embraced the logic of Texas justice. The murder was Mac's means of getting rid of a man who was hurting his family. He had assumed the role of taking care of his siblings from the time when he was a college student. She could rationalize that the killing of John Douglas Kinser fell into the category of protecting his family. Unlike her brother Bill, who would have acquitted Mac under the paramour defense had only he pled guilty, Nora Ann decided that there were no circumstances under which she could excuse the murder of Kinser. She thanked her "lucky stars" that she hadn't been "taken in by his handsome figure" and married Mac, as her heart had urged her to do.

Nora Ann knew nothing of Mac's dalliance with Josefa Johnson, nor of Lyndon Johnson's interest in the case.

As a Roman Catholic who then entered the Trappist (Cistercian) monastery of St. Joseph's Abbey, and would be ordained to the priesthood in 1963, Henry Scarborough is a more credible source than many. Scarborough discovered a Johnson connection to the case, and wrote the following:

"I had a friend in Tejas who had political connections. He told me that the woman in the case was Lyndon Johnson's sister, who was supposed to be a nymphomaniac. Johnson was a senator at the time. His informant told him that Johnson had flown to Austin secretly and registered at the Stephen F. Austin Hotel from which he summoned the DA and told him to drop the case or he was finished politically. My friend is dead now, but Governor Mark White was his first cousin. So I do know he had political connections."

Mac Wallace held a victory party, something in bad taste, Henry Scarborough thought. The only thing to be celebrated was that Mac was not going to prison, although he had been convicted of first-degree murder. Mac insisted that Henry attend the party, at which he heard Mac exclaim, "Too bad the jury did not do the right thing. All the evidence was circumstantial."

Several jurors telephoned John Douglas Kinser's parents to apologize for voting for the suspended sentence. Threats had been made against their families, some claimed. One juror made a trip to Bob Long's office.

"Mr. Long, if we'd tied that jury up and had a hung jury, would he have been tried again?" he asked.

"Yes," Long said. Then, according to Long, the man wept.

Years later, Johnson adversary Senator Ralph Yarborough was asked by would-be author Stephen Pegues about the Kinser trial verdict.

"It was supposed to look like rivalry over a woman but it was much deeper than that!" Yarborough said.

"Was the murder over Andre Wallace's affair with Kinser?" Pegues persisted.

"NO!" Yarborough said, raising his voice.

"Had the incident anything to do with a certain senate majority leader?"

"BINGO!" Yarborough said, according to Pegues. Yarborough never clarified his assertion or spoke about the Kinser trial for the record.

Three months after the Kinser trial, in May 1952, Bob Long wrote to a New York acquaintance named Ben Kaplan. (R. V. Long's oral history for the LBJ Library newly unredacted in May 2016 reveals that his belief that "perversion" was behind the Kinser killing was based on his having learned that Andre at the time of the trial was having an affair with an Austin minister's wife, and that the minister and his wife both attended the trial. So "the whole thing wasn't somebody screwing a man's wife," Long said. He remained convinced that "the man that was killed was a pervert.")

"I did not prove a motive for the killing," Long wrote. "I would like some day to know the true motive for the killing for my own satisfaction." No reply from Kaplan was available.

Later, when rumors swirled about a Lyndon Johnson–Mac Wallace connection, and Josefa's name was whispered, Long made a point of insisting that he had had no contact with Lyndon Johnson during the Kinser trial. Long's oral history reveals that Lyndon Johnson and Bob Long enjoyed a long acquaintance. They had met all the way back when Johnson was working for Dick Kleberg, in the mid-1930s. Their friendship continued when Johnson ran the National Youth Administration for Texas. Lyndon and "Bird," as Lady Bird was known among friends, would come out of an evening because the Long place was the coolest in Austin. Later Long helped out in Johnson's 1941 campaign for the Senate. Long was already district attorney in Austin. Asked whether he had been "under any pressure from the Congressman's [sic] office to knock that off," Long replied, "None. In any shape, form or fashion." "But you were accused of it," interviewer Frantz persists. "Lord, you were accused of it!"

On Election Day in Austin in 1954, Bill Carroll ran into Bob Long on Congress Street. Years earlier Carroll had written Long off as a person lacking in "polish and class," a "second-rate lawyer" and a "lethargic man given to fits of temper." They shook hands.

"Carroll, if I lose today," Long said. "You and I will know why." The Kinser trial and its irregularities hovered beneath the surface of their conversation.

"Yes, we will, Mr. Long," Bill Carroll said.

On that day, which was their first opportunity since the Wallace trial to express what they thought of the performance of their district attorney, the voters of Travis County booted Bob Long out of office. He was defeated in the Democratic primary race by Leslie Clay Proctor, one of his assistants. If the rumor Henry Scarborough heard was correct, and Lyndon Johnson had instructed Long not to pursue the case with rigor or effectiveness, nonetheless Long's old friend Lyndon, who in the company of Lady Bird had embraced the cool of the evening many a time in Long's backyard, certainly had not helped him to remain in office.

After the Kinser trial, Mac Wallace's warfare with Andre resumed. On April 29, 1952, two months after he walked out of the Travis County courthouse a free man, Andre left him again. On May 1, he filed for divorce in Dallas County. In his petition, Mac charged Andre with "alcoholism, cruelty, belligerence, [and] insulting behavior." This language suggested the intolerable humiliation he claimed to feel because of Andre's affair with John Douglas Kinser. He asserted that Andre "no longer cared for him." Her conduct had affected his "health and well-being, causing him much mental disturbance and anxiety."

Granted the divorce, on June 6, 1952, Mac Wallace received full custody of their two children, Michael Alvin Wallace and Alice Meredithe Wallace. Andre had to remain content with visitation rights.

On May 1, 1952, Mac Wallace had been hired by the Jonco Aircraft Corporation, based in Shawnee, Oklahoma, a subsidiary of Fairchild Engine and Airplane Corporation. When Wallace joined Jonco, they were manufacturing moving assemblies for a superjet. In business for only one year, Jonco had received a $750,000 government loan from the Reconstruction Finance Corporation under the Defense Production Act. The Cold War signaled a military buildup, the re-arming of America; the Southwest was a major recipient of these contracts. There is no apparent explanation for this unlikely scenario. A convicted murderer, in the same year as his trial, was employed by a defense contractor of growing significance.

Before he moved to Oklahoma, Wallace's arrest record was transmitted by the Austin Police Department not to Jonco, but to the Luscombe Airplane Corporation. Since 1950, Luscombe had been a wholly owned subsidiary of the Texas Engineering and Manufacturing Company (TEMCO), headed by David Harold (D. H.) Byrd, a defense contractor and significant Texan supporter of Lyndon Johnson. Even the records of the Office of Naval Intelligence, which began to investigate Mac Wallace at the time of the Kinser trial, offer no explanation for how a convicted murderer could be hired by a defense contractor. It seems apparent, however, that a job with TEMCO had already been arranged and that the hiatus in Oklahoma was what would later be termed a "place maker." Coincidentally or not, Admiral Richard E. Byrd, the cousin of D. H. Byrd, who explored the Antarctic, flew in a Fairchild aircraft.

On November 15, 1952, Mac Wallace was in Texas. On that day, he was charged with being "drunk in a judge's office" in Georgetown, Williamson County, west of Austin. Having a spent a night in the Williamson County jail, he was released the next day after paying an eighteen-dollar fine.

On December 21, 1952, Mac remarried Mary Andre. The whole family went to live in Shawnee, Oklahoma. Michael Wallace would remember the family in Oklahoma working together to dig a tornado cellar in their backyard. They dug a pit, put down scrap wooden boards to create steps, and a tarp, and then replaced the dirt. Michael, age four, proudly carried the family's prized possessions outside and placed them in the tornado cellar.

As Jonco prepared to hire 150 new workers, Mac served as the company's labor relations manager in charge of union contract negotiations, grievances, and arbitrations, a position of executive responsibility. For his final six months at Jonco, he would be personnel manager, handling recruitment, first aid, plant security, and the safety program. Maintaining his academic interests, he taught two courses in economics for one semester in 1953 at Oklahoma Baptist University in Shawnee.

The Wallaces remained in Shawnee for less than two years. When they returned to Texas, they moved into A. J. Wallace's house in Dallas, joining the world of Mac's brothers and sister. Among the Wallaces, Andre was ill-at-ease and combative. She got into frequent arguments with her in-laws.

In 1954, Mac Wallace went to work for TEMCO, which had been founded in 1946 as another fruit of the postwar boom that came to Texas. There is no record of how he came to secure this plum, a job one would not expect to be extended to a convicted murderer. TEMCO enjoyed contracts with the U.S. Navy and the U.S. Air Force. As a member of the Senate Armed Services Committee, and the Select Committee on Post-War Military Policy, Lyndon Johnson had been in a position to send contracts TEMCO's way and at that time he was close to D. H. Byrd, as their correspondence at the LBJ Library makes apparent.

By the time he employed Mac Wallace, D. H. Byrd had long been indebted to Lyndon Johnson. Building, overhauling, and converting aircraft, TEMCO had not only had contracts with the U.S. Navy, but was lending properties to them, in the manner of Herman and George Brown, so that there was no separation between the corporations and the military. TEMCO's surplus in 1953 was more than $245 million; its defense contracts totaled $92,900,000.

In 1954, the year Wallace joined the company, TEMCO built the Convair B-58 and was designing airborne electronics for the Navy and the Army Signal Corps. In Dallas, they constructed a Naval Industrial Reserve Aircraft.

"Texas is still the land of great opportunity," Byrd believed, "thanks to the American system of free enterprise." He would go on to run fifty-two companies, some related to oil and gas, some to aviation, some to real estate. Byrd admitted in his self-published autobiography, *I'm an Endangered Species: The Autobiography of a Free Enterpriser*, that to accomplish his purposes, he created a rapport with "the politicians who ran things." "Where you have capitalism, you have capitalists," Byrd wrote.

Byrd acknowledged in his autobiography that "among the men I could go to at any time that I wanted action" was Lyndon Johnson. "It's wonderful to have your friendship," Johnson wrote to Byrd on September 2, 1956. Johnson was instrumental in TEMCO's gaining the contract for the Corvus air-to-surface missile at a cost to the Navy of $1,600,000. In turn, Byrd donated generously to Johnson's political campaigns. Johnson then sponsored such Byrd projects as the Civil Air Patrol, an Air Force affiliate Byrd cofounded in 1941.

In D. H. Byrd's correspondence with Lyndon Johnson in the 1950s and '60s there is no mention of Byrd's having hired Mac Wallace. There is evidence of their shared symbiotic relationship. "Dear Harold," Johnson wrote to Byrd in June 1965, "You've done so much to be helpful to me. I can never thank you enough." The correspondence began in 1953 when Byrd expressed interest in bills before the Armed Services committees of the Senate and of the House. In an April 13, 1953, letter, Johnson invited Byrd to name a time when they might "get together." Johnson furthered the application of Byrd's Natural Gas Pipeline Company of America. February 22, 1956, found Johnson offering, "Let me know when I can be of service." On March 9, 1956, Johnson was able to report to Byrd that the Civil Air Patrol (CAP) was pending before the House Committee on Armed Services.

"It means a lot to me to know that you are behind me 100%," Johnson wrote to Byrd on May 31, 1956. "I do wish you would give me your views from time to time on issues in which we are both interested." On January 23, 1958, Johnson wrote, "I will always be grateful for your friendship." On January 7, 1959, Johnson wrote, "I am comforted to know that I have friends like you and Mrs. Byrd." When in May 1960 the Russians took down Francis Gary Powers' U-2 spy plane, Byrd offered his suggestions, and Johnson replied (on February 24): "I hope that you will continue to let me have your advice and counsel." That year Byrd had difficulties with the telephone service at one of his farms, and Johnson intervened personally. On June 25, 1960, came one of Johnson's most effusive notes to Byrd: "And, for your every other expression and deed in my behalf, my heartfelt thanks. I'll never forget you."

He knew exactly how to flatter Byrd. It is worth quoting these many letters and the frequency of their communication through the 1950s until Johnson's fortunes rose, at which point Johnson's staff sent the thank-you notes.

Over the years, there were gifts from Byrd to Johnson beginning in January 1954 when Johnson acknowledged a box of "real Texas Grapefruit." A similar thank-you note came on January 12, 1956, also about grapefruit. A year later (January 11, 1957) came gratitude for grapefruit that "does for me what ambrosia does for the gods."

The gifts continued into Johnson's vice presidency. Johnson sent a personal thank-you note for a box of preserves on February 12, 1961. On February 7, 1964, Johnson acknowledged a gift from Byrd of a photograph of Mrs. Johnson, Darrell Royal, and himself, taken three years earlier. On June 8, 1964, Byrd sent Johnson "a very generous supply of onions" shipped from his farms.

Johnson continued to cultivate D. H. Byrd into 1962. Byrd sent a cable immediately upon the assassination of President Kennedy, which Johnson acknowledged on November 30, 1963; and Christmas 1963 brought a fruit-cake from Byrd that Johnson acknowledged personally.

When Byrd and his wife were not invited to the inauguration in 1964, Byrd was miffed. He wrote Johnson on January 19: "You have all forgotten two of the oldest most loyal friends you've had in Texas for many years." But in 1965

Byrd resumed his gift-giving, sending LBJ "a lovely, inscribed copy of the Holy Bible." On January 11, 1966, Lady Bird acknowledged a gift of "luscious apples." On September 1, 1967, Byrd acknowledged receiving a photograph, "the Presidential family portrait." A white Bible came to the Johnsons from Byrd at Christmas 1968.

Byrd repaid Johnson certainly by providing employment to people Johnson favored. Mac Wallace was not the only Johnson acquaintance to gain employment with Byrd's TEMCO. Another such recipient of a job with D. H. Byrd was Raymond Fehmer, the father of Johnson's personal secretary, Marie Fehmer. Billie Sol Estes' comment on the subject decades later bears consideration. "Mac Wallace never worked for Byrd. Always he worked for Johnson."

By 1954, George Parr's fortunes were on the wane in South Texas. The malfeasances of Box 13 would not go away. In a February 5, 1954, article in the *Daily Eagle*, listed among the wrongs emanating from Duval County was George Parr's fixing the senatorial election of 1948. The *San Antonio Light* of February 12, 1954, suggested that the fight by Governor Allan Shivers against George Parr "may very well be aimed at toppling Senate minority leader, Lyndon Johnson."

As reported in the *Houston Press* of February 3, 1954, thousands of dollars were paid out annually by the Duval County school district to maintain the "reign of George B. Parr as monarch of this kingdom of mesquite and mayhem." Those willing to fight "the dictatorship of George B. Parr" were compared in "their heroism with that of men who died at the Alamo and Valley Forge."

Eusabio Carrillo Jr. had been issued funds from the district, although he was not employed by the district. Carrillo was the brother of D. C. Chapa, the tax collector of Duval and Parr's first lieutenant. The press in Texas seemed bent on exposing George Parr's corruption, large and small, and the courts were emboldened to take action as they had not been in past times.

Simultaneous with these revelations, public anger against Parr surfaced. A Jim Wells County grand jury indicted two Texas Rangers on charges of assault with intent to murder George Parr in a courtroom scuffle at Alice, Texas. A Duval County grand jury met to investigate the misuse of public school funds in the county. There was a threat from Governor Shivers to declare martial law or send five or fifty rangers to crush what he called "ballot gangsters" in Duval County. Shivers declared he was going to clean up "boss rule in Duval County."

CHAPTER 9

Two Faustian Bargains: Little Lyndon and Billie Sol

*"You've got Bobby Baker and Billy [sic] Sol
Estes and Lyndon Johnson has the colossal
nerve to say, 'Let us continue'?"*
—CONGRESSMAN WILLIAM MILLER
RUNNING WITH BARRY GOLDWATER
IN THE GENERAL ELECTION OF 1964

Given his obsession with power, described so well by Robert Caro, it should surprise no one that Lyndon Johnson easily became minority leader in 1953. Entering the Senate, he had gone over "every member of the Senate—his drinking habits, his sex habits, his intellectual capacity, reliability, how you manage him." Each individual was to be the subject of a particular Johnson strategy. Historian Robert Dallek writes, quoting Bryce Harlow, that as soon as Johnson entered the Senate he provoked conflicts in a compulsive effort to be noticed. At a House-Senate Armed Services Committee conference, Harry Byrd, Sr. of Virginia denounced the Seventy Group Air Force as "an advertising slogan of the Secretary of the Air Force." Johnson then demanded an apology from Byrd, as Dallek writes, "for impugning the character, motives, and intelligence of Seventy Group supporters, of whom he was one." Byrd capitulated. The year was 1949, and Johnson was the most junior of senators. Dallek terms this Johnson's "first big move to the leadership of the Senate."

From Senate page Bobby Baker, then messenger to the Senate minority, assistant to the Senate doorkeeper, chief telephone page to the Senate majority, and assistant clerk to the majority conference, Johnson sought advice: "I want to know who's the power over there, how you get things done, the best committees, the works." Lyndon Johnson remained in the shadows as Joseph

McCarthy ran amok in the Senate and elsewhere and was chastised by Drew Pearson. In late 1950, as Robert Dallek tells the story, McCarthy launched a vicious physical attack on Pearson at the Washington Sulgrave Club, kneeing him in the groin and slapping him repeatedly across the face. Pearson appealed to Lyndon Johnson for help. Johnson replied, "Drew, you've not been kind to me lately." Publicly Johnson adopted the strategy of standing by until McCarthy attacked conservatives, which took some time.

Johnson ran for party whip at Bobby Baker's suggestion against Alabama Senator John Sparkman, and succeeded—in 1951—with the help of Georgia senator Richard Russell, whom Johnson cultivated throughout his career in the Senate. It was Russell who ensured Johnson's leadership: "Saw L. Johnson & buttoned up leadership for him," Russell wrote on November 10, 1952, on his desk calendar.

Far from being toppled, as the *San Antonio Light* had predicted he would be, when the Democrats gained control of the U.S. Senate in 1955, Lyndon Johnson was re-elected easily. He was elected majority leader through a deal with Wayne Morse, who had become an independent and perceived Lyndon Johnson to be the person without convictions that he was. "Lyndon Johnson represents Lyndon Johnson," Morse said. A telephone call from Johnson to Morse closed the case. "You could have any committee assignment that a *Majority leader* has to offer," Johnson said. Morse agreed to vote with the Democrats and Johnson became majority leader.

As majority leader, Johnson facilitated two particular Faustian bargains. He became a silent partner with Billie Sol Estes, a corrupt farmer and wheeler-dealer based in West Texas. In Washington, D.C., Johnson relied upon Bobby Baker, a young man of breathtakingly few scruples. "I wanted to meet you," Johnson said at their first encounter, leading with flattery, as was his wont. "My spies tell me you're the smartest son of a bitch over there."

Robert Gene Baker began his career in Washington as a child. Fourteen-year-old Baker was sent to Washington from his hometown of Pickens, South Carolina, in 1942 by his postmaster father to serve as a Senate page. He assumed his duties on January 1, 1943. Within two years, he was chief Senate page, shedding his knickers for a black suit. He met Lyndon Johnson in December 1948. When Johnson became minority whip, Baker was elected Assistant Secretary to the Senate Minority.

"I understand you know where the bodies are buried in the Senate," Johnson added at their first meeting. Baker was twenty years old, Johnson forty. Baker soon went on to earn a law degree at night, although he was never to practice law. His "firm" was called Tucker and Baker and occupied offices at 2000 P Street. As majority leader, Johnson controlled the election of Baker as Secretary to the Majority.

Bobby Baker took on the assignment of facilitating the awarding of campaign funds to those senators who voted the way Johnson preferred. Support of the oil depletion allowance, so important to Johnson's Texas oilmen friends, was a given. As Baker served as Johnson's intermediary with senators whose votes he sought, he became Johnson's eyes and ears, his courier and messenger, errand boy, bookkeeper, and propagandist. Still, Bobby Baker found time to moonlight, enriching his own coffers, more often than not by illegal and semi-legal means.

Baker admired his mentor in those palmier days. He noted that Johnson "seemed to *sense* each man's individual price and the commodity he preferred as coin." Baker would approach a senator and say, "The Leader would like to know what your position is on this issue." Always Baker dangled a bribe. Many senators were not shy about specifying what they wanted: "Can you send me on a trip? My wife wants to go to Paris or Rome." Or "we've never been to Tokyo." Baker called these bribes "a little lollypop." "How would you like to take a NATO trip?" he would ask. "You'll go to Paris and to Brussels and to Bonn and to Athens and Rome in a two-week period."

Baker's cynicism was matched by the ease with which he fulfilled his maneuvers. Baker later acknowledged: "I could arrange a trip right quick." In addition to the NATO trips, there was an "Interparliamentary Union" that financed trips abroad for senators. For meetings of this association of "parliamentarians," senators and congressmen traveled free of charge to England, France, Germany, or Japan. As majority leader, Johnson decided "who got to take what trip where."

Baker later revealed: "I would say nine times out of ten they would be delighted, especially when they would tell their wives about it, because most wives felt like they were abused and neglected, so they got to be somebody on these trips. It was a very key weapon that we had to protect our flank."

Together, Johnson and Baker kept dossiers on each senator. They recorded that Estes Kefauver of Tennessee had "a severe whiskey problem, and a woman problem." Styles Bridges of New Hampshire accepted five thousand dollars from Baker. The list of senatorial capitulations grew long.

After Johnson became majority leader, the two grew personally close. Lyndon Johnson "made you such a part of the family," Baker would remember. "You never knew when he'd call up and say, 'Why don't you and your wife come to dinner; why don't you come to brunch; why don't we go together; why don't we go to this place?'" At cocktail receptions, among Baker's duties was that he taste each drink to ensure that it was light enough so that Johnson would not get drunk.

According to Baker, Johnson told him, "You're closer to me than I was to my father." Baker surmised that Johnson "wanted a son more than any human being that I've ever known in my life." Later this sentiment would be echoed by Johnson's older daughter, Lynda Bird: "How unfair for this person not to have a son to carry on his name." (That Johnson chose not to acknowledge his illegitimate son, Steven, the child he shared with his Texas mistress Madeleine Brown, was left unsaid.)

Johnson publicly offered Bobby Baker fulsome praise that found its way into the Congressional Record of 1956. Johnson lauded Baker for his "alertness, his diligence, his devotion, his dedication and his insistence that things be done right." Baker was, Johnson said, "one of the outstanding Americans." Baker and his wife moved to a $125,000 house in the Spring Valley section of Washington, D.C., near where Lyndon Johnson lived.

Sometimes Johnson withheld his approval. One time when Johnson ordered Baker to the Senate cloakroom where they sometimes conferred and Baker "didn't move fast enough . . . with one long step, Lyndon Johnson caught up to him, grabbed each of Baker's narrow shoulders in a huge hand and shoved him violently down the aisle." Before long, Baker was dubbed "Lyndon Junior" or "Little Lyndon," or, later, "the Mole." Johnson described Baker as "one of the most trusted, most loyal and most competent friends." To Baker, Johnson was simply "the Leader."

Among the errands Bobby Baker ran for Johnson was to ensure that Ralph Yarborough be kept from a place on the Senate Judiciary Committee. Baker whispered to Johnson-friendly senators: "We cannot let Yarborough go on that committee because then Lyndon Johnson would lose his hand on Texas judicial patronage."

There was no politician Johnson detested more than Yarborough, no doubt because Yarborough, with his support from labor, exposed the hypocrisy of Johnson's claims to liberalism. Yarborough's very existence exposed Johnson's political duplicity. As Yarborough put it, he stood for "the poor, underprivileged, and exploited Americans of Mexican descent, blacks . . . leaders of the campus intellectual community, labor unions, teachers and followers of progressive politics," constituencies to which Senator Lyndon Johnson offered little support. Arch Underwood confided to Holland McCombs, "Lyndon would like to break his [Yarborough's] neck . . . but he made that deal with big labor to lay off." In Texas, organized labor stood solidly behind Ralph Yarborough; as the recipient of Herman Brown's favor, Lyndon Johnson was against the unions and opposed union organizing at his radio station. He voted for and was known to support the open shop.

As soon as Yarborough was elected in 1957 in a special election, he went to war with Johnson over Texas patronage. The struggle for the appointments to federal judgeships was particularly bitter. They eventually settled upon a compromise, Yarborough later explained. Each would trade off and take turns making recommendations.

Yet Yarborough concluded that this system was being used to diminish his popularity, because every time an LBJ selection did not get appointed they would be told Yarborough had blocked the nomination. Lawyer Byron Skelton, a figure deep in Texas politics, believed that they split up the patronage, so that Ralph got the marshals, and Lyndon got the judges; each of them had a veto power over the nominees of the other. Once Johnson became Vice President, according to Bobby Baker, to appease Johnson, John F. Kennedy awarded Johnson a virtual monopoly over patronage in Texas.

As a longtime administrative aide to Johnson, John Connally did errands for Johnson in Texas to undermine Yarborough's credibility. Although Yarborough was now the senior senator from Texas, when Kennedy visited El Paso in the summer of 1963, Yarborough was not invited to attend the event. Yarborough saw personal ambition in John Connally's acting to exclude him.

In an interview in 1978 with the House Select Committee on Assassinations, Yarborough described how "LBJ urged JFK to ignore him [Yarborough] and not be seen in public appearances with him. LBJ allegedly told JFK of Yarborough's declining popularity in Texas and repeatedly emphasized that Yarborough was not respected or well thought of in Texas politics—and that he would be a 'drag' on the ticket."

Yarborough went on to explain: "A friend of his had asked John Connally why he attacked Yarborough so bitterly and John Connally replied that LBJ had made it clear that if they didn't stop and discredit Yarborough he eventually would take over control of Texas politics." "Whenever they had an event planned," Yarborough added, "the Connally interests would schedule a similar fund-raising event at a more prominent location on the same day and force loyalties."

In 1964, Connally said that "much of my trouble with Yarborough stemmed from Lyndon Johnson's trouble with Yarborough." Connally added in the same interview: "Yarborough was the only statewide man in Texas who was an all-out liberal. I am not that liberal. The real friction was between Yarborough and the Vice President." The Connally-Johnson relationship was summed up by Bill Moyers, who saw John Connally as the dominant force in Texas politics, the heir to the Johnson organization once Johnson moved on to the vice presidency.

Obsessive about how he was depicted by the media, Johnson decided that columnist Drew Pearson, although he might have the appearance of being pro–civil rights and anti-oil and anti-gas interests and support the rights of the little man, was in fact "a whore: he was for hire." Yet Johnson drew close to Pearson and admitted him into his inner circle. Johnson frequently used the epithet "nigger" in discussing a civil rights bill and boasted, "I'll have them niggers voting Democratic for two hundred years." He described the Brown v. Board of Education ruling desegregating the public schools as "all hell had broken loose." Such statements suggest that Lyndon Johnson's support of the Civil Rights Act was about his creation of a public image and furthering his own personal ambition.

By the time of the 1960 presidential campaign, Bobby Baker viewed Johnson as "very very pro-military, very hawkish, very distrustful of the United States and the Russians and the Cold War and the Chinese." Baker added: "If you were going to survive in Texas politically, you had to be pro-defense." As the Texas oilmen and defense contractors saw it, Lyndon Johnson, with what Baker shrewdly called his "Machiavellian mind," was the perfect antidote to John F. Kennedy.

Because Baker and LBJ had a symbiotic relationship, each man understanding the essential opportunism of the other, Bobby Baker was free to pursue a number of scams designed to enrich himself. J. Evetts Haley, an outspoken Johnson antagonist in Texas, summed up Baker's enterprises in this way: "He dealt in everything; brokerage on American beef in Haiti with Texas millionaires; questionable building promotions in Washington; business with notorious Las Vegas gamblers; and especially, lucrative friendships with the choicest call girls."

Baker owned 28 percent of a vending company called Serv-U. He entered into million-dollar contracts with vendors before Serv-U even owned any vending machines and at a time when they boasted no employees on the payroll. Baker also masterminded the construction of a flamboyant motel in Ocean City, Maryland, called the Carousel, at whose opening the guests of honor on July 22, 1962, were Lyndon and Lady Bird Johnson.

Another Baker project was the Quorum Club, which provided women for "top-level aides to Johnson." Among the women Baker procured was Elly Rometsch, later to become notorious for a liaison with President Kennedy until the president's brother Robert F. (Bobby) Kennedy and special assistant Ken O'Donnell spirited her and her hapless husband, a West German Army sergeant assigned to the German military mission in Washington, out of the country. Baker also served as the middleman with an insurance broker named Donald Reynolds, among the few publicly to expose Lyndon Johnson, in a hearing for bribery.

Behind the Baker maneuvers, the mob hovered. There was a connection to the InterContinental Hotel in the Dominican Republic where Baker represented Ed Levinson, who owned the Fremont Hotel in Las Vegas, and was close to Meyer Lansky and Sam Giancana. (The vending machines of Serv-U were manufactured by a company owned in part by Giancana.)

Baker attempted to acquire gambling rights for Levinson in Latin America. The trajectory involved Baker contacting a friend at Pan American Airways named Samuel Pryor, of whom Baker requested an introduction to someone at Pan Am to help Levinson get hooked up with a gambling casino in the Caribbean. The contact was John Gates, chairman of the board of InterContinental Hotels Corporation, a subsidiary of Pan American. InterContinental owned resorts with gambling licenses in Curaçao, Santo Domingo, and Puerto Rico. When Gates discovered that Levinson's brother, Louis, who was to be involved in the casino, had a criminal record, the deal fell through. Things progressed further in Santo Domingo. In 1955, Baker and Johnson were invited to the first casino opening. (They did not attend.)

Another of the more imaginative Baker scams in which there is substantial circumstantial Lyndon Johnson participation involved Clint Murchison Jr.'s meat-packing company in Port-au-Prince, Haiti. HAMPCO had failed to pass the sanitation requirements of the Department of Agriculture that would permit it to export meat to the United States. HAMPCO was even denied an export license to export its meat to Puerto Rico, the designated destination. The year was 1960. Bobby Baker arrived—whether in Haiti, or certainly in Puerto Rico, where he traveled frequently—and HAMPCO received its export license from the Department of Agriculture, courtesy of a new inspection.

Bobby Baker acknowledged accepting a kickback from HAMPCO, in collaboration with José A. Benitez, chief of the Democratic Party of Puerto

Rico. Lyndon Johnson's name does not appear in any of the writing about Baker and HAMPCO, although it is difficult to believe that "Little Lyndon" could have procured that reversal of the sanitation ban and an export license on his own. The spoiled meat was "ground up to make sausages, frankfurters, bologna and even some hamburgers."

Puerto Rico was not the final destination for the tainted meat. A more highly placed wheeler-dealer than Bobby Baker stepped in: I. I. Davidson, the registered lobbyist for both the government of Haiti and the Murchison interests. Davidson, an arms dealer for CIA, and a reliable FBI informant, made the deal: The HAMPCO meat went to Chicago.

Davidson paid Ernest Tucker, Baker's ostensible law partner, and Baker almost 10 percent of the net profits, up to thirty thousand dollars a year. The checks were made out to Tucker. Before it was over, Baker was being paid both by William Kentor, at Chicago Packing and Provision Company, and by HAMPCO and Clint Murchison Jr. This arrangement continued into 1963 without Lyndon Johnson's name ever surfacing.

An especially unsavory Baker episode was revealed after the alleged suicide of Alfred Novak, a Baker partner in the Carousel motel-resort that was among Baker's most flamboyant projects. A Washington, D.C., builder, Novak had loaned Baker twelve thousand dollars early in 1960 so that he might pursue a stock tip. They split the profits fifty-fifty. Baker came away with $37,660. Mrs. Novak had been an employee of the Senate Small Business Committee for more than twelve years.

The Novaks, who had known Baker and his wife from the time Baker was appointed Secretary to the Senate Majority, were partners with Baker on his stock in the Mortgage Guaranty Insurance Corporation (MGIC) of Milwaukee and on the Carousel Motel project. In 1959, the Novaks had bought the property on which the Carousel Motel would sit. As the Carousel ran into financial problems, Baker kept requesting more money from the Novaks.

On March 23, 1962, Alfred Novak, age forty-four, was found dead in his automobile parked in the garage with the engine running and a door open a scant inch. It was said that Novak had panicked as the project seemed to be tanking. Novak was discovered with a large bruise on his head, belying the suicide verdict. The Washington, D.C., *Daily News* termed Novak's a "mystery death." On the day of Novak's funeral, his wife said later, Bobby Baker went to her house with his associate, Ernest Tucker, and carried away all the motel accounts. Mrs. Novak accepted Tucker as the lawyer for her husband's estate.

Baker told Mrs. Novak he had found a buyer who would assume the Carousel's liabilities and reimburse their investments with promissory notes to be liquidated out of the motel's future receipts. This buyer turned out to be Serv-U, Baker's vending machine company, and the notes were signed by Ernest Tucker, Carousel's attorney. At that point, Mrs. Novak hired another lawyer.

Billie Sol

"I want you to know I appreciate everything
you have done, and will never forget it."
—LYNDON JOHNSON TO BILLIE SOL ESTES,
NOVEMBER 19, 1960

During his time as a United States senator, Lyndon Johnson drew close to another connoisseur of scams, a provincial Texas version of Bobby Baker, named Billie Sol Estes.

During the war, serving in the Merchant Marine, Estes had bought "stuff and sold it to the boys overseas." Clark Tabor, the former postmaster of Clyde, Texas, Estes' hometown, revealed to Holland McCombs that Estes had been involved in a "sort of black market." Noticing this enterprising young fellow, Johnson's man in Texas, Cliff Carter, encouraged him to purchase old barracks, like those at Fort Clark, that Estes went on to refurbish and then sell. The year was 1947. Estes sold the ramshackle buildings to farmers for cotton pickers' shacks or to "Negroes" as barns. Estes spent two hundred or three hundred dollars on the refurbishing and sold the shacks for three or four thousand dollars each, taking back mortgages in lieu of full payment.

At the turn of the 1950s, Estes moved to a West Texas farming backwater called Pecos, population approximately twelve thousand. Soon, wrapped in Christian fundamentalism and a pseudo-puritanical lifestyle, Estes emerged with a three-ring circus of scams that depended upon the cooperation of federal authorities who were to remain nameless.

In one scam, Estes purchased the cotton allotments of farmers whose land had been confiscated by the government through eminent domain for public works projects. There were strict acreage controls for the growing of cotton in exchange for price supports. The allotment stayed with the land, with the exception of land taken by eminent domain. Then the cotton allotment could be transferred to other land bought by the same person. The farmers retained the ownership of the allotment, which was useless to them without land. They then sold the allotment to Estes in exchange for a piece of land too narrow for farming. Estes took back a mortgage. The farmer came away with more cash money than he had had before.

It was all prearranged. The farmer would default on his payment to Estes, and the land would revert to Estes, who just happened to own an adjacent parcel. This allowed Estes to plant cotton where the farmer could not; his planting was dependent on his having first secured the legal allotment from the farmer. The agreement was contingent, however, on approval from the Agriculture Department's Stabilization and Conservation Service, which Estes received until one particular Texas-based agriculture department official looked into the matter.

Along the way, Estes bypassed government regulations regarding how much cotton a farmer was permitted to grow. Estes was assisted not only by Lyndon Johnson, but by Johnson's nemesis Ralph Yarborough. Estes also drew on the favor of a congressman named J. T. "Slick" Rutherford—until the West Texas voters kicked Rutherford out of office. On the ground in Texas, Johnson aide Cliff Carter was present to smooth the way. That Carter represented Johnson was widely known in Texas. "He was a very sharp operator," Ralph Yarborough said. "Lyndon could trust him to pick up the money and keep his mouth shut."

That Carter spoke for Lyndon Johnson there was no doubt in anyone's mind. One source was Estes himself. Another was Frank Cain, an attorney for the Pacific Finance Corporation, one of the institutions to which Estes was in debt. Cain told Holland McCombs that around March 1961 Estes made calls to Johnson's Washington office while he was being investigated by federal and state agencies, saying he would have Lyndon stop the investigation. "I'll get a-hold of Lyndon and get him to call it off," Estes said. By "it," he meant the investigation.

The federal help he received to further his scams included efforts by Ralph Yarborough as well as Johnson. In Washington, Estes frequently took Yarborough and members of his staff to dinner, and, McCombs wrote, "he practically used Yarborough's office as his Washington headquarters and had Yarborough running around taking him to see officials of the Agriculture Department." At other times, he took members of Senator and later Vice President Johnson's staff out to dinner.

Frank Cain, the closest person to Estes who was willing to speak to a journalist, told McCombs: "LBJ will change the history of the country. FDR took a poor country and made it rich. LBJ is taking a rich country and milking it . . . this power structure was built by FDR and is reflected in LBJ. This is not a Texas practice or phenomenon. It is a political practice. The Texas flavor comes in the wheeling and dealing in politics."

In a second scam, and certainly with the assistance of Lyndon Johnson, Estes developed so mammoth a surplus grain storage operation that by the late 1950s he was receiving millions of dollars a year from the federal government. The plan was to use the income from the grain storage operation to pay off bills he had run up in an effort to gain control of the anhydrous ammonia fertilizer market. (Estes enjoyed an annual income of between five and seven million dollars from government-guaranteed grain storage alone.) This would still leave Estes with millions of bushels of grain in storage and continuing income from the government. All the while, Estes claimed that he "just wanted to make the farmers a good deal." With all this cash, Estes bought businesses in Pecos, among them a funeral home and a newspaper.

Estes began buying grain elevators in 1958 with money furnished by a company called Commercial Solvents of New York. Before long, Estes was storing in Plainview, Texas, alone 23,107,000 bushels of grain. Billie Sol Estes became the largest recipient of government contracts for grain storage in the Southwest. Holland McCombs discovered that Lyndon Johnson had a controlling interest in how government grain was shipped, but could go no further in discovering the specifics. "There is that grain storage outfit in Houston," McCombs writes, "which Lyndon is supposed to have a piece of. Its growth was phenomenal to say the *least!* (from some $25,000 to some $6 million within a few years. If report checks out). . . "

That Billie Sol Estes received preferential treatment from the Department of Agriculture in accumulating contracts for the storage of surplus grain there is no doubt. In 1961, a Department of Agriculture employee named William E. Morris wrote Estes suggesting that he expand his West Texas operation "by creating a world-wide empire to sell or trade surplus grain." On March 27, he wrote Estes that he might "obtain government surplus ships to carry the surplus grain and that that first one be named the S.S. Pecos Trader."

The third scam had Estes attempting to corner the market in anhydrous ammonia fertilizer, which was necessary to the local farmers, by drastically underselling his competitors. As Bill Adler wrote in the *Texas Observer*, "he sold it cheap, so cheap that by the end of 1958 he'd become the biggest—and nearly the only—anhydrous ammonia dealer in West Texas, and among the nation's biggest."

Manufactured tanks for storing liquid fertilizer were good collateral for loans. Estes mortgaged fertilizer storage tanks to farmers. The farmer would buy the tank on credit, and sign a mortgage and then lease the tank back to Estes. He eventually mortgaged 33,500 tanks, although only 5,000 tanks actually existed. Estes borrowed from finance companies using fictitious tanks as collateral. To cover himself, he obtained serial numbers for the nonexistent tanks and had each one engraved on a plate which he would move around from tank to tank should an investigator come snooping.

Through 1961, Estes was safe so long as he kept his warehouse bond of seven hundred thousand dollars, which amounted to favoritism. The government issued warehouse receipts for all grain stores, which were negotiable paper and prime collateral, paying thirteen and a half cents a bushel annually for the storage. When the bond was raised to one million dollars on January 18, 1962, Estes flew to Washington and appeared at the Agriculture Department. The higher bond was waived. Soon, however, back in Texas, Attorney General Will Wilson, a Lyndon Johnson adversary, charged federal favoritism.

In his heyday, Estes accumulated so much cash that he was able to offer the politicians who were helping him (Johnson and Yarborough) fifty thousand to one hundred thousand dollars at a pop as "campaign contributions." (In Texas and Louisiana it was legal to donate money to candidates even at times when they were not running for office.) Yarborough and Johnson were both beneficiaries of Estes' largesse. In Billie Sol Estes' gallery of luminaries there hung signed photographs of both Johnson and Yarborough, as well as of John F. Kennedy. According to Estes, he funded LBJ's (unsuccessful) campaign for the 1960 Democratic Party nomination.

Johnson had conferred great favor on Estes with respect to keeping his bond required for the storage contracts low, as well as in the profusion of those contracts, and he expected a significant return. An envelope containing fifty thousand dollars that Estes gave to Yarborough, and that represented money the unions had collected for the Democratic national campaign, came to light. The money was bound for Arthur Goldberg, then a Washington, D.C., labor lawyer, and ultimately for Johnson.

Sometimes Estes would deliver the money destined for Lyndon Johnson to Cliff Carter from the back of a hearse. Yarborough called Cliff Carter Johnson's "bag man." Twenty percent of Estes' gross sales went, he would claim, to the Johnson "slush fund." Billie Sol would dine out for years on how once when he was tardy in delivering a one-hundred-thousand-dollar payment to Johnson (the amount varied in the telling and rose to as high as two hundred thousand dollars) Johnson rang him up at two in the morning and demanded that Billie Sol get himself to the airport and personally see to it that the cash was sent on its way.

"They'd run the money through me and I'd funnel it to Lyndon," Estes explained later. It was a symbiotic relationship. "If Billie Sol builds the storage facilities," Estes quoted Johnson as promising, "I will make sure they stay full." Estes told people "just to call Lyndon Johnson" if there were any questions about his business practices.

Meanwhile Estes remained wrapped in his cloak of fundamentalism and religiosity. He attended the Church of Christ, taught Sunday school, and sent disadvantaged black youth to local religion-based colleges. He claimed that he neither smoked nor drank nor danced. At his swimming pool, adult men and women were permitted to swim only separately, at fixed hours. Estes lived in nouveau riche splendor with his family in a pink stucco mansion with a tennis court and pool. A pet monkey was chained to a perch in the living room. He commanded three private airplanes that he put at the disposal of Lyndon Johnson to ferry Johnson friends and supporters back and forth between Texas and Washington, D.C.

Politically, Estes was an unlikely liberal. He supported integration, a position that won him few friends in the West Texas of the late 1950s and early 1960s. His hero, he said, was Harry S. Truman. Yet always he courted success of the worldliest variety: Success was synonymous with how much money you had accumulated and in how many ways you could flaunt it. "I have always worshipped money," he would admit.

There is documentary evidence of the close connection between Billie Sol Estes and Lyndon Johnson during these years. A 1958 memo has Johnson assistant Lloyd Hand quoting Cliff Carter, who had referred to "Billie Sol Estes, in whom we are very interested. He has 26,000 acres of crops and stands to lose $250,000 if labor is not available for harvesting."

"I hope you will never hesitate to call on me if I can be of service," Johnson wrote Estes in 1959 in a locution very similar to one he used in his correspondence with D. H. Byrd. A note of November 19, 1960, was even more fulsome. "I don't know how I could ever repay you for all the things you have done for me," Johnson says. "But, I want you to know I appreciate everything you have done, and will never forget it. I know you were working against tremendous odds, and it is a tribute to your intelligence and your perseverance that the result came out like it did." The content may be opaque, but the tone is unmistakable.

By the fall of 1960, Estes was in debt to the IRS for two years of income taxes. Estes was to tell IRS investigator Walt Perry that he had passed ten million dollars in bribes to Lyndon Johnson. From 1962 to 1966, the IRS conducted an audit of Billie Sol Estes' records. Estes' books were judged to be "in balance." But the source is his daughter Pam in her memoir of her father. In 1984, Estes had close to thirty-five million dollars in federal tax liens filed against him and his family.

CHAPTER 10

Enter the Office of Naval Intelligence

*"Who could be so strong and powerful in politics
that he could get a clearance for a man like
this?"*

—CAPTAIN CLINT PEOPLES, TEXAS RANGERS

To be employed by TEMCO in 1954 required a security clearance at least at
the level of SECRET. This clearance would be issued by the Defense Logistics
Agency and be supported by the Defense Investigative Service.* The evidence
that Lyndon Johnson secured a clearance for Mac Wallace is circumstantial.
That Johnson was in the habit of obtaining security clearances for his people
is reflected in his chief aide, Walter Jenkins, being awarded a "Q" TOP
SECRET clearance in 1958. This entitled Jenkins to "secret information about
the design, manufacture, or use of nuclear weapons and materials."

Since TEMCO manufactured weapons for the Navy, its employees were
subject to scrutiny by the Office of Naval Intelligence (ONI). Almost from the
day Mac Wallace began to work for TEMCO, with the exception of one year,
the ONI maintained an unrelenting decade-long effort to strip him of his
SECRET security clearance.

A confidential ONI report dated July 12, 1957, notes that Mac Wallace had
been arrested for "Murder." Equal to felony murder in the Navy's mind was
the iron hand of "Communism." The Navy focused on a sentence in the FBI's
investigation of Wallace that "revealed he was in contact with two CP

---

* DISCO, the Defense Industrial Security Clearance Office, was established only in 1965 as
part of the FBI's Division 5, its security service that had been organized by J. Edgar Hoover
and William Sullivan. DISCO was also tied to Army Intelligence. There are no records
indicating how Mac Wallace attained his security clearance in those years prior to the
creation of DISCO.

[Communist Party] members apparently for personal gain, but he was not known to be a CP member or open supporter of CP aims."

One of these Communists was Elgin Williams. The other was Stuart Chamberlin. Neither of these friendships bore on whether Wallace was a "security risk" in working for TEMCO. Yet "subversion" would be a charge the Navy repeatedly leveled against him in its efforts to strip him of his clearance.

Since the time he and Mac Wallace had known each other, Elgin Williams had led a peripatetic life. In 1949, he was an Assistant Professor of Economics at the University of Washington. Before long he moved on to Reed College in Portland, Oregon. That year, Williams published his dissertation, *The Animating Pursuits of Speculation: Land Traffic in the Annexation of Texas.* Williams refers to the annexation of Texas to the United States as a form of "land speculation." His eloquent title derives from the pen of Sam Houston.

In 1950, Williams published an article called "The Left and the American Way of Life" in the Marxist *Monthly Review* magazine. Retaining the socialist ideals of his university days, Williams argued that the focus of the left should be on raising the standard of living, and so offering people "something to fight *for*, a really creative, satisfying way of life."

Reed College fired Williams in 1951. That fall he was appointed Professor of Economics and Sociology at North Texas State College at Denton. According to Reed officials, Williams was fired because of a drop in student enrollment at the time of the Korean War, and not for his progressive views. That Reed fired Stanley Moore, a Professor of Philosophy, in 1954 for invoking his Fifth Amendment rights before the House Un-American Activities Committee casts some doubt on this explanation.

On February 29, 1956, Williams suffered what was termed a "psychotic episode." He underwent shock treatments at John Sealy Hospital in Galveston. Something went wrong during the electric shock therapy and he died. Williams was thirty-four years old.

In 1956, Mac Wallace was listed in the Dallas City Directory as an "economist" with TEMCO. His responsibilities included analysis of defense budget trends. At the time, TEMCO was manufacturing a broad line of military products, including aircraft, missiles, transmitters, and commercial products like environmental test equipment. Within TEMCO's corporate program, Wallace was listed as "Supervisor of Business Forecasts."

On February 28, 1957, accompanied by Polk Shelton, who presented the motion to the court, Wallace stood once more before Judge Charles O. Betts.

Five years to the day of his conviction for the murder of John Douglas Kinser, Wallace swore that since that time he had not been convicted of a felony "in this State or any other State." He had been "an upright and law-abiding citizen for the past five years." His criminal record was now wiped clean. Bill Carroll was sitting in the University of Texas law library on that winter day when he felt two strong hands on his shoulders. It was a smiling Mac Wallace, delighted to run into Nora Ann's younger brother.

Judge Betts' action gave the ONI pause. "I am not sure that we still have a conviction of applicant for murder," a Navy investigator wrote into Wallace's ONI file, evaluating Mac Wallace's life since 1952.

From the moment he walked out of that Austin courtroom until he left Texas at the turn of the 1960s, Wallace lived a conventional life as a husband and father. He was a heavy drinker and kept an open bottle of bourbon on the floor of his automobile. Still, he went to work every day and returned home on time for dinner. He read his children bedtime stories, choosing tales of Greek mythology rather than children's books. Years later, Meredithe would remember how her father talked about figures out of the Greek myths, like Odysseus, as if they were people he knew personally. Odysseus was a grand person, someone he admired.

Mac was ambitious that his children acquire knowledge. He taught them a game called "Encyclopedia." You were to open the encyclopedia and put your finger on a word, arbitrarily. Then you were obliged to dissect it, tracing its etymology, and make up a story that illustrated the meaning of the word. Once he bought Michael a record player and three or four records, classical music that did not appeal to a boy his age. "You might end up liking them," Mac told Michael.

Most years there wasn't enough money for many presents. The first Christmas that Michael Wallace remembers, his father bought him three pairs of pants for school. There was one bountiful Christmas that came at a time when Mac and Andre were separated. Mac sent Meredithe a cosmetics case filled with practical items, like shampoo and bubble bath. To Michael, he sent a chemistry set and Legos, which did not interest him, and a bicycle, which did. Later Michael Wallace concluded that this had been his father's way of offering alternatives from which to choose what he might become.

Michael became a youth who kept to himself and made no emotional demands on anyone. Not only did he show no interest in his parents attending his basketball games, but if he discovered they were present in the gym, he refused to play.

Michael admired much about his father, particularly his graciousness. Once, his father's friend Stuart Chamberlin and his family came to stay with the Wallaces for a week. The house grew stifling and crowded, unpleasantly so.

"When you have a guest," Mac told his son, "whatever they want, it's theirs." Hospitality toward friends was a given.

To his children, Mac Wallace seemed to be a kind man, never blaming anyone for something if he could help it. His children were given no hint of his sacrificed hopes, and he did not complain. He was even-tempered, not given to shouting. A child had to do something really dangerous to earn a spanking. Once Michael threw a bamboo spear at his sister from a long distance and it sailed right through an open window. He earned a spanking for that. Mac was not demonstrative or physically affectionate; this was not the Wallace family way. But he made a point of treating his children equally to compensate for Andre's obvious partiality for Michael.

Michael Wallace recalls his father taking him to the Terrell Hospital to visit his grandmother. Alice Marie Riddle Wallace called Mac "Mikey," his child-hood name. It was a long drive, but one they made at least once a month, far more often than any other of her children, until she died in September 1959.

According to Meredithe Wallace, there was "an elephant in the room" during those years, a shadow that hovered over the family. There were sealed boxes in the garage connected to the murder and trial that were never mentioned. Meredithe had been too young to read during the first years after the event; she had been fourteen months old when John Kinser was killed. Later she saw no point in looking into the Kinser case until one day when she discovered a box of clippings, all about "Dad murdering a man." She figured out that "it was over Mother."

One day in 1956 Mac took the children for a ride into the Hill Country, near the LBJ Ranch. Meredithe was six, Michael eight. They drove down a dirt road. "I bet you can't guess what I threw out the window," Mac Wallace said as they rolled toward Johnson City. "This is where Lyndon Johnson lives," Mac said. "I know him."

In Johnson City, they saw men in black suits wearing dark glasses. "Those are some of his bodyguards," Mac said, referring to Senator Johnson. He revealed that he hadn't exactly thrown the gun with which he shot John Douglas Kinser out the car window. He confessed to his children that he had lodged it in a tree stump.

By 1958, the relationship between Mac and Andre, never harmonious, had further deteriorated. Andre went to live with a man, surname Bailey, one of two she would go on to marry. Michael remembers that Andre sent the children to stay with a family they scarcely knew, but who lived within walking distance of their school. The children saw her on weekends.

One Friday afternoon that year, Andre had promised to pick them up outside the school. Michael, now in fifth grade, and Meredithe, a third grader, sat waiting for her on the school steps. Two hours passed and Andre did not appear. Then their father happened by coincidence to drive by and picked them up.

"You're going to live with me from now on," Mac said.

Mac and Andre were remarried on New Year's Eve, 1959. It was a strange version of *La Ronde*, a late-nineteenth-century black farce by Austrian playwright Arthur Schnitzler, featuring interlocking scenes between lovers. Sexual passion alone motivated the characters, as over these years Mac and Andre, ill-suited to each other as they were, could not break free of the centrifugal force of their connection.

Mac was drinking ever more heavily. When Meredithe was nine years old, she was sexually molested three times by her father. There was oral sex, Meredithe remembers, and, twice, sexual penetration. "It hurt," Meredithe says. She didn't scream. I have to act as if I'm asleep, she had thought. "He killed this man. Maybe he would kill me." Each time he was drunk.

On the final occasion, he pulled her onto his lap and tried "to feel me," as she puts it. "I was scared and jumped and ran out of the room." He was trying "to groom me," she concluded. "It happened," she says simply.

One day he picked her up at school. "I did something I'm not proud of," he said. "I did it to you. I'm sorry." How can I get out of this car? she thought.

Meredithe kept silent about these traumatic episodes for two years, until she told her mother. Andre arranged for her to talk to her priest (Episcopal) and to a psychologist. Both were men. Meredithe couldn't find the words to express what she felt and confined herself to reporting what had happened. Neither the priest nor the psychologist provided her with any solace or insight.

She grew depressed. Sometimes she could hardly move. Her grades remained high, but often she would sit in the schoolyard by herself, melancholy at the prospect of getting through another day. "God gave me the tool of denial," she concluded. "I hid from life." Her motto was "simply reality." Whatever took place, it was "simply reality." This was what you could expect from life.

One day when Meredithe was twelve or thirteen, she was driving with Andre. Impetuously, Meredithe hugged her mother around the neck. Andre pushed her away. "That's what lesbians do," Andre said.

Years later, when Meredithe was already married, her mother told her, "You know, your brother doesn't believe your story." Yet one day, her brother's wife, referring to Mac Wallace's third child, remarked, "When Elaine was molested . . . " Startled, Meredithe had to wonder. She blamed the incestuous episodes on alcohol. "He must have been drinking, blacked out, and did this to me," she says. Her mother, who also drank a great deal, finally went to Alcoholics Anonymous. Not so her father.

In 1958, in a brief hiatus, the Office of Naval Intelligence had made no investigation into Mac Wallace's TEMCO clearance. That changed dramatically in 1959. Between 1959 and 1961, Mac worked at positions of high responsibility connected to the Navy's Corvus missile contract. He was assigned "to take a one-year assignment in the Corvus Weapon System as General Supervisor over the Program Master Plan and Control Section." Mac's title was "Control Supervisor."

On July 10, 1959, the Navy issued "Navy 8ND/922E," a memo requesting another "up-to-date" investigation of Malcolm E. Wallace. A naval intelligence document dated two days later repeats the 1957 locution that Mac Wallace had been in contact with two CP members, "apparently for personal political gain." In charge of the 1959 investigation was Special Agent A. C. Sullivan. Sullivan had been assigned to determine whether Wallace might not be "of counterintelligence interest" because of the "Communist Party members he knew in the past." So the Navy continued to weave its way through the byways of McCarthyism, pursuing Mac Wallace's nonexistent subversive tendencies in their effort to revoke his security clearance. Mac Wallace and Elgin Williams had become targets of McCarthyism without either of them knowing that they were victims alike.

On July 18, 1959, John H. Traynor, a security specialist at the Bureau of Aeronautics, working for the ONI, noted that Mac Wallace was still employed at TEMCO Aircraft Corporation "with access to SECRET Material, and his position is that of general supervisor, master scheduling." On August 13, under "undeveloped leads," Traynor wrote "None." The 1959 ONI report on Mac Wallace was one page long, suggesting that the ONI effort had run its course.

Yet the ONI was not done in its stubborn effort to revoke Mac Wallace's security clearance. The term that appears repeatedly in his ONI file is "revoke and deny." On February 8, 1960, they requested another "up-to-date" investigation of Mac Wallace. R. L. Lacey, the special agent now leading the search, noted that Mac Wallace was "carried in the files of the DO-8BD as an individual of counter intelligence interest in view of his past contact with Communist Party members." On March 29, Robert W. Ellis, an industrial relations supervisor at TEMCO, reported that Mac Wallace was still employed there.

Under "Character of Investigation," the Navy wrote "SUBVERSIVE ACTIVITIES." They uncovered no new evidence to warrant this further investigation. Lacey wrote: "DIO-8ND files contain no information regarding this subject not already reported." Reading the FBI file yet again, Navy investigators concluded that Mac Wallace was not a "pervert," by which they meant "homosexual." None of the ONI reports refer to Mac Wallace's alcoholism. Nor had the Navy come up with any new information that would allow it to succeed in removing his security clearance.

In 1960, now thirty-eight years old, Mac Wallace was ready to move on. He composed a three-page, single-spaced résumé. Under Education, he noted that he had done an additional year of graduate work in economics and statistics beyond his master's degree at Columbia University in New York. An unusual component of this résumé is the following: "My security clearance is SECRET." Mac Wallace viewed his clearance as an asset, one that he expected would aid him in his search for future work.

Andre filed for divorce from Mac for the final time on November 17, 1960. She accused him of having engaged in incestuous relations with Meredithe, and Meredithe backed her up. No one else in the Wallace family believed her. The divorce was granted on January 30, 1961. Mac moved into the home of a friend, a Dallas accountant named Henry A. Schupbach, and his wife, Josephine.

On February 2, three days after the divorce was granted, at one fifty A.M., Mac was arrested on a charge of drunk and disorderly conduct. According to the police report, "Subject was staggering eastward on public sidewalk on the 6400 block of Gaston Avenue." He had been spending the evening at a piano bar on the corner of Gaston and Abrams. The police found him to be "intoxicated to a degree whereas he found difficulty, extreme difficulty, in walking. His breath was strong of alcohol, and his speech was slow and uneven." He was convicted and paid a five-dollar fine.

It was time to "regroup his life," as one of his brothers put it. On February 19, 1961, Mac quit his job at TEMCO. He invested his accrued retirement account in his brother Jerry Neal Wallace's insurance business and went to work for Ling Electronics, which had merged with TEMCO and the Chance Vought Corporation, and which did fourteen million dollars of business a year. James Ling had been friendly with Lyndon Johnson and was reported personally to have contributed a quarter of a million dollars to the 1960 Kennedy-Johnson campaign.

On his own and with friends and employees, James Ling had contributed generously to the Kennedy-Johnson ticket. In return LTV became "the recipient of generous government contracts—and some of them prime contracts." Interviewed by reporters later, James Ling insisted that he did not remember the name "Mac Wallace."

On June 1, 1961, Mac Wallace's SECRET security clearance was renewed and countersigned by his supervisor at Ling. Having left Meredithe and Michael in Texas with Andre, he was now living in Orange County, California. His arrival at Ling prompted the Office of Naval Intelligence, through the Inspector of Naval Material at Losa, California, to conduct its most comprehensive investigation to date.

A nineteen-page report, dated 20 July 1961, with attachments, was the result. The Navy pictured Mac Wallace as a man "of muscular build, ruddy complexion, and tortoise-rimmed glasses." On behalf of the Navy, A. C. Sullivan requested Mac's file from the Austin Police Department. On November 9, Sullivan received the "Offense Report" for Case Number 78693, along with the statements of the witnesses at the Pitch & Putt, initiating a new investigation of the murder of John Douglas Kinser a decade after the fact.

Among those they tracked down was Lieutenant T. S. "Pete" Weaver of the Austin police. Weaver, who had worked alongside Bob Long's chief investigator, Onis Doherty, talked about "strange aspects" of the Kinser case. He focused on how charges of homosexuality and perversion had played "a prominent part in the background factors of the murder, although they did not surface at the trial."

Doherty had "screened out" the hearsay report "and the salacious innuendos that crop up in any murder investigation where the possibility of a 'triangle' exists," Weaver said. Leslie Clay Proctor, now District Attorney of Travis County, remained indignant at the outcome of the Kinser trial. Mac Wallace, Proctor said, was "a man who murdered another in cold blood and got away with it." The suspended sentence represented a "travesty of justice." Proctor had retained a list of the jurors to ensure that none of them would be impaneled in any future case that his office tried. He noted that the sentence had created a stir in political circles and resulted in the electoral defeat of Bob Long.

Accompanying Proctor to his meeting with the Navy investigators were Billy Roy Wilder and Richard C. Avent, both of whom had been assistant district attorneys under Bob Long. Wilder now offered a startling piece of hearsay. There had been a persistent rumor that Long had "been the recipient of valuable property in the city of Austin as the result of his suppression of certain aspects [of the Wallace case] involving political ramifications," a further suggestion, if circumstantial, that Long had negotiated with Lyndon Johnson at the Stephen F. Austin Hotel during the Kinser trial, as Henry Scarborough's source has confided.

Avent suggested that Mac Wallace had killed John Douglas Kinser because Andre "sucked off" Kinser, and it was this "unnatural and perverted oral copulation" that fueled Wallace's anger. Although Avent requested that his remarks be "off the record," they appear in the Navy's written report.

Onis Doherty and his team had also interviewed other of Kinser's lovers. One told the police, "I know that he is not a pervert." Kinser "was sexually hungry and he was very potent. We had normal relations." Grace Hewitt, the woman who had introduced Andre to Kinser, termed Kinser "a forceful man" and a "dictator." She added that he was a liberal and "sympathetic to Dr. Rainey."

Puzzled by the profusion of contradictions, innuendos, and irregularities, the Navy attempted to locate a transcript of the Kinser trial. The court reporter, Henry Beck, admitted that he had never transcribed his record of the trial. There had been no appeal, Beck explained. He had kept his notes longer than the required year. When the courthouse was renovated, Beck had destroyed all his old notebooks, including the one chronicling the Wallace trial.

There was little in writing in Austin about Mac Wallace. The deputy sheriff of Travis County told the Navy that the files of the sheriff's office contained no records on Mac Wallace. The Department of Public Safety's Criminal Intelligence Section claimed that it held no file on Mac Wallace. There were "homosexual files," but Mac Wallace's name did not appear in any of them. A clerk suggested that Captain Clint Peoples, "who worked with Mr. Onis Doherty . . . may have kept custody of SUBJECT's investigative files."

Onis Doherty had included in his report that the FBI file "indicated nothing in regard to Communist activity on the part of Wallace nor did it indicate that he was a pervert." Still, the Navy pondered whether "homosexuality and perversion . . . played a prominent part in the background factors of the murder."

In the 1961 report, the Navy noted that Mac Wallace had no criminal background. Other than the Kinser murder, all they could find of interest was that on his personnel security questionnaire, which he was obliged to submit annually, he had omitted his February 2, 1961, arrest for drunk and disorderly conduct. Then they noticed that he had filled out the form prior to his arrest. The arrest sheet indicated that Mac Wallace was to be remanded to Corporation Court #2 on February 9, at nine A.M. This had not taken place.

It seemed that someone was looking out for him.

The Navy interviewed no liberals, no one with views similar to Mac Wallace's. His political adversaries were consulted, among them Mac's former classmate Arno Nowotny, who had risen to the position of Dean of Student Life at the University of Texas. Nowotny had despised Homer Rainey and on November 10, 1961, lied to the Navy investigator who interviewed him, concealing Rainey's wide support among the faculty. He accused Mac Wallace of being a "radical," which he was not, and leading the students to "march against the state legislature," which Mac had never done. Nowotny said Dr. Rainey's views were "at variance . . . with the other professors of the University of Texas"; in fact Rainey enjoyed unanimous faculty support.

About Mac Wallace, Nowotny was vicious. Wallace had only become president of the student body, Nowotny claimed, because he had arrived at the university during wartime when mostly "old women and cripples" were in attendance. He denounced Mac Wallace as "a liberal and radical . . . the only man I know who shot and killed a man in cold blood and got away with it by keeping his mouth shut."

Dr. Charles P. Boner, director of the Defense Research Laboratory, created a false image of a revolutionary Homer Rainey. Rainey "advocated a new social order in the 1940s," Boner claimed. He had incited the faculty and students to "riot" against the legal governing order of the university. So mythological depictions of Mac Wallace had begun to follow in his wake.

On November 12, 1961, the Navy caught up with Onis Doherty, who was now working as an investigator for the State Board of Dental Examiners. Doherty told them that "SUBJECT is a homosexual and pervert," although he wasn't able to prove it. Kinser too, Doherty said, was a "confirmed pervert." Mac had "found out about this [Andre's] perversion with a competitor." With little stomach for revisiting the story of Mac Wallace, Doherty said he "momentarily expected visitors" and ushered the investigators out the door.

During this 1961 ONI investigation of Mac Wallace, Texas Ranger captain Clint Peoples met with Navy inspector A. C. Sullivan, who had worked on the 1959 investigation. Peoples had not forgotten the Kinser trial. Now he zeroed in on what he considered to be an anomaly.

"How in the world," Peoples asked Sullivan, "could Wallace, an obvious security risk, have received [such a] high security clearance?"

"He would have to have been extremely well connected politically to maintain that security clearance," Sullivan said.

"Who could be so strong and powerful in politics that he could get a clearance for a man like this?" Peoples said.

"The Vice President," Sullivan said.

Peoples agreed. Lyndon Johnson had to have been "a factor behind Wallace's employment with the defense contractors." Peoples believed that "you can't put this fellow in a classified job in government."

"Lyndon Johnson may have played a role in Wallace's getting a job with Ling-TEMCO-Vought," Sullivan said.

The Office of Naval Intelligence failed again in 1961 to revoke and deny Mac Wallace's SECRET clearance.

CHAPTER 11

Some Faustian Bargains Come Due: The Falls of Billie Sol Estes and Bobby Baker

"Who told him he could do that?"
—HERMAN BROWN

From his earliest youth, Lyndon Johnson professed to have wanted to be president of the United States. Robert Caro quotes Johnson's cousin Ava speaking of Johnson three years after he graduated from high school and had decided not to go on to college: "His 'big talk' grew bigger; he was frequently predicting now that he would be 'the President of the United States' one day."

So it should not be surprising that Johnson saw his opportunity as early as 1957, when President Dwight Eisenhower was running for office for the final time. Johnson was head of the Texas Democratic Party delegation to the Chicago convention in 1956. He chose a panel of three to head up the Texas delegation.

One member of that panel was lawyer John Cofer, who had worked on Johnson's legal team during the 1948 election, conferring more heat than light, but an imposing figure. Cofer had gone on to mastermind Mac Wallace's successful defense. On the Saturday before Easter 1956, Cofer arrived at the LBJ Ranch to pitch the idea that Lyndon Johnson should declare for the Democratic Party nomination for the presidency that year.

When John F. Kennedy offered Lyndon Johnson a spot on his ticket four years later as a conservative Southerner who would appease the oil interests, and help Kennedy carry Texas, Johnson hesitated. One version of how Kennedy came to choose Johnson as his running mate has it that in addition to Phil Graham, publisher of the *Washington Post*, and right-wing journalist Joseph Alsop, Joseph P. Kennedy argued for Johnson's presence on the ticket. Kennedy even offered Johnson one million dollars to settle his campaign debts, which Johnson accepted. That Bobby Kennedy vehemently opposed the idea of Johnson running for Vice President made no difference.

Believing that this was the only way Lyndon Johnson would ever become president, Bobby Baker urged him to accept Kennedy's offer and run for Vice President. Herman Brown, on the other hand, was livid at the very idea. When he learned that Johnson was to be Kennedy's running mate, Herman was apoplectic.

At his redoubt, Suite 8F of the Lamar Hotel in Houston, he vented his rage. "Who told him he could do that?" Herman exploded. He called Johnson a "goddamn traitor." From Herman Brown's point of view, given Johnson's seniority in the Senate, his becoming Vice President was "a ridiculous thing." The legislative bills supported by the Browns, the contracts that came their way, all would be in jeopardy.

Brown nephew Harry Austin concluded that Herman's "main purpose was to try to see that Texas had top influence in the Congress." Now Johnson had exposed himself as a man consumed by ego, and Herman "just didn't want anything to do with Lyndon after that." Frank "Posh" Oltorf, a Brown & Root factotum based in Washington, D.C., commented that Herman had always "thought he [Lyndon Johnson] was a little devious."

In Texas, with Lyndon Johnson on the Kennedy ticket, jokes abounded. A reporter supposedly asked Johnson if it was true that if elected, Kennedy planned to build a tunnel to the Vatican. Johnson's reply was that he had heard of no such plan, but that the project was fine with him provided they would hire Brown & Root to build it! When Lyndon Johnson was nominated for Vice President, all charges against George Parr, civil and criminal, including embezzlement, murder, and income tax malfeasances, were dropped. The Supreme Court granted a writ and Parr was rescued by Johnson intimate Abe Fortas, whose efforts before Justice Hugo Black had catapulted Lyndon into the Senate in the matter of Box 13. On June 13, 1960, by a vote of six to three, the Supreme Court reversed all the convictions against Parr.

Parr's fortunes continued in their jagged trajectory. In November 1960, the State of Texas foreclosed on his Dobie Ranch to satisfy his "debt to Duval County for the half-million dollars he had dipped out of the Road and Bridge Fund in 1945 for its purchase." As John E. Clark points out in his book about Parr, the foreclosure sale on the steps of the Duval County Courthouse brought $1,575,000 from the successful bidder; Parr pointed to the price "as evidence he had invested the county's money wisely."

*　*　*

The two years, ten months, and two days of Lyndon Johnson's vice presidency were characterized by bad decisions and threats that his illegal activities would be brought to light. His behavior on the rainy, foggy night of February 17, 1961, not even a month after the inauguration, exposed yet again his dark side. On that night Johnson insisted that his pilots, based in Austin, pick him up at the ranch and fly him to Washington, D.C.

The tower control at Austin municipal airport advised against flying. Visibility was scant. Harold Teague, the chief pilot, suggested to Johnson that it was too dangerous; he preferred to wait until the next day rather than fly blind in the rain and hail, dense clouds and fog.

"Get up here right away!" Johnson exploded. "What do you think I'm paying you for?" Teague had been with Johnson for two years, had flown for him during the presidential campaign, and was an accomplished aviator with eleven thousand hours of flying time behind him. The co-pilot, Charles Williams, was new and had flown for Johnson only a few times.

When the plane did not arrive, Johnson telephoned his neighbors, asking them to check their landing strips and keep a watch for lights and fires. The charred remains of the pilots were discovered the next morning on a nearby hillside. When the plane crashed, their bodies were thrown from the aircraft.

Within forty-eight hours, $250,000 was made available to Johnson to divide among the families of the dead pilots. In the ensuing cover-up, the Johnson spokesman insisted that the plane did not belong to Johnson, but had been chartered from oilman John Mecom for the campaign. On documents the date of the sale was forged. Finally it emerged that the bill of sale to the LBJ Company was dated March 29, 1960.

When the registration was sent to the FAA a month after the crash, it was in the name of Brazos Tenth Street Corporation, another Johnson company. The registering agent for the plane was a Johnson crony named R. Max Brooks. When reporters attempted to sort all this out, the insurance agent, Roger Beery of Beery Insurance Company of San Antonio, said, "It is not public information. It is sort of a doctor-patient relationship."

When Holland McCombs looked into the crash, he found that the plane had been sold to Johnson on February 1, 1961. Sometimes the "LBJ Company" was named as the owner, at other times it was "Brazos Tenth Street Corporation." Only after the crash was the title transferred to Brazos Tenth Street. The officers of Brazos Company were the same as the Clark law firm partners. One name that did not appear on any of the records was "Lyndon Johnson."

The Fall of Billie Sol Estes

> *"It's those dern, crooked politicians that got my*
> *boy in trouble."*
> —JOHN ESTES, FATHER OF BILLIE SOL ESTES

After Johnson became Vice President, his relationship with Billie Sol Estes continued. On January 12, 1961, Johnson, eight days away from being sworn in as Vice President, wrote again to Estes. Thanking him for the gift of some roses, Johnson said, "It's wonderful to have friends like you."

After the inauguration, Estes received an invitation from Cliff Carter: "Call on me in the Vice-President's office as we can serve you." During inauguration week, the third week of January 1961, Billie Sol Estes hosted a dinner at the Sheraton Park Hotel in Washington, D.C. His newspaper, the *Pecos Daily News*, pictured him chatting with Lynda Bird Johnson. On May 22, 1961, Carter reiterated the invitation: "Please call when we can be of service."

Yet Estes' castles built of air and sophistry had begun to crumble. Underselling the fertilizer producers cost him dearly and he began to borrow from Commercial Solvents. In 1957, Estes lost $475,755. In 1958, he lost $1,258,915. By the end of 1958, he owed Commercial Solvents alone more than $500,000. Yet he requested a loan of $900,000, which the president, Maynard C. Wheeler, believed was "particularly advantageous . . . because it gave the Company an opportunity to sell its ammonia in a rapidly expanding and prosperous market." The $900,000 included $540,000 to cover Estes' previous debt and $225,000 to enable Estes to make a down payment on grain storage facilities. The rest would be applied against the cost of ammonia purchases in 1959.

In 1959, Estes lost $2,132,281. In 1960, he lost $3,198,058. He paid Commercial Solvents $88 a ton, and sold the fertilizer for $60 a ton, and sometimes for as low as $20. His debt rose to six million dollars. He called Frank Cain, a lawyer for the Pacific Finance Corporation of Los Angeles that would go on to sue him, "father." Once Estes told Cain, "Father, with your wisdom and my zeal, there is no end to what we can accomplish."

At first, the problem seemed manageable. Estes' grain storage bond remained at a low seven hundred thousand dollars. When Estes fell into debt, Walter Heller, a Lyndon Johnson friend, offered him an unsecured seven-million-dollar loan through the Heller Corporation of Chicago. Estes' collateral now amounted to his assertion that Lyndon Johnson was his sponsor.

The finance companies had grown suspicious. Frank Cain discovered that despite the mortgages Estes held from farmers, "there aren't any tanks." Before long, Estes was in debt to twelve finance companies. "I will make it work," he reassured Cain, "based on my contacts in Washington."

Commercial Solvents eventually held a mortgage on everything Estes owned, except his home and automobile. He was in to the Murchisons alone for a million dollars' worth of fertilizer. Clint Murchison Sr. himself went to Pecos and put his own man in charge of "Estes Agriculture, Inc." Yet despite all his losses, in 1961 Estes claimed that he was worth more than four hundred million dollars. He had paid no income tax for four years.

Later Frank Cain told Holland McCombs, "Without political help Estes could not have gone anywhere much. But with political help he damned near went all the way to many millions."

Among those in on Estes' schemes were Coleman D. McSpadden, Superior Manufacturing's major stockholder, and Harold E. Orr, its Vice President. Superior, of Amarillo, Texas, was the company through which Estes sold his discounted mortgages to the twelve finance companies.

Seeking still to control the market on anhydrous ammonia, Estes found himself short two hundred thousand dollars. "We don't have it," Orr said.

"Well, if I go down the river, so does Superior," Estes said. Estes handled all the price changes himself. When the company stopped sending Estes ammonia, he issued a threat. "Well, I'm taking a tape recording of this conversation," Estes told Superior. "I'll have a Senate Investigating Committee seeing you in a few days." Threatening adversaries with incriminating tapes would be a lifetime Billie Sol Estes tactic.

After a while, Estes instructed his receptionist to act as if she did not know Harold Orr. Orr retaliated by publicizing that there were no storage tanks.

Henry Marshall, a local agriculture official, penetrated Estes' cotton allotment fraud. Having been persuaded by Cliff Carter to approve 138 of Estes' cotton allotment transfers, Marshall experienced second thoughts; he demanded that a farmer appear in person before the county committee to certify that he was buying land from Estes instead of selling him a cotton allotment, which was illegal. Marshall had figured out that Estes was buying cotton allotments and signing mortgages that would be defaulted on by design, pre-arranged to foreclose. While the farmers were sent off with a pittance, Estes accumulated land on which to grow more cotton.

On January 17, 1961, Marshall informed Billie Sol's lawyer, John P. Dennison, that he would not approve any further Estes arrangements to buy allotments. Should illegalities be discovered, prosecution would follow. Marshall's own signature was now required on each transaction. A. B. Foster Jr., the manager of Billie Sol Enterprises, met with Henry Marshall. Gaining no quarter, Foster wrote to Cliff Carter, requesting that he intervene personally. The new regulations are "unreasonable," Foster pleaded. (Among those soon to turn on Estes was Foster, who would recall three thousand acres of land being transferred as cotton allotments from local farmers to Estes. (The land was worth only fifty to one hundred dollars per acre raw, but rose to between $250 to $350 if there were a cotton allotment attached.)

At first, Estes wasn't worried. "I never saw a man who wouldn't take a promotion," he said, by which he meant a bribe. With Lyndon Johnson now Vice President, Henry Marshall was offered the position of Assistant Secretary of Agriculture, a job that would bring him to Washington, D.C. Marshall declined. An offer to work in Brazil was dangled before him. Marshall rejected this, too. Henry Marshall preferred life in rural Texas, especially on his small ranch in Franklin, Robertson County.

In February 1961, Lyndon Johnson met with Ward Jackson, a Commercial Solvents executive, and a Billie Sol Estes creditor to the tune of $550,000. Jackson was offered "special services" by Cliff Carter. Later, Jackson wrote to Estes that he had discussed "in general the situation in Texas and in the overall business area" with Vice President Johnson. Among the many rumors now circulating was that Mrs. Johnson was a heavy investor in Commercial Solvents.

Johnson and Secretary of Agriculture Orville Freeman discussed "changes in regulations governing the transfer of cotton allotments from farms whose owners have been displaced by agencies having the right of eminent domain." Apparently unwitting, Freeman wrote Johnson: "There have been some abuses of the law in this regard" which "had the effect of an outright sale of the pooled allotment by the displaced owner under subterfuge practices." This letter was forwarded to Billie Sol Estes with a memorandum from the office of the Vice President: "If I can again assist you, let me know." It was signed "LBJ."

Texas publications now wondered out loud about the relationship between Lyndon Johnson and Billie Sol Estes. "How do Lyndon Johnson and his enterprising wife fit into the Estes enterprise?" *Farm and Ranch* magazine asked. On April 28, 1961, Johnson, traveling to Austin for Mayor Tom Miller's funeral, met Billie Sol Estes at the Midland-Odessa airport. Johnson's government plane was parked at some distance from the terminal, according to Estes, and was guarded by the Secret Service.

Two men, Billie Sol Estes and a lawyer, were escorted onto the plane. They remained for an hour. The records of that day's flights were then sealed by government order. According to Estes, Lyndon Johnson advised him to keep quiet and he would take care of things. Estes later claimed that there had been a witness to his boarding the plane, his friend Kyle Brown, only later to say that he had been mistaken and Kyle Brown had not been there.

Never short of bravado, in the midst of all his troubles, with a bankruptcy hearing a year in the future, Estes purchased two one-thousand-dollar tables at President Kennedy's May 27 dinner, celebrating his May 29 birthday. Vice President Johnson sat on the dais, directly above Estes.

Having filed a report of his findings with the Agriculture Department, Henry Marshall made plans to travel to Washington, D.C., on Monday, June 5, 1961. Marshall had organized a meeting with Attorney General Robert F. Kennedy, his goal being to expose Billie Sol Estes' cotton allotment fraud and to involve the Justice Department in the matter.

On Saturday, June 3, Marshall drove to his ranch in Franklin. He was a fifty-one-year-old man, six feet two inches tall, and a wiry 215 pounds. His leathery skin reflected that he had spent much of his life out in the Texas sunshine. Marshall parked deep into his ranch. Then he sat in his Chevy pickup truck awaiting a visitor he had arranged to meet, one who was familiar with the layout of his ranch. There were in fact two visitors, Billie Sol Estes would confide to Clint Peoples twenty-three years later, two people at the scene.

When the visitors arrived, Marshall got out of his truck to greet them. These were no friends of his, however. One smashed Marshall on the left side of his head with such force that his eye was split open. Either this assailant or the other pushed him up against the side of his truck, breaking Marshall's arm.

An assailant forced a plastic bag over Marshall's head, pushed him into the truck, and turned on the ignition, attempting to facilitate a death by carbon monoxide poisoning. But Marshall eluded him and escaped from the truck. The killer then grabbed Marshall's .22 bolt action rifle and shot him, at least six times, turning the rifle around and working the action with his thumb for each shot; it was necessary to pause to pump the rifle to eject the previous shell each time. When Marshall's body was discovered, there was 30 percent carbon monoxide in his lungs. The apparatus that had been placed over his head for inhaling the carbon monoxide was gone.

It was an era in Texas when "the sheriff was king, the deputy his vassal," said former Robertson County District Attorney John Paschall in 2012. A sheriff wielded more power than a district attorney. If a sheriff claimed that the sun was going to come up in the west, then people did not doubt it. When Henry Marshall's brother-in-law discovered the body, he called Sheriff Howard Stegall.

"The sonavabitch shot himself!" Stegall declared. Under Stegall's sway was the Robertson County coroner, a justice of the peace performing double duty and a man with no medical training. Lee Farmer dutifully wrote "suicide" on the death certificate. Later Clint Peoples was brought in on the case. "If he can kill himself with that gun," Peoples said, "then I'll ride a jackass to the moon!"

Half a page long, the offense report ignored the bruise on Marshall's face entirely. It did not mention that there was blood on the side of the truck. No fingerprints were lifted from Marshall's truck, no blood samples taken. Marshall's brother-in-law had the truck washed the next day, making the collection of any forensic evidence an impossibility.

"It looked like murder," said Manly Jones, the mortician. There was no way Marshall could have killed himself, wounded as he was, and then fired the rifle with his opposite hand. No one paid the mortician any mind. Marshall's death was ruled a suicide.

In July 1961, with the assistance of Ralph Yarborough, Billie Sol Estes was appointed to the National Cotton Advisory Committee. He remained confident that Lyndon Johnson would prevent any real trouble from befalling him. According to Estes, Lyndon Johnson had reassured him "he'd have grain storage unless the Capitol fell down."

Josefa Johnson was now married to a man named James Moss, who was employed as a social security representative of the Department of Public Welfare for South Texas. In the early morning hours of Christmas Day 1961, Josefa was discovered by her husband dead in her bed. It was three fifteen A.M. They had returned home only a few hours earlier from a Christmas Eve party at the LBJ Ranch, where the sole guests were John and Nellie Connally. Josefa was forty-nine years old.

The cause of death was first announced as a heart attack. Then it was changed to "cerebral hemorrhage." There was no autopsy, no inquest. Dr. J. Hardin Perry, the doctor who signed the death certificate, had not bothered to examine the body of the deceased. Josefa was embalmed on Christmas Day.

On December 26, she was buried hastily at the family cemetery on the LBJ Ranch.

Lyndon Johnson told the newspapers that Josefa had been "extremely active in the political campaigns of her brother and was a member of the State Democratic Executive Committee from the Twenty-first Congressional District of Texas." (Holland McCombs discovered it was "actually the Sixteenth Senatorial District.") Then Josefa's death faded into obscurity. "Josefa died?" Holland McCombs wrote back to *LIFE* magazine during his 1964 investigation of Lyndon Johnson. "When? Under what circumstances?" (Ace reporter William P. Barrett, who covered the Estes case for the *Dallas Times Herald*, discovered that Josefa was in bad health.)

McCombs' researcher wrote him a note: "In Fredericksburg there was no one willing to say that Mrs. Moss had had a drinking problem though my information has been that she was the sister who has often been described as something of a wanton." Neither Robert Caro in *The Passage of Power* nor Robert Dallek in *Lone Star Rising* or *Flawed Giant* mention Josefa's death.

Nineteen sixty-two would be the year of Billie Sol Estes' fall from grace, a fall now precipitous, inevitable, and uninterrupted. On January 15, Estes met with Lyndon Johnson's chief aide, Walter Jenkins. Jenkins said that money was required to grease the wheels. Estes then sent Cliff Carter three cashier's checks totaling $145,015. When Robert Kennedy invited Estes to lunch, Carter told Estes to play along. "Lyndon will take care of things," Carter said.

Three days later, on January 18, in an ominous development, Billie Sol's grain storage bond was raised to one million dollars from seven hundred thousand dollars. C. H. Moseley, director of the Dallas commodity office, and John White, of the State Commission of Agriculture, supported Estes. White, close to both Estes and Johnson, said he checked two of the Estes grain elevators and found "the inventories exactly right." This victory was pyrrhic.

"Billie Sol, we know you have been giving a lot of money to Lyndon," Bobby Kennedy purportedly said. "Just tell us how much and when and we can give you immunity." According to Estes, Bobby Kennedy himself telephoned him. This was in March 1962.

"I don't know what you're talking about," Estes said.

That month, Estes gave Cliff Carter "about ten tickets to a hundred-dollar-a-plate Democratic fund-raising dinner in Washington."

On March 17, 1962, Estes met with Maynard Wheeler, President of Commercial Solvents, which had financed his fertilizer tank leases. On March 28, he sought the advice of Frank Cain. "That guy didn't kill himself," Estes said, referring to Henry Marshall. He reassured Cain that the investigation of Estes' businesses would lead nowhere. "I can stop all that," he said. "I'll get Lyndon Johnson on the phone." Three times in Cain's presence Estes telephoned Cliff Carter, pointedly dialing an unlisted telephone number at the White House.

The biweekly *Pecos Independent and Enterprise* had opposed Estes' election to the Pecos school board and had, Estes believed, contributed significantly to his defeat. Soon Oscar Griffin Jr., the city editor of the *Independent,* at the encouragement of owner John Dunn, a dentist, began an investigation into Estes' activities. That November (1961), the storm seemed to have passed. Henry Marshall was dead and the F B I's investigation into Estes had been called off. Estes was reappointed to the National Cotton Advisory Committee, a boon to his credibility.

At the *Pecos Independent,* John Dunn, later smeared by Estes as a Bircher, was ready to expose Estes' cotton allotment fraud. Later people told Holland McCombs that Dunn hadn't been a member of the John Birch Society at all; that had been slander propagated by Estes. But Dunn certainly was conservative and had opposed Estes' integrationist views.

In February and March 1962, Oscar Griffin at the *Independent* wrote four articles exposing Estes' crimes. He revealed that Lyndon Johnson had given Estes a loan of five million dollars. The series carried no byline. Griffin later said he began his investigation when he heard some local farmers talking about Estes in a café.

"It's like pennies from heaven," one said. A farmer named, coincidentally, L. B. Johnson had a verbal agreement with Estes that he would be held harmless on the purchase agreement when he defaulted. Griffin discovered that Estes had cheated many farmers like Johnson. Letters of credit addressed to the farmers had been written on five different typewriters and on five different stationeries with five different sets of secretaries' initials. Each listed the amount of credit each farmer had been issued and his standing at the time.

On March 28, Griffin interviewed Billie Sol Estes and asked if the fertilizer tanks existed. "He told me that there weren't as many tanks as the mortgages showed," Griffin wrote. "That sure was the understatement of the year."

Griffin's articles did not mention Billie Sol Estes by name; they referred to him only as a "businessman" whose Byzantine scheme involved nonexistent fertilizer storage tanks being used as collateral on a twenty-four-million-dollar loan. There was no doubt in anyone's mind as to who that "businessman" was. Griffin would receive a Pulitzer Prize in 1963 for "distinguished local reporting" for these articles. Needless to say, Lyndon Johnson was not mentioned, either.

Fearful that Bobby Kennedy would use his connection to Estes to remove him from the 1964 presidential ticket, Lyndon Johnson turned to his close friend, J. Edgar Hoover. Johnson requested that "the Bureau talk to the editor of the weekly newspaper in Pecos, Texas . . . people with that paper have this incriminating tape." This tape contained farmer L. B. Johnson's explanation to Oscar Griffin of how Billie Sol Estes' cotton allotment scam worked. This very conversation with Hoover implicates Lyndon Johnson in Estes' activities.

Johnson told Hoover that Griffin and Dunn were now offering the tape to an investigative reporter for CBS. Unless measures were taken, there would be a national scandal in which Johnson might be implicated in Estes' illegalities. Hoover promised to "get on it right away."

Lyndon Johnson had a final suggestion. It was that Hoover involve FBI assistant director Cartha DeLoach in his Estes-related troubles. A plan was devised. Johnson "would have his assistant, Walter Jenkins, get in touch with Mr. DeLoach in such instances." When an obstreperous Republican from Florida named Bill Cramer announced that he was preparing impeachment proceedings against Lyndon Johnson based on his and Lady Bird's association with Billie Sol Estes in two grain storage operations, Johnson dispatched Jenkins to pay a call on DeLoach.

Jenkins requested that DeLoach arrange to have the FBI "interview Cramer immediately." Mr. Hoover "would, of course, want to be of every possible assistance to the Vice President," DeLoach said. DeLoach suggested that the information come from a third party, rather than from the Vice President's office. Thomas Corcoran, a Johnson intimate, was enlisted. "Cramer is a loud-mouth," Hoover remarked.

Hoover saw to it that Oscar Griffin was removed from the Estes story. Furious, John Dunn kept up his attack, exposing that the ammonia tanks Estes was mortgaging did not in fact exist. Dunn forwarded this information to the FBI—in care of the Department of Justice. Before long, seventy-five agents descended on Pecos, along with sixteen federal auditors and IRS agents, courtesy of Bobby Kennedy. Kennedy persisted with such zeal that a retired IRS investigator named Ken Bradberry later revealed that "the unspoken word in the IRS was that our orders were to get Billie Sol Estes."

Bradberry had come to believe that Estes "wasn't guilty of all the charges we eventually brought against him. This whole case was predicated upon politics involving the Kennedy and Johnson factions."

Estes' claim that all he need do was contact Lyndon Johnson to stop the proceedings against him was wearing thin as the State of Texas entered a penalty judgment against Billie Sol Estes for violating anti-trust laws. He owed the IRS ten million dollars. "I'll never go to jail because I'll drag in too many with me," Estes said.

Billie Sol Estes was arrested on March 29, 1962, by a U.S. marshal. The charge was that he had transported chattel mortgages on allegedly nonexistent fertilizer tanks across state lines. On April 5, he and three associates were indicted on fifty-seven counts of violating interstate commerce laws with respect to the fertilizer mortgages. Among the charges were conspiracy; interstate transportation of falsely made, forged, altered, and counterfeit chattel mortgages on nonexistent anhydrous ammonia tanks; and "transporting bogus tank mortgages across state lines." The chattel mortgages alone amounted to more than thirty-four million dollars. State charges were filed on April 25. Estes was only thirty-seven years old, and it seemed that he already had lived out several lifetimes.

On May 5, at a press conference called by the Department of Agriculture, N. Battle Hales, an employee, said Agriculture officials gave Estes "the equivalent of favoritism" on certain matters. At times the cover-up was crude, as collateral damage accumulated. A secretary in the agriculture department named Mary Kimbrough Jones, according to Senator John J. Williams of Delaware, a Republican, had been "railroaded" into a mental institution "for no reason other than that she knew too much about the Estes case and because she refused to cooperate in covering up corruption in the Department."

"Everything will be all right," Cliff Carter told Estes in a telephone call, according to Estes. On May 25, 1962, Billie Sol Estes graced the cover of *Time* magazine. "The Billie Sol Estes Scandal" compared Estes to the Murchisons. "Like the Murchisons," *Time* wrote, "from cotton and cheap housing, Estes rapidly branched out into many other businesses—selling fertilizer and farm implements, digging wells, lining irrigation ditches, providing other agricultural services." The story speculates that Estes' ambition was to be like the Murchisons: "He wanted to get as rich as the Murchisons, the most famous of Texas' big-rich clans. He had some theories about how to get Murchison-rich." There is no quotation from Estes on the subject of the Murchisons.

If it reached the point where he would have to go to prison, Estes told Holland McCombs in a long interview during this time, he would be dead, or living in Brazil—or he would talk. He threatened to reveal everything and bragged that he was "the only one who can tell the whole story." But Lyndon Johnson had already taken steps to dissociate himself from Billie Sol Estes. Horace Busby termed Estes "a small-bore burglar who stole from both neighbors and national corporations."

Reporter William Barrett uncovered an undated, unsigned confidential memo proposing "a major public relations campaign against Estes" by the Johnson forces. At least twenty letters to Billie Sol Estes from either Lyndon Johnson or someone on his staff over a four-year period were made public. Walter Jenkins denied that either of the Johnsons ever had any contact with Estes. Exposed by a letter from Lady Bird Johnson to Estes, Walter Jenkins laughed. "I guess I lied," he said.

Columnist Drew Pearson reported that when Texans had telephoned Johnson's office to arrange for their trip to Washington, D.C., for the Kennedy-Johnson inaugural, they received a return call within a matter of minutes from Billie Sol Estes inviting them to fly on his private plane. Reporters now requested a list of every government passenger who had flown on an Estes plane.

Lyndon Johnson's Vice Presidential office was inundated with letters and telegrams from outraged Texas citizens. One postcard read: "Who in hell is going to believe you, Lyndon?" Another asked Johnson whether "Mr. Estes ever contributed to any of your campaigns." The managing editor of the *Odessa American* asked Johnson whether he recalled "if Mr. Estes contacted your office, through any means, in regard to his problems." A Texan named Tom H. Canfield wrote in a letter to the *New Republic* magazine: "His [Estes'] closest political connections were with Lyndon Johnson, a fact which the press has conveniently ignored and which the Vice President's propaganda mill is trying to hide."

Johnson marshaled some support in the press. *Time* magazine blamed as "the real villain" the "vast tangle of the farm price-support system of production controls and surplus storage." There was no mention of the Vice President.

On April 4, 1962, George Krutilek, Billie Sol Estes' accountant, was found dead, another "suicide" by carbon monoxide. This was the day before Estes was indicted by a federal grand jury on fifty-seven counts of fraud. Krutilek had represented the farmers who had signed ammonia tank mortgages, selling Estes their credit. Interviewed by FBI agents on April 2, Krutilek had admitted that he had encouraged farmers who were his clients to invest in Estes' schemes. He was scheduled to testify before a federal grand jury about his relationship with Estes. After the FBI interview, Krutilek was never again seen alive.

An autopsy revealed that there was no carbon monoxide in his lungs. The hose was not even connected to the exhaust pipe when the body was discovered in a cotton field. A local sheriff, R. S. Bailey, declared, following the Stegall scenario, that Krutilek, "very despondent," had committed suicide. Krutilek had a deep bruise on the side of his head as he sat, stiff as a board, behind the wheel of his car, a bruise similar to the one found on Henry Marshall. Rigor mortis had set in before Krutilek had been placed behind the wheel.

"Cardiac arrest," the local coroner ruled.

Obsessed with Billie Sol Estes, Lyndon Johnson discovered that Estes was scheduled to meet on May 14, 1962, with I. Lee Potter, a Republican political activist and one-time Eisenhower staffer and troubleshooter, at the Hilton Plaza Hotel in San Antonio. Johnson contacted Owen Kilday, sheriff of Bexar County. Kilday had been close to Johnson since the 1948 election and was friendly with George Parr.

Kilday now hired a private detective named Charles S. Bond to bug Potter's hotel room and record his conversations with Billie Sol Estes. Bond rented the room next door to Potter's and to justify his presence alerted the hotel assistant manager, R. H. Gross, falsely, that "someone was coming in as a killer to have a contract on someone." Detective Bond checked the hotel coffee shop in search of Billie Sol Estes, but Estes was nowhere to be found.

Lyndon Johnson would never have been so blatantly exposed in his interest in Billie Sol Estes had Sheriff Kilday not furnished incriminating documentation of the scheme. On May 22, Kilday wrote a letter to Vice President Johnson:

> As per your request, I put a private detective on the Potter case. I was forced to do this because I did not have a plainclothes man available. An extreme urgency existed, so I employed Charles S. Bond. He covered Potter, but Billy [sic] Sol Estes did not show up. I am sorry, but I had to run up a bill on account of the speed necessary to investigate. I regret we were not successful. Potter met with all the Republican candidates who were in San Antonio at the time.

Included with this note was a bill for $484.56. When these documents were discovered by *Austin American Statesman* reporter Mike Cox, the Johnson forces had no alternative but to lie. "Knowing Kilday," Walter Jenkins said, "I would guess the surveillance was his own idea." Later Billie Sol Estes would recite what would become his habitual mantra: "If I had attended the meeting and talked about the relationship [with Lyndon Johnson], I would have been dead before nightfall."

In May 1962, at the urging of Henry Marshall's widow, Sybil, an inquest into Marshall's death was begun in Robertson County. Among those who testified was Billie Sol Estes, who appeared on June 13. Estes sheltered under his Fifth Amendment privilege at least seventy-five times. Attorney General Will Wilson, who filed an anti-trust suit against Estes, claimed that he had refused to answer some one hundred questions.

Estes was represented by John Cofer, who would not be shy about admitting his distaste for Estes, whom he termed a "most uncooperative client" with "all kinds of money hidden away." Signing on to represent Estes, Cofer was handed twenty-five thousand dollars. Privately, Estes said the figure was eighty-five thousand and that the money originated with Lyndon Johnson. Cofer managed to persuade the grand jury to state for the record that they didn't consider Billie Sol Estes to be a suspect in Henry Marshall's death.

A dominant presence at the inquest was Sheriff Howard Stegall, whose son-in-law, Pryse Metcalfe, just happened to be a grand juror. Metcalfe ran a feed store in town. Three other grand jurors were kin to the Stegalls. Present as well was Barefoot Sanders, U.S. attorney for the Northern District of Texas and one more recipient of Lyndon Johnson's largesse. Sanders, who reported back to both Bobby Kennedy and Lyndon Johnson, although his loyalty was to Johnson, succeeded in quashing a subpoena that would have made available to the Robertson County grand jury the Agriculture Department's 175-page report on Billie Sol Estes' cotton allotments.

Marshall's body was exhumed and an autopsy was performed by veteran Houston medical examiner Dr. Joseph Jachimczyk. Jachimczyk termed the head wound alone "incapacitating." His conclusion was that "if in fact this is a suicide, it is the most unusual one I have ever seen during the examination of approximately fifteen thousand deceased persons." Yet Dr. Jachimczyk proved unwilling to challenge the local officials. "Possible suicide, probable homicide," he waffled. "I don't have nothing to say now," said Lee Farmer, the coroner and justice of the peace.

The only witness of merit was a Billups service station attendant named Nolan Griffin. Strangers were a rarity in Franklin, Texas, and so Griffin remembered vividly how a year earlier, on Saturday, June 3, a stranger had turned up asking where "the Marshall place was." The same man had returned the next day.

"You gave me the wrong Marshall," he said. "But that's all right. I got my deer license." This man was about forty-five years old, Griffin said. He was heavy, over six feet tall, and had a round face, heavy acne scars, and horn-rimmed glasses. A Department of Public Safety artist drew a composite.

Present at the Marshall inquest was Captain Clint Peoples, who examined the composite. It did not resemble anyone he had ever seen, he said. Peoples flew to Odessa to interrogate a suspect who had been identified by Griffin as the man who had come to his gas station. Griffin had signed a statement about this suspect in the company of county attorney Bryan Russ, with Sheriff Stegall present. (Later Griffin remarked that he had signed the statement without reading it.)

In Odessa, Peoples tracked down the suspect only for him to be "checked out and completely cleared." He passed a polygraph. A week after the composite became public, Nolan Griffin received an anonymous telephone call. The caller knew where Griffin lived, and revealed details about his children. He ordered Griffin to "back off." Ted Shipper, a private detective who had been hired by Sybil Marshall to investigate her husband's death, revealed that he had resigned after he began receiving anonymous telephone calls threatening his family. "They asked me how my family was doing," Shipper said. "I knew they meant it."

Judge W. S. Barron halted the inquest "abruptly." Three witnesses who had been subpoenaed and were scheduled to testify were never called. The grand jury affirmed "suicide" as the cause of Henry Marshall's death. Later, several grand jurors requested that county attorney Bryan Russ subpoena Judge Barron himself because he had halted the hearing so precipitously. Someone had "got to" the judge, they concluded. Russ refused.

Later Judge Barron revealed that Robert F. Kennedy had telephoned him every day requesting details of the day's testimony. Some days he called twice. "I talked to John Kennedy one time and I talked to Robert Kennedy nine or twelve times," the judge said. He had also heard from Lyndon Johnson. "Lyndon got into it, took a great interest in it," the judge said. "Cliff Carter wired down and called me about it two or three times." Johnson had claimed he wanted "a complete investigation made," Judge Barron added. He "put on a good act." Judge Barron concluded that Cliff Carter and Lyndon Johnson wanted not the truth, but a continuation of the cover-up of how Henry Marshall had died.

One of the grand jurors remarked that Pryse Metcalfe had "used all his influence to be sure the grand jury came out with a suicide verdict."

On June 21, a federal grand jury in El Paso brought out a new indictment of twenty-nine counts against Billie Sol Estes, naming as well Harold E. Orr, Ruel W. Alexa, and Coleman D. McSpadden. A front-page headline in the June 24, 1962, *McAllen (TX) Valley Evening Monitor* read, LBJ, YARBOROUGH LINKED WTH ESTES, stating that either Lyndon Johnson himself, or Lady Bird Johnson, had a 43-percent ownership in Estes' Plainview grain elevator.

On July 13, 1962, Billie Sol Estes was declared a bankrupt. Many of his assets were scooped up by Morris Jaffe, a close friend of Lyndon Johnson and a major supporter of Johnson for the 1960 presidential nomination. Jaffe came away with thousands of acres of irrigated land, ranch holdings, and the multimillion-dollar grain complex. For all this, he paid one hundred thousand dollars. Jerry Holleman, a former Assistant Secretary of Labor—an appointment he owed to Lyndon Johnson—joined the Jaffe firm in San Antonio.

According to Holland McCombs, Holleman had been fired as Assistant Secretary of Labor because he took money from Estes "and one of Lyndon's Austin boys." McCombs considered that if there was any link between Billie Sol Estes and Lyndon Johnson that might be proven, it was Holleman. From sources in Austin, he heard that Holleman was viewed as a "political crook" and wondered whether that fifty thousand dollars Billie Sol had given to Yarborough had gone through Holleman.

McCombs learned that after Estes was arrested, he put in twenty-eight calls to Yarborough's office in the space of sixteen hours. A West Texas former Estes employee and school classmate recounted to McCombs that "Billie Sol liked for you to know how buddy-buddy he was with Johnson and all those big shots in Washington. He's run up a telephone bill in my house of two hundred and two hundred fifty dollars a month talking to Johnson, Yarborough, and big guys in Washington."

McCombs also uncovered that the federal government had prevented the Pecos postmaster from revealing records of money orders because they would have exposed the cash flow from Estes' deals. McCombs' source was attorney general Will Wilson. McCombs concluded that "when the FBI first began investigating Estes, about a year before he was caught, they were called off by Kennedy or Johnson." McCombs asked rhetorically in his notes: "Why haven't they found out and exposed everyone they could possibly connect with the Billie Sol case? The answer seems to be that it would lead to all those murders."

In August, a federal grand jury in Dallas indicted Estes on charges of misrepresenting his financial position to the Commodity Credit Corporation in connection with his grain storage deal with the government.

On April 28, 1962, an editorial in the *New York Herald Tribune* had called upon Senator John L. McClellan of Arkansas to investigate the circumstances surrounding the friendship between Billie Sol Estes and "an aide to Vice President Lyndon Johnson," Cliff Carter. McClellan was a close friend of Johnson. Although his Senate subcommittee on investigations looked into the activities of Estes, Lyndon Johnson's name did not appear in the final report, which was released on September 30, 1964.

Following suit, the House Inter-Governmental Relations subcommittee absolved "high officials" of any wrongdoing in the Billie Sol Estes case. It placed the blame on the Agriculture Department and other agencies that had failed to discover "the fraud behind Estes' cotton and grain manipulations." Johnson staffers attended the hearings of both committees, under instruction to note if Lyndon Johnson's name came up. In the released McClellan Committee hearings, there is only a glancing reference made by agriculture official Bill Mattox to a "Cliff Carder." A copy of the full report is available at the LBJ Library in Austin.

Before the Senate committee, Coleman McSpadden of Superior Manufacturing testified that Billie Sol Estes had bragged that he was building a ten-thousand-bushel storage elevator in Hereford, Texas, and that one eighth of the spoils would go to Lyndon Johnson. This testimony does not appear in the 2,812 pages of testimony released by the McClellan Committee. After Lyndon Johnson became President, the McClellan Committee's findings on the matter of Billie Sol Estes were sealed, even from Congress.

Offering up a 439-page report, the House committee concluded that "there was no evidence that Mr. Johnson ever knew Estes." Holland McCombs concluded that among the reasons that Lyndon Johnson did not take a public stand against Ralph Yarborough was that Yarborough was helping in the cover-up on the Estes case.

Out on bail, Estes was a legal pauper sporting a three-thousand-dollar wristwatch with diamond hours, and driving a cream-colored Fleetwood Cadillac. He now resided in a lakefront mansion with a private dock and fishing pier, where he employed inside and outside servants. He was observed shopping at the local Safeway store with crisp one-hundred-dollar bills.

Estes affected confidence still that Lyndon Johnson would come to his rescue. "I'll call Orville," Estes said, referring to Secretary of Agriculture Orville Freeman, "and if he can't help us I'll call Lyndon, and if I have to, I'll call Jack." The Johnson staff was now denying that they had ever heard of Billie Sol Estes. "Mr. Estes has made no campaign contributions to Mr. Johnson," Walter Jenkins said. Estes even approached Barry Goldwater for help.

Among Estes' more desperate actions at this time was a visit he paid to Wilson C. Tucker, deputy director of the Agriculture Department's cotton division. If the investigation of his activities were not halted, Estes threatened, he would embarrass the Kennedy administration. "The cotton allotment matter has already caused the death of one person," Estes said. "Do you know who Henry Marshall was?"

Estes remained a free man throughout 1963 and into 1964. One trial was on March 11, 1963. There were trials in El Paso and in Tyler. Holland McCombs wondered in his notes how Estes could afford to "keep the high-priced Cofer law firm working on this almost full time," but he did. One observer told McCombs that fighting the court actions must be "costing over two hundred thousand, maybe more." The Cofers, father and son, worked on the Estes trials for two years.

At one proceeding, Cofer distributed Nolan Griffin's composite of the man who visited his gas station on the day of Henry Marshall's murder, then asked every prospective juror whether they had ever seen this man. Estes' daughter Pam thought Cofer was planting "a suggestion in the mind of the jurors that Daddy might also be wanted for murder." Billie Sol did resemble Nolan Griffin's composite with his horn-rimmed glasses, black hair, and round face.

At the trials in Tyler and El Paso, Cofer rested the case for the defense without putting a single witness on the stand. He neglected to demonstrate that the finance companies that had provided loans to Estes were well aware that there were only a handful of fertilizer tanks. This would have gone some distance toward refuting the fraud charge. Estes claimed that "not a single fertilizer tank payment was past due."

Cofer spent "more time using delay tactics than defending me," Billie Sol complained later. Estes had assumed that at the end of each day he would meet with Cofer to review what had happened and to plan the next day's strategy. This never occurred. When Billie Sol whispered suggestions on how someone's testimony might be refuted, Cofer ignored him.

He had told Cofer that he wanted to testify, only for Cofer to refuse to put him on the stand. According to Estes, he attempted to fire Cofer, only for Cofer to refuse to be fired. He had already been paid, he said. The judge saw it Cofer's way. Estes had another lawyer in mind, Warren Burnett of Odessa, whom he had already agreed to pay thirty thousand dollars. Cofer remained.

Estes lost in Tyler. He was granted a retrial because there had been a circus atmosphere, and in El Paso he lost again. After Estes was convicted on March 29, 1963, in El Paso, Cofer took the case to the Supreme Court, which refused to review the conviction. The ruling came down in January 1965, at which point the El Paso judge ordered him arrested.

In state court, the jury found Estes guilty on the count of swindling (they could on that occasion convict him legally only on the one count). El Paso judge R. Ewing Thomason stated that Estes had been "the author and perpe-trator of one of the most gigantic swindles in the history of our country." A man sitting next to Holland McCombs remarked, "*That* jury was not fooled!"

Seemingly unperturbed, John Cofer vowed to file for yet another trial. "We've got ten days!" he said. McCombs concluded that "the Cofers have pretty well stacked things up with technical maneuvers, legalistic confound-ments and confusion." Cofer himself exuded such an aura of confidence that McCombs thought Estes would surely get off or receive a very light sentence.

Estes was sentenced on January 24, 1963, to eight years in the state peni-tentiary and on April 15 to fifteen years in federal prison. Cofer's appeal was rejected by the Fifth Circuit. The U.S. Supreme Court denied certiorari, refusing to review the Estes conviction yet again. Cofer then filed a petition for a rehearing by the Supreme Court based on the presence of television cameras in the courtroom at the November 1962 trial in Tyler. By now it was moot. Estes had settled down to life at Leavenworth prison.

"If I had testified against him," Billie Sol said, referring to Lyndon Johnson, "he would have gone to prison and I would have gotten immunity." He would have a decade in prison to nurture his anger at Lyndon Johnson and to come up with a suitable revenge.

In the coming years, an epidemic of deaths of people connected with Estes and his businesses erupted, adding to the murders of Henry Marshall and

George Krutilek. On February 28, 1964, Harold Orr, President of Superior Manufacturing, who had been arrested with Estes in April 1962, died in an accident while supposedly working on the family car. The tools scattered about in his garage would have been of no use in repairing the automobile.

Coleman Wade, an Oklahoma building contractor who had constructed grain elevators for Estes, met with Estes in Pecos in 1963 only for his plane to crash shortly thereafter. Howard Pratt, a Chicago office manager for Commercial Solvents, was found asphyxiated in his car on August 21, 1970. The ruling was "suicide by carbon monoxide poisoning."

None of these deaths was adjudicated in a court of law. There were no eyewitnesses to these deaths—no suspects even.

Surveying all the human wreckage that accumulated in the wake of the Billie Sol Estes scandal, Holland McCombs concluded that Lyndon Johnson would never be implicated in any of the Estes crimes; only "a Johnson stooge."

The Fall of Bobby Baker

> *"He acted like he didn't even know me."*
> —Bobby Baker

Billie Sol Estes was not yet in prison when Baker's scams began to unravel in 1963. From Estes' problems, Lyndon Johnson, with a scrupulous effort by John Cofer, was able to conceal his own involvement.

Even greater scandal and personal exposure confronted Vice President Johnson when Bobby Baker's scams became public. By 1963, the Baker-Johnson Faustian bargain was nearing collapse. Publications in Texas had begun to expose Lyndon Johnson to public scrutiny.

Fifteen years after the events of Box 13, when Johnson was serving as Vice President, the *Texas Argus* summoned the indignation felt by many in Texas regarding the 1948 senatorial election. The *Argus* published "The Story of George Parr's Ballot Box No. 13" in April 1962. In a sidebar, ironically addressed to "Mr. President," they addressed Lyndon Johnson directly:

> May we impiously ask: In the span of a few years, Lyndon, you have gone a fur piece and done well, particularly for LBJ. You have covered the distance from the Pedernales to the Potomac in strides that would put Hiawatha to shame. As fellow Texans, we would like to brag about you, and point with pride to your fantastic

accomplishments; but we can't because of the sordid facts revealed
in a scrutiny of your record.

The *Argus* depicted Lyndon Johnson "as a sort of two-timing scalawag son-
of-a-gun; an ambitious bush-whacker with his eye on the White House; whose
voice was that of Jacob, but whose hand was that of Esau, ready and willing to
dry gulch any and all who got in his way."

The beginning of the end came for Bobby Baker when he was sued by one
of his victims, Ralph Hill, President of Capitol Vending Company in
Washington, in September 1963. Hill claimed that through Baker he had
received a vending machine concession from Melpar, Inc., a Virginia electronics firm, only for Baker to demand a monthly cut from Hill for his services.

In August 1963, Capitol Vending had canceled its contract with Serv-U
Corporation. Bobby Baker threatened Ralph Hill that were he to make trouble
"he might meet with an unfortunate—and probably fatal—accident." Hill
sued anyway. He alleged that Baker had obtained vending machine contracts
for Serv-U because "as Secretary of the Majority, [he] was able to, and did
represent . . . that he was in a position to assist in securing defense contracts."

At the time, Serv-U was making $3.5 million a year from aerospace compa-
nies. As *LIFE* magazine put it, in an exposé researched by Holland McCombs,
"Hill charged that Bobby, like a coin machine that fails to drop the gumball,
had not delivered influence for which he had been paid" and had tried to
install the vending machines of another company [Serv-U] in which Baker
himself had an interest. Hill sued Bobby Baker for three hundred thousand
dollars. A codefendant was Fred Black, the lobbyist for North American
Aviation.

Johnson instructed his Press Secretary, George Reedy, to maintain strict
silence on the subject. Then Johnson consulted his lawyer, Abe Fortas. He
wasn't all that close to Bobby Baker, Johnson claimed. Walter Jenkins was able
to scuttle a story by White House reporter Sarah McClendon and remove it
from every newspaper in Texas. But a small wire service, the North American
Newspaper Alliance, sent it out, and one newspaper picked it up, the *Des
Moines Register*. The story appeared on September 18, 1963.

There it was: the story of the "protégé" of Lyndon Johnson. As Robert Caro
explains, McClendon's article offered up the details of the lawsuit against
Serv-U, identifying Fred Black as one of Baker's codefendants. She went into
the Carousel Motel interest and stated that Baker was Johnson's "protégé and
close personal friend." Jenkins called her into his office and, as Caro writes,

"ordered her to stop trying to 'peddle' the story . . . you are not to print this story." McClendon told Caro that the impression Jenkins gave her was that no one would print the story, that he had closed off all avenues, and that she was about to be fired.

In the autumn of 1963, President Kennedy pushed an investigation of Baker, which would have provided him with ample reason to remove Johnson from the 1964 presidential ticket. Baker resigned as Secretary to the Senate Majority on October 7, 1963, in the wake of the exposure of a bribe he had passed to Senator Thomas J. McIntyre for seventeen thousand dollars. Asked to meet with three senators, including John J. Williams, the Delaware Republican who had taken an interest in the Estes case, and Everett Dirksen, the Illinois Republican, Baker capitulated.

By November, Baker was under twenty-four-hour surveillance. J. Edgar Hoover refused to bug Baker's telephone lines, so the Narcotics Bureau had been enlisted by the Justice Department. Drew Pearson confided to his diary, "Lyndon is worried sick over the developments. This, of course, could knock Lyndon off the ticket for 1964." Pearson had long observed that Johnson was a man fearful of personal risk, citing as a prime example "during the McCarthy era when he refused to stand up and fight and also when he cow-towed [sic] before the gas lobby."

On November 1, 1963, the Senate Rules Committee was voted fifty thousand dollars by the Senate for an investigation of Bobby Baker. The Senate Permanent Subcommittee on Investigations chaired by Senator John McClellan should have been the body investigating Baker. But the powerless Rules Committee, chaired by a Lyndon Johnson acolyte, B. Everett Jordan, who also had a personal relationship with Baker, received the assignment.

Jordan spoke vaguely about how the Baker affair "is a reflection on something in the Senate," so that even *LIFE* magazine had to term this an understatement. *Life*'s exposé of Bobby Baker's scams did not mention the role Lyndon Johnson had played in Baker's rise to financial success. The accumulating scandals included the resignation on October 14, 1963, of Navy Secretary Fred Korth, who was using Navy stationery to transact private business, and was a Johnson appointee.

When Clint Murchison's Washington-based lobbyists, Thomas Webb Jr. and Francis E. Law, testified before the Rules Committee, the hearings were conducted behind closed doors. William Kentor testified that he had paid $9,842.33 in commissions to Baker's law firm as the condition for doing business with HAMPCO, Clint Murchison's meat business.

Exposed to the glare of daylight, Bobby Baker's figures and financial dealings were chimerical, untraceable, and the fruit of illegal wheeling and dealing. In three months of 1962, Baker had deposited more than fifty-three thousand dollars in cash in his bank account. He sold the Carousel Motel to Serv-U for four hundred thousand dollars even as Clint Murchison's Tecon Corporation had offered $1.5 million for it.

Baker concealed his assets, which included stock in twenty-seven corporations including six banks in six states between January 1, 1959, and November 1, 1963. Some said it was eighteen banks in eight states. He participated in sixty-five loans totaling $2,784,520 from twenty-six banks, businesses, and individuals. Most of the time he dealt in cash. He had parlayed a $19,612 a year salary into close to $2,000,000. His net worth in 1954 had been $11,025.

Abe Fortas defended Bobby Baker—at Lyndon Johnson's suggestion.

Holland McCombs interviewed Congressman Robert Ashton "Fats" Everett, who remarked that Bobby Baker "was so high up there with Lyndon and Kerr and the big boys that there was just not much that I, a mere congressman, could do for him." Baker termed Senator Robert S. Kerr of Oklahoma his financial mentor; his earliest investments had been in the Kerr-McGee oil company.

Everett noted that there was "a lot of Texas oil money coming to Bobby from the Murchisons and some of those people out there." Everett asked McCombs: "Some people wondered how much he might be involved with Lyndon. Have you found anything about his Lyndon involvements?"

Behind the scenes, Bobby Kennedy enlisted J. Edgar Hoover to persuade the Senate leadership that the Senate Rules Committee not mention Elly Rometsch. The Rules Committee obliged. *LIFE* magazine published a photograph of the sultry "German Call Girl." If *Life* knew of Elly's liaison with President Kennedy, they weren't saying. That the scams and projects of Bobby Baker splashed onto the Kennedys made it more likely that they would remove Lyndon Johnson from the 1964 presidential ticket.

Only one individual elicited the courage and indignation to lift the corner of the curtain concealing Lyndon Johnson's relationship with Bobby Baker. This was Donald Reynolds, a Silver Spring, Maryland, insurance agent who had been blackmailed by Baker. Baker had known Reynolds since Baker had once brokered an abortion for one of Reynolds' girlfriends after Reynolds had asked him for "some way to get rid of the baby."

Furious still at Baker, Ralph Hill introduced Don Reynolds to Senator John Williams, a member of the Rules Committee. Reynolds told Williams what he knew. It was the testimony of Don Reynolds that jeopardized Lyndon Johnson's credibility, and might well have accomplished his comeuppance.

Reynolds had used Bobby Baker as the intermediary to sell life insurance to Lyndon Johnson when he became Vice President. Baker arranged for Lyndon Johnson to purchase two fifty-thousand-dollar life insurance policies from Reynolds. Johnson then enlisted Bobby Baker and Walter Jenkins to persuade Reynolds to kick back some of his eleven-thousand-dollar commission. Reynolds was ordered to purchase $1,208 worth of advertising on the Johnson KVET television station in Austin. Reynolds later testified that Walter Jenkins had demanded that he buy a minimum of *three thousand dollars worth* of advertising time.

Reynolds succumbed. Knowing it was absurd that, based in Maryland as he was, he could sell insurance to anyone in Austin, Reynolds sold the television time to a pots and pans dealer. In a sworn statement Walter Jenkins denied he knew anything about the arrangements for Reynolds to purchase the advertising.

In addition to the advertising time, Johnson wanted something more from Reynolds. From a catalogue, Lady Bird selected an expensive piece of stereo equipment, a Magnavox costing $542.25. Bobby Baker arranged for the stereo to be sent over to the Johnson home. A similar stereo went to Bobby Baker.

In recounting how he came to be blackmailed by Bobby Baker and Walter Jenkins, Reynolds used the term "shakedown." (Baker had called it a "kickback.") It would be the only time Lyndon Johnson's name surfaced in the Baker hearings.

Reynolds had also been involved in a bid for the nineteen-million-dollar District of Columbia stadium. He turned over 40 percent of his commission on the performance bond to Bobby Baker because Baker had introduced him to the builder, Matthew H. McCloskey Jr. Out of the $109,205.60 that went from McCloskey's company to Reynolds, at least twenty-five thousand went to Baker.

There had been another four thousand dollars to Baker, and a twenty-five-thousand-dollar campaign contribution to Lyndon Johnson's bid for the 1960 presidential nomination. Later Reynolds contributed fifteen thousand dollars to the "Johnson-Kennedy campaign," as he put it. What is clear is that mountains of cash changed hands along a chain that ran from Bobby Baker to Lyndon Johnson.

Reynolds also testified that on a trip to Hong Kong as Vice President, Johnson drew one hundred thousand dollars in government money to buy gifts for his friends.

On November 22, 1963, Don Reynolds sat before the Senate Rules Committee recounting his financial escapades with Bobby Baker and Lyndon Johnson. Later he was to characterize the senators' questioning of him as hostile. However, the senators found his testimony so riveting that they did not adjourn for lunch. Reynolds was testifying at the moment that the shots rang out in Dallas, transforming him into a witness against the President of the United States. The participants did not learn until later in the afternoon that President Kennedy had been killed.

Representing Reynolds was Johnson lawyer Abe Fortas. Soon Fortas would resign as Bobby Baker's lawyer. The hearings were suspended and would not resume until January 8, 1964. There would be no further discussion of Reynolds's relationship with Lyndon Johnson.

What remained was damage control. At a news conference on January 23, 1964, President Johnson said, "The Baker family gave us a stereo set. We had exchanged gifts before. He was an employee of the public and had no business pending before me and was asking for nothing and so far as I knew expected nothing in return any more than I did when I had presented him with gifts."

Early in 1964, the Senate voted not to extend the Baker inquiry by a vote of forty-two to thirty-three. All forty-two votes came from Democrats. Among tidbits coming to the attention of the Warren Commission as it investigated the Kennedy assassination was that Don Reynolds had been heard to say "the FBI knew that Johnson was behind the assassination." Reynolds denied that he had ever said such a thing. He did reveal that during the swearing in of John F. Kennedy, Bobby Baker had said, "The S.O.B. will never live out his term and will die a violent death."

On January 17, 1964, the Senate Rules Committee voted to release Don Reynolds's testimony to the public. The most damning moment came when Reynolds recounted under oath that one day Bobby Baker had opened a satchel full of paper money, which he said was a one-hundred-thousand-dollar payoff to Lyndon Johnson for pushing through the seven-billion-dollar TFX fighter plane contract that had gone to General Dynamics, a Texas corporation. Close to bankruptcy, General Dynamics was far less qualified than Boeing, its chief competitor.

General Curtis LeMay was dumbfounded. In each of four evaluations Boeing had revealed itself to be the best contractor for the job. "It never entered my mind what was actually going to happen," LeMay said. "I couldn't foresee anything like this happening. Boeing had even put in a lower bid." For the first time in LeMay's memory, the Secretary of the Air Force made the decision: "We should give the contract to General Dynamics." LeMay was chief of staff of the Air Force, and the selection should have been his.

"I'm sure it was a political decision," LeMay concluded, a result of "Mr. Johnson's own Texas background." With the assistance of Abe Fortas, Johnson arranged to halt the publication of the Reynolds testimony.

Johnson's office leaked Don Reynolds's FBI file, which came to Lyndon Johnson courtesy of J. Edgar Hoover. It included classified Air Force records and details of Reynolds's black market dealings when he was a foreign service officer. On February 5, a *Washington Post* story exposed that Reynolds had lied about his grades at West Point (he had flunked out). He had supported Joseph McCarthy and had made anti-Semitic remarks in Berlin.

The *New York Times* then reported that Lyndon Johnson had smeared Reynolds with information from secret government documents. Johnson aides had tried to pressure newspaper editors not to release information from Reynolds's testimony. There were no consequences. By now Lyndon Johnson was President of the United States.

On February 25, 1964, Baker testified before the Rules Committee in a lavender coat with a lavender silk lining and a velvet collar, in mockery of the hearings. Lavender had been the color of the carpeting in the townhouse he had purchased illegally for his mistress Carole Tyler, a former "Miss Loudon County" (Virginia). To secure the sale, Baker had claimed she was his cousin. Perched on his head in jaunty contempt was a blue fedora. As *Time* magazine described Baker, his "bright eyes stole briefly across the gathered crowd and looked away again."

On the stand, Baker admitted only that when he was hard up, he had gone to Vice President Lyndon Johnson for "advice." Otherwise, as Billie Sol Estes had done, Baker sheltered beneath his Fifth Amendment privilege and refused to surrender any documents to the committee. Among the questions the Rules Committee put to Bobby Baker is: "Was it true that you received ten thousand dollars from Fred Black, North American Aviation's man in Washington, in hundred-dollar bills to be used for one particular friend who was a candidate for the Democratic Presidential nomination in 1960?"

Black was a close friend and associate of mobster Johnny Rosselli. He had promised an additional ninety thousand dollars to the same nameless candidate. The senators inquired as to what service Baker had performed to continue to receive the HAMPCO kickback. Baker did not slither off in ignominy. He had been elected as a South Carolina delegate to the 1964 Democratic Party Convention.

Only a few spoke out on the Baker-Johnson connection. Henry J. Taylor wrote in the June 4, 1964 *Dallas Herald American* that "Baker's political salt came from Johnson's table." Taylor called Johnson "the decisive participant," and charged that Johnson had condoned the Senate Rules Committee's stalling tactics. The committee had refused to summon at least twenty important witnesses, among them Johnson's chief aide, Walter Jenkins. The lid is on, Taylor wrote, "only because Mr. Johnson permits it."

Once his relationship with Baker came to light, Lyndon Johnson pretended not to know him. Johnson did not contact his former disciple again. Instead, Lady Bird telephoned Bobby Baker. "Lyndon and I just want you to know we love you," she said. "You are like a member of the family and we are so grateful for all you've done for us." It was Lady Bird fulfilling her own Faustian bargain in a marriage her daughter Lynda would define as "a little oppressive."

Among Johnson's antagonists in Texas was rancher and amateur historian J. Evetts Haley who, even as Johnson ascended to the presidency, self-published a diatribe called *A Texan Looks at Lyndon: A Study in Illegitimate Power* (1964). Haley moves from Johnson's specious "victory" in the 1948 senatorial election to the scams of Billie Sol Estes. In a chapter titled "L.B.J.: Friends and Favors," Haley revisits the Kinser case, strongly implying that Lyndon Johnson sent Mac Wallace to murder Kinser because of his affair with Josefa. (Haley does not mention that Andre Wallace had had an affair with Kinser as well.)

Bobby Baker appears only in passing. But with respect to Hoover's leaking of Don Reynolds's FBI file to Johnson, Haley wrote: "Does the White House have the authority—ethically, anyway—to order J. Edgar Hoover to turn over its secret files any time the Administration wants to crack down on an embarrassing witness or a political opponent?"

In retrospect, Haley emerges as a stronger historian than has been suggested by Johnson's mainstream biographers. He was the first to break the Box 13 story in book form. That Lyndon Johnson had ascended to the presidency did not inspire Haley to engage in self-censorship. If there are some errors of fact in his book, few historians can claim otherwise. Many engage in errors of omission.

A Texan Looks at Lyndon created a sensation in Texas. In one day it sold eight thousand copies. At the Liberty Lobby bookstore, Haley's book was featured. One Houston business distributed five hundred copies of the book only to be visited shortly thereafter by two IRS agents, who kept watch over that firm's finances for the next two years.

The source is Houston attorney Douglas Caddy, who later represented Billie Sol Estes; the anecdote came to Caddy because the IRS had harassed friends of his mother. Caddy concluded it was "typical LBJ retribution against my mother's friends for their purchasing and distributing Haley's book during the presidential campaign." His mother purchased twenty copies of Haley's book that her friends had in storage.

In 1967, Bobby Baker was found guilty of seven counts of theft, fraud, and income tax evasion, including stealing campaign contributions. At his trial, he testified, again, that when he was hard up, he had gone to Vice President Lyndon Johnson for financial advice. It was the time when he was having trouble meeting the payments on his Carousel, motel at Ocean City, Maryland. Lyndon Johnson had referred Baker to Senator Bob Kerr, who immediately got him a loan of one hundred eighty thousand dollars from an Oklahoma City bank. Johnson's relationship with Kerr was longstanding: When Johnson had set out to destroy Leland Olds of the Federal Power Commission on behalf of the oil and gas interests, oilman Kerr had been his ally. Kerr, Drew Pearson wrote, had "carried the ball." In their book *The Case Against Congress*, Pearson and his co-author and successor Jack Anderson wrote that "Robert S. Kerr, oil millionaire, uranium king, cattle baron and Senator from Oklahoma . . . dominated the Senate's back rooms in the late 1950s and early 1960s."

Lyndon Johnson asked powerful Washington lawyer Edward Bennett Williams to represent Bobby Baker at his impending trial. A grand jury spent eighteen months hearing 170 witnesses. Although Baker "had done his best to delay and avoid trial," he went to trial on January 9, 1967, a full year after he was indicted. The jury took only a day to convict Baker on all nine counts; some jurors told reporters that they believed Baker had lied on the stand.

Federal prosecutor William O. Bittman, Evan Thomas writes in his biography of Edward Bennett Williams, "suspected Justice steered the ultimate indictment away from areas that might be politically embarrassing to congressmen or officials in the Johnson administration." LBJ didn't dare make the case go away, but Williams was present to see that Johnson's name was not mentioned, just as John Cofer had done in the trials of Billie Sol Estes.

Baker was sentenced to three years in federal prison. He entered Lewisburg federal penitentiary in 1970, and was released after sixteen months. The distinguished criminal attorney Michael Tigar, who assisted Williams in representing Bobby Baker, offered the most trenchant analysis of the Johnson-Baker affair. "The prosecution chose to prosecute him," Tigar said, "while ignoring his superiors who'd conducted themselves in much the same manner, and it labels him as a wayward bad boy, not as part of a generally corrupt system in order to protect the government's reputation and image . . . the government chose to make Baker the subject of scrutiny it would not risk bringing against others."

Well into Lyndon Johnson's presidency, Carlos Marcello, Louisiana and Texas crime boss, made Baker an offer. According to Baker, Marcello asked if Johnson was "your dear, great friend." When Baker acknowledged that he was, "although he was a coward at my trial," Marcello made him an offer: "I have a million dollars in cash that I would love to give to him or whoever he assigns, to get a presidential pardon for Jimmy Hoffa." Baker replied: "Mr. Marcello, the greatest coward in America when it comes to something like this is Lyndon Baines Johnson."

CHAPTER 12

Mac Wallace in California

Life is too damn short to worry about anything
very much, Nora Ann, so don't you do it.
—MAC WALLACE TO NORA ANN CARROLL,
JULY 17, 1946

While Lyndon Johnson was devoting no small measure of his time as Vice President to preserving his reputation and credibility, concealing his connections to Billie Sol Estes and Bobby Baker, Mac Wallace had settled into his California life. Among his responsibilities as a "control supervisor" at Ling Electronics was frequent travel to Stanford University, where Ling operated a linear particle accelerator. As Mac Wallace pursued his duties at Ling, the Office of Naval Intelligence persisted in its efforts to lower his security clearance.

In September 1962, the Navy sent investigators, probably FBI agents who performed such duties for the Navy, to Timpson, Texas, to interview Andre at her home. Andre told the Navy that in August 1961 she had married an Air Force veteran, now a truck driver, named Delmer Lee Akin, and had moved to Henderson, in Rusk County.

Despite this fresh start, her bitterness against Mac Wallace remained alive and well. Mac had been "very possessive of her and did not want her to have social contact with anyone," Andre said. It was at Mac's request that they had engaged in "unnatural perverted sex acts" over a period of ten or twelve years. Mac Wallace, Andre insisted, was a "sexual pervert," an unstable person. On about "100 occasions," he requested that she "participate in a sex act with another man while he remained a spectator." Among fresh charges Andre leveled against her former husband was that Mac had suggested "joint suicide pacts."

Now Andre introduced the Navy to the incest charges that she had leveled against Mac Wallace at the divorce hearing. Andre announced that Mac Wallace had had "incestuous relations with his nine-year-old daughter." The

resulting report, dated December 27, 1962, and signed by a Navy captain, an
Army lieutenant colonel, and an Air Force officer, concluded, yet again, that
"a favorable finding as to granting of access authorization is not warranted."
Their recommendation was that Mac Wallace's SECRET clearance be
revoked. To mediate the conflict between the ONI and Defense Intelligence
which, persistently, had refused to grant the Navy's recommendation, an
arbiter was brought into the case.

His name, appropriately as it turned out, was Charles C. Wise, and he was
a "security adviser" to the Industrial Personnel Access Authorization
Screening Board. On February 1, 1963, Wise sent a memorandum on the
subject of Mac Wallace's security clearance to the chairman of "Screening
Board Panel #1." It was six single-spaced pages in length.

Wise summarized the Navy's reasons for recommending that "the existing
authorization be revoked," ranging from the Kinser murder to Mac Wallace's
having been twice arrested and fined for being drunk and yet not having
disclosed these arrests on his personnel security questionnaire. Wise was
more concerned with the arrests having been omitted than that the subject
was an alcoholic.

Wise added: "He may be a sex pervert; he may have communist or
subversive inclinations." Wise did not ignore Andre's charge that Mac had
"performed cunnilingus on their minor daughter." Nor could he conceal his
outrage. Mac Wallace, he wrote, had "all the least desirable elements of an
utter bum."

More worldly than the trio of Onis Doherty, Clint Peoples, and A. C.
Sullivan, Wise acknowledged that reading Mac Wallace's file was a "frus-
trating experience." It felt as if he were reading about two different people. "If
all the facts alleged are true, applicant is a real Dr. Jekyll and Mr. Hyde." Wise
noted the positive moments in Mac Wallace's history: his leadership at the
University of Texas; his master's degree and postgraduate work. He even
quoted the student at Long Island University in New York who had told the
FBI that Mac Wallace was "one of the best instructors I have ever had."

Wise suggested a motive for Mac Wallace's killing of John Douglas Kinser,
the "illicit, immoral and perhaps bizarre adulterous intimacies between the
deceased and applicant's wife." He acknowledged that the murder had been a
crime of passion and implied that the paramour defense might well have
been invoked had Mac Wallace entered a plea of guilty.

Charles Wise was appalled by Andre's behavior; for Andre, Wise could
summon little sympathy. She had "on every possible occasion blackened her

Holland McCombs: In 1963 and 1964, McCombs worked on an exposé of Lyndon Johnson under the auspices of *LIFE* magazine. COURTESY OF KAREN ELMORE, UNIVERSITY OF TENNESSEE AT MARTIN.

Herman Brown and George Rufus Brown, proprietors of Brown & Root: As the recipient of Herman Brown's favor, Lyndon Johnson was against unions and opposed union organizing at his radio station. He voted for the open shop. COURTESY OF FONDREN LIBRARY, RICE UNIVERSITY.

WALLACE   Malcolm E.
Enl   3Nov39
Taken   10Nov39

Mac Wallace at the
moment when he joined
the U.S. Marines in 1939:
His character, the Marines
determined, was
"excellent." COURTESY OF
THE NATIONAL ARCHIVES,
ST. LOUIS.

In September 1943, at the
University of Texas, Mac
Wallace met Nora Ann
Carroll, the woman who
would turn out to be the
love of his life. COURTESY
OF NORA ANN STEVENSON.

Mac Wallace at the University of Texas c. 1943. He fought for democratic governance of the university with the students enjoying significant influence. COURTESY OF THE DOLPH BRISCOE CENTER FOR AMERICAN HISTORY, THE UNIVERSITY OF TEXAS AT AUSTIN.

Mac Wallace marching in the demonstrations in support of University of Texas President Homer Rainey, 1944. COURTESY OF THE DOLPH BRISCOE CENTER FOR AMERICAN HISTORY, THE UNIVERSITY OF TEXAS AT AUSTIN.

In 1944, Mac Wallace addressed a sea of students, men, and women in equal numbers, surrounding him on all sides. Behind him on a balcony, two students held up a banner: WE FIGHT HITLERISM ABROAD/WE'LL FIGHT IT AT HOME. COURTESY OF THE DOLPH BRISCOE CENTER FOR AMERICAN HISTORY, THE UNIVERSITY OF TEXAS AT AUSTIN.

Scene at a restaurant. Andre Wallace (RIGHT) and Mac Wallace (TO HER RIGHT), ill-suited to each other as they were, could not break free of the centrifugal force of their connection. COURTESY OF MICHAEL WALLACE.

Lawyer John Cofer: He was a connoisseur of sophistry, and his efforts would weave through Lyndon Johnson's political career and the lives of those with whom Johnson forged his Faustian bargains for many years. COURTESY OF THE ASSOCIATED PRESS.

Billie Sol Estes (LEFT) and his attorney John Cofer arriving at the federal courthouse in El Paso, May 23, 1962. AP PHOTO/FERD KAUFMAN.

Bobby Baker and LBJ: "I wanted to meet you," Johnson said at their first encounter, leading with flattery, as was his wont. FROM *LIFE* MAGAZINE, NOVEMBER 8, 1963.

Mac Wallace during the Kinser trial: "It was supposed to look like rivalry over a woman but it was much deeper than that!" Senator Ralph Yarborough said. COURTESY OF NEAL DOUGLASS, AUSTIN PUBLIC LIBRARY.

David Harold (D. H.) Byrd acknowledged in his autobiography that "among the men I could go to at any time that I wanted action" was Lyndon Johnson. FROM *I'M AN ENDANGERED SPECIES: THE AUTOBIOGRAPHY OF A FREE ENTERPRISER* BY D. H. BYRD.

John F. Kennedy attempting to restrain Lyndon Johnson during the 1960 presidential campaign.

Lyndon Johnson with his sister Josefa. She died suddenly, under mysterious circumstances in 1961, after attending a Christmas Eve party at the LBJ Ranch. COURTESY OF THE LBJ LIBRARY.

Photograph of Lyndon Johnson inscribed to Billie Sol Estes: At least twenty letters to Estes were sent from either Lyndon Johnson or someone on his staff over a four-year period. FROM *BILLIE SOL ESTES: A TEXAS LEGEND* BY BILLIE SOL ESTES.

Henry Marshall had figured out that Estes was buying cotton allotments and signing mortgages that would be defaulted on by design, pre-arranged to foreclose. COURTESY OF THE ASSOCIATED PRESS.

Workers prepare to remove the body of Henry Marshall from its grave in Franklin, Texas, May 22, 1962. "Possible suicide, probable homicide," said the medical examiner who testified at the inquest. COURTESY OF THE ASSOCIATED PRESS.

Composite of the man who asked for directions to Henry Marshall's ranch on the day he was murdered. This photograph first appeared in print in "The Killing of Henry Marshall" by Bill Adler, *Texas Observer*, November 7, 1986.

Clifton Crawford Carter with Lyndon Johnson: Carter represented Johnson on the ground in Texas. According to Emmett Shelton, Carter did Johnson's "work and dirty work for many years."
COURTESY OF THE LBJ LIBRARY.

King Ranch CEO Robert J. Kleberg Jr., brother of Richard Kleberg, at left with Mamie and President Dwight David Eisenhower at Belmont Park racetrack, Elmont, New York, June 3, 1961. Bob Kleberg saw no reason to offend his moral sense by granting any favors to either Archer or George Parr. GETTY IMAGES.

LBJ and Lady Bird with Charles Luckman at the dedication of the re-designed Los Angeles International Airport, 1961. Johnson's choice of Luckman parallels his relationship with Herman and George Brown. COURTESY OF LOYOLA MARYMOUNT UNIVERSITY, WILLIAM H. HANNON LIBRARY, BOX 6, FOLDER 8.

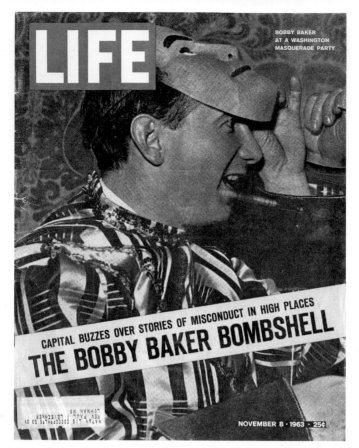

Bobby Baker on the cover of *LIFE* magazine, November 8, 1963.

LIFE

BOBBY BAKER AT A WASHINGTON MASQUERADE PARTY

CAPITAL BUZZES OVER STORIES OF MISCONDUCT IN HIGH PLACES

THE BOBBY BAKER BOMBSHELL

NOVEMBER 8 · 1963 · 25¢

Nora Ann and Mac reunited in California in the summer of 1963: Their photograph shows a happy smiling couple who might have been on their honeymoon. "God in the form of a roving street-photographer entered the restaurant just after we sat down," Nora Ann said. COURTESY OF NORA ANN STEVENSON.

Lieutenant Commander David Edwin Lewis recovering aboard the USS *America*: "I don't care if the *Liberty* sinks," Johnson said, as Dave Lewis remembered it. Or maybe it was, "I don't give a damn if the ship sinks." Johnson certainly said, "I will not embarrass an ally!" COURTESY OF THE LIBERTY VETERANS' ASSOCIATION.

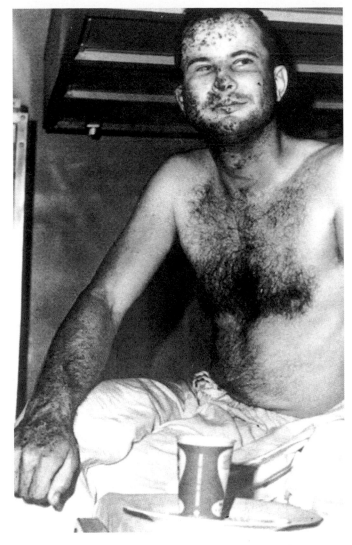

The USS *Liberty* ambushed by the Israeli Defense Forces, June 8, 1967. COURTESY OF DON PAGELER.

CERTIFICATION OF VITAL RECORD

TEXAS DEPARTMENT OF HEALTH
BUREAU OF VITAL STATISTICS

STATE OF TEXAS 032-01-2 057-01 CERTIFICATE OF DEATH E8150 65 STATE FILE NO. 07899

1. PLACE OF DEATH
a. COUNTY CAMP
2. USUAL RESIDENCE (Where deceased lived. If institution: residence before admission)
a. STATE TEXAS b. COUNTY DALLAS

b. CITY OR TOWN (If outside city limits, give precinct no.) PITTSBURG
c. LENGTH OF STAY in 1 b.
c. CITY OR TOWN (If outside city limits, give precinct no.) DALLAS

d. NAME OF (If not in hospital, give street address) HOSPITAL OR INSTITUTION M AND S HOSPITAL
d. STREET ADDRESS (If rural, give location) 610 TENNISON MEMORIAL RD

e. IS PLACE OF DEATH INSIDE CITY LIMITS? YES YES☐ NO☐
e. IS RESIDENCE INSIDE CITY LIMITS? YES YES☐ NO☐
f. IS RESIDENCE ON A FARM? YES☐ NO NO☐

3. NAME OF DECEASED (Type or print)
(a) First MALCOLM (b) Middle EVERETT (c) Last WALLACE
4. DATE OF DEATH 1-7-1971

5. SEX MALE 6. COLOR OR RACE WHITE 7. Married☒ Never Married☐ Widowed☐ Divorced☐
8. DATE OF BIRTH OCTOBER 15, 1921
9. AGE (in years last birthday) 49 IF UNDER 1 YEAR Months Days IF UNDER 24 HRS Hours Minutes

10a. USUAL OCCUPATION (Give kind of work done during most of working life, even if retired) Salesman
10b. KIND OF BUSINESS OR INDUSTRY newspaper
11. BIRTHPLACE (State or foreign country) TITUS COUNTY, TEXAS
12. CITIZEN OF WHAT COUNTRY? U. S. A.

13. FATHER'S NAME A. J WALLACE
14. MOTHER'S MAIDEN NAME unknown

15. WAS DECEASED EVER IN U.S. ARMED FORCES? (Yes, no, or unknown) (If yes, give war or dates of service) YES
16. SOCIAL SECURITY NO. 457-14-3252
17. INFORMANT /s/ David Wallace   brother

18. CAUSES OF DEATH (Enter only one cause per line for (a), (b), and (c).)
IMMEDIATE CAUSE (a) Compound Comminuted skull fracture with
DUE TO (b) probable basal skull fracture
DUE TO (c)
INTERVAL BETWEEN ONSET AND DEATH

PART II. OTHER SIGNIFICANT CONDITIONS CONTRIBUTING TO DEATH BUT NOT RELATED TO THE TERMINAL DISEASE CONDITION GIVEN IN PART I(a)
19. WAS AUTOPSY PERFORMED? YES☐ NO☒

20a. ACCIDENT☒ SUICIDE☐ HOMICIDE☐
20b. DESCRIBE HOW INJURY OCCURRED. (Enter nature of injury in Part I or Part II of item 18.)

20c. TIME OF INJURY Hour Month Day Year a.m. p.m.
20e. PLACE OF INJURY (e.g., in or about home, farm, factory, street, office building, etc.)
20f. CITY, TOWN, OR LOCATION Pittsburg COUNTY Camp STATE Texas

WORK☐ NOT WHILE AT WORK☐ State Highway 271

21. I hereby certify that I attended the deceased from D-O-A 19 71 to 19 and last saw the deceased alive on the date stated above, and to the best of my knowledge, from the causes stated.
Death occurred at 8:00 p.m. on the date stated above.

22a. SIGNATURE [signature] MD
22b. ADDRESS 412 Quitman St. Pittsburg, Tex.
22c. DATE SIGNED 1-11-71

23a. BURIAL
23b. DATE JANUARY 10, 1971
23c. NAME OF CEMETERY OR CREMATORY NEVILS CHAPEL CEMETERY

23d. LOCATION (City, town, or county) RFD, MT PLEASANT, TITUS CO. TEXAS
24. FUNERAL DIRECTOR'S SIGNATURE [signature]

25a. REGISTRAR'S FILE NO. 8
25b. DATE REC'D BY LOCAL REGISTRAR Jan 12, 1971
25c. REGISTRAR'S SIGNATURE [signature] J H Miller

E515159

This is to certify that this is a true and correct reproduction of the original record as recorded in this office. Issued under authority of Section 191.051, Chapter 678, Health & Safety Code, 1989.

ISSUED JAN 0 5 1996

[signature] RICHARD B. BAYS STATE REGISTRAR

WARNING: IT IS ILLEGAL TO DUPLICATE THIS COPY.

ANY ALTERATION OR ERASURE VOIDS THIS CERTIFICATE

RECD FEB 22 1971 BUREAU OF VITAL STATISTICS

BUREAU OF VITAL STATISTICS 1971

TEXAS DEPARTMENT OF HEALTH RECD FEB 12 1971 BUREAU OF VITAL STATISTICS

The death certificate of Malcolm Everett Wallace was laced with inaccuracies. Mac's brother Harold David Wallace supposedly provided the information to the doctor yet did not sign the death certificate. David, if it was he, was unable to provide their mother's maiden name, "Riddle."
FROM THE FILES OF J HARRISON, COURTESY OF WALT BROWN.

Billie Sol Estes leaving prison in December 1983: "There's one thing I want you to tell me," Texas Ranger Clint Peoples said. "Who murdered Henry Marshall?" AP PHOTO/RON HEFLIN.

Texas Ranger Clint Peoples: "Who could be so strong and powerful in politics that he could get a clearance for a man like [Wallace]?" COURTESY OF THE TEXAS RANGER HALL OF FAME AND MUSEUM.

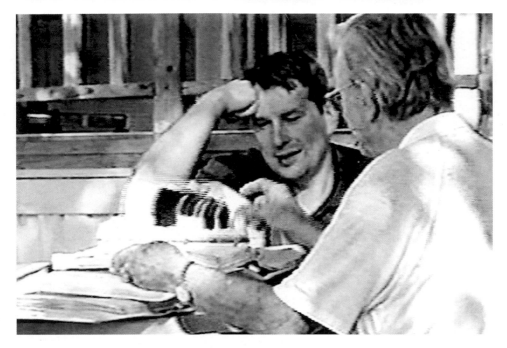

J Harrison with Mac Wallace's FBI file. For eight years, J Harrison attempted to pry this file from the hands of the government. To his Freedom of Information Act request, the Bureau finally replied on September 30, 1998, with a blizzard of paper. Nearly half the writing was buried beneath heavy black redactions. FROM AN UNFINISHED VIDEO BY WILLIAM REYMOND.

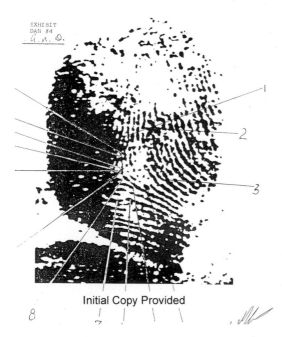

Initial Copy Provided

National Archive Image CE 656 #29

An unidentified fingerprint located in the exhibits of the Warren Commission, found on the sixth floor of the Texas School Book Depository, was mistakenly thought to belong to Mac Wallace. The corrected identification was made by Robert J. Garrett of Idman Forensics.
COURTESY OF ROBERT J. GARRETT.

husband's reputation." This included her lying to the authorities at the time of the trial "when the truth would have provided a defense that almost certainly would have won acquittal from a Texas jury." Andre's demeanor repelled Wise more than Mac Wallace's actions. "In any event we have no evidence that could be submitted to a hearing board to prove applicant is a pervert of any kind," he wrote. Andre was too unstable to be taken seriously.

She was "an admitted alcoholic or ex-alcoholic, a lesbian adulteress and a liar." The supposed acts of "perversion" of which she accused Mac Wallace were "under cover of the marriage relationship" and were hardly crimes. Wise did not "believe we can invade the privacy of the marriage bed and allege as perversion anything taking place therein." He noted that Andre admitted that her husband never forced her to perform any specific act. "I think this woman's testimony must be entirely discredited," Wise concluded.

On the political charges, Wise revealed himself to be as politically provincial as earlier investigators. He termed Mac Wallace "an extremely aggressive radical in student politics," which he had never been.

"Is Mr. Wallace, a highly unstable and unsuitable person, to be barred from access, or is he a Texas gentleman suffering in silence the slurs of an estranged and vicious ex-wife?" Wise asked in his report. Had there been evidence that Mac Wallace had had a "nervous breakdown, psychiatric treatment, personality defect or is otherwise unstable," he might have changed his mind, but no such evidence existed.

Wise concluded that the killing of John Douglas Kinser did not have "serious security significance." Mac Wallace's arrests for being drunk, and his concealing those arrests, did not reveal "any real intent to deceive the Government . . . they would hardly seem of substantial security significance." Mac Wallace was not a threat to national security. Yet the Navy "felt strongly and would make outraged reclamation" were Wise to recommend that the case against Mac Wallace be dropped and so he did not go that far and did not dismiss the case. He did not refuse to lower Mac Wallace's security clearance. Lyndon Johnson's name does not enter the copious Office of Naval Intelligence reports.

At Ling, Mac Wallace met a young woman named Virginia Ledgerwood. Before long, they became lovers. Virginia had questions. Answers were not forthcoming, although on one occasion Mac said he regretted some things that had happened. "I've been in the newspapers twice," he said, "once for something very good and once for something very bad."

The "something very good" was the student movement at the University of Texas. He never relived those days with Virginia. Instead, he talked, matter-of-factly, about participating in Homer Rainey's failed gubernatorial campaign. Virginia came to think of him as a damaged man whose despair was exacerbated by alcohol.

Virginia became pregnant in January 1963. She and Mac Wallace were married in Ensenada, Baja California, on April 30. Whether he had left behind his obsession with Andre is open to question. A month after Mac married Virginia, on May 31, 1963, a farmer residing three miles east of New Summerfield, Texas, telephoned the police to report that a drunk had driven through his vegetable patch. The man had done about forty dollars worth of damage. Not bothering to stop, the driver had continued in the direction of Henderson, Rusk County, the residence of Mary Andre Dubose Barton Wallace Bailey Akin.

Mac was arrested for driving under the influence. He didn't bother to deny that it was he who had wrecked the farmer's vegetable patch. There was an open bottle of bourbon in his car. On June 1, waiving a jury trial, Mac pled guilty to "driving while intoxicated." He was sentenced to three days in jail and a fifty-dollar fine. His Texas driver's license was suspended for six months.

Nora Ann Carroll Cary was now the mother of four children. In the years since she had known Mac Wallace, Nora Ann endured unanticipated trials in her marriage. Ted Cary had become a tortured individual, and an alcoholic, an epidemic disease among men of his and Mac's generation. Nora Ann blamed Ted's free-floating anxiety on the sad fate of his father. Cary senior had been a founder of the Piggly Wiggly supermarket chain. Having lost all his money in the Great Depression, he shot himself.

Before long, Ted's alcoholism included his being picked up by the police, on more than one occasion, for driving while intoxicated. Exasperated, when he called one night and asked her to bail him out, Nora Ann refused to arrange for his release; he spent that night in jail. One day in 1959, Ted arrived home late and locked himself in the toilet. In the morning, Nora Ann discovered his body. He was thirty-five years old. Their children were nine, eight, seven, and two and a half.

Possessing still the abundant energy with which she had blazed a trail through the University of Texas, and beyond, Nora Ann decided now to pursue a master's degree in musicology. During the summer of 1963, she signed up to participate in a two-week string workshop at the University of California at Santa Barbara. Their mutual friend Pat Elliot had kept in touch with Mac Wallace. So it was that he received the news that the love of his life was heading west.

As if he had not a care in the world, summoning the wit and charm of his youth, Mac Wallace wrote to Nora Ann for the first time in a decade. His letter, dated July 3, 1963, and composed on the stationery of Ling Electronics, reveals how much in love with Nora Ann he remained.

> Dear Mrs. Cary:
>
> It has come to our attention that you will soon be honoring our area with your presence.
>
> You of course know that California is now the nation's most populous state. However, we are on our part equally well aware that this recent recognition of our state's outstanding attractiveness is indeed a dwarfed honor in comparison to your decision to visit us.
>
> This corporation wants to do everything possible to acknowledge and be worthy of the benefit you are bestowing upon us. Consequently we are assigning to you the twenty-four-hour attention and service, to be on-call as required, of one of our outstanding young executives: Mr. Malcolm E. Wallace.
>
> Mr. Wallace has been selected for this most pleasant duty for the simple reason that he has loved you for at least twenty years.
>
> So you just catch the plane and relax, dear. No problems.
>> Very truly yours,
>> LING ELECTRONICS
>> Mac
>> M. E. Wallace
>> Materials Manager.

His tone is euphoric. He lets Nora Ann know that he is still in love with her. Their marriages to other people; his having committed the unspeakable act of murder; fifteen years of separation—these have done little to diminish his ardor. Mac Wallace is elated at the prospect of seeing Nora Ann again.

Never having mentioned his wedding only three months earlier, Mac Wallace was waiting at the airport when Nora Ann arrived, armed with gifts: a corsage of an orchid, a black lace mantilla, and a bottle of Balenciaga perfume. The ship of their youth had sailed. Neither expected that they would be able to revive those turbulent zones. Yet their attraction to each other remained intact.

Mac handed Nora Ann a copy of his curriculum vitae which Nora Ann at once mailed to her mother for safekeeping. "He has changed so much," Nora Ann wrote to Lelia Carroll, "is so mature, kind and very entertaining and well read. I was showered with attention . . . best of all, he seemed happy to enjoy the pleasure of the moment and is not too concerned over my plans."

When Nora Ann's string workshop concluded, Mac picked her up in Santa Barbara and they toured the countryside. They strolled around Solvang, a miniature facsimile of a Danish town, then headed south. They ate lunch on the roof of a San Diego hotel overlooking the ocean. They toured the zoo. Then they crossed the border at Tijuana, where they attended a bullfight. As to how many days they spent together, Nora Ann was evasive.

Their photograph was taken in a restaurant, a happy smiling couple who might have been on their honeymoon. "God in the form of a roving street-photographer entered the restaurant just after we sat down," Nora Ann remembered years later. She wore a blue dress with white piping, and had tied the jacket around her waist to conceal a stain. During the day she had inadvertently sat down on someone's abandoned Popsicle.

At dinner, Mac spoke to Nora Ann for the first time about the murder of John Douglas Kinser. He exhibited, she thought, "a sense of deep remorse." He told her that he "had been enraged not so much because *he* had been betrayed, but because Kinser had taken advantage of Andre during a time when she was ill and confused yet was on her way to recovery." To Nora Ann, Mac never mentioned the name "Josepha Johnson," not that she had been his lover, not that she had been Kinser's lover, too.

He confided that Andre had been enrolled in a master's program in the English department at the University of Texas only to drop out midway. Her fees had been forfeited. Money was scarce during his time with Andre; forfeiting school fees should have been unthinkable. Andre had tried interior decorating. She had not been committed to that either and had been unable to contribute to the family's strained finances.

For the first time, they spent a night together at a motel. "It seemed very right to do so," Nora Ann remembered, "since we had been in each other's lives for two decades . . . it was the only night we ever had."

When they parted, Mac gave Nora Ann a telephone number where she could reach him. She dialed it, and the woman who answered became very upset when she heard Nora Ann's voice. The woman handed the telephone to Mac. "Never call this number again!" Mac said harshly, and Nora Ann concluded that her call had been an embarrassment to him.

Soon she learned the truth, that he had remarried a few months earlier and he and his new wife were awaiting the birth of a child. Virginia Ledgerwood Wallace would later recall that Mac Wallace had never been an affectionate husband. All the time she knew him, Mac had loved another woman. Virginia remembered her name as "Carol Ann," close enough to Nora Ann Carroll.

Mac remained interested in everything Nora Ann did, everything she thought. "There is so much turbulence (of a most pleasant type) in me these days that a letter might run on for twenty or thirty pages and ramble over dozens of subjects," Mac wrote to Nora Ann on August 10, while she remained in California.

On October 10, after Nora Ann had departed, Mac wrote again. He invoked "old Socrates" and his role in Athenian life, then went on to praise Nora Ann's critique of a Spanish program in which she had enrolled. He leavened his remarks with brotherly teasing. "If I were the director, I'd spank your bottom, young lady, for the excess of scorn in your language," he wrote. He needed to keep talking to her, to restore their connection and preserve her presence in his life very much as he done in his Christmas letter of December 1943.

In the envelope, he included photographs of his children, sent from Texas "where relations lately are so good they scare me." Another photograph was of Nora Ann, "a close-up with the naval vessels in the background" that "breaks my heart." Referring to the photographs of Nora Ann, he added, "I love them all because I love you."

Elizabeth Elaine Wallace was born in California on October 17, 1963. Two weeks later, unable to remain with a husband who loved another woman, Virginia left him. "We called it quits," she says. She moved out of a home that had never been hers and returned to her parents' house in Fullerton. When Mac moved to Corona del Mar, Virginia took Elaine to see him every other Sunday.

Michael Wallace moved to California that year. He was fifteen years old now, and in the tenth grade. He chose to live with his father rather than his mother because he believed he would receive a better education in California than in rural Texas. His mother's erratic lifestyle was another factor. Only after Michael moved to California did he discover that he had a stepmother named "Virginia."

Looking back, he viewed his father as a man of a particular era. He smoked, sometimes cigars. He drank. He was not forthcoming about his feelings.

Only rarely did Mac mention the Kinser trial. When he did, Michael cut him off. "I don't know what you're talking about," Michael said. He respected his father too much to permit the shooting of John Douglas Kinser to become an issue between them.

Michael knew that his father was paying his uncle James Eldon Wallace and his grandfather installments to reimburse them for having covered his legal fees for the Kinser trial. Once in a while, Mac mentioned Lyndon Johnson, but only in the context of his having known Johnson "way back when." Mac spoke of Johnson neutrally; there was no apparent emotional charge in his mentioning that he knew Lyndon Johnson. They had parted as friendly acquaintances. Mac Wallace was not an introspective man and he did not talk about whether his connection to Johnson had been detrimental or beneficial to his well-being.

At Ling, Mac worked long hours and excursions were rare. During the two years they lived in Corona del Mar, Mac occasionally took his son to a bullfight in Tijuana. Mac and Virginia remained apart. Michael took care of household chores, his father giving him money for grocery shopping or to pick up the dry cleaning. After school, Michael did his homework, then took a walk on the beach. Sometimes his father stopped for a drink after work with some cronies. Unlike others whom Lyndon Johnson took under his wing, people who attained worldly success like John Connally, Barefoot Sanders, and Lloyd Hand, Mac Wallace led a diminished life of ever decreasing prospects.

In the summer of 1964, Ling Electronics sent Mac Wallace to Detroit to purchase equipment for the linear particle accelerator at the Lawrence Livermore National Laboratory. On his way back to California, he visited Nora Ann at her home in Ann Arbor. He had no money for gifts, but one of the salesmen at the Detroit firm where he was doing business presented him with two small framed landscapes painted on velvet. He gave these to Nora Ann.

It was not a "hot reunion," as Nora Ann puts it. All passion had been spent. Nora Ann had studied nuclear chemistry and she could discuss his work with him. Mac seemed healthy and in good spirits. He stayed at a Holiday Inn near the interstate and invited Nora Ann's youngest daughter, Page, and her friend Jill, to swim at the hotel pool. There he frolicked with the children, tossing them over his shoulder, splashing in the water and having a "grand time," as Page recalled. Years later, Page Cary remembered Mac Wallace during that hot summer as joyous, friendly, and kind, a pleasant man in a khaki or yellow bathing suit.

In conversations with friends and family, Mac Wallace remained fond of playing the devil's advocate, stirring the pot, taking unpopular positions to stimulate discussion. He made few friends in California. Michael remembers only one man, who was Asian, being close to him. He took some camping trips to Mexico with co-workers. Ling had a baseball team, but Mac Wallace, once a proud athlete, was not on it.

Always he wore a suit, never jeans, never shorts. Food didn't interest him. He would buy quantities of Swanson chicken pot pies. "A great invention," he said. "They have all the necessary food groups." Always he was devoted to his children. After Elaine was born, he bought three small pictures in identical frames, one for each of his children. He had done this, he explained, "to unite his three children." He wanted them to be close to each other.

Sometimes he said he was afraid he would lose his mind, like his mother. He feared that he would die like his mother.

On July 29, 1964, Charles Wise, still the arbiter of the military panel over-seeing Mac Wallace's security clearance, produced another memorandum. Titled "WALLACE, Malcolm Everett," it was directed to a Mr. Lewis, Chairman of Screening Panel Board #1. "I see no basis for alleging sexual perversion," Wise wrote. "Any funny business seems to have been within the marriage rela-tionship." The Navy counsel recommended that the "charge involving the daughter" be deleted "as only proof is the wife or hearsay deriving from her." Wise added that "in the light of her background, I do not think DOD (the Department of Defense) could seriously offer her as a witness."

Wise had interviewed fourteen people. Only five believed that Mac Wallace's "general reputation and character defects would preclude his access authoriza-tion." On the matter of Mac Wallace's killing John Douglas Kinser, Wise took into account Andre's admission to Onis Doherty that "she had had sexual rela-tions with Kinser." Like many of Mac Wallace's Texas friends, Wise believed that killing in a crime of passion was mitigating, the paramour defense.

That Mac Wallace's credit report disclosed "unsatisfactory credit ratings with three unpaid accounts" confirms his son's observation that Mac was always short of money. If he was Lyndon Johnson's hit man—which he would be charged after his death with having been—he was committing those murders free of charge. In Wise's final "Statement of Reasons," dated September 18, 1964, the false claims that he was "a sex pervert" with "commu-nist or subversive inclinations" were dropped at last.

Deferring to the Office of Naval Intelligence, choosing to avoid further conflict with the Navy and not for reasons of substance, the Screening Board recommended "suspension of existing access authorization." They ruled that Mac Wallace "may retain access authorization at a level no higher than CONFIDENTIAL, pending final action." Once he lost his SECRET security clearance, Mac Wallace was demoted at Ling Electronics. The work he was authorized to oversee was curtailed and he became "Director of Purchasing and Subcontracts," then "Manager of the Contracts Department, including Contracts Administration, Master Scheduling, and Cost Estimating."

Joe Bloomberg worked under Mac Wallace in the contracts department. Bloomberg remembered that Ling had put up with Mac's problem with alcohol for a long time. With a clearance only at the level of CONFIDENTIAL, he was not permitted to read some of the paperwork that had formerly been part of his job. Bloomberg had to do it for him. Without his SECRET clearance, he could no longer travel to observe the particle beam accelerator at Stanford. "I always liked him," Bloomberg said. "Everyone did. He was very intelligent and performed his job quite well." At work, Mac never talked about his personal life, or about politics.

In 1965, Nora Ann returned to California. When she telephoned, Mac told her he had given up smoking and had grown quite fat. The mood was dark and "bore no resemblance to the joyous reunion" of two years earlier. There was no hope that they would find their way back to each other. Elaine, now two years old, "seemed to hover over us," Nora Ann remembered, both at Fisherman's Wharf and in the fog of their parting at midnight on the steps of her bus. She was on her way to visit their teacher, Clarence Ayres. Mac's gentle kiss on the steps was a chaste final farewell.

During the second half of the 1960s, Mac lived with Michael, with Virginia an intermittent presence. He urged Michael to pursue his dreams; he encouraged self-reliance. Once the two got into an argument and Michael went off to live in a friend's garage. His father sought him out. "Whatever works and is necessary for you to come home, I'll do," Mac said. Michael returned home. His father was like a rock, always there.

One day Michael got into a fight and appeared worse for the wear. "What did the other fellow look like?" Mac said. The Wallaces were like that: taciturn, not emotional. When Michael was sixteen or seventeen, he took a job as a busboy at the local Denny's. Wielding a butcher knife, a Mexican cook opened his fly and said, "Get down and take care of it!"

When Michael reported the incident to his father, Mac told him he had done the right thing in making a quick getaway. "Maybe you should quit working there," Mac said. This was what Michael had already done. Mac was upset, but he urged his son not to do anything in retaliation. Violence was not his first option.

In March 1966, Virginia and Mac Wallace were reunited. He had put her through Fullerton State College as she earned her teaching credentials, only for her to have left him again. Now they were back together. He was sympathetic as she confided the struggles of her first year teaching.

For sixteen-year-old Meredithe, life with Andre and her stepfather, Del Akin, came without frills. Akin had begun to drink heavily and they were now living in Colorado at a motel called the Smuggler's Inn. Andre and Del Akin had lost their house, and their belongings were stored in the parking lot of the motel. When Mac invited her to Dallas to spend Christmas 1966 with the Wallaces, Meredithe accepted. She would see her brother, whom she called her "savior," and her sister, Elaine. She spent that Christmas with her grandfather and her cousins. The Wallaces had known about the incest, but there were no overtones now.

When Mac urged Meredithe to live with them in California, she agreed. Virginia did all the chores. No one pitched in to help.

CHAPTER 13

Lyndon Johnson as President, Part I

*What are we to do? Tell our children that this
is the way to success? Are we to teach our
children that rough and ruthless politics as
practiced by Lyndon is a virtue—and the way
to become President of the United States?*
—HOLLAND MCCOMBS TO WILLIAM
LAMBERT, *LIFE* MAGAZINE, UNPUBLISHED

We've never had a President just like this one.
—HOLLAND MCCOMBS IN CONVERSATION
WITH ONE OF HIS SOURCES (UNNAMED)

When Lyndon Johnson succeeded to the presidency, Billie Sol Estes had been convicted, but had not yet gone off to serve his time. It would be five years before Bobby Baker went to prison. Johnson was uneasy. Among his first acts as President was to request of J. Edgar Hoover that he send over to the White House "tapes and memoranda documenting some of Johnson's own questionable activities—sexual and financial." These were duly "lifted from the raw files of the FBI and sent over to the White House," never to be seen again.

At four A.M. on November 23, fourteen hours after the death of President Kennedy, Lyndon Johnson consulted with his loyalists, Jack Valenti, Bill Moyers, and Cliff Carter. He already had conceived in detail the programs that would come to be known as the "Great Society," as if, one might speculate, he had foreknowledge of the assassination. Certainly he was well prepared for this moment.

There remains only the thinnest circumstantial evidence pointing to Lyndon Johnson's foreknowledge of the Kennedy assassination. It comes in the form of a single source, Johnson's disgruntled mistress, Madeleine Brown.

A petite redhead with a mop of curly hair, and a round baby face, Brown bore Lyndon Johnson a son named Steven Mark Brown in 1950. Johnson never acknowledged this child, who apparently resembled him. There is an extant letter from Johnson lawyer Jerome T. Ragsdale assuring Madeleine Brown that Johnson would take care of her and the child financially.

For years, Brown would claim that on the evening before the assassination of President Kennedy she and Johnson were both guests at a party at a house belonging to Clint Murchison Sr. Emerging from behind the closed doors of a meeting with his confreres, Johnson supposedly reported to Brown that "after tomorrow those Kennedys, they will never embarrass me again. That's no threat. It's a promise." But Brown's tale has been undermined by the changing guest list at that party; at one point she named Mac Wallace as a guest, at another, George Rufus Brown of Brown & Root. Later, these figures disappeared from her accounts of the party.

According to Jack Valenti, during the meeting early on November 23 Johnson said, "I'm going to get Kennedy's tax cut out of the Senate Finance Committee . . . I'm going to pass Kennedy's civil rights bill . . . without changing a single comma or word." He would initiate legislation allowing black people in the South access to the vote, adding, "and I aim to pass Harry Truman's medical insurance bill that got nowhere before." On that first morning of his presidency, there was no mention of Vietnam.

Johnson's first official meeting as President was with Director of Central Intelligence John McCone. This fifteen-minute meeting in the oval office that still contained John F. Kennedy's possessions took place later on November 23 and was initiated by McCone. Ostensibly McCone was giving Johnson an intelligence briefing, to "reassure" the new President "that he and the Agency stood ready to support him in every way." Johnson told McCone that he "looked to CIA for firm recommendations" with respect to Cuba. McCone and Johnson agreed that this would mean a "hardening up of President Kennedy's November 18 statement." This was a reference to a speech Kennedy had given in Miami Beach before the Inter-American Press Association, where he talked about the Alliance for Progress and spoke of a "hemisphere of nations living in peace."

McCone now promised to brief Johnson personally every morning for the next several days. Johnson requested that the director "bring any urgent matters to my attention at any time, day or night." (That John F. Kennedy did not trust Lyndon Johnson is reflected in the revelation that Kennedy had instructed CIA "under no circumstances" to share the President's daily briefing statements, then called the President's "intelligence checklist," with Vice President Johnson.)

The assassination of his predecessor was never far from Lyndon Johnson's thoughts. His confidant was J. Edgar Hoover. There is an extraordinary fourteen-minute gap in the transcription of a telephone conversation held on November 23, the same day he met with McCone, between Johnson and Hoover. The subject was accused assassin Lee Harvey Oswald and the ambiguities of a visit Oswald had made to Mexico City in September.

On Sunday morning, November 24, Johnson telephoned the operating room at Parkland Hospital in Dallas where Lee Harvey Oswald lay dying, or dead, to request that the surgeon obtain a deathbed confession. When the *Journal of the American Medical Association* accused Dr. Charles A. Crenshaw of inventing the story, Crenshaw sued and won libel damages. The telephone operator who put through the call confirmed that it had been Lyndon Johnson on the line. Johnson had also stationed an armed officer in the trauma room.

From the moment Lyndon Johnson assumed office, he had his eye on the 1964 general election, less than a year away. The Estes scandal had provoked opposition in Texas; the Bobby Baker hearings had assumed national significance, and had been featured in *Time* and *LIFE* magazines. Johnson knew that he was not a popular figure, and that it was unlikely that he would have been elected to the presidency in normal times.

Nothing if not shrewd, a gifted thespian, Johnson then discovered the formula he required. To persuade the Kennedy cabinet and loyalists to stay on for the remainder of the year, until the 1964 election, he promised that he would see to it that President Kennedy's policies became law. Knowing perception counted for more than reality in politics, Lyndon Johnson wrapped himself in two mantles: He would be the reincarnation of his old mentor Franklin Delano Roosevelt, creating "Great Society" programs to rival those of the New Deal. "If you looked at my record, you would know that I am a Roosevelt New Dealer," he said without basis. And he would devote himself to perpetuating the legacy of John F. Kennedy.

In the aftermath of the assassination no one was about to challenge him, even as foreign leaders had already had their doubts. During his vice presidency, Johnson had gone to dinner in London with British prime minister Harold Macmillan. "A Texan, an acute and ruthless 'politician,' but not (I would judge) a man of any intellectual power," Macmillan wrote in his diary for November 28, 1960, about Lyndon Johnson.

And so Johnson played the role of the humble servant, whose role was to honor and uphold the principles of his predecessor. That he had few principles or convictions of his own—he had long opposed the rights of labor, and had voted against civil rights—assisted him in this Herculean effort. His modus operandi had always been to be all things to all people.

The strategy worked. Even Kennedy's counsel, friend, and confidant Ted Sorensen, normally clear-thinking, shrewd, and uncmotional, fell for the claim that his continued service was needed to help Johnson enact John F. Kennedy's policies. "I wanted to help commit LBJ to carrying on Kennedy's program for 1964, and Kennedy's legacy for the ages," Sorensen would acknowledge later, regretting that he had stayed on with Johnson as long as he did. He would stay on long enough to work on Johnson's first State of the Union speech.

Johnson, whose views on unions were shaped by Herman Brown, a fierce proponent of the open shop, told labor leaders like George Meany, President of the American Federation of Labor and Congress of Industrial Organizations (AFL-CIO), that he needed their help. Flattered, they succumbed to his blandishments. He told Martin Luther King Jr., who invoked John F. Kennedy's "great, progressive policies," that he was "gonna support them all, and you can count on that." And all the while Johnson exuded self-deprecation, depicting himself as inferior to John F. Kennedy.

"I need you more than President Kennedy needed you," he would say, describing himself as lacking "the education, culture and understanding that President Kennedy had." He summoned Ambassador to the United Nations Adlai Stevenson to Washington, where, once more wrapped in a mantle of humility, he oozed unctuous flattery. "By all rights, you, Adlai, should be sitting here," Johnson said. "But the office fell to me. I need your support and advice."

Boldly, calmly, and with breathtaking poise, on November 27 in his first public speech as President, Johnson addressed a joint session of Congress and announced that he would be pursuing a Civil Rights bill.

In his draft of Johnson's speech, Sorensen had written the line, "I who cannot fill his shoes must occupy his desk." Johnson excised it. Otherwise, Johnson connected his Civil Rights legislation to Kennedy, calling it a bill "for which he [Kennedy] fought so long." He depicted the transition from Kennedy's presidency to his own as an unbroken chain. "Let us continue," Johnson intoned, invoking Kennedy's "let us begin." Shrewdly, he placed the tax cut first on his agenda.

He bemoaned "poverty and disease and illiteracy," and "the problem of inequality." To oppose him would be "a posthumous repudiation of John F. Kennedy." Shivering in the implications of the assassination, the political classes embraced him gratefully. Johnson had determined that to be elected in his own right, he had to shed his identity as the Southern conservative that he was. "We could have beaten Kennedy on civil rights," Senator Richard Russell of Georgia, a Johnson mentor, remarked, "but we can't [beat] Lyndon."

Taking credit (with President Kennedy) for the Civil Rights Act of 1964, as if social change were the province of politicians, Johnson neglected to award credit where it should most properly have been placed: on the suffering and sacrifices of the civil rights movement that alone made passing such a bill mandatory were civil order to be maintained. But Johnson was not about to offer credit to such people as Malcolm X; Robert (Bob) Moses, the brilliant, selfless leader of the Student Nonviolent Coordinating Committee (SNCC); and others.

Author Clay Risen has noted that credit for the passage of the Civil Rights Act belongs in equal measure to Hubert Humphrey and other liberal senators whose efforts dislodged the Civil Rights Act from committee. Humphrey later remarked of Johnson's actual participation in the crafting and passage of the civil rights act, "We did give him regular reports on the progress of civil rights over at the Tuesday morning breakfasts. But the President was not on the spot. He was not enlisted in the battle particularly."

Johnson's biographers have viewed his commitment to civil rights as genuine. At one point early on, his rhetoric may have seemed authentic as he explained why he would pursue a civil rights bill: "so that we can say to the Mexican in California, or the Negro in Mississippi or the Oriental on the West Coast or the Johnsons in Johnson City that we are going to treat you all equally and fairly." Johnson's actual history belies this rhetoric.

Privately, Johnson questioned the viability of "Great Society" programs like the Job Corps. Doubtful that it would succeed in getting young people jobs, Johnson confided to a friend that it might at least ready them for another government institution, the U.S. Army. "Scrub 'em up, get some tapeworms out of their bellies and get 'em where they can get up at six o'clock in the morning, work all day," he said in August 1964. At the time the Army was turning away draftees for lack of physical fitness. "We think we can clean 'em up this way and shoot 'em on in there," Johnson said. "And maybe—maybe even teach 'em to be a truck driver, or, something."

Johnson's racism is well documented. As a boy he delighted in throwing rocks to drive black children out of the local swimming hole. Robert Caro, who insists upon Johnson's sincerity with respect to the Civil Rights Act, himself tells the story of how, when he visited Texas at the time he was serving as a congressman, Johnson liked to put a snake, sometimes a rattlesnake, into the trunk of his car, then drive to a gas station where he would ask the black attendant to examine his spare tire. "You should have seen that big buck jump!" Johnson said on one such occasion. At a meeting about civil rights at the White House, attended by Seymour Trammel and Alabama governor George Wallace, along with Nicholas Katzenbach, Bill Moyers, and Burke Marshall, Johnson burst out with these words: "I am G-damned tired of hearing 'bout those G-damned niggers on the G-damned news." As an elected official he had voted against repealing the poll tax, against President Truman's bill against lynching, and against Medicare.

Among those who came to doubt him was Martin Luther King Jr. By 1967, Dr. King had twice canceled private meetings Johnson had set up with him. When asked what the civil rights movement had ultimately done for blacks, King pointed not to Johnson's legislation, but to "positive self-identity."

Johnson invited King to Congress when the Voting Rights Act was being introduced in 1965. King went instead to Selma. Later Dr. King would say on the television news program *Face the Nation* that "the Great Society with its very noble programs, in a sense has been shot down on the battlefields of Vietnam."

Johnson had his eye on how he would be remembered and the "Great Society" and his subsequent "War on Poverty" were his first shots across the bow of history. He admitted as much to biographer Doris Kearns Goodwin: "John Kennedy had died. But his 'cause' was not really clear. That was my job. I had to take the dead man's program and turn it into a martyr's cause."

Johnson even visited Ted Kennedy, recovering from a plane crash in a hospital, to garner his support for the Voting Rights Act. The presidential recordings reveal a Ted Kennedy who all but chokes on the words "Mr. President" when speaking to LBJ. Still, Senator Kennedy could not deny Johnson his support. In reality, although Johnson took the credit, the Voting Rights Act was equally the work of unsung heroes like civil rights activist and President of the Potomac Institute Against Racial Discrimination Harold

Fleming and Stephen R. Currier (David Bruce's son-in-law) and the Taconic Foundation.

On one policy, Lyndon Johnson immediately rejected John F. Kennedy's thinking entirely. Johnson issued National Security Memorandum (NSM) 273 on November 26, 1963, opening the door to the decade-long war to come, and overriding NSM 263 issued by President Kennedy and announcing the beginning of the removal of American forces from Vietnam. While insisting with lip service that he was honoring President Kennedy's goal of withdrawing a thousand men by the end of 1963, Johnson simultaneously revealed his plan to increase military operations against North Vietnam. NSM 273 promised that the war, a war "against communism," would be won; the United States was committed to assisting the people of South Vietnam. There was no mention of troops coming home.

Guided by General Douglas MacArthur, who told him that the United States could not win a land war in Asia, and that it would be a "mistake," John Kennedy had withstood unrelenting pressure from his cabinet to pursue that war. NSM 273 exposes the hypocrisy of Johnson's rhetoric about how he was continuing the programs of President Kennedy and bringing them to fruition.

In the 1964 general election, Lyndon Johnson cashed in on the credibility he had gained by casting himself as the legatee of John F. Kennedy. He had persuaded the entire Kennedy cabinet to serve him, and had signed a civil rights bill. His persona was now that of the reasonable man, the opposite of his opponent, the militaristic Air Force veteran Senator Barry Goldwater, who had voted against the Civil Rights Act.

Seizing upon Goldwater's aphorism borrowed from Cicero that he recited in his nomination acceptance speech, "extremism in the defense of liberty is no vice, moderation in the pursuit of justice is no virtue," Johnson portrayed Goldwater as an extremist, the implication being that Goldwater was certain to lead the country into an endless quagmire of war. The strategy worked. Johnson won 61.1 percent of the popular vote. Later Goldwater called him a "hypocrite," a man who "used every dirty trick in the bag."

Indeed, Lyndon Johnson's escalation of the war in Vietnam had been long planned. At a surreal cabinet meeting on November 24, 1963, two days after the assassination, Johnson assembled his brain trust: McGeorge Bundy, the national security adviser, to be replaced in 1966 by W. W. (Walt) Rostow, a true extremist; Secretary of State Dean Rusk; Secretary of Defense Robert McNamara; and Undersecretary of State George Ball, a fish out of water in this company with his (mildly) dissident views about the American involvement in Vietnam. Present as well were John McCone, the director of Central Intelligence, and Henry Cabot Lodge Jr., ambassador to South Vietnam.

"We are on the road to victory," Lodge said. McCone dissented, urging "a program that would involve escalation significantly beyond anything considered by McNamara and Johnson." The war in Vietnam would be, equally, CIA's war, for those who noticed.

He would "win the war," Johnson promised; and he "didn't want as much effort placed on so-called social reforms." Firmly, he said "we have to see that our objectives are accomplished." He wanted "no more divisions of opinion." We "cannot retreat," Johnson, said, declaring that we "are closer to an end than most people realize." Dean Rusk, a "hawk" through and through on the subject of Vietnam, and a fanatical cold warrior, replied with what Drew Pearson later called "a flamboyant American Legion–type speech." (About Lyndon Johnson, Pearson wrote in his diary for November 27, 1963, "a lot of people thought he never had the qualities to be President.")

Later, as he escalated the war in 1965 and thereafter, Johnson told McNamara, "I want you to go out and kill a bunch of people." No one in the inner circles should have been surprised. On Christmas Eve 1963, a month after the assassination, Johnson promised the military that he would pursue a war in Vietnam vigorously. So he reassured the Joint Chiefs of Staff: "Just let me get elected," Johnson said, famously, "and then you can have your war." It seems apparent that Lyndon Johnson knew exactly what was expected of him, which was, as historian Stanley Karnow wrote, the "deeper military plunge."

In January 1964, as Johnson settled into office, D. H. Byrd, the defense contractor, who owned the Texas School Book Depository on the day of the Kennedy assassination, was awarded a contract to build a jet bomber from Johnson's 1965 budget before the budget was approved by Congress. February saw Ling-TEMCO-Vought being awarded a contract to build an A-7 Corsair II, a plane that would see service in Vietnam. Mac Wallace, now in California, was still working for Byrd: Ling Electronics, which employed Mac, was a subsidiary of TEMCO.

Barry Goldwater's charge of hypocrisy against Johnson is illuminated by a telephone conversation between Johnson and Senator Russell on May 24, 1964.

"What do you think about this Vietnam thing?" Johnson asks.

"It's the damned worst mess I ever saw," Russell says.

"That's the way I've been feeling for six months," Johnson says.

Russell suggests pulling out. Johnson invokes a military man he knows who has "six kids." Just thinking of this man being sent to Vietnam, Johnson says, "makes the chills run down my back." By the end of the conversation, Russell, an honest man, says, "I see no terminal date."

The human costs of the Vietnam War cannot be laid entirely at Lyndon Johnson's door. The United States was entrenched in Vietnam even before the French defeat at Dien Bien Phu in 1954. As soon as he arrived in the United States in 1951, posted as liaison to CIA, Philippe Thyraud de Vosjoli, an officer of the French clandestine services (Service de Documentation Extérieure et de Contre-Espionnage, SDECE) brokered the U.S. funding of the French war in Indochina. President Kennedy, seduced by the James Bondish lure of Special Forces, had sent sixteen thousand plus "advisers" to Vietnam. Lyndon Johnson fulfilled a deadly mandate not entirely of his own devising.

In October 1964, Walter Jenkins was arrested in the basement of a YMCA for giving oral sex to a sixty-year-old divorced Army veteran. At once Johnson ordered his resignation. It was the second time that Jenkins had been arrested at this YMCA, the first having been in 1959.

In 1965, Johnson swung into a massive acceleration of the war. "We had to go ahead with it," he later claimed to Drew Pearson. At the head of the line to profit was Brown & Root, now a Halliburton subsidiary. Herman Brown had died, but George still served the company. Bell Helicopter, General Dynamics, Bechtel, and others followed close behind on the gravy train.

To justify the war, Johnson enlisted the clichés of cold war propaganda. The Vietnamese were "spurred by Communist China," he claimed, although China was Vietnam's hereditary enemy. "We must halt the extension of the Asiatic dominion of Communism." Johnson was well aware that this war was a lost cause. "I don't believe they're ever gonna quit," he said in a private conversation. "We think they're winning and if we think they're winning, you can imagine what *they* think." Presidential adviser Clark Clifford warned Johnson at a Camp David meeting on July 25, 1965. "I hate this war," Clifford said. "I do not believe we can win . . . we could lose more than fifty thousand men in Vietnam." Johnson ignored him and proceeded without restraint.

In 1965, Johnson also dispatched troops to Santo Domingo under the pretext that there was a "Communist pattern in the hemisphere" that could be "traced back" to Vietnam. Pretexts were now his stock in trade. The most notorious was the Gulf of Tonkin episode, in particular the second incident of August 4, 1964, when the United States falsely accused the North Vietnamese of firing in international waters on the USS *Maddox* as a pretext for retaliatory bombing. It was a false-flag operation, in which the United States fired on its own ship.

Later, on September 18, Johnson admitted to McNamara, "When we got through with all the firing, we concluded maybe they hadn't fired at all." His national security adviser Walt Rostow had already confessed, on August 6, at a State Department luncheon, that the supposed attack on August 4 probably had not taken place. In a 2003 documentary, *The Fog of War: Eleven Lessons from the Life of Robert S. McNamara,* McNamara finally admits that the attack of the second incident never happened.

The lie served its purpose, however. On August 7, 1964, Johnson extracted a joint resolution from Congress, the "Gulf of Tonkin Resolution," allowing him to "take all necessary steps" to support South Vietnam, a political entity that had specious political legitimacy to begin with. Johnson was to use this "resolution," built as it was on a lie, to justify his further escalations in Vietnam.

The false-flag operation in the Gulf of Tonkin bore a remarkable resemblance to a scheme suggested by General Lyman Lemnitzer during his term as chairman of the Joint Chiefs of Staff in 1960–62 in his "Operation Northwoods" list of paramilitary acts designed to remove Fidel Castro from power in Cuba. Another scheme involved airplanes crashing into a building that bore some resemblance to the attack on the World Trade Center on September 11, 2001.

Operation Northwoods had been rejected by President Kennedy after it was presented to the Joint Chiefs. Its schemes included the United States firing on its own people and blaming a "foreign power." Apparently "Northwoods" had remained on Robert McNamara's desk to be enacted, not against Cuba, but Vietnam.

Johnson embraced being President, entertaining at his Texas ranch foreign dignitaries, like the German chancellor, the press, and politicians. His character may be illuminated by his telephone call in 1966 to the brother of a man he had destroyed, but who was now dead. From Robert J. Kleberg Jr., Johnson sought advice on stocking the LBJ Ranch with exotic wildlife to amuse visiting "drugstore cowboys" from Congress.

A worldly man, Kleberg laughed and offered to send Johnson a herd of Nilgai antelopes. They were "perfectly delicious eating," although "hard to catch." Next came a needle. "Nobody will know what the hell they are," Kleberg said, indulging in a private joke at the expense of this man who at best he did not take seriously, at worst despised. Unlike Edward Kennedy, Kleberg not only choked on the locution "Mr. President" when talking to Lyndon Johnson, but never used it.

"They're native to Indo-China and Cambodia," Kleberg said.

Johnson laughed nervously, sensing that the joke was on him. By 1966, when this conversation took place, every mention of Vietnam was fraught with irony. Nilgai antelope were native not to Vietnam, but to India and East Pakistan. Kleberg was no opponent of the Vietnam War, of course. "I agree with everything you're doing up to a point," he said, "and internationally one hundred percent."

The Kennedy assassination continued to bedevil Johnson throughout his presidency. Johnson's preoccupation with the assassination is revealed in a February 10, 1966, document from the files of Johnson secretary Mildred Stegall. Johnson ordered that the Justice Department investigate lawyer and assassination researcher Bernard Fensterwald. Fensterwald had worked for Senator Estes Kefauver, for the State Department, and as chief counsel for Senator Edward V. Long of Missouri, who chaired the Senate Judiciary Committee. Fensterwald's interest in the assassination troubled the President. The ensuing report revealed a minor infraction that occurred when Fensterwald was in the U.S. Navy. Otherwise his record was impeccable.

During his presidency, Lyndon Johnson still faced some media scrutiny for his habitual selling of government contracts for his own profit. The *Chicago Tribune* reported in 1966 that Charles Luckman, a contributor to Johnson's fund-raising President's Club, "had been granted an unusual favor," a contract to build a veterans' administration building in California. The *Tribune* neglected to mention that Johnson's relationship with Luckman dated back to the 1950s. This deal was but one more quid pro quo between the two men. As in all media attempts to penetrate Johnson's private interests, the matter soon disappeared from public attention.

Johnson continued in the pursuit of his financial interests, using as his partner and front man Judge A. W. Moursund of Johnson City. In the press, Moursund was described as "an attorney who has represented Johnson interests and who has been associated with the President in ranching ventures." By 1964, Johnson "had acquired or is acquiring or is attempting to acquire some fifty thousand acres around Santa Rosa and Clovis, New Mexico," Holland McCombs discovered.

There was a method to Johnson's acquiring ranch properties not only in New Mexico, but in old Mexico as well. In the waning days of his vice presidency, Johnson had learned from a boyhood friend from Johnson City, Dick Richardson, a former U.S. Army officer, about a treasure of gold bars, and pure gold, some dating from the Spanish colonial period and others of more recent vintage. The trove was said to be hidden in caves at Victorio Peak, a small mountain in the Hembrillo Basin on leased government land in the White Sands Proving Ground in New Mexico, a missile testing base. The person who had discovered the treasure originally was one Milton Ernest "Doc" Noss, who was later murdered by a man named Charlie Ryan of Alice, Texas, home territory of George Parr. Richardson had learned about the treasure from Doc Noss.

On June 5, 1963, Johnson, along with President Kennedy himself, had visited White Sands ostensibly to view a demonstration of the Nike Hercules, Pershing, Talos, and Zeus missiles, and to examine a proposed landing area for the return of spacecraft. By helicopter, they visited Victorio Peak. Kennedy was interested in gold artifacts found in the caverns. "This belongs to all of us," Johnson said. "This is our treasure and we have control of it all."

Once he was President, Johnson began to extract the gold, ordering Attorney General Robert F. Kennedy to help him organize a military escort to handle the gold that would be taken to his ranch, according to a former U.S. Marine source, Hugh James Huggins; John Clarence, co-author of an extensive study of the story of the Victorio Peak treasure and its fate, identifies as a "B-24 Pilot." All this was illegal. Stored at Victorio Peak were also World War Two contraband, such as two wooden crates of Russian fine china; coins. In the mix were also old helmets, lances, and swords that seem to have come from the era of the conquistadores.

A witness named Lloyd Gorman Tucker, a CIA asset and an LBJ friend, witnessed Johnson himself opening one of the crates. Tucker admitted to carrying a box of the Russian china to her car for Lady Bird Johnson. Tucker was an expert in handling, mining, smelting, and refining gold and had traveled the world in that capacity. He held a "gold license" issued by the Treasury Department, a license arranged by President Johnson. This license allowed Tucker to move gold bullion around legally. Helping to remove the gold was also a group of investors calling themselves Expeditions Unlimited. Among them was Johnson supporter Clint Murchison Jr. Years later, Tucker would report that he had witnessed underground bunkers at the LBJ Ranch in Texas, presumably where gold had been stored.

To facilitate the theft of the gold, Johnson utilized not only New Mexico properties. He purchased a ranch called Las Pampas from former Mexican President Miguel Alemán, whom he entertained at the LBJ Ranch, a property in Mexico that consisted only of an airstrip. Johnson accumulated 110,000 acres of land in Chihuahua, Mexico, all in the service of extracting gold from Victorio Peak. As President and after, Johnson was to remove six million troy ounces of gold bullion from the Noss treasure.

It was in the late fall of 1964, after he was elected to the presidency, that Johnson began to remove gold bars from Victorio Peak. He had the gold flown to Mexico from the United States. As President, Johnson made four secret trips to Chihuahua, charging the Department of Defense for the equipment needed to remove the gold. That gold was resmelted in Chihuahua. Then it traveled to Europe. In Switzerland it reappeared as currency. In the process, Johnson violated several laws, among them that a President was not to leave the country secretly. He ignored Federal Aviation Administration regulations, violating Mexican airspace and more.

Funds for the "War on Poverty" shriveled. By 1967, considerable treasure of the country had been expended in Vietnam. Johnson now endorsed a plan for the assassination of Prince Norodom Sihanouk of Cambodia, who was an outspoken critic of the U.S. war in Vietnam and an influential figure among the "neutral" countries, as they were then called. As author Ralph Schoenman puts it, "the assassination of Prince Sihanouk would have prepared the way for Generals (Cambodian) like Lon Nol to allow U.S. forces to operate in Cambodia and sanction the bombing of the entire Mekong Delta. Marvin and CIA were demanding that the assassination of Sihanouk by Marvin would be tied to U.S. Special Forces operations on the ground." The CIA case officer was John McCarthy and the operation to murder Sihanouk was named "Project Cherry." The project to assassinate Sihanouk was not a Special Forces mission. McCarthy, later a whistleblower, was court-martialed in January 1968.

A CIA officer relayed the assignment to murder Sihanouk to Special Forces leader Dan Marvin. "This mission is from the 'highest authority,'" CIA told Marvin.

"Did he think I was stupid?" Marvin wondered. "Who else but President Johnson, our highest authority for sure, could order the assassination of

Sihanouk?" Johnson refused to meet Marvin's condition, which was to block the use of Cambodian sanctuaries by river that were being used by the National Liberation Front of South Vietnam. American forces would have been required to meet that condition and the U.S. role in the secret bombing of Cambodia, as well as in the assassination of Prince Sihanouk, would have been exposed.

Documents released in 2000 reveal that the Air Force began bombing the rural regions of Cambodia along its South Vietnam border in 1965; it is at LBJ's door that the decimation of Cambodia began in full, an operation that met its final moment in the incursion of the Khmer Rouge. To maintain the fiction that the United States was not making war on Cambodia, the plan to murder Prince Sihanouk was abandoned. It isn't only the devastation of Vietnam that is Lyndon Johnson's legacy, but the destruction of Cambodia for which he should be blamed.

In the second half of the 1960s, there was widespread public outrage against the war in Vietnam. Vietnamese monks burned themselves in images shown on national television along with crying Vietnamese children, and American soldiers shooting captured Vietnamese, who did not look like combatants but peasants tending to their rice fields. Johnson and his family could not enter a public building by the front door without encountering demonstrators, some-times a handful, sometimes hundreds, holding up signs and chanting, "Hey, Hey, LBJ, How Many Kids Did You Kill Today?"

The 1968 re-election campaign loomed. Johnson now viewed his younger brother, Sam Houston Johnson, with alarm as a possible embarrassment and took steps to ensure that Sam Houston be kept far from public scrutiny. For the year 1967 Sam Houston Johnson was confined to the Kimbrough Army Hospital at Fort Meade, Maryland, "stashed" in this army hospital, as Army doctor Samuel D. Axelrad, who was stationed there as part of his war service, puts it.

Sam Houston Johnson was not suffering from any illness. Yet he lived as a patient at the hospital. He descended from his room for meals at the hospital cafeteria and returned immediately to his isolation afterward. He spoke to no one and no one spoke to him. Sam Houston Johnson had been arrested several times for driving under the influence and his brother considered it prudent to keep him out of sight. To a stranger on an airplane in 1975, Sam Houston called his brother "the meanest man I ever knew."

As the casualties in Indochina mounted, with no end in sight, Johnson was urged to seek peace. He replied that he "couldn't possibly live with himself or the Congress if he stopped bombing North Vietnam." He told Drew Pearson that "if he could get out of the war in Vietnam, 70 percent of the criticism would disappear." Then he added: "Whenever you bomb you have civilian casualties. When the military first gave me their bombing recommendations, they said we would probably kill about one hundred civilians with each raid. I said multiply that by five, and it will probably be more accurate. But we had to go ahead with it."

Fully supporting the continuation of the war was Johnson's national security adviser, Walt Rostow, whom State Department security officer Otto Otepka had sought to deny the security clearance required for him to enter government service when the Kennedys put forth his name in late 1960. A conservative, relying on his instincts, Otepka felt there was something not quite right about Rostow. His loyalty to the United States was questionable.

The wiliest of politicians, having brokered the unforgivable, the killing of at least two million Vietnamese and the decimation of a country that had never threatened U.S. security, Johnson would have a reply to those appalled by the Vietnam War at the ready, an argument for a viable legacy. He told Drew Pearson in a formal interview on January 16, 1967, that he had put "one million students through college through loans, scholarships and jobs in college." He had got "two million nine hundred thousand more people jobs." He had put "nine million people under the minimum wage law." He had placed "three and a half million people under Medicare and [had given] seven million kids an elementary education." Plus, he had put "seven hundred eighty thousand people through job training courses. Under Kennedy there had been only forty thousand trained and none under Eisenhower," he claimed.

Waiting outside the room where Johnson and Pearson talked was Walt Rostow. "I can think of no one I would rather keep waiting more," Pearson added in his diary. This was six months before the attack on the USS *Liberty*.

CHAPTER 14

Lyndon Johnson and the USS *Liberty*: Lyndon Johnson as President, Part II

"I don't give a damn if the ship sinks."
—PRESIDENT LYNDON B. JOHNSON

For one particular violation of his oath of office committed by Lyndon Johnson, history can discover no justification, no ameliorating circumstances. It might be argued that it was not the Civil Rights Act that defined Johnson's presidency but, rather, his action in response to the attack on the USS *Liberty*. That Johnson's role in these events was covered up so assiduously by Johnson himself, and every subsequent President and Congress, alone suggests its significance.

The incident derives, like the false-flag attack in the Gulf of Tonkin three years earlier, from Lyman Lemnitzer's "Operation Northwoods." As Lyndon Johnson's Secretary of Defense, Robert McNamara retained custody of this document. "A 'Remember the Maine' accident could be arranged in various forms," Lemnitzer suggested in the document. "We could blow up a U.S. ship in Guantanamo Bay and blame Cuba." The foreign power enlisted in this devilish adventure, which was carried out on June 8, 1967, would turn out not to be Cuba, but someone else.

The USS *Liberty* was a Navy surveillance (spy) ship reporting to the Naval Security Group, and ultimately to the National Security Agency (NSA). In the research spaces several levels below deck, sailors engaged in "technical research." Forty-five antennae stretched across the deck listening to the communications of countries unfriendly to the United States, in particular the Soviet Union and the United Arab Republic (Egypt and Syria). Were they to intercept messages from friendly nations, like the United Kingdom or Israel, the communications technicians were instructed, according to chief intelligence officer Lieutenant Commander David Edwin Lewis, they should not be translated. There was no Hebrew translator aboard, no one who spoke fluent Hebrew.

A parabola-shaped satellite dish bounced intercepted messages off the moon and back. It was all about signals intelligence, Morse code, and teletype. There were four Browning .50 caliber machine guns on deck, and light arms in a locker, but the USS *Liberty* had no means of defending itself were it to be attacked.

On May 24, 1967, having trolled along the coast of West Africa, *Liberty* was anchored at Abidjan, the largest city in the Ivory Coast. Early that morning it was summoned with all deliberate speed to Rota, Spain. At the dawn of the Six-Day War, six linguists were hurried on board. Three worked for the NSA and were Arabists. Three were U.S. Marines. One of these, Bryce Lockwood, was a Russian linguist. The other two Marines spoke Arabic.

Liberty was dispatched to the eastern Mediterranean, to a position twelve and a half miles off the coast of Egypt. There it would troll in international waters with no particular interest in Israel's invasion of Egypt, Jordan, and Syria during the week of June 5. The Johnson White House stated publicly that the United States was not a participant in any way in the Six-Day War. (Of the Six-Day War, Dr. King noted drily: "It has given Johnson the little respite he wanted from Vietnam.")

Later it would leak out that unmarked American reconnaissance planes, bearing no insignia as to their nation of origin, had participated in the lead-up to the war on the side of Israel. These planes had taken off from the U.S. base at Torrejón de Ardoz, Spain, which at that time accommodated the largest bomber aircraft in the Strategic Air Command. The pilots wore nondescript uniforms. Their task was to supply high-quality surveillance photographs of the Egyptian airfields. The destruction of the Egyptian air force on the first day of the war would not have been possible without the participation of these U.S. F-4 planes.

When the photographs were later published in *LIFE* magazine, they were falsely identified as having been taken by Israel—which at the time lacked the capacity to create such sophisticated aerial photographs. The Egyptian airfields had been bombed courtesy of the United States.

With the agreement of Captain William McGonagle, and wary of the turbulent zones toward which they were sailing, Lieutenant Commander Lewis requested that the Sixth Fleet, five hundred miles away, provide *Liberty* with an escort in the form of a Destroyer. The Sixth Fleet commander, Rear Admiral William Inman Martin, denied the request.

A later argument stated that the presence of a Destroyer by its side would have exposed *Liberty*, whose mission was secret, but where they were going and who they were was common knowledge in Rota. Sailing from Spain, *Liberty* was tracked by Soviet ships that followed her most of the way. Admiral Martin's public excuse in turning down the request for an escort was that *Liberty* was an unarmed, well-marked noncombatant sailing in international waters and flying the flag of the United States of America. She didn't require an escort.

Liberty sailed along, with 294 sailors on board, a solitary American presence in the area, into which, however, the Soviet Union had moved twenty warships. Later it was claimed that NSA had sent a message that *Liberty* be moved a further one hundred miles away, only for a series of mishaps to result in the message failing to arrive. In reality, the arrival of the message would have made no difference to what followed.

From the yardarm of *Liberty* an American flag unfurled in the soft Mediterranean breeze. Emblazoned on its gray hull were the letters GTR5, which marked its unique identity. In *Jane's Fighting Ships*, a compendium known to all who sailed the seas, *Liberty* was described as an "electronic intelligence ship."

By June 8, the fourth day of the war, Israel had captured the Sinai and East Jerusalem, easily defeating Egypt and Jordan. All that remained for the taking were the fertile lands of the Golan Heights, and any other Syrian targets Israel had in mind.

Beginning at dawn that day, the sailors aboard *Liberty* began to observe in rapid succession, stretching through the morning, at least eight overflights, reconnaissance aircraft examining the ship. Some of these were "flying boxcars." They were French-made Noratlas aircraft and they swooped down so low that their pilots could be observed taking photographs of *Liberty*. Larry Weaver, a boatswain's mate, spotted the Star of David on a reconnaissance plane, as did engineer Jim Ennes.

They flew so low that the sailors could wave to the pilots. "I could see the brightness of his teeth—that's how damn close he was," Weaver recounted later. One of the pilots waved to the sailors and they waved back. They were in the presence of an ally and this increased their sense of security. There are photographs taken that morning of smiling, shirtless men sunbathing on the deck of *Liberty*.

In the early afternoon, as he had done assiduously several times as they made their way to the Eastern Mediterranean from Abidjan, Captain

McGonagle conducted a drill, preparing the sailors for an attack. If he had an inkling of what was to come, he never said. "General Quarters, General Quarters. All hands man your battle station!" was the call at one P.M.

A klaxon punctuated the order. Each man headed for his General Quarters duty station. They had three minutes. Then all hatches were sealed and the watertight integrity of the ship was established. The captain timed how long it would take for everyone to be prepared and in a state of readiness. A brief moment of respite followed.

At one fifty-eight P.M., *Liberty* was attacked by three Mirage III fighter planes firing rockets, cannon, and machine guns. They were as black as American U-2s, or the U.S. planes that had flown from Torrejón. The besieged sailors had no leisure to consider whether there was any connection between the reconnaissance flights of the morning and these attackers. If anyone had the presence of mind to think anything, it was that their attacker was either Egypt or the Soviet Union.

With single-minded intensity, the Mirage fighter planes delivered heat-seeking missiles to the coil of each of the forty-five antennae on deck. Obviously well prepared, they knew exactly how to strike the coil that generated heat at the base of an antenna. With precision, the attacking aircraft rendered every antenna and its transmitter inoperative. The first order of business was a premeditated and systematic effort to eliminate any possibility that *Liberty* call out for help.

The fighter planes then targeted each man visible on deck, hitting him with shrapnel. Scrambling, bleeding, the sailors rushed for cover. Rockets and cannon fire and machine gun fire hit each moving target as sailors were picked off one by one. Those manning the machine guns died instantly. When one of the machine guns began suddenly to fire, this was owing to the heat of the gunfire setting it off. The sailor who had been behind that machine gun had long since been killed.

Soon the deck was awash in blood. Men risked their lives to help the wounded find cover. The ship's one doctor, Richard Kiepfer, was an easy target. Bleeding profusely, Dr. Kiepfer strapped on a life jacket and pulled it as tight as he could so as not to bleed to death. Then he set on a Herculean effort to save lives. With makeshift equipment, he performed blood transfusions. Those who were not themselves bleeding out, donated their blood.

One antenna alone had been "cold" or inoperative. It had been shut down by sailor Terence Halbardier, who was in charge of maintaining this equipment. Ignoring the gunfire, Halbardier dashed over to the cold antenna, dragging a cable from an unused transmitter. Spotting this moving target, a gunner on one of the attacking planes took him down.

Halbardier was hit three times as he attempted to activate the one available antenna. His body now riddled with shrapnel, Halbardier connected the cable to the cold antenna and activated the transmitter. All the while, the firing planes, in the interlude between firing their rockets, jammed all of *Liberty*'s transmission frequencies. They knew exactly how to jam the frequencies because the information had been made available to them. They were, after all, an ally.

A radioman found a moment between the bombardments when a frequency was open. And so Rockstar, which was *Liberty*'s code name, was able to send one distress call to the Sixth Fleet. When the Sixth Fleet, incredulous that some hostile power had launched an attack on this unarmed American ship, demanded *Liberty*'s identifying code, someone managed to look it up.

Because those on *Liberty* did not know, Rockstar did not identify by whom she was being attacked, only that rockets were exploding all around. On the USS *Saratoga*, which received the call, the sound of rockets could be heard in the background.

Quickly, however, the identity of the assailants became known. An eavesdropping EC-121 U.S. Air Force plane with Hebrew linguists on board intercepted the words of one of the attacking pilots. This pilot was perplexed and deeply distressed as he spoke to his handler at ground control. "It's an American ship! It's an American ship!" he shouted. Surely there was some mistake. The pilot was reluctant to fire on the USS *Liberty*. Air Force intelligence also intercepted the reply to the pilot: "You have your orders! Attack it!"

Liberty's flag was reduced to tatters by the rockets and machine gun fire, and so a signalman grabbed the giant holiday ensign, seven by thirteen feet in size, and hoisted it up. (The "holiday flag" was raised on holidays like the Fourth of July or Memorial Day when the ship was in port, never at sea.) There was never a moment during the nearly two-hour attack when *Liberty*'s Stars and Stripes was not visible.

When the attacking Mirage jets ran out of ammunition, they were replaced by two French-made Super Mystère IV fighter-bombers loaded with canisters of napalm. It was the war in Vietnam now turned against American innocents. As soon as the napalm was tossed onto the deck, a profusion of fires erupted. Sailors grabbed hoses and tried to extinguish the fires. Flying low, the attacking planes deliberately shot holes into the hoses. When sailors carried stretchers onto the deck to rescue the wounded, the planes took aim at the stretcher bearers. The attack was systematic and vicious. The mission of the enemy, whatever its identity, was clear. It was to sink *Liberty* and everyone on it. There were to be no survivors.

At about two twenty-seven P.M., three motorized torpedo boats arrived in a V-formation. Certain of victory now, the attackers no longer bothered to conceal their identity. The torpedo boats sported small Stars of David on their sides. Five torpedoes were launched. They aimed for the boiler in the engine room. Had a torpedo struck the boiler, the ensuing explosion would have sunk the ship instantly and the mission to sink *Liberty* would have been accomplished there and then.

The captain's "talker" came over the loudspeakers. "Stand by for torpedo attack, starboard side." There was no defensive action available. All you could do was hunker down under a desk and hope for the best. One torpedo managed to strike *Liberty*, hitting below the waterline on the starboard side of the ship, creating a nearly forty-foot gaping hole into the spaces where the Naval Security Intelligence Group accomplished its work and where only moments before Lewis had ordered classified material in the form of coded key cards to be burned.

The explosion lifted the ship out of the water as the torpedo took out the bulkheads and the entire deck where the cryptologists and communications technicians worked. Water rushed into the spaces. Power was lost. The space was plunged into darkness as water rose around the trapped men.

Twenty-six sailors died instantly. Among the dead were the Arab linguist, Allen Blue, and two of the Marine linguists. In a twisted irony, Blue had worked as a volunteer in Lyndon Johnson's 1964 presidential campaign. Allen Blue was a civilian employed by the NSA when he was rushed to Spain to meet up with *Liberty*. For the first time upon leaving for an assignment, Blue had been "teary," his wife Pat would remember for the rest of her life.

Dozens were wounded and tossed among the shattering bulkheads. Bones were broken, legs hanging useless. Unable to move, men lay waiting to die as water rose around them. The hatches had been locked following the drill, creating watertight integrity, so that should there be an attack, water could not rise to the upper levels of the ship. This meant that the wounded, unable to walk or to move, unable to see their way to the ladder that would enable them to proceed through the hatch once it was opened, were locked in the flooded compartment. Facing certain death, most were unable to free themselves from the debris of the shattered bulkheads. If they managed to wrench themselves loose, they still faced the dilemma of how in the rising water to find the ladder in the darkness.

At the moment that the torpedo hit, Lieutenant Commander Lewis was blinded by exploding paint that sealed his eyes shut. His eardrums were blasted through. His skin was covered by black paint so that it seemed as if his face and body had been wildly tattooed. Jim Ennes describes this moment in his 1979 landmark account of the attack:

> The single exit from this flooded room was a narrow ladder leading through a hatchway to the deck above. The hatch was closed, as was a manhole in the hatch cover. Lewis was thrown to the top of the ladder and found himself waist-deep in swirling water, hanging on the quick-release wheel for the manhole . . . He was simply trying not to be swept away in the water that was around him.
>
> With Lewis were roly-poly Robert "Buddha" Schnell and John Horne. Horne pried Lewis loose from the handle so that the door could be opened. Schnell exited first and joined the group around the hatch. Then he helped Lewis, Horne, and the others through.

Dave Lewis was in a state of shock and would not remember Buddha Schnell pulling him to safety. Schnell had earned the nickname "Buddha" because of his habit after returning to the ship intoxicated following a raucous evening in port of assuming the lotus position and remaining motionless until he sobered up. Now he ascended to the status of hero, as did all of those who struggled to save their comrades, ignoring the danger to themselves.

Marine Staff Sergeant Bryce Lockwood was one of three men in this story with an ancestor who had sailed to the New World on the *Mayflower*. (Another was Dave Lewis.) He had been trained at the Defense Language Institute in Monterey, California, and had been assigned hastily to *Liberty*. It was as if trouble had been expected, as if there had been foreknowledge of what was to come, even as the United States was not officially a combatant in the Six-Day War. Lockwood's task was to intercept messages from the Soviets, put them into electronic format, and forward them to the NSA.

Now Lockwood was caught with the others in the rising water. He managed to find the ladder and bang fiercely on the closed hatch, which could be opened only by the commanding officer, the captain. But by now Captain McGonagle himself was wounded and bleeding even as he maintained his post on the bridge on deck. The Damage Control Officer intervened to open the hatch and Lockwood went back down to extricate wounded drowning men. He pulled sailors, one by one, through the hatch to safety. In this way, he rescued three men.

Then Lockwood descended yet again into the pitch-black research spaces in search of more of the wounded caught in the rising, swirling water. This time, Lockwood went down to the surveillance room only to find no one remaining alive. Bryce Lockwood is uneasy with being called a hero. "What was I supposed to do?" he says. "Leave them there to drown?"

Sailors attempted to use pumps to rid the research spaces of the rushing water. The ship listed at nine degrees, in danger of capsizing at any moment. The captain from his perch on deck ordered that they prepare to "abandon ship." Life rafts were released into the sea and inflated so at least the wounded might be carried to safety. The "captain's gig," an elegant small boat with a cabin made of wood that could hold eight to ten sailors, used to transport sailors to shore, had been rendered totally inoperable, having been hit by rockets and napalm.

An officer named Lloyd Painter, arrived on deck in time to observe one of the torpedo boats machine-gunning a life raft to ribbons. A torpedo boat seized another of the life rafts and carried it off as a trophy. Soon this raft would reside in the Hall of Heroes at the Israeli naval museum in Tel Aviv. In the display, the raft was accompanied by a photograph of the captain of the boat that had fired the torpedo that hit *Liberty* successfully.

In the third act of this macabre attack on unarmed American sailors, two helicopters arrived at the scene. One descended with its doors open. In the doorway were soldiers dressed in camouflage, with rifles and machine guns in their hands, ready to complete the job and drown those pesky sailors who had managed to keep their ship afloat and remain alive. They were about to board *Liberty* and finish off the survivors while sending the listing ship to the bottom of the sea. On the side of these helicopters, the Star of David was visible.

Sailor Glenn Oliphant made eye contact with a soldier standing in an open helicopter door. The man held a machine gun. He aimed it directly at Oliphant. Their eyes met.

Captain McGonagle, still on deck, wounded and dazed, his leg oozing blood, issued an order: "Prepare to repel boarders!" It would be hand-to-hand combat, even as the sailors were armed only with World War Two–issue M-1 rifles, .45 caliber automatic pistols—and their bare hands. Phil Tourney and Rick Aimmetti rushed to the small-arms locker to extract the pistols only to find that it was secured with a huge steel lock. No one could locate the key. Tourney and Aimmetti grabbed the fire ax and tried to break the hinges. The box would not budge and the Master of Arms was nowhere to be found.

Emerging on deck, Tourney observed a helicopter hovering no more than ten feet off the starboard gun mount. One of the commandos sat on the side of the helicopter with his foot on the skid. Neither said a word. The other helicopter was circling the ship.

Then, suddenly, the helicopters whirled away. What had transpired that led to the decision of their attackers to abandon the operation and permit the surviving sailors to live would be concealed for twenty years.

Now the sailors of the USS *Liberty* had to face, with sickening certainty, that they were alone and abandoned, the seaworthiness of their ship questionable. Against all odds, with breathtaking heroism, they had sent out their distress message only for no one to heed their call. There had been no response from the USS *Saratoga*, or anyone else.

When the Sixth Fleet received the SOS from *Liberty*, it did respond. Using the Critical Intelligence Communications network, or Criticom, an instantaneous communications signal, they contacted the White House and the Pentagon so that both the President and the Joint Chiefs were alerted. Admiral Martin authorized that rescue planes be rushed to the scene of the attack. There is some anecdotal evidence, since covered up, that the Joint Chiefs at once ordered retaliation at the torpedo boat basin at Haifa, only for the order to be rescinded.

At Port Lyautey, the naval station in Morocco, routing the Automatic Voice Network (Autovon), an unclassified worldwide telephone service of the U.S. military serving the Mediterranean area, NSA communications technician and petty officer Julian ("Tony") Hart was listening in. There were "ready" aircraft, two sets of planes authorized to take off. Two jet aircraft carrying "nuclear-tipped" weapons had been dispatched by Captain Donald D. Engen on the USS *America* to Cairo. These were recalled seven minutes from their target as the rescue planes were dispatched to *Liberty*. That *Liberty* did not sink at once canceled the attack on Egypt.

The rescue aircraft had scarcely taken to the air when Rear Admiral Lawrence Geis, commander of the Mediterranean Carrier Strike Force, received a telephone call from Robert McNamara. The Secretary of Defense spoke on an unsecured open line, so urgent was his message. He ordered Admiral Geis to call back the planes that had been dispatched to the USS *Liberty*. Julian Hart heard McNamara identify himself.

Admiral Geis found McNamara's order incomprehensible. He was incredulous. These were American sailors under attack, unable to defend themselves. At that moment the admiral did not know by whom the United States was being attacked. The sailors on *Liberty* in their rushed distress call hadn't communicated that Israeli reconnaissance aircraft had flown over the ship about eight times that morning.

Finding it inexplicable that he should be forbidden to come to the assistance of American sailors under siege, Admiral Geis obeyed McNamara's order and recalled the planes he had dispatched to the aid of *Liberty*. Perhaps there had been a misunderstanding. Perhaps McNamara believed that the planes carried nuclear bombs. On instructions from Admiral Geis, Captain Tully of the USS *America*, which carried nuclear-armed planes, now launched aircraft armed only with conventional weapons.

These were rescue aircraft that could not possibly be interpreted as carrying nuclear weapons. Once more rescue planes took off, bound for the USS *Liberty*. Admiral Geis then sent a Criticom straight to the White House, informing McNamara that he was dispatching planes without any nuclear capability.

McNamara responded to this Criticom instantly.

"I told you to get those damned aircraft back!" McNamara snarled. "Call them back!"

Admiral Geis refused. He required higher authority than a mere Secretary of Defense to abandon American sailors to their deaths in violation of the code of military justice. These were men for whose lives he was responsible. Calling back the rescue planes violated every principle for which he stood.

And now Lyndon Johnson himself came on the line, the commander-in-chief in whose custody the lives of America's fighting men ultimately resided. They were on the open line, Autovon.

"I don't care if the *Liberty* sinks," Johnson said. Or maybe it was "I don't give a damn if the ship sinks." Johnson certainly said "I will not embarrass an ally!" In his panic that the operation be uncovered, Johnson revealed that he knew the identity of the attackers, and that the attack itself had been a collaboration. The 40 mm. tracer rounds used by the torpedo boats had been made in the United States. The French-made planes had been purchased with U.S. dollars. The napalm tossed onto the deck of *Liberty* had been manufactured by Dow Chemical.

"Call back those planes!" Johnson ordered. Once Admiral Geis received such specific orders from his commander-in-chief he had no alternative but to obey. W. D. "Bill" Knutson was among the pilots who had been participating in the nuclear-loading exercise involving the planes that had been bound for Cairo from the *America*. He then became the pilot of the lead plane launched to fly to the side of *Liberty*. Knutson set forth at maximum speed, full throttle, knowing only that Rockstar was under attack by "unknown forces." He was about five hundred miles away and had a lot of sky to cover.

Fifteen or twenty minutes into the flight, Knutson was called back. He asked at once if Rockstar was all right. No explanation was forthcoming. Knutson was told only to return to the USS *America*. Whether or not there was sufficient time for the Sixth Fleet rescue planes to have reached *Liberty* to prevent the torpedo from penetrating the hull of the ship, Lyndon Johnson's intent was clear. Johnson's telephone conversation would never have come to light, would have been lost to history, except that Admiral Geis was deeply troubled by the action he had been compelled to take.

"I sent jet aircraft with nuclear-tipped weapons to Cairo," Captain Engen told the survivors of the attack at one of their annual reunions. This operation was in direct contradiction of any effort to rescue the besieged sailors. The planned bombing of Cairo was predicated on there being no survivors from the USS *Liberty* to bear witness to the fact that they had not been attacked by Egypt—or the Soviet Union. The U.S. attack on Cairo would be represented as retaliation for *Egypt*'s bombing of *Liberty*.

A Navy aviator named Brad Knickerbocker was about to take off for Cairo from the USS *Saratoga*. Prior to his departure, Knickerbocker had been briefed by officers using large maps of Egypt. They highlighted surface-to-air missile sites, antiaircraft emplacements, port facilities, and other military targets. Knickerbocker was part of an operation against Egypt that was already well advanced.

"My flight did not launch . . . my combat initiation would have to wait for Vietnam," Knickerbocker wrote drily in an article published many years later in the *Christian Science Monitor*

So it has emerged that the attack on *Liberty* was to be a Northwoods-like false-flag operation. Israel had attacked the United States, but Egypt would be blamed, and the United States, using small nuclear arms, would retaliate by bombing Cairo. The United States (and Israel) would rid themselves of a disputatious head of state named Gamal Abdel Nasser. Israel would be rewarded by seizing the next day, with impunity, not only the Golan Heights, but Damascus as well. That there were nuclear bombs on the USS *America* is demonstrated by their having been conducting a Single Integrated Operational Plan (nuclear) drill at the very moment of the attack on *Liberty*. Returning from their mission to Cairo, the planes that had been carrying nuclear weapons were ordered to Crete, since with those bombs aboard they could not land on an aircraft carrier.

It had not been anticipated that *Liberty* would summon the wherewithal to send a distress signal and call for help after the Israeli bombs had systematically taken out the antennae on deck, one by one. But once it did receive the distress signal, the Sixth Fleet honored it.

"We're on the way," a pilot on one of the planes launched by the *Saratoga* and bound for *Liberty* was heard to say. "Who is the enemy?" It was all on a need-to-know basis. Even the admirals had not been briefed on the operation. As soon as *Liberty* completed its SOS, the planes that had been sent to Cairo were called back. Rescue planes were sent twice. As soon as McNamara telephoned, the rescue planes sent to *Liberty* were called back, too.

Seventeen hours passed. On the morning of June 9, the USS *America* and lesser ships of the Sixth Fleet arrived at the side of the USS *Liberty* and medical services at last were offered to the wounded.

Among those undergoing surgery in the hospital facilities on the USS *America* was Dave Lewis. He had been wrapped up in sheets, placed into a basket, and hauled up onto a helicopter. The corpsman attending to him, confusing his head with his feet, had sat on his head all the way. The roar of the helicopter had prevented Lewis from making known his distress; he couldn't breathe. By the time he was unloaded onto *America*, he had turned purple. And he thought: "What an ignominious way to die, after having survived a torpedo attack!"

Dr. Peter Flynn removed the bandages from his eyes, then lanced open Lewis' eyelids. There was no anesthesia. "Don't move your eyeballs or I can't guarantee where the scalpel will go," Dr. Flynn, a hard-boiled type, said. "Stare straight ahead and don't blink." A few days later, Lewis's bandages were removed. He could see!

Admiral Geis had left word that Lewis should report to him as soon as he was ambulatory and had regained his vision. It wasn't long before the admiral had discovered how many sailors had died on *Liberty*. It was thirty-four. One hundred seventy-four men had been wounded, some with injuries that would endure for the rest of their lives, many suffering from what would later be termed post-traumatic stress disorder (PTSD). To the crew of 294 men, 208 purple hearts would be awarded. So it was that Dave Lewis arrived at the admiral's stateroom, his headquarters aboard the USS *America*.

"I have to tell someone what happened," Admiral Geis said. It was as if he were trying to absolve his conscience by confessing to someone who would understand. He swore Dave Lewis to secrecy for the duration of his own lifetime. Lewis suggests that Admiral Geis chose him as the person in whom to confide because he was the senior officer available on the *America* who had survived the attack and was likely to keep his confidence.

Then, obviously distraught, Admiral Geis described Lyndon Johnson's intervention: "I don't give a damn if the ship is sunk and all the sailors die. I don't want to embarrass an ally."

Aboard the USS *Little Rock,* Admiral Martin offered a similar confidence to a *Liberty* communications technician named Moe Shafer. Moe too had been rescued by Buddha Schnell. Now Admiral Martin sat on Moe's bed and told him that when he received the distress call from Rockstar, he had launched four jets from the USS *Saratoga* armed with conventional weapons, their destination the USS *Liberty.* He had earlier dispatched four jets armed with nuclear warheads from the USS *America,* their destination Cairo. In a few minutes they would have been bombing Cairo, had they not been called back.

The planes bound for Cairo were seven minutes from the target when they were recalled.

An hour after Lyndon Johnson made his call to Admiral Geis, the announcement came that the aggressor had been Israel. The Israeli government summoned the U.S. naval attaché, Ernest Castle, and revealed that a U.S. ship, "maybe Navy," had been erroneously attacked. As James Ennes writes, "At 1614, *Liberty* time, a Flash precedence message from the American embassy reported the Israeli apology to everyone concerned, including COMSIXTHFLT, the White House and the Department of State."

Implausibly, Israel offered the excuse that they had mistaken the surveillance ship with its many antennae and parabolic dish and Stars and Stripes in plain sight, with its writing in English, not Arabic, for the Egyptian horse carrier *El Quseir,* a vessel considerably less than half the size of *Liberty* and at that moment in port at Alexandria. Later, Dave Lewis was told by lawyer Ron Gotcher, who learned about it from the Air Force Security Forces, that Air Force Intelligence had been speculating as to which Israeli city would be wiped out in retaliation.

The travail of the 294 men on the USS *Liberty* is not mentioned once in Lyndon Johnson's White House diary for June 8, 1967, although there are four conversations listed for the day of the attack with Soviet premier Alexei Kosygin. The subject of the first message at nine forty-eight A.M. is "status of cease-fire." Kosygin does not elucidate actually to what "status of cease-fire" refers, nor does he mention the USS *Liberty*.

There is no available summary of the content of this message, which came from Kosygin. Perhaps an incredulous Kosygin wanted to know why Israel was committing an act of war against its chief ally, the United States. Perhaps Kosygin was threatening that should the U.S. bomb Cairo, they could expect swift retaliation from the Soviets, whose own nuclear submarine had been trolling the area and was aware of the entire charade.

Years later, a Soviet submarine captain, his ship armed with nuclear weapons, would relate that he had been on alert to retaliate should the U.S. bomb Cairo.

Lyndon Johnson spoke again at eleven A.M. with Kosygin. He lied and said he had instructed the carrier *Saratoga* "to dispatch aircraft on the scene to investigate the attack on the USS *Liberty*." In fact, Johnson had done the reverse. He had canceled any air support for *Liberty*. As his White House diary does make clear, on June 8 Lyndon Johnson was preoccupied with his re-election campaign, and not with the unprovoked attack on an unarmed American surveillance ship.

The record suggests that the attack on *Liberty* neither surprised nor distressed Johnson. At ten A.M. he was engaged with his secretary in compiling a list of the states he had visited since he became President. Eliminate 1964, Johnson ordered, and compile only 1965, 1966, and 1967. The 1968 presidential election was looming and, as American sailors lay wounded and bleeding, his re-election was of first importance in Lyndon Johnson's mind.

According to White House records, Johnson did not make his way from his bedroom to the Situation Room until late morning. Where he was when he ordered the planes to be recalled, whether he had made his way to the Situation Room, we do not know since neither Johnson nor anyone who worked for him ever was to admit that McNamara and Johnson had recalled the rescue planes. After Johnson's death, McNamara would be asked by writers about the incident. Repeatedly, McNamara denied that he remembered anything about *Liberty*.

Soon Johnson, aided by Robert McNamara and national security advisor Walt Rostow, would be orchestrating so airtight a cover-up that the Israeli act of war against the United States would be known only to the "happy few."

The gaping hole in the side of *Liberty* was covered with plywood, and even mattresses, as the sailors, led by chief engineer George Golden, who had survived two torpedo attacks during World War Two, kept the ship afloat. *Liberty* was now dispatched limping to Malta for dry dock repairs. Souda Bay, in Crete, was sixteen hours away, as against one hundred and twenty-four hours for Malta, and some wondered if there had been sufficient concern for the well-being of the survivors. Petty Officer First Class Ron Kukal says that "the excuse was given that at Souda Bay they didn't have facilities to repair our severe damage." The risk in making it to the more secluded confines of Malta was embraced by higher authority. In Malta, they could keep an inquisitive press at bay.

In Malta, Kukal and his team descended into the ruined watery spaces for the grisly task of retrieving bodies and body parts of the men who had died when the torpedo struck so that they might be returned to their families for burial—if they could be identified. Local newspapers were forbidden from photographing the battered ship. The sailors were ordered not to talk to reporters. The name of the aggressor would not appear on the tombstone at Arlington National Cemetery where the unidentified dead would be buried in a mass grave. It read: "Died in the Eastern Mediterranean, June 8, 1967."

A Naval inquiry into the incident was initiated by four-star admiral John S. McCain Jr., Commander-in-Chief, U.S. Naval Forces, Europe (CINCUSNAVEUR), and father of the bellicose Arizona senator-to-be John S. McCain III. Placed in charge was three-star admiral Isaac Kidd, who was given a scant week to investigate. Admiral Kidd was not granted authority to travel to Israel to do any investigating there.

Admiral Kidd first deposed Captain McGonagle, who offered up a bouquet off lies. Having guided his battered ship to port in Malta, Captain McGonagle, whose naval career was about to end, initiated the cover-up. He made no complaint about having been compelled to sail to distant Malta on a ship where safety was questionable. Testifying for the official Naval inquiry, McGonagle claimed that the attack had lasted five to six minutes, at the most eight, when in fact the bombardment had continued for close to two hours.

He claimed that the first Israeli reconnaissance flight had arrived at ten thirty A.M., when others recalled the flights had begun at five fifteen A.M. and been ongoing. He insisted that he had never given an order to abandon ship, when he had. At that moment, his second in command, George Golden, had taken charge, surreptitiously countermanding the captain's orders. Nor did Captain McGonagle mention that the torpedo boats had machine-gunned the inflated life rafts.

Then Admiral Kidd turned to the sailors. In a flamboyant gesture of ostensible solidarity, he removed the stars from his lapel. Talking to the survivors in groups, he posed as an ordinary sailor, sympathizing with those who had been attacked. He pretended to listen to their accounts, assuring them that their testimony would appear in his final report.

Later several of those whom Kidd had deposed discovered that their testimony had not been taped, and so had not been included in the six-hundred-page report. Lloyd Painter's testimony of how he personally had witnessed the torpedo boats machine-gunning the life rafts does not appear, although he had testified for two hours. Dr. Richard Kiepfer put it this way: "Never before in the history of the United States Navy has a Navy Board of Inquiry ignored the testimony of American military eyewitnesses and taken, on faith, the word of their attackers."

Lyndon Johnson and Robert McNamara ordered Admiral Kidd to conclude in his naval inquiry that the attack had been a case of "mistaken identity," that the Israeli Defense Forces had not known that *Liberty* belonged to the United States. "Ward, they're not interested in the facts," Admiral Kidd confided to his legal counsel, JAG Captain Ward Boston. "It's a political matter and we cannot talk about it." Instead they were to "put a lid on it."

Captain Merlin Staring as "Force Legal Officer" for Admiral McCain had been enlisted to evaluate the draft of the inquiry report and offer his comments and endorsement. Staring began and soon revealed that he was having serious problems with the evidence to support the conclusion that the attack had been a case of "mistaken identity." In less than twenty-four hours Captain Staring was ordered to return the draft to Admiral Kidd. His assessment would not be required after all.

Ward Boston would keep silent for thirty-seven years. Then in an affidavit dated January 9, 2004, he spoke out. "The evidence was clear, Captain Boston wrote. "Both Admiral Kidd and I believe with certainty that this attack . . . was a deliberate effort to sink an American ship and murder its entire crew . . . I recall Admiral Kidd repeatedly referring to the Israeli forces responsible for the attack as 'murderous bastards.' It was our shared belief based on the documentary evidence and testimony we received first hand that the Israeli attack was planned and deliberate, and could not possibly have been an accident." He terms the attack a "war crime."

"I am outraged," Boston continues, "at the efforts of the apologists for Israel in this country to claim that this was a case of 'mistaken identity.'" He relates that Admiral Kidd had told him "that he had been ordered to sit down with two civilians from either the White House or the Defense Department, and rewrite portions of the court's findings."

The Naval Court of Inquiry transcript was now heavily redacted. Removed were transcriptions of intercepted instructions from Israeli commanders to their pilots ordering them to "sink the American ship!"

Each sailor was ordered never again to speak of the attack, on penalty of a court-martial; a lengthy stay at Leavenworth federal prison; and a heavy fine, up to one hundred thousand dollars. Careers in the Navy and other government agencies were at stake. Lloyd Painter, who joined the Secret Service following his Navy commitment, received his Purple Heart in Germany. "Don't tell anyone where you got it!" he was ordered. The sailors were now dispersed so that no two were posted together. For more than a decade, no one talked about the incident.

Lyndon Johnson went on television to announce to the American public that "ten" American sailors had been killed "in a six-minute accidental attack." Johnson's Press Secretary, George Christian, also lied and told reporters that planes "went to the area" when they learned that the ship had been attacked.

The cover-up would be successful despite the massive evidence that the Israeli attack had been planned and well organized. Director of Central Intelligence Richard Helms would remark, "There could be no doubt that the Israelis knew exactly what they were doing in attacking the *Liberty*. I have yet to understand why it was felt necessary to attack this ship or who ordered the attack." What CIA knew in advance about the operation has not been made part of the scanty released record. Later Johnson's own Secretary of State, Dean Rusk, came to the conclusion that the attack had been well planned and premeditated.

James Scott, son of a *Liberty* sailor, noted in his book about the attack that on the afternoon of June 8, a mass rally was held in Lafayette Park in Washington, D.C. Its purpose was to express solidarity with Israel. The event endorsed Israel's aggressions in the Six-Day War. Johnson aide and speechwriter Larry Levinson suggested to the President that he send a message to the rally in support of Israel.

"You Zionist dupe!" Johnson reportedly said, raising his right fist. "Why can't you see I'm doing all I can for Israel!" Yet there are photographs of Lyndon Johnson shaking hands with pro-Israel demonstrators on that day. (Yet another of John F. Kennedy's policies that Johnson reversed was Kennedy's demand of Israel, renewed as late as July 1963, that the Israeli nuclear reactor at Dimona be subject to inspections in accord with international standards to verify its peaceful intent.)

The cover-up extended to several government agencies, of which CIA was only one. Undersecretary of Defense Cyrus Vance ordered NSA director Marshall Carter, as Carter later revealed, to "Keep my mouth shut!" Carter then added, "Those were his exact words."

Captain McGonagle received the Medal of Honor, along with an otherwise unlikely promotion and a new ship to command, rewards for his complicity. Lyndon Johnson defied precedent. He did not invite this particular captain to the White House for the presentation of his medal, as tradition demanded. Instead Captain McGonagle received his award at a Navy yard from the Secretary of the Navy. The Chairman of the Joint Chiefs was not in attendance. There was no accompanying press release. For betraying his men, McGonagle was rewarded with disrespect by the president with whom he had forged his own Faustian bargain.

Two years before his death, and thirty years after the attack, McGonagle plaintively requested of President Bill Clinton that he elicit the truth from Israel. Neither Clinton nor Israel obliged. Dave Lewis suggests that if anyone deserved the Medal of Honor it was Dr. Richard Kiepfer.

For twenty years, Lewis, who became a full commander in the U.S. Navy, kept Admiral Geis's confidence. At the twentieth-year reunion of the survivors of the attack, Lewis stood talking with Admiral Thomas H. Moorer. Admiral Moorer was a four-star admiral, the highest rank the U.S. Navy affords. He had twice been chairman of the Joint Chiefs of Staff and was then President of the *Liberty Alliance*, an organization he had founded with the goal of making known the truth about the events of June 8, 1967. Through the years, Admiral Moorer had supported the sailors in their quest for justice.

The secret of Lyndon Johnson's recalling of the rescue planes had weighed heavily on Dave Lewis. Now he mentioned the call Johnson had made to Admiral Geis, along with the promise he himself had made not to reveal Johnson's role in the events during Admiral Geis's lifetime.

Admiral Moorer told Lewis that Admiral Geis had died. So he was free to tell the truth, a decision Admiral Moorer supported. Lewis made no mention of what he knew that night to the assembled survivors. He was not a man for whom notoriety, or public notice, held any attraction.

Lewis grew up in rural New Hampshire, poor and humble. Beginning at the age of seven or eight, he worked on farms, pitching hay. As a teenager, for five years he was employed as a gravedigger. As he was completing an indifferent high school education, he spotted a notice on the bulletin board of the local post office, announcing that university entrance examinations would be held there on the following Saturday. Lewis did not bother to read the fine print explaining that these exams were for entrance into the service academies. His acceptance into the Naval Academy at Annapolis came as a surprise.

Twenty-eight of the men who died on the USS *Liberty* had worked for Lewis, who had told them all to call him "Mr. Lewis," ignoring rank. Two had arrived at his office, retirement papers in hand, prior to their departure from Norfolk. Both agreed to accept one last deployment—for him. Lewis was tortured for years by the thought that they wouldn't have died had he not urged them to join what would be *Liberty*'s final voyage.

Rather than make an announcement about Lyndon Johnson's telephone command to Admiral Geis at the reunion, Lewis waited until he arrived at home. Then he wrote a half-page description of what Admiral Geis had told him about Johnson's demand.

There was no dramatic response from his comrades, no outpouring of indignation other than that they thought something like that must have happened. This verifiable evidence that their commander-in-chief had consigned them to their deaths was inflammatory. In the coming years, many survivors, preferring to cast the blame for the attack entirely on Israel, would prove willing to be content with a half-truth. Published two decades after Lewis revealed the truth about Lyndon Johnson's intervention and his role in these events, James Scott's book about the travails of *Liberty* and its sailors does not even mention Johnson's recalling the rescue planes. A 2014 Al Jazeera documentary participated in the same cover-up.

Lyndon Johnson had violated the Uniform Code of Military Justice, Article 99, which prohibits abandoning a fellow combatant—as well as a vessel—belonging to the United States in battle, as well as Article 118. The code defines murder at war as "unlawful killings" which are the consequence of "committing an act inherently dangerous to others" and exhibiting "a wanton disregard of human life." The accused must know that death or great bodily harm is a "probable consequence" of his conduct. This definition derives from "Principle VI," adopted by all members of the United Nations and defined by the Nuremberg War Crimes Tribunal.

According to Rear Admiral Merlin Staring, who became the Navy's judge advocate general, Lyndon Johnson was guilty of a war crime; by the universally accepted definition adopted at Nuremberg, Johnson's behavior on June 8, 1967, classified him as a war criminal. That he be deemed guilty did not require that his actions be aimed "at anyone in particular." It does not require that the rescue planes would have arrived in time to stop the torpedo boats. Johnson's action revealed a "wanton disregard of human life."

On June 8, 2005, the USS *Liberty* Veterans' Association filed a War Crimes Report with the Secretary of the Army, who served as the executive agent for the Secretary of Defense, at the Pentagon. It describes Lyndon Johnson's behavior, but does not mention his name. There was no response. The *Liberty* veterans were given to know that there would be no further investigation, nor had there ever been any investigation apart from the hasty, corrupted Naval inquiry.

It is a life-changing moment to embrace a truth that turns your entire worldview upside down, let alone one that compels members of the military to reexamine the integrity of the country they had served with unconditional loyalty and dedication. In an effort to understand why some have been hesitant to take the full measure of Lyndon Johnson's abandonment, one might turn to how the most honorable sea captain in literature, Joseph Conrad's Captain Marlow in *Heart of Darkness,* handled a similar moment.

A sworn enemy of lying, a man who believes that lies carry the "taint of mortality," Marlow lies to protect the reputation of the ivory trader Kurtz, a man who had descended into corruption and degeneracy. Once Kurtz had been a stalwart of the empire and an example of European high culture. Kurtz's dying words, "the horror, the horror," explode the myth that the empire served by both Marlow and Kurtz was in any way worthy of their dedication. Kurtz represents the very civilization that Marlow served all his life. For Marlow to repudiate Kurtz would amount to a moral judgment on himself and his own life. Marlow cannot face being alienated from the system by whose values he defined himself all his life. He cannot imagine existing as an outsider.

"It would have been too dark altogether," Marlow says. So we may understand why so many naval officers took so long to come forward with the truth about *Liberty,* why they continued to abide by the stricture on their freedom of speech. It took three decades for Ward Boston to speak out.

In a declassified cable, CIA revealed that a horrified Israeli general, working under Moshe Dayan, leader of the Israel Defense Forces at the time, had opposed the attack. This officer, whose name CIA redacted and has continued to conceal, had termed the assault on this unarmed American ship "pure murder."

The director of the National Security Agency at the time of the attack Marshall Carter was the brother of Lyndon Johnson's factotum Cliff Carter. Powerless to break the cover-up, Marshall Carter was appalled by Isaac Kidd's Naval Inquiry. He thought the attack was well-planned and premeditated. His deputy, Louis Tordella, was more outspoken. "A nice whitewash," he scribbled onto the Israeli navy's "Yerushalmi report." Marshall Carter had been appointed by Lyndon Johnson but, unlike his brother, he was too honorable to lie for him.

Hothead though he was, Dayan had hesitated before finally approving Israel's June 9 attack on Syria, the final act of aggression of the Six-Day War. Yet some have sought to place the blame for the *Liberty* attack on Dayan. It had been an act of war against the United States, a reckless endangerment of the Zionist project. Or was it? Evidence suggests that Israel did not pursue the operation alone, although Israel over the years has accepted full responsibility.

Suggesting U.S. foreknowledge of the incident, a unit of the U.S. Air Force, the 601 Direct Air Support Squadron based in Germany, was placed on stand-by alert on June 8, 1967. The pilots were not briefed as to why.

More chilling is that the Strategic Air Command commander-in-chief, in the early morning hours of June 8, had directed its nuclear-armed planes, to be placed on alert. Jim Nanjo was an Air Force pilot serving with the 744 Bomb Squadron, 4556 Strategic Air Wing, at Beale Air Force Base north of Sacramento, California. His orders were clear. On receipt of the proper coded message, he was to take off in his nuclear-armed plane and proceed toward a designated target where he would "deliver nuclear weapons."

Nanjo described for author Peter Hounam that between two and four A.M. Pacific Time, the klaxon went off. Nanjo had two and a half minutes to dash to his plane, start the engines, and listen for an incoming message from the Strategic Air Command headquarters at Offutt Air Force Base in Omaha, Nebraska. By the dark of the moon, Nanjo took his hydrogen-bomb-armed B-52 to the end of the runway and waited.

The "go-code," which could be given only upon direct orders of the President of the United States, never arrived. There would be no bombing of

Cairo. Nanjo remained in his bomber ready to take off for four hours. Then he was ordered to stand down. That *Liberty* did not sink, that there were survivors to tell the tale, put closure on the operation. Whether the Soviets would have then retaliated is a matter of speculation. Bryce Lockwood subsequently learned that the entire nuclear force of the United States was on alert from the early morning of June 8.

In his memoir *The Vantage Point: Perpectives of the Presidency, 1963–1969*, published in 1971, Lyndon Johnson would repeat the falsehood that "ten men of the *Liberty* crew were killed and a hundred were wounded." He characterized the episode as "heartbreaking" and a "tragic accident" even as he lied yet again that "carrier aircraft were on their way to the scene to investigate."

Had Lyndon Johnson's order that no rescue planes be dispatched achieved its intended result, the sinking of *Liberty*; had Egypt (with Soviet assistance) been blamed for the attack, as was also intended; had the United States then retaliated by bombing Cairo with those nuclear weapons at the ready on the USS *America*; had the Soviets then responded with a nuclear retaliation on Israel, as a Soviet submarine commander has testified that they were prepared to do; and had the Strategic Air Command then further retaliated with its hydrogen bombs, raising the ante, Lyndon Johnson's legacy would have been World War Three. He came close.

Coda: One week after he consigned the sailors of the USS *Liberty* to their deaths, Lyndon Johnson nominated Thurgood Marshall to the United States Supreme Court. Richly deserved, it was a historic nomination, the first African-American ascending to the court. For more than twenty years, Marshall had heroically and at great personal risk sown the seeds of a civil rights movement that would culminate in his victory in Brown v. Board of Education (1954), which promised an end not only to legal segregation but to inequality before the law.

At the same time, Johnson welcomed Marshall into the establishment, an environment from which Marshall could inflict the least harm on the status quo, while simultaneously burnishing Johnson's own civil rights credentials.

CHAPTER 15

Downward Spirals

"John, why do they hate me so?"
—LYNDON JOHNSON TO JOHN CONNALLY

By the late 1960s the lives of Lyndon Johnson and Mac Wallace had begun a simultaneous and uninterrupted downward spiral. Having been obsessed with the re-election campaign of 1968 for several years, Johnson chose not to run again. In his memoir, he wrote, "I felt that I had used up most of my capital as President." This was true, no matter that Johnson felt compelled to add, "I am convinced that if I had run again I would have been re-elected." For the historical record, his Vice President, Hubert Humphrey, disagreed. Johnson decided against running again, Humphrey said, because "he knew he couldn't make it."

Mac Wallace had long been out of touch with Johnson, although they had parted on good terms. When Michael Wallace received his draft notice, his summons to serve in Vietnam, Mac asked his son what he wanted to do. He could contact Lyndon Johnson, Mac suggested, and get him off. Michael rejected the offer and Johnson's help was not enlisted. When Mac referred to Lyndon Johnson in conversation with his son, Michael felt, there was no tension, no intimation of dark secrets in his tone. There was no hint that he had anything to hide that was connected to Johnson.

In the late sixties, Michael and Meredithe Wallace returned to Texas. Mac was chafing at his job at Ling Electronics. He complained that Ling wasn't loyal to people when they reached retirement age. He began to drink even more heavily, bourbon and Hiram Walker Canadian Club whiskey. Exasperated, his superiors at Ling told him to take three months off and "do what you have to do to get clean." He had been a functioning alcoholic for many years, Meredithe notes, but he couldn't function any longer the way he once had.

Accepting Ling's suggestion, Wallace took three months off with the understanding that he was expected to rid himself of his alcoholism. Yet he didn't stop drinking. Instead he settled into an inexorable downward spiral.

By 1967, Lyndon Johnson was already a tormented man. To a gathering of state senators, John Connally, governor of Texas, recounted how Johnson had called him after midnight "the other night" from the White House. Johnson was weeping. "John, why do they hate me so?" Johnson had said, according to Connally, who recounted the moment for *Texas Monthly* magazine with scorn for Johnson's weakness. Johnson had done much for Connally, but with their Faustian bargain completed, he emerged with only contempt for the man.

Lyndon Johnson announced on March 31, 1968, that he would not run for re-election. He had planned to announce his resignation in his January 1968 State of the Union speech. Then he hesitated, obsessively consulting polls and his approval ratings. His announcement revealed that he had learned little from the travail of the Vietnam War. Johnson threatened that "the Communists may renew their attack any day" and insisted that he "could not in good conscience stop all bombing so long as to do so would immediately and directly endanger the lives of our men and our allies." This was the same man who had consigned the sailors on the USS *Liberty* to watery deaths.

As in his first public address as President, Johnson had invoked the policies of John F. Kennedy, so now Johnson attempted again to connect himself with the fallen leader whose stature had grown over the years. He quoted from Kennedy's inaugural speech in which JFK invoked a generation of Americans willing to "pay any price, bear any burden, meet any hardship, support any friend, oppose any foe to assure the survival and the success of liberty." John F. Kennedy did not have a ground war in Vietnam in mind, so for Johnson to use his words in this context was to cloak himself in hypocrisy.

Johnson's preference as his successor was Nelson Rockefeller, the Republican governor of New York, apparently on the ground that Rockefeller was "the one man who could beat Robert Kennedy, no small asset in Johnson's mind." When some of his staff came out for Kennedy, Johnson rebuked them. The animosity between Robert Kennedy and Lyndon Johnson had long been visceral.

Kennedy depicted Johnson as "murderous" and "a very mean, mean figure . . . he's mean, bitter, vicious—an animal in many ways," meanness being the very quality Johnson's brother, Sam Houston, had invoked. Ed Clark, Johnson's lawyer, later recounted that the name "Bobby Kennedy" provoked a telling gesture from Johnson: "Raising his big right hand, he would draw the side of it across his neck in a slow, slitting movement." Johnson told Clark, speaking of Bobby Kennedy, "I'll cut his throat if it's the last thing I do."

Among the policies Johnson supported during the waning days of his presidency was the eighteen-year-old vote for which Mac Wallace had fought in 1944 in his campaign for the presidency of the student body of the University of Texas. As the Vietnam War raged on, Johnson returned to the rhetoric of the "Great Society." On Labor Day, he urged all Americans to "open their hearts and work with a new sense of purpose to help the disadvantaged enter the mainstream of our society."

In these last months of his presidency, Johnson was a whirling dervish of programs, from food stamps to signing an agreement to ban the spread of nuclear weapons. Only the Soviet invasion of Czechoslovakia that summer prevented him from traveling to Moscow. When Chief Justice Earl Warren retired from the Supreme Court ahead of schedule, in June 1968, so that his successor would be nominated by a Democrat—many were concerned a Republican would win in 1968—Johnson wanted to make his old crony Abe Fortas the new chief justice.

Among those opposing the idea was Johnson's adversary Ralph Yarborough, who spoke out against Fortas' attempts to dissuade Alaska senator Ernest Gruening from opposing the Vietnam War. Yarborough argued that Fortas as a sitting justice had "violated the separation of powers and the judicial code of ethics." When the Senate would not confirm Fortas, Warren's retirement was delayed and it fell to Richard Nixon to nominate his successor, Warren Burger.

After Bobby Kennedy was assassinated in June 1968, Johnson considered changing his mind about not running again. Polls declared that only 40 percent of Americans disapproved of his performance in office. He thought Humphrey was too soft. "The trouble with you, Hubert, is that you're just too damn good," Johnson said. "Somebody comes along and kicks you in the face, and you pat their leg. I give them nothing."

Anti-war protests being held outside the Chicago Democratic National Convention during August 1968 made Johnson's appearance there inconceivable. The idea of his renewed candidacy evaporated. Although he did not attend the convention, he successfully pushed through a plank in support of his Vietnam policy, thereby ruining Humphrey's chance to be President. That Johnson went on to provide lip service to his support for Humphrey, while undermining his candidacy, was typical of his lifelong modus operandi.

A lifetime leaker of self-serving intelligence, Johnson refused to leak information he had obtained from renowned Greek journalist Elias P.
Demetracopoulos that the Greek colonels had contributed more than a half
million dollars to Nixon's campaign. Johnson apparently had no quarrel with
the vicious Greek colonels. Nor was he about to do anything to help Hubert
Humphrey be elected.

Lyndon Johnson attributed the profound public and press disenchantment
with him and his presidency to, among other factors, animosity of easterners
toward Texans, and hence "toward anyone that comes from my area."
Wallowing in self-pity, he attacked the *New York Times* and the *Washington Post*
and spoke of how "ugly things" had been said about him and his family, how
he had been abused and harassed by the media. His last act as President was
to establish a Franklin Delano Roosevelt Memorial Park.

In 1968, still together, Mac and Virginia Wallace purchased a house in
Placentia, Orange County. They moved in before the school term began in late
summer. Mac's diminished life and his alcoholism had descended into
suicidal depression. He talked often to Virginia about Nora Ann Carroll.
There was a near accident on a freeway.

Early in 1969, Mac was fired by Ling Electronics. He was only forty-seven
years old, and yet his options had been exhausted. Beset by medical problems,
he decided to return to Texas and the bosom of the Wallace family. Before his
departure, Mac requested that Virginia have Elaine baptized. Any Christian
order would do. Virginia chose Episcopalian. Mac had told his older children
that he believed in the value of a strong spiritual foundation, even if one never
went to church. Once Michael had made a disparaging remark about nuns
and monks, people who renounced the world.

"You should respect them," Mac said. He was talking about respect for all
other people, not just about religion, Michael thought. Mac remained unemployed and was living on his meager savings. On August 1, 1969, he and
Virginia separated for good. When he left for Texas, she was relieved. They put
the Placentia house on the market. It had been rented out, but they owned it
for too short a time for there to be any profits from the sale. It was purchased
by the tenants.

On that same day, August 1, Alice Meredithe Wallace, age nineteen, married
a farmer named David Paul Nix and moved to Troup, Texas. She had married
young, but she had found the right man, a good man. Her mother-in-law was

Baptist and Meredithe attended her church. She became less a Wallace. She hadn't heard much about God from either of her parents. Now she heard the gospel and "was saved."

When Mac left for Texas, Michael promised that he would graduate from college. His father had done his best, financing Michael's education, only for him to drop out of school. Now Michael returned to his studies.

Mac Wallace had an aversion to flying. He drove back to Texas, passing through Arizona during that first week of August 1969 in another of his battered used cars, a 1964 Chrysler. Mac had always warned Michael against hitchhiking, a ban Michael ignored. But on his way to Texas Mac picked up a hitchhiker. Mac passed out in what Virginia believes was a diabetic coma. The hitchhiker grabbed the wheel and gained control of the car. Mac was rendered unconscious and suffered a bad concussion, but the hitchhiker had saved his life.

When he regained consciousness, Mac's brother Jerry Neal Wallace told Virginia later, and the police requested his address, Mac named his father's house at 610 Tenison Memorial Road in Dallas. Virginia took this as an affront, as if she had never existed for this man, as perhaps in some profound sense she had not.

Virginia soon filed for divorce. The summons and complaint were mailed to Mac in Texas on December 9. Four days later, before a notary public in Dallas, Mac signed his assent to a settlement. Custody of six-year-old Elizabeth Elaine Wallace went to her mother.

There was little property and Mac was described on the document as "unemployed." His assets were the heavily mortgaged house, his clothes, and his books. They owned two automobiles, a 1964 Rambler and the Chrysler. Mac had three hundred dollars in his bank account. The court ruled that he was "without funds or property to maintain or support said minor child." Child support for Elaine was set at a minimal one hundred dollars a month. The divorce became final on February 16, 1970.

That year Mac Wallace distributed his revised résumé far and wide throughout the state of Texas. No one offered him a job. His brother Jerry later explained to reporters that prospective employers "would often tell him that he was overqualified." He helped run his brothers' insurance agency, although there wasn't much for him to do; the Dallas City Directory nonetheless listed him as "one of three proprietors of the Robinson-Wallace Insurance Agency."

On his 1970 résumé, Mac listed his work from "mid-1969 to the Present" as "Robinson Wallace Insurance Agency, Assistant Manager." He described his marital status as "married with 3 children, one son, age 21, and 2 daughters, ages 19 and 6." His brothers also ran a real estate operation renting out properties in the Texas panhandle and on occasion Mac worked there. Nora Ann Carroll Cary, now Stevenson, viewed this as a descent into "mediocrity . . . a nondescript family member in a rental operation." He taught as an adjunct at the Texas A&M campus at Arlington where once he had been a student.

Mac found someone to cover his classes and he returned to California one week in 1970 to visit his daughter Elaine. With Michael, he shared the irony of a hitchhiker having saved his life, given how often he had railed against Michael's practice of hitchhiking. One day they set out for a walk. Before their eyes, a little boy ran out into the street just as a speeding car rounded the curve at the end of the block. Mac rushed out into the road and tackled the child, covering him with his body. He emerged with cuts and bruises, but he had rescued the boy.

The health of both Lyndon Johnson and Mac Wallace, a much younger man, seemed to decline at the same pace. "No Johnson has ever lived beyond the age of sixty," Johnson said often. "Everyone has died of a heart attack before that." He had suffered a major heart attack in 1955 at George Brown's Middleburg, Virginia estate, Huntland, and believed that his days had been numbered ever since.

Mac's health was also failing. On April 27, 1970, he wrote out his will, choosing as his executor his brother Jerry Neal, who was ten years his junior. Mac had taken out three life insurance policies, leaving each of his children ten thousand dollars. Michael would be the administrator.

Meredithe's first child, a daughter, was born on November 22, 1970. On January 7, 1971, Mac Wallace drove to Troup to meet his granddaughter for the first time. He arrived unannounced, as if sensing that had he telephoned, he might not be invited. Meredithe was living in a mobile home. Suddenly there was her father standing on the steps outside.

"I didn't want him in my house or in my life. I had a daughter to protect," Meredithe says. "But he came on purpose to meet her." They chatted as if they were old acquaintances. Mac told her that he was planning to have a full medical workup at a veterans' hospital, either in El Paso or in the panhandle. Meredithe was surprised because she had never heard him complain about his health. He was a man who never complained about anything. He was a man who did not blame others for his troubles.

He hadn't sent a gift for the baby. Now he gave Meredithe fifty dollars to "buy her something." She did not offer her father coffee. She didn't even offer him a glass of water. She did not want to cook supper for him. "I didn't have any graciousness about me," Meredithe says. "I was not gracious to my father." She remembers that he was not drunk.

Mac Wallace was so delighted to see the baby that the visit ended on an upbeat note. He remained for one hour and then he left. On his way back to Dallas, he said, he planned to visit one of his aunts in Mount Pleasant. It was between seven thirty and eight P.M. on a clear night when Mac left Meredithe's trailer. The roads were dry. He arrived at a bridge eight miles south of Pittsburg, Texas. There was a concrete approach as traffic moved from the outer road onto the bridge.

Mac bypassed the cement upright and his car tumbled onto the road alongside the bridge, moving into the space where the bridge left the ground. Running off the highway, the car struck the bridge abutment and wound up on the wrong side of the railing. There was massive damage to the passenger side of the vehicle. He always drank in the car, Meredithe thought when she learned of the accident. Maybe he had reached down for a bottle.

According to Ronny Lough, the police officer at the scene, the driver had lost control of his car. Lough described the incident this way:

> The passenger side was caved in as if the car had hit a pole, not a bridge. There was a dead body in the car. The door was damaged on the passenger side. The front fender was a bit buckled, and the roof . . . the picture shows a person inside with his finger pointed out, sitting in the middle of the strong seat. His hand showed with the finger pointing up at the roof, which was a bit bucked [sic] too. No damage to the driver side. Yet there was no one in the car but Mac Wallace.

Mac Wallace was pronounced dead on arrival at seven fifty-eight P.M. at the Medical and Surgical (M & S) Hospital in Pittsburg by a Dr. P. W. Reitz. His massive head injuries seemed out of keeping with a one-car accident. Almost immediately anomalies surfaced. The medical report vanished from the M & S Hospital. The report from the office of Doyle Johnson, the local sheriff, vanished without a trace.

When Virginia was notified, she drove to Michael's house. Michael Wallace was not a man given to crying, but he burst into tears and wept. Later Virginia speculated that Mac may have fallen asleep at the wheel as a result of his narcolepsy, a condition that causes sudden and deep sleep, rather than a "diabetic coma." "I think he had a lot of traffic accidents in Texas because of this," she said. Nora Ann at first speculated that Mac must have taken his own life. Then she concluded that he would not have done so in his daughter's neighborhood and on so happy an occasion.

Jerry Neal Wallace paid $942 (about $5,322 in today's money) for the coffin, according to the Mount Pleasant funeral home. David Wallace tied one of his own neckties around his brother's neck. He could not find a tie among his brother's effects. At the service, Bobbie Wallace, David's wife, grabbed her nephew and made Michael march up and look into his father's casket.

Michael resisted, but then he walked up and looked. The man he observed in the coffin was his beloved father, casting doubt at once on the assertions of those promoting Mac Wallace as an urban legend who did not die in 1971 but lived on in secrecy. Michael's cousin Connie, Jerry's daughter, was also led up to the coffin. Connie looked and saw her uncle lying there. "The body was easily recognizable," James Eldon Wallace said later.

Mac Wallace was forty-nine years old. He would not have reached his fiftieth birthday until the coming October.

Not only were the accident and hospital and sheriff's reports missing, but the death certificate was laced with inaccuracies. Harold David Wallace supposedly provided the information to the doctor, yet David did not sign the death certificate. No one signed it. David, if it was he, was unable to provide their mother's maiden name, Riddle. The death certificate reads "Unknown."

Under "married," the death certificate stated that Mac was married, which he was not. Under "employment," the certificate says that Mac was a "salesman for a newspaper," something he had never been. Years later, Jerry Neal Wallace would tell reporter David Hanners that he didn't know for whom Mac was working at the time of his death. He did not mention the family insurance company.

Several distinctive handwritings drift over Mac Wallace's death certificate, and there are obvious erasures. This flawed document was submitted to the Texas Department of Health, Bureau of Vital Statistics, in Austin. Clerk T. H. Miller returned the document to Camp County for correction. On February 22, the death certificate was stamped "Received" by the Department of Health in Austin. Again it was returned to Camp County for "additional information and/or correction." On March 2, Mac Wallace's death certificate arrived in Austin for the third and final time. David Wallace still had not signed it.

Mac Wallace was laid to rest in the Wallace family plot at the Neville Chapel Cemetery in Mount Pleasant, Titus County, beside his brother Alvin J. Wallace, who had died before his first birthday. The gravestone would be supplied by the Veterans Administration.

The discrepancies with the death certificate, and the extent of the injuries sustained in a one-car accident, led some to speculate that Mac Wallace did not die in 1971. Captain Clint Peoples looked into the federal witness protection program, but could not find Mac Wallace embedded there. Some, embracing the urban legend that Mac Wallace had served as a paramilitary arm of Lyndon Johnson, purportedly spotted him at the Horseshoe Casino in Las Vegas run by mobster Benny Binion. There is no credible evidence that Mac Wallace was ever seen again after his funeral. Michael Wallace, who, of course, had seen his father in his coffin, is convinced that had his father lived, he surely would have contacted him. Their bond was that strong.

Other than the insurance policies taken out in the names of his three children, Mac Wallace's estate had no value. The Application to Probate Will and For Letters Testamentary reads "in excess of $1,000." The will was to be probated twice, once when the "probate cause" was filed on March 15, 1971, and again on April 4, 1984, when the Inventory and Appraisement was approved. The normal time for the issuance of the approval was four years or less. The value of the estate when probate was completed in 1984 was $0. Real estate and personal property were each valued at $0. Jerry Neal Wallace's second appearance in probate court was not recorded on the Registry of Actions of Mac Wallace's probate file, as protocol decrees that it be.

In January 1969, Lyndon Johnson returned to his ranch in the Hill Country of Texas. He remarked that he was "sure he had less power [as President] the day he left office than the day he entered after the assassination of President John F. Kennedy." By now, many who had served in his administration and observed him up close viewed Johnson as a ruthless man capable of anything. McGeorge Bundy, who had facilitated the Vietnam War with such enthusiasm, saw an extreme psychological disintegration in Johnson at the end. A tinge of violence had always lurked beneath the surface of Johnson's locutions. Kennedy aide and historian Arthur Schlesinger called Johnson "dangerous."

Supporting Schlesinger's conclusion was that Johnson was heard to say about someone, "I hate that man! Kill this man!" Once, Johnson said of his partner, lawyer A. W. Moursund, the principal trustee of the Johnson family business interests, that Moursund "could whup Sonny Liston." "There were no Marquess of Queensberry rules," Holland McCombs concluded.

Schlesinger remarked on the "curious resemblance between Khrushchev's account [in his memoirs] of the life around Stalin—the domineering and obsessive dictator, the total boredom of the social occasions revolving around him, the horror when invited to attend and the even greater horror when not invited—and Albert Speer's account of the life around Hitler." McGeorge Bundy assented. "When I read Khrushchev," he replied, "I was reminded of . . . my last days in the White House with LBJ."

In 1968, having resigned from service to Johnson, Bill Moyers, who had worked for Johnson since the Kennedy assassination, noted that Johnson was now "well sealed off from reality." Moyers was appalled by Johnson's single-minded pursuit of the Vietnam War, as well as by Johnson's having assigned him to enlist the FBI to investigate members of Barry Goldwater's staff, and White House staffers as well. "I work for him despite his faults and he lets me work for him despite my deficiencies," Moyers told the *New York Times* with grace and characteristic humility the year before he resigned. Moyers talked about Johnson's "manic-depressive cycle," terming him a "sick man." Moyers pondered the difficulty of constructing a credible narrative that included "Johnson the private monster" and "Johnson the public statesman."

Moyers invoked the word *paranoid*, as did former Kennedy aide Richard Goodwin. When Tom Johnson, Lyndon Johnson's Deputy Press Secretary, arranged a book party for Bill Moyers in Austin and asked Johnson to attend, Lyndon Johnson was angry and accused Tom Johnson of divided loyalties. He hung up the telephone and didn't speak to his aide for weeks.

Lyndon Johnson in his retirement was not yet done at Victorio Peak. On December 5, 1967, three months before he announced he would not seek a second term, Johnson had organized the LaRue Corporation, part of the cover he would need in his effort to remove gold from Victorio Peak. The LaRue Corporation was set up by Johnson and John Connally, with the help of an El Paso lawyer named Pat E. Dwyer, who was close to Connally, and another crony named Ray Pearson. Pearson had set up the corporation as a favor to Connally and Johnson.

In the summer of 1969, Johnson visited Victorio Peak in the company of John Connally. For ten days, they remained at a large motor home in Orogrande, New Mexico, forty-seven miles from the treasure trove. A convoy of military vehicles with Johnson and Connally, in attendance would visit the

Hembrillo Basin in the daytime and return home at night. Johnson brought the Secret Service agents assigned to him. One of the security guards talked to journalist Tom Whittle, as did the pilot of the B-24 Liberator plane used to move 120 tons of gold bars. Between 1969 and 1970, Johnson removed gold from Victorio Peak.

In February 1971, President Richard Nixon appointed John Connally as Secretary of the Treasury, according to John Clarence, author of *The Gold House: The True Story of the Victorio Peak Treasure*, suggesting an alliance between the two Presidents in which Connally played a role as gatekeeper for the Victorio Peak gold.

His accretion of great wealth notwithstanding, isolated at his ranch, deprived of power, Johnson was now "bitter and tormented," as his longtime lawyer, Jerome T. Ragsdale, put it. He turned "old, weary and battered," as if overnight. He drank heavily, smoked two to three packs of cigarettes a day, and ate hamburgers and other forbidden foods so that he grew "excessively fat." He refused to have his now-gray hair cut, and it grew long and curled under at his neck. His fingernails remained unclipped.

The staff at the LBJ Ranch was instructed not to admit anyone from the press. "The damn press always accused me of things I didn't do," Johnson remarked. "They never once found out the things I did do." He oversaw the creation of the LBJ Library, which has religiously sanitized its records, even as it is part of the country's National Archives. He attended football games. He was restless, and defensive, isolated and given to brooding.

On the subject of Vietnam, Johnson defended his policies. "No man worked harder or wanted peace more than I," he claimed. Johnson dictated this sentence to Horace Busby, who had been pressed back into service to author a statement from Johnson on the subject of the cease-fire in Vietnam.

There were moments of startling honesty. Johnson acknowledged to an interviewer, Leo Janos, that when he took office as President he found "we have been operating a damned Murder Inc. in the Caribbean." If he was referring to the attempts on the life of Fidel Castro, Janos doesn't say. Doubting that Lee Harvey Oswald had acted alone in the murder of John F. Kennedy, Johnson said he had asked Ramsey Clark, who became attorney general in March 1967, to look into the Kennedy assassination only for Clark to report back that he "couldn't find anything new."

"I thought I had appointed Tom Clark's son," Johnson said, referring to the Supreme Court justice. "I was wrong." For decades Ramsey Clark, inaccurately, would argue that Jim Garrison, the District Attorney in New Orleans investigating the Kennedy assassination, had allowed homophobia to deter-mine his prosecution of an innocent man, Clay Shaw. (Garrison had indicted Shaw, a local CIA asset, for participation in a conspiracy connected to the Kennedy assassination.) When Lyndon Johnson felt free to be honest, he was brutally so.

If he regretted anything, Johnson said, it was waiting eighteen months before pouring more troops into Vietnam in 1965. His other regret was that he had not imposed censorship on the media so that people would not have been able to view on nightly television graphic evidence of the atrocities committed in Vietnam that day. Later presidents, among them George W. Bush and Barack Obama, would remedy this transparency. Smoking "like a fiend," now a chain smoker, Johnson suffered another massive heart attack at the Charlottesville home of his daughter Lynda in April 1972.

Few cared to visit the LBJ Ranch. One person who did come to call was Johnson's former acolyte, Bobby Baker. From the moment Baker resigned in October 1963, and through his 1967 trial, they had communicated only through intermediaries, supporting Baker's contention that Johnson would not accept a million dollars from Carlos Marcello because he was too timid.

In October 1972, Johnson invited a surprised Baker and his wife to visit. Baker arrived to discover his mentor pale, white-haired, and fat. "I wonder what it was he had to fear," Baker wrote in his memoir, *Wheeling and Dealing*. During this visit, Baker suggested that Johnson telephone Nixon crony Charles "Bebe" Rebozo on his behalf. Baker hoped that Johnson might dispel any suggestion that Baker had a Watergate connection. Would Johnson please "put in a good word" for him?

In palmier days, Baker later told Senate historian Donald A. Ritchie, he had found Rebozo "a real warm friend of mine. He was always calling me, when Nixon was President, to see if I could furnish him anything about Larry O'Brien." O'Brien was Democratic National Committee chairman at the time of the Watergate break-in. Richard Nixon had suggested of the Internal Revenue Service that they search for embarrassing information in the income tax files of George McGovern and O'Brien. The IRS declined. But in October 1972 the winds had shifted.

Johnson refused. "It'd be in big black headlines," he said. He would have liked to "turn off the investigative machinery but he feared the political as well as the legal risk," Baker wrote. Johnson's personal risks trumped Baker's needs.

Baker asked again. "I don't want to go back to jail," he pleaded. Now Johnson turned cold, outraged at Baker's pursuing the point. He was the same man he had always been; everything was to be evaluated for its impact on him. Johnson refused to grant what seems to have been a simple favor.

His presidency had been "sold out and gone sour," Johnson complained. He did not invite Baker to sign the ranch guest book, as it was customary for departing visitors to do. It hurt Baker deeply. "He was ashamed of me," Baker said later, embracing the insult.

Later, Bobby Baker spoke benignly of Lyndon Johnson. He covered for Johnson in his connection to Billie Sol Estes. In his memoir, Baker depicts a scene in which President Kennedy asks him, "Bobby, how about this damned Texas tycoon, what's his name? Billy [sic] Sol Estes? Is he a pal of yours?" Estes "was never an LBJ man," Baker replies, "but was in the political camp of Ralph Yarborough of Texas." Still later, Bobby Baker stated that Johnson was "a real, warm, Christ-like character in certain areas." In 1983, he referred to Johnson's "intellectual superiority" and his "political superiority." In Johnson's ability to charm others, Baker added, "he was a genius."

Johnson returned to rattling around the ranch, most of the time alone. His fingernails were now claw-like. Loyal always to a man who had so often been disloyal to her, Lady Bird escaped when she could. Johnson wasn't entirely idle. He talked incessantly on the telephone. During the four years of his retirement, he doubled the size of his estate.

Still, his mood was grim. Repeatedly, he listened to Simon & Garfunkel's "Bridge Over Troubled Water": "When you're weary, feeling small, when tears are in your eyes . . . and friends just can't be found . . ." The accumulation of the terms of engagement of his life came to weigh upon him in the end. He had made a Faustian bargain with himself and paid the price.

In December 1972, Lyndon Johnson attended a civil rights conference held at the LBJ Library and attended by civil rights leaders, from Thurgood Marshall, who owed him his seat on the U.S. Supreme Court, to Roy Wilkins, Julian Bond, and Barbara Jordan. Missing was the hero of Mississippi Summer, Bob Moses, who had done so much to advance the voting rights of African-Americans.

Dr. Martin Luther King Jr. had been assassinated in April 1968. By the last year of his life, King had challenged decisively the efficacy of Lyndon Johnson's civil rights efforts. "It is transparently immoral to pay the outrageous price of a reckless military adventure while cutting out the very heart of our domestic social programs," King said. In 1967, funds for the Head Start program for preschool children had been cut. King initiated the Poor People's Campaign as his response to the Johnson "Great Society" legislation. It was to culminate in a garbage workers' strike in Memphis and a sit-down in Washington, D.C., creating a shantytown reminiscent of the years of the Great Depression.

King was also skeptical of the Voting Rights Act. "I've come to believe that we are integrating into a burning house," he said, speaking of "a failed system" where "a small privileged few are rich beyond conscience and almost all others are doomed to be poor at some level." King's struggle was not focused on struggling African-Americans alone, but on everyone.

Now, at the LBJ Library on a December day, for the last time, Lyndon Johnson reached for the rhetoric in which he had wrapped his support for the Civil Rights Act: "To be black in a white society is not to stand on level and equal ground . . . unless we overcome unequal history, we cannot overcome unequal opportunity." Johnson closed with the title of the civil rights movement anthem, "We Shall Overcome," a strategy he was resurrecting from a 1965 speech.

Lyndon Johnson succumbed to a heart attack at the LBJ Ranch on January 22, 1973. He was alone in the house with his Secret Service contingent, Lady Bird having gone to Austin. He telephoned for help but the agents on duty did not reach his room in time. "Well, we expected it," Lady Bird said when she heard the news.

Lyndon Johnson was only sixty-four years old, but already a very old man. He was buried on an icy day in Stonewall, where he had been born. General William Westmoreland, who had implemented the war in Vietnam, placed a wreath that was a gift from Richard Nixon at the foot of the coffin. A peace agreement with the Vietnamese was a week away.

George Parr, who had played so instrumental a role in Lyndon Johnson's political career, committed suicide on April 1, 1975, with a .45 caliber firearm.

Into the 1970s, the Treasury Department held gold bars for Lady Bird Johnson, which were subsequently delivered to her. Sources reported to Tom Whittle that in 1977, during Operation Goldfinder, yet another expedition to extract gold from Victorio Peak, Lady Bird called the White Sands Missile Range every day for the latest news. When Whittle telephoned her assistant later, he was told that Lady Bird "had never heard of Victorio Peak."

CHAPTER 16

Billie Sol Estes Creates an Urban Legend

*Hegel remarks somewhere that all great
world-historic facts and personages appear, so
to speak, twice. He forgot to add: the first time
as tragedy, the second time as farce.*
— KARL MARX, THE EIGHTEENTH
BRUMAIRE OF LOUIS NAPOLEON

If Lyndon Johnson and Mac Wallace were linked only tenuously in their lifetimes, in the decades that followed their deaths, and into the twenty-first century, their relationship devolved publicly into one of inseparable co-conspirators. Single-handedly, Billie Sol Estes was responsible for this mythology. In Estes' telling, Wallace was Lyndon Johnson's personal hit man, his right- hand man to the point that Wallace, on Johnson's orders, had participated in the assassination of President Kennedy. Wallace had also murdered all those witnesses who, had they lived, might have testified to Johnson's role in the scams, crimes, and misdemeanors of Billie Sol Estes. That these witnesses died is a fact. None of the deaths has been adjudicated, leaving whoever was responsible safe from blame, and others open to unprovable accusations.

Estes' assertions united Wallace and Johnson in death as they had never been in life. It never emerged exactly how much Billie Sol Estes knew about those killings; it is likely that he knew quite a bit, certainly enough to know that those murders had benefited both himself and Lyndon Johnson, and there was no one to demonstrate otherwise. Whether Wallace murdered John Douglas Kinser out of jealousy over his relationship with Andre, or so that Kinser would not live to repeat whatever Josefa Johnson had told him about her brother, this reality would also be buried in the graveyard of Johnson cover-ups. Whether Johnson had sent Wallace with instructions to murder Kinser has also drifted in the smoke of these events. No clear answer has been forthcoming.

* * *

In 1971, having served six years, four months, and one week in prison, Billie Sol Estes was released. Soon he was wheeling and dealing in the company of questionable "Italian" (Estes' term) companions, and spending as much time, "considerable time," in Las Vegas as he did in Texas. He was, he would write, "making deals and having fun." He took a mistress. Now openly a man who no longer recognized limits, the former teetotaler indulged excessively in alcohol.

Before long, Estes was arrested again. He was charged with mail fraud and conspiracy to conceal assets to avoid paying income taxes. "How could I be accused of not paying taxes on non-existent assets?" Billie Sol complained. The authorities were not impressed. He was arrested in Dallas on August 12, 1977. Once more Billie Sol found himself in a courtroom. This time he took the stand.

"Regretfully," Estes confided to the jury, "I have become a liar." Once his money was gone, he admitted, he had "turned to lying and bragging." He was signaling that no one should grant undue credence to anything he said.

In 1979, Billie Sol Estes went off to La Tuna penitentiary in El Paso to serve a second prison term. On his journey, he was accompanied by Clint Peoples. Now in late middle age, Peoples had been appointed a U.S. Marshal. "Henry Marshall very definitely did not commit suicide," Estes remarked according to Peoples. "He was murdered. You're looking in the wrong direction. You should be looking at the people who had the most to lose." So began the long revenge Billie Sol Estes was to exact against Lyndon Johnson, and, by extension, Mac Wallace.

"Should I be looking in the direction of Washington?" Peoples reported that he had asked Billie Sol Estes.

"You are [now] very definitely on the right track," Estes said.

In late 1983, Billie Sol Estes walked out of federal prison and back into the world. At La Tuna, he had made the acquaintance of an inmate named Jimmy Day, who had been the Austin lobbyist for a rich Texan named Shearn Moody Jr., an insurance heir and trustee of the family Moody Foundation. The family fortune had been the legacy of W. L. Moody, a nineteenth-century Galveston cotton trader and insurance king.

In 1968, Shearn Moody had been worth about three hundred million dollars and owned 100 percent of the W. L. Moody & Co. bank in Galveston. He had built Empire Life Insurance of America with a half billion dollars of insurance in force. The Moody Foundation dispensed five million dollars a year in philanthropic contributions. Shearn Moody lived on a six-hundred-acre ranch with bulletproof windows, patrolled by German shepherd dogs, its swimming pool inhabited by penguins. He traveled with a suitcase filled with cash and was fond of quoting his grandfather: "Use your money the way you would use an army, deploying only what is necessary, and maintaining plenty in reserve."

Moody collected Hitler memorabilia, including a copy of Leni Riefenstahl's film *Triumph of the Will*. Politically, he termed himself a General MacArthur conservative. He was also a supporter of Alabama governor George Wallace. By the late 1950s Moody had been so profligate with the family money that Texas attorney general Will Wilson appointed three outsiders to the Moody Foundation board, among them John Connally.

A startling detail of Shearn Moody's biography is that in 1960 he met Lee Harvey Oswald's assassin, Jack Ruby, on a trip to Dallas. At the Carousel Club, Ruby provided a special strip show for Moody and his friends and presented Moody with a card inviting him to return. Moody's name appeared on a notepad discovered among Jack Ruby's effects after his death. Among the CIA-connected foundations investigated by Texas Congressman Wright Patman was the Moody Foundation. These were foundations used as fronts or cover for CIA's domestic operations as "pay throughs." Patman's investigation of CIA's use of these foundations took place from 1964 to 1967.

Labeled "the sleaziest man in Texas," inhabiting the underbelly of American culture, Moody was Billie Sol Estes' type, a person with contempt for the U.S. legal system and notorious for his Mob connections. Moody's Gold America National Insurance Company was invested heavily in Nevada casinos like the Sands. An ex-military explosives expert signed an affidavit alleging that Moody had hired him to "blow the legs off" a friend he thought had betrayed him. Moody wanted him to "possibly get a sniper rifle with a silencer and just blow him away."

In 1982, at La Tuna, Jimmy Day, whose two fraud convictions were in cases that had nothing to do with Shearn Moody, introduced him to Billie Sol Estes. Moody fancied himself a history buff, having written several tracts, including *A History of Galveston* and *Comparison of the Governments of Alexander of Macedonia and Genghis Khan of the Gobi Desert*, both published in 1954, as well as a book called *The Texas Ranger*.

For Moody, Billie Sol Estes was a figure in history. That Estes had been betrayed by Lyndon Johnson appealed to Moody, who despised Johnson acolyte John Connally; Moody had accused Connally of attempting to take over the Moody Foundation and had sued Connally for allowing American

National Insurance to make large, low-collateral loans to Mob-connected Las Vegas casinos, a suit Moody won.

In 1982, Estes poured out to Moody his tale of how he had functioned as Lyndon Johnson's "bag man." Estes talked about making public the story of his relationship with Johnson and Cliff Carter (Mac Wallace was not mentioned). Moody listened. Choosing an admitted liar, con man, and convicted felon as a witness to history may seem an odd choice, but not for Shearn Moody. To support Estes in his attack on Lyndon Johnson, Shearn Moody would simultaneously be taking revenge on John Connally for his attempt to take over the Moody Foundation.

Houston attorney Douglas Caddy remarked to the author in a 2013 interview that the only person Billie Sol feared was John Connally, who was "more ruthless than LBJ." It was in the 1970s that Moody tangled with Connally; in 1970 Connally had been in line for one of the foundation's outside trusteeships. "Shearn Moody Jr. on numerous occasions told me how John Connally had attempted to take over the Moody Foundation of Galveston, Texas," Caddy said. "At one time the foundation was placed in the hands of strangers and only through a lawsuit filed by Moody did the Moody family regain control. Moody provided me with documents showing that one means by which Connally utilized his power illicitly was though Project Southwest, which was instituted by the Internal Revenue Service under the Nixon administration." At the time, John Connally was Secretary of the Treasury under Richard Nixon, who appointed him in 1971.

Connally used IRS Project Southwest to go after his political enemies in Texas, and later Watergate Special Prosecutor Leon Jaworski from Texas indicted Connally in part in retaliation for devising Project Southwest. The indictment charged that Connally accepted a bribe while serving as Secretary of the Treasury, although a Washington, D.C., jury found him not guilty. But documents unearthed by the Senate Watergate Committee revealed that there was a "Project Southwest," the goal of which was to harass wealthy Texans, and that Connally had been briefed on Project Southwest by the IRS in March 1972.

Douglas Caddy was to conclude that "had Watergate not erupted and had not Connally been swept up in its wake, he might well have succeeded in using his position as Secretary of the Treasury to steal the Moody Foundation from the Moody Family. Discussions that took place in the Oval Office in the White House would seem to support this. Shearn Moody Jr. had good reason to be on guard against Connally's ambitions." Connally stepped down in 1972.

To facilitate a grant for Estes, Moody contacted Douglas Caddy, who had been a founder of Young Americans for Freedom. In 1964, Caddy had supported Barry Goldwater in his bid for the presidency, and had been counsel to the "Conservative Caucus, Inc." He was soon to be counsel to the Texas Policy Institute, in line to receive a $250,000 grant from Shearn Moody. Caddy had defended Watergate conspirators E. Howard Hunt and Gordon Liddy and had earlier provided Hunt with a glowing reference before he was hired by the Nixon White House. Later, Caddy underwent a political transformation. He described himself as a "progressive liberal" and supported Al Gore in 2000 and Howard Dean in 2004. He joined the American Civil Liberties Union (ACLU).

Shearn Moody told Caddy he had eighteen million dollars a year to give away. One day Moody told Caddy, "I'm going to put Billie Sol Estes on the line." Moody planned to make a grant of $350,000 available to Estes so that he could write a book. The money would be issued to Abilene Christian University, which would disburse the funds to Estes. To facilitate this grant, Douglas Caddy made at least half a dozen trips from Houston to Abilene. As for Lyndon Johnson, Moody told Caddy that he had "heard on reliable authority that Johnson had created a secret financial empire while holding public office."

In 1983, just as Billie Sol Estes was about to be released from prison, Shearn Moody was removed from the board of trustees of the Moody Foundation for financial irregularities, including having approved hundreds of thousands of dollars in grants to a series of bogus foundations that were in fact fronts for paying his own legal bills. That year, Moody filed for bankruptcy and spent a week in jail for refusing to make his foreign bank records available. Estes would not receive any money from Shearn Moody. The $350,000 Estes had been promised vanished in the smoke of time.

A free man, Billie Sol Estes put Douglas Caddy in touch with Clint Peoples as Estes set forth on his path to destroy Lyndon Johnson's reputation. "I'm ready to talk to you," Estes told Peoples, who had been waiting for five years for him to come forward. He trusted Peoples, Estes explained.

"There's one thing I want you to tell me," Peoples replied. "Henry Marshall? Who killed Henry Marshall?"

"Mac Wallace!" Estes now declared. To confuse matters, there was a Texan named Mack Wallace, who served between 1983 and 1985 as chairman of the Railroad Commission, a regulatory agency. "Mack" had been the spelling

Estes had offered to Holland McCombs when he interviewed Estes in 1964 in connection with the exposé McCombs was writing for *LIFE* magazine. Estes was to occupy a considerable portion of that article, and McCombs traveled to Estes' home before he went to jail the first time.

To provide Estes with a platform, Clint Peoples contacted John Paschall, the District Attorney of Robertson County where Henry Marshall had been shot.

On March 20, 1984, Billie Sol Estes, a short, round-shouldered, dumpy one-time farmer, his eyes blinking behind horn-rimmed, Coke-bottle eyeglasses, arrived at the courthouse in the dusty town of Franklin, Texas. It had now been twenty years since Estes' scams had caught up with him. Accompanying him was Clint Peoples. "He said he'd do it [testify] for me because he wanted to get his life straight with the Lord," Peoples explained to reporters. Henry Marshall was "killed because he was in the way of people he didn't have to be in the way of."

John Paschall had arranged for state immunity for Billie Sol Estes, but only in the matter of the murder of Henry Marshall. He would not testify about any of the other litany of murders that followed in the wake of his fall, the deaths of all those who had in common that they could implicate Lyndon Johnson in Estes' illegal schemes. Estes rambled on for four and a half hours. An investigator from Paschall's office surreptitiously manned a tape recorder, although it was illegal to tape grand jury proceedings, which are always held in secret. Soon the tape would be in the hands of Texas reporters hungry for copy about the colorful Billie Sol Estes.

At the inquest into the death of Henry Marshall at this same courthouse twenty years earlier, Estes had claimed his Fifth Amendment privilege. Now he swore to reveal what he knew about Marshall's murder, still on the books as a suicide.

Lyndon Johnson gave the order for Marshall's murder, Estes said. It was in January 1961 during the snowy week that John F. Kennedy took office. At Johnson's Washington home, the newly inaugurated Vice President had gathered his right-hand man, soda bottler Cliff Carter; Estes himself; and a young Texan named Mac Wallace, a former president of the student body of the University of Texas whom Johnson had gathered under his wing. These four supposedly trooped out into the snow-covered backyard. (Although Horace Busby later challenged Estes' version of how much snow there was and what actual home Johnson was living in, Busby himself was not in fact present.)

"It looks like we'll just have to get rid of him. He will have to go," Johnson said, referring to Henry Marshall, who had twice refused to be bribed into silence. His voice low and weak, Estes claimed on the stand that "Mac Wallace was awarded the assignment to kill Henry Marshall." At that moment, Estes converted Mac Wallace into Lyndon Johnson's hit man, a hatchet man implementing the crimes of the man who had done Estes wrong. Mac Wallace, Lyndon Johnson, and Cliff Carter had all been dead for more than a decade.

After Marshall was murdered, Estes claimed, he, Carter, and Wallace had gathered at Estes' Pecos home. Wallace described to them how he had waited for Marshall at his ranch, planning to use carbon monoxide to kill him. Wallace was in the process of gassing Marshall when he heard a car approach. Panicking, he had shot Marshall with Marshall's .22 caliber rifle. There was, Wallace purportedly said, an "awful scuffle."

"You sure did botch it up," Carter said.

Interviewed by Holland McCombs, Estes had mentioned Wallace only as an errand boy for Johnson, a hatchet man shaking down Texas businessmen. Now, twenty years later, with both Johnson and Wallace dead, there was no one but Mac Wallace's family and Lyndon Johnson's former staff to challenge the story that Mac Wallace had murdered Henry Marshall on orders from Lyndon Johnson.

In fact, Mac Wallace had a credible alibi, indicating that he was not in Texas on the day of Henry Marshall's murder, nor on the day after when the killer returned to Nolan Griffin's service station where on the day of the murder he had asked for directions to the Marshall farm. Mac Wallace was living in Anaheim, California, working for Ling Electronics. On that June weekend when Henry Marshall was murdered, Mac entertained his brother Harold David Wallace and his family. It was the weekend after the Dallas public schools had recessed for summer vacation. David, as he was known, brought along not only his own children, but Mac's son, Michael, who had not seen his father since he had moved to California.

Michael was to celebrate his thirteenth birthday at the end of the month, and welcomed this opportunity to celebrate with his father. The weekend was memorable for another reason: He was being taken to Disneyland by his father and uncle. Harold David Wallace, his family, and Michael arrived in Anaheim on June 2, the day before Henry Marshall was murdered. Later Harold recounted that they had spent June 3 at the beach. "We were there all day long, along with Mac, until evening," he said.

Gas station attendant Nolan Griffin testified that a stranger who had asked directions to the Marshall ranch on the day of the murder had returned the next day, June 4. Had Mac Wallace absented himself from his guests for two days, as would have been required, either Harold David Wallace or Michael would have remembered. Wallace's presence in California on June 1 is documented; on that day, at Ling, he filled out a portion of his application for the renewal of his security access.

District Attorney John Paschall reasoned that Henry Marshall's killer had to have been somebody Marshall knew was coming to visit, someone familiar with his ranch. He had parked his truck in the middle of the property rather than at the front gate. That ruled out Wallace, since there is no evidence that Wallace ever met Marshall. Further challenging Estes' tale, Johnson's longtime assistant Horace Busby pointed out that the scene Estes pictured as the meeting place of Johnson, Estes, Carter, and Wallace described "the Elms," the mansion Johnson was not to occupy for another six months. Wary of the Mac Wallace component, Paschall nonetheless concluded, referring to the murder of Henry Marshall, that Estes and Johnson "were in it together."

The resulting headlines were flamboyant. BILLIE SOL ESTES SAYS LBJ ORDERED OFFICIAL KILLED was typical. "Marshall had information that could link former President Lyndon Johnson to Estes' illegal schemes and a multi-million-dollar political slush fund that Estes claimed was being run by Johnson," *Dallas Morning News* reporter David Hanners wrote. A source told the *College Station (Texas) Eagle* "that Estes claims he can link former President Lyndon Johnson to seventeen mysterious deaths in West Texas."

Many Texas newspapers noted that Estes had not presented a shred of evidence. "We see no reason to buy anything from Estes—especially this story," one paper said. A grand juror confided to a reporter from the *Dallas Times Herald*: "It's just the word of an admitted con man." In that paper, Peter Hecht called Lyndon Johnson "the first elected President accused of arranging a murder." In the *Texas Observer*, Bill Adler wrote that "perhaps Billie Sol saw in Wallace the believable hit man, the made-to-order character to fit his plot line." Having committed one murder, who would doubt that he would commit others?

Texas attorney general Will Wilson, a longtime Johnson adversary, defended Estes. "I see no reason why he's not telling the truth," Wilson declared. He claimed that it had to have been "Johnson's political influence" that earned Mac Wallace his freedom after his trial for killing John Douglas Kinser. *Dallas*

Times Herald reporter William P. Barrett quoted an anonymous source who remarked that Johnson had seen to it to keep Wallace's punishment for shooting Kinser "light" to keep his family name out of the news reports.

Writing for the *Dallas Morning News*, David Hanners searched for Mac Wallace's files at the National Archives. The government (Hanners refers in his article to "security officials" and "two former intelligence officers") denied that there had ever been a series of Office of Naval Intelligence investigations of Wallace, and that Wallace ever possessed a security clearance. With these ONI files in hand, we can conclude safely that those officials were lying. Hanners contacted the Defense Investigative Service office in Washington, D.C., that had awarded Wallace his SECRET clearance. Dale Hartig, chief of the Office of Information and Public Affairs of the Defense Investigative Service, admitted that there was a Mac Wallace file in the Defense Central Index of Investigations. Yet Hartig claimed that the file did not contain any background investigations. Nor, he contended, did it indicate that Mac Wallace ever held a security clearance.

Jim Crossland, a spokesman for the Vought Aero Products Division of Ling, which in 1961 had merged with TEMCO, told Hanners, "I don't see any way that he wouldn't have a security clearance, working in the programs he was working on." A spokesman at Vought echoed Crossland: It was "inconceivable that Wallace could have held a management position on a missile contract and not have had a security clearance."

Hanners tracked down A. C. Sullivan, who had worked for the Office of Naval Intelligence on the Mac Wallace investigation. Requesting that his name not be used, Sullivan admitted that "there was an investigation: that I can verify . . . why there isn't a Navy file, I'm puzzled." Hanners was unable to discover how extensive the ONI's file on Mac Wallace had been, how on a virtually annual basis the Navy had attempted to rescind Wallace's clearance. The ONI files have since emerged and speak for themselves.

David Wallace reminded reporters that Billie Sol Estes was "internationally known as a fraud and a cheater." Interviewed by reporter William P. Barrett, Virginia Wallace said, "Mac had been acquainted with the Johnsons. He told me he knew Mrs. Johnson better than Mr. Johnson." He had spoken of knowing "the Johnson family."

After Estes testified before the Robertson County grand jury, Abilene Christian University withdrew from its participation as recipient of the grant. No grant was ever approved and Estes never received Moody Foundation grant money. Shearn Moody was the only trustee who was interested in supporting Estes and he soon was to face legal difficulties sufficient to distract him from the idea.

At the end of March, the death of George Krutilek was reopened by Sheriff Mike Davis, but nothing came of it.

Testifying before the Robertson County grand jury was only Estes' opening salvo. With Douglas Caddy to assist him, Billie Sol was ready to bring his accusations against Lyndon Johnson and Mac Wallace before federal prosecutors at the Department of Justice. In the spring and summer of 1984, Caddy sent to the Justice Department a list of the murders Mac Wallace allegedly committed on orders from Lyndon Johnson. Taking Estes' accusations on faith, Caddy traveled to Washington, D.C., where at the Department of Justice he met with Stephen S. Trott, an assistant attorney general in the criminal division. Accompanying Caddy was Edward Miller, a former assistant director of the FBI.

Caddy took with him newspaper clippings describing Estes' appearance before the Robertson County grand jury, but otherwise Caddy possessed no evidence supporting Estes' accusations because Estes had not provided him with any corroboration of the charges.

At their second meeting, Trott promised to request of FBI director William Webster that he assign agents to search the files to determine whether there was justification for the Justice Department to talk to Billie Sol Estes. Caddy says that the reply came back in the affirmative. On August 9, 1984, Caddy wrote to Trott, accusing Lyndon Johnson of being the mastermind behind a laundry list of murders, and of being part of a group, brothers in crime, that included "Cliff Carter and Mack [sic] Wallace."

"Mr. Estes was a member of a four-member group, headed by Lyndon Johnson, which committed criminal acts in Texas in the 1960's," Caddy wrote. He then provided a list of the murders ostensibly committed by this group:

1. The killing of Henry Marshall.
2. The killing of George Krutilek, Estes' accountant
3. The killing of Ike Rogers [sic] and his secretary. His secretary was named Thelma Lanelle Ensley. Rodgers killed his secretary with a .22 caliber bullet to her head. She was thirty-nine years old. It was ruled a murder-suicide.
4. The killing of Harold Orr, a Vice President of Superior Manufacturing in Amarillo.
5. The killing of Coleman Wade, an Oklahoma builder of grain elevators for Estes.

6. The killing of Josefa Johnson.
7. The killing of John Douglas Kinser.
8. The killing of President John F. Kennedy.

John Douglas Kinser is sandwiched among those for whose deaths there is no corroborating evidence of Mac Wallace's—or Lyndon Johnson's—involvement. Josefa Johnson appears among those allegedly killed by Wallace, although he was not present at the Christmas Eve party at the LBJ Ranch that preceded her sudden death. Except for Josefa, and President Kennedy, none could be connected to LBJ. Marshall, Krutilek, Orr, Wade, and possibly Rodgers were connected to Estes' business enterprises; none could be linked to Lyndon Johnson.

Caddy promised Trott that Billie Sol Estes was "willing to testify that LBJ ordered these killings, and that he transmitted his orders through Cliff Carter to Mac [now spelled correctly] Wallace, who executed the murders." Caddy had accepted Estes' contention that he had had "conversations" shortly after each murder with Cliff Carter and Wallace. Caddy added that in 1971 Carter had told Estes that there were in fact "seventeen murders." Estes had also related that his friend Kyle Brown had been present at the 1971 meeting and was willing to testify to what he had heard. Caddy quoted Estes as calling Wallace a "stone killer" with "a communist background."

In his memoir, Estes was to claim that Wallace "recruited Jack Ruby, who in turn recruited Lee Harvey Oswald." President Kennedy's killer was Wallace, who "fired a shot from the grassy knoll in Dallas, which hit JFK from the front during the assassination." Madeleine Brown, who claimed to have been LBJ's mistress, would echo Estes' charge. Mac Wallace "was one of the shooters behind the picket fence overlooking Dealey Plaza," she wrote in her 1997 memoir, *Texas in the Morning*. Brown also accused Mac Wallace of murdering her black nanny because the nanny had inadvertently witnessed Johnson and Brown in one of their steamy sexual encounters.

Caddy had injected into his August 9 letter to Stephen Trott that he himself had learned all this information "yesterday for the first time." Tapes, he contended, had been made "as a means of Carter and Estes protecting themselves should LBJ order their deaths." Then Caddy went out on a limb. "I wish to declare, as Mr. Estes' attorney," he said, "that Mr. Estes is prepared without reservation to provide all the information he has."

In exchange for evidence about the murders, Estes demanded a deal from the Justice Department. He requested a pardon for the offenses for which he had been convicted, as well as immunity from any further prosecution. He wanted relief from his parole restrictions and a recommendation that his "long-standing tax liens" be removed.

Trott agreed to a "detailed debriefing of Mr. Estes" on the condition that he provide the Justice Department with all the evidence in his possession, including the 1971 Cliff Carter tape. Estes was expected to provide the sources of all his information and the extent of his own involvement in the crimes. Nothing Estes said would be used against him in a court of law—provided that he respond "completely, truthfully and without guile."

Trott demanded that Estes submit to a polygraph. Estes and Caddy were to sign a copy of Trott's letter, testifying to their acquiescence in these conditions. The Justice Department would be free of any agreements with Estes should any of Estes' statements turn out to be "false, misleading or materially incomplete, or if he knowingly fails to act with total honesty and candor." Caddy added that Estes had in his possession not only records of his telephone calls, but tape recordings that supported his assertions.

Stephen Trott dispatched three FBI agents to Abilene to meet with Billie Sol Estes. Caddy flew to Texas from Washington to join the group. It was September 1984. Estes arrived at the meeting place, a hotel atrium, in the presence of his daughter Pam. From an upper level of the atrium, the FBI agents peered down in anticipation.

When he faced the federal agents, Estes unexpectedly did an about-face. He had changed his mind about providing evidence, he said. Then he fled from the building. In his memoir, Estes would explain that he had walked off because he had received "a series of telephone calls from my Italian friends . . . they insisted if I appear to be going through with the discussion, my life would end." To his dumbfounded lawyer, Estes related none of this, only that "as a member of the Church of Christ, I know I'll have to answer for what I've done in this life."

"You had your chance," Douglas Caddy told Estes. "What did you expect the Justice Department to do?"

In a January 20, 2006, interview conducted via e-mail, Caddy noted that he was never at any time provided with evidence that confirmed Estes' accusations. Kyle Brown, a close friend of Estes who supposedly held the tapes in his custody during Estes' time in prison, has said only that they reveal that Lyndon Johnson was "a cold-blooded killer," but "we already knew that." He claimed he had helped transfer cash to Johnson and Cliff Carter.

In a more recent conversation, Caddy reflected that even Billie Sol Estes "was unfamiliar" with some of the seventeen murders he claimed had taken place. Caddy noted that Estes had been evasive, and revealed nothing so much as that he "feared LBJ." Caddy emerged from his relationship with Estes feeling as if he had been an actor in a drama not of his own making, "messed up by Billie Sol Estes."

To the moment of his death on June 22, 1992, Clint Peoples insisted that Mac Wallace, along with Josefa Johnson and John Douglas Kinser, was homosexual. He called Mac Wallace a "Communist" and said Homer Rainey and Wallace were "communistic friends." Only after Estes' accusation that Wallace had murdered Marshall did Peoples decide that Wallace fit the composite drawing produced by Nolan Griffin as "absolutely right."

Peoples told his biographer that he had questioned the person involved in murdering Henry Marshall, but that, without concrete evidence, "he will not be able to prove anything." He had not interviewed Mac Wallace, and so had to be referring to someone else. When Peoples requested that the State of Texas open an investigation into Mac Wallace's death, he was chastised by three Texas judges.

At one point, contradicting his grand jury testimony, Billie Sol Estes claimed to Clint Peoples that there were *two* people present at the scene of the murder of Henry Marshall. He talked about a "mysterious car" at the location. "We hope they didn't get any long-range photographs of the situation," Estes said. He knew who had been there, Estes said, but he refused to give Clint Peoples the information. "Mack [sic] Wallace and somebody else," he said.

Estes later admitted to Tom Bowden, the ghostwriter of his 2005 memoir, that he and his younger brother, Bobby Frank, who died in 1966, "had been present at one of the murders." Bobby Frank had long lived under Billie Sol's sway as his "faithful follower." According to Bowden, Estes deleted passages from his memoir that implicated himself. The book was "edited by him to remove certain material which would have incriminated him in some of the murders," Bowden said. Estes never came up with a shred of corroborating evidence for the accusation that Mac Wallace had killed anyone other than John Douglas Kinser, or that Lyndon Johnson had ordered any of the Estes-connected murders.

In the ensuing years, Estes also changed other aspects of his story. In his memoir, Estes wrote, "Kyle Brown was not at the meeting with Cliff Carter." If in 1984 he had instructed Douglas Caddy to tell the Department of Justice that Mac Wallace had killed George Krutilek, now the certainty was gone. "I would speculate that Malcolm Wallace murdered George Krutilek," he wrote. Tom Bowden told people, such as historian Larry Hancock, that he had listened to a 1971 tape with Cliff Carter speaking only to remark that it "could be taken to implicate Lyndon Johnson as a murderer." Bowden told the author that he questioned Estes' veracity.

At the millennium, a Texas carpenter named Floyd Stephens began talking about how, when his father died, among his papers were clippings about the murder of Henry Marshall. Stephens hinted that his father had been a participant in Henry Marshall's death. Then Stephens the younger died suddenly, taking with him whatever he knew. Even as Henry Marshall's death had been finally declared a "homicide by gunshot wounds" six months after Billie Sol Estes testified before the Robertson County grand jury, a fog of uncertainty settled over the event.

In June 2010, this author drove southwest from Dallas through Fort Worth in search of the elusive Billie Sol Estes. Estes had hunkered down in Acton, a small, unincorporated community seven miles outside of Granbury. It was a stifling, hot Texas afternoon. There, within a nondescript, but gated, community, was Estes, a wrinkled old man uneasy with questions. His daughter, Pam, had enlisted a friend to guide me to Billie's house. Pam herself could not accompany me because father and daughter were not on speaking terms. The issue was Pam's guardianship over Estes' finances. The house was comfortable, if plain.

In our conversation, Lyndon Johnson inhabited every one of Billie Sol's sentences. Johnson was all-powerful. Johnson was a horrific human being. Johnson represented pure evil. No one in Texas could evade his power. In a cluttered room, part kitchen, part sitting room, in the semi-darkness, Billie Sol sat back on his recliner, a frail, eighty-five-year-old man lost in his memories of the man who had destroyed his life. His second wife, Dorris, stood nearby, solicitous, concerned, kindly, and silent.

Johnson was so powerful that no person could be elected to office in Texas without his support, Estes said. I thought of Richard Kleberg and John Lyle. While up to this moment Estes had been slow and lethargic, suddenly he grew animated. "Don't paint him as a man that loved the common man!" Estes warned. He pointed to a tree outside the window. "Draw the trunk of a tree!" he ordered. "That's Lyndon Johnson. All the branches emanate from him!" Then he added: "Anything Lyndon wanted, he got."

In the waning light of that Texas afternoon, Estes recalled Johnson's words to him: "You're going to do what I tell you and you will do what I told you!" As dusk fell, Billie Sol Estes embellished his portrait of a megalomaniacal sociopath.

"Hitler was a sissy compared to Lyndon," Estes said. "Lyndon controlled the CIA and Hoover. He just told them what to do. He was Jesus to Cliff Carter. Everyone hated him. No one understood Lyndon. I think he was from outer space. He was bigger than life!" Asked about Herman and George Brown, who figured so profoundly in Lyndon Johnson's rise to power, Estes scoffed. "Lyndon got them everything they ever had," he said. "Lyndon controlled everything!"

"I own it. I am the government," he had heard Johnson say. "The Kennedys should have had more sense than to come to Texas." John F. Kennedy had been "like a buck deer caught in the headlights. Lyndon got everything done." There it was, the accusation that had been Estes' theme for two decades. Lyndon Johnson had been behind the Kennedy assassination and was its chief sponsor. Estes made it clear to me that Lyndon Johnson had been behind the Kennedy assassination.

Near the close of this fascinating if rambling performance, a trace of Estes' old sycophancy toward Lyndon Johnson surfaced. "He had a heart of gold," Estes said. "That war killed his spirit. There will never be another like him." Although in a later telephone conversation Estes told me that Mac Wallace "would kill as easily as he would drink a Coke," on that sweltering Texas afternoon the name "Mac Wallace" did not pass his lips.

Billie Sol Estes' accusations against Mac Wallace and Lyndon Johnson bore fruit. In the millennium, a steady stream of books, beginning in 2003 with Barr McClellan's *Blood, Money, & Power: How L.B.J. Killed J.F.K.*, began to appear. They all blamed Lyndon Johnson for the Kennedy assassination, which they claimed had been organized for him, alternately, by his lawyer, Ed Clark, or by his factotum Cliff Carter. Estes himself published two memoirs that included new details, such as that Mac Wallace had access to the garage of Michael and Ruth Paine where Oswald stored his rifle. Wallace knew Oswald's wife, Marina, Estes claimed, and had met Oswald's CIA handler, George de Mohrenschildt, in the mid-1940s at the University of Texas.

In *The Man Who Killed Kennedy: The Case Against LBJ*, published in 2013, former Nixon political operative Roger Stone talks of "the assassin Mac

Wallace" as if this were a given. In Max Allan Collins's pulp novel *Ask Not*, Wallace is surly and has "socialist ways." When a detective shoves him "face first into the toilet bowl," the reader is encouraged to believe that he deserves it.

Estes was also instrumental in an account by Stephen Pegues. An amateur who had never published a book, Pegues worked under the auspices of Estes, whom he taped at great length. Although it was never published, the manuscript for "Texas Mafia" portrays Johnson as sending Mac Wallace to Austin "to deal with Kinser," a fact for which there is no evidence. Boldly, Pegues recreates the murder of Henry Marshall. "Mac Wallace approached the land owner with his snake charming appeal," Pegues writes. "He flexed the muscles in his jaw as he tried to incapacitate the victim with one thrust . . . things were weird and Mac liked weird." Pegues writes that Mac Wallace "generically committed pre-meditated, cold-blooded murder," *generically* being an unusual choice of adverb, but offering a clue that he was not really writing about Mac Wallace at all, but that Wallace's name was being substituted for others. The Pegues manuscript contains no source notes.

Pegues does challenge a few of Estes' assertions. He does not place Mac Wallace at the backyard meeting "where it was decided that the agriculture agent [Henry Marshall] had to be eliminated." Realizing that Mac Wallace was not present at the Christmas Eve party at the LBJ Ranch preceding her death, Pegues writes, "Johnson poisoned the wretched sister with the loose mouth." As for Estes, Pegues presents him as a saint in the midst of scoundrels. "Stop!" he interjects into his narrative. "This is not Billie Sol Estes. He would rather eat cow chips on rye than take a life!" Pegues died before his book could be published.

Even more outlandish is a 2003 effort, Glen Sample's and Mark Collom's *The Men on the Sixth Floor*, in which at the 1961 funeral of Sam Rayburn, Mac Wallace is said to have recruited a new character in the Kennedy assassination scenario, a Chickasaw Native American named Loy Factor. Two years later, according to Sample and Collom, Factor was driven to Dallas, where he met Jack Ruby and discovered that Ruby had recruited Lee Harvey Oswald. The Factor myth is revisited in a documentary film directed by Lyle Sardie called *LBJ: A Closer Look* in which Factor actually appears. Prone, weak, Factor is shown a photocopy of a photograph of Mac Wallace and is asked to identify it. "W-A-L-L-A-C-E," he groans, scarcely audible, less than convincing.

Some have speculated that Factor learned what he did about the Kennedy assassination while reading books when he was in prison for murder. Behind director Sardie's back, Billie Sol Estes laughed. "We make sausage meat out of people like him," Estes said.

In Barr McClellan's *Blood, Money and Power: How L.B.J. Killed J.F.K*, Mac Wallace appears in the company of Lee Harvey Oswald. Both were Marxists, McClellan says, although in fact neither was. "We know they did meet," McClellan writes without any evidence. Certainly Mac Wallace was never, as McClellan writes, a radical who "wanted to make the world safe for extreme socialism." Nor does he offer any credible evidence that Mac Wallace shot John Douglas Kinser "to protect Johnson's interests." When an innocent worker wanders onto the sixth floor of the Texas School Book Depository on November 22, 1963, McClellan has Wallace "[decide] to kill him."

In McClellan's version of events, Johnson's lawyer, Ed Clark, organized the Kennedy assassination. McClellan's Clark devoted his time entirely to advancing Lyndon Johnson, who was determined "to do anything to become the most powerful person in the world." In reality, Clark managed the political campaigns of Johnson rival Ralph Yarborough, Senator John Tower, and Texas governors Allan Shivers and Price Daniel. Clark also on occasion represented Herman and George Brown. His uncle didn't have "the courage to be involved in the assassination," says nephew Guy Cade Fisher, a Clark partner.

In Estes' own memoir, the role of Ed Clark is assumed by Cliff Carter. Estes names Carter as the source for the information that Mac Wallace "shot from the grassy knoll and was the one who did the head shot." Estes has the assassination planned at a poker table on the second floor of Brownie's restaurant in Dallas by mobster Benny Binion; John Melvin Liggett, an embalmer who supposedly altered the body of John F. Kennedy prior to its return to Washington, D.C.; and a hit man high school classmate of Mac Wallace's named R. D. Matthews. Inaccurately, Estes places Mac's father A. J. Wallace's office on the second floor of Brownie's. Estes also writes that in December 1963, a month after the assassination, he met with Cliff Carter and Mac Wallace at the Driskill Hotel in Austin.

Part of Estes' strategy as he devoted himself assiduously to destroying Lyndon Johnson's place in history was to connect him with the underworld. According to Estes' memoir, Johnson obstructed legislation that would have hindered racing wires and slot machines. Estes charges that Johnson represented the interests of the underworld in Washington, for which "Fat Jack" Halfen and Congressman Albert Thomas paid him fifty thousand dollars a year. (Mobster Jack Halfen was found guilty of bribery of a laundry list of

Texas politicians from Supreme Court Justice Tom Clark and Albert Thomas to Sam Rayburn. Johnson pardoned him in 1966.)

In Estes' version of events, it was not Ed Clark or Cliff Carter, but Mac Wallace who was entrusted "to build the hit team for the actual murder." "Lyndon should not have authorized Mack [sic] to kill the President," Estes concludes, portraying Wallace's "real job" as "doing dirty tricks for Lyndon."

Yet another of the books focusing on Lyndon Johnson as the perpetrator of the Kennedy assassination is Phillip Nelson's *LBJ: The Mastermind of JFK's Assassination*, published in 2013. Nelson begins from the assumption embraced by all these books, and treated as so obvious that it no longer requires substantiation, that Mac Wallace was Lyndon Johnson's hit man.

Nelson claims Wallace drove to Dallas "to get a gun from an FBI agent friend of his." He says Ed Clark arranged for Wallace's bail when he shot Kinser, an event with which Clark had nothing to do. He writes that Wallace had a TOP SECRET security clearance, which was never the case. Armed with "Secret Service credentials" provided by Lyndon Johnson, Nelson writes, Wallace was present at Dealey Plaza "to help frame Oswald at the scene." Nelson amends the customary scenario: "Malcolm Wallace was there . . . not as a shooter but as a supervisor who would ensure that the planted evidence included shells that matched the Mannlicher-Carcano, which would be found in the 'sniper's lair,' and the rifle would be stashed along the stairwell on the fifth floor."

All of these books base their theory that Lyndon Johnson was the organizer of the Kennedy assassination on two premises. One, the story told by Madeleine Brown, went that on the night before the assassination, at a Dallas party, Lyndon Johnson had revealed to her his foreknowledge of the assassination, asserting that "after tomorrow" the Kennedys would never bother him again. Her story, oft told, has been riddled with inconsistencies; the guest list has varied as partygoers have come and gone. No one has corroborated her story of Johnson's admission of foreknowledge of the assassination.

The other premise is that an unidentified fingerprint found on the sixth floor of the Texas School Book Depository belonged to Mac Wallace. In the custody of the Warren Commission, this print matched no police officer on the scene. It did not belong to Oswald, nor to any other employee of the depository. This "one square inch of human sweat" proved to be Lyndon Johnson's undoing, Barr McClellan insists.

Residing at the National Archives, unidentified, this fingerprint became the main piece of evidence convicting Lyndon Johnson as the planner, the "mastermind," of the Kennedy assassination.

CHAPTER 17

The Fingerprint

"You could go to the bank with the I.D. of that print."

—JOHN FRASER HARRISON

John Fraser Harrison, a veteran who had served in military intelligence and with the Dallas police, became a researcher into the Texas roots of the Kennedy assassination. Studying a "security index" of Texas figures who might bear watching, his attention was drawn to Mac Wallace. On November 22, 1963, Harrison was assigned to the Criminal Intelligence Section of the Special Service Bureau of the Dallas Police Department, investigating extremist groups of the far left and the far right who might make their presence felt during the President's visit. Harrison was asked to perform covert surveillance of a Black Muslim church. Informants had reported that members of this church were planning to create a disturbance somewhere along the parade route.

Harrison was a small, intense man with a piercing gaze and dark blond hair. Thin-lipped, he looked at you shrewdly through giant Coke-bottle eyeglasses. He was a man of his generation, sporting a short 1950s haircut, a man without personal vanity. In his later years, he took on a grizzled look. Like all successful law enforcement officers, Harrison was skilled in making himself seem invisible. He even signed his e-mails ".-," which was Morse code for "J," dot dash, dot dash. (He insisted upon being addressed only with the letter "J," no punctuation, and not as "Harrison.") One would not look at him twice. J Harrison preferred it that way.

John Fraser Harrison was born on November 8, 1933. He grew up in Portland, Maine, the only child of a branch manager for the Burroughs Adding Machine Company. His parents ran the Ogunquit Playhouse, in Ogunquit, Maine, some of whose productions featured Katharine Hepburn, who became a family friend. Harrison's ancestry dated back to five Pilgrim passengers who made the voyage to the New World on the *Mayflower*. Genealogy would forever beguile him. In later years he became the certified genealogist for the Texas Supreme Court Historical Society.

Early in 1953, Harrison found himself engaged in what he termed "the Korean police action." The Army trained him in intelligence gathering. Returning to the United States, he was assigned to the Joint Chiefs of Staff Communication Center at the Pentagon. He earned all necessary security clearances and for six years participated in a Reserve Strategic Intelligence Research and Analysis (SIRA) team. Along the way he did graduate work at Mac Wallace's alma mater in Austin.

Harrison arrived at the Texas School Book Depository building four minutes after the shots were fired. He compiled a list of all the vehicles parked behind the picket fence where some shots, by copious witness testimony, had been fired, along with their make, model, and license tags. Then he turned his notebook over to the Dallas police. He would never see it again, although he requested its return. Later that day, Harrison served on the guard team for Governor John Connally at the intensive care unit at Parkland Hospital.

On March 25, 1964, Dallas Police sergeant Don Francis Steele, testifying before the Warren Commission, commended "J.F. Harrison" for recognition as the officer who had been with him during the assassination and its aftermath. A year later, Harrison received a certificate of merit for exemplary conduct signed by Dallas Police chief Jesse Curry. On the day of the assassination Curry had remarked to Harrison that the security threat with which he was most concerned was the local Communist Elgin Williams, Mac Wallace's friend who had died in Galveston in 1956.

From the moment of the assassination of John F. Kennedy, Harrison was obsessed with discovering who was behind the heinous deed. He worked in the shadows, viewing personal notoriety as a detriment to a serious investigation. I "creep around unknown," he once said.

"I want to be part of the answer, not part of the problem," Harrison said, "and there are more parts of the problem in this whole scenario than there are parts of the answer." The copious files he created were based on documentary evidence. He even eschewed witness testimony since anyone could lie, anyone might misremember. "The names of the people involved in the Kennedy assassination," Harrison came to believe, "could wrap around the earth five times." He concluded that at least four people had to have been shooting on November 22. He did not center his suspicions on Lyndon Johnson.

Harrison joined the Unsolved Closed Case Association within the Dallas Police Department. He attended their meetings, discussing the JFK case frequently. He was willing to be wrong, and he urged the young researchers who were his protégés to figure things out for themselves. Rarely did he make definitive statements. He spoke through implication and indirection so that you had to interpret for yourself what he meant. Harrison was likely to call at an odd hour. He seemed always to know where someone was when he needed information.

Often he invited people on field trips to explore assassination sites. He took Doug Horne, the chief analyst in the late 1990s for military records for the Assassination Records and Review Board staff, on a tour of Dallas cemeteries. They visited the graves of Lee Harvey Oswald; J. D. Tippit, the Dallas police officer who was killed shortly after Kennedy's shooting; and Rose Cheramie— real name Melba Marcades—who had been a stripper in Jack Ruby's night-club. Harrison included the headstone of John Liggett, the mortician whom he suspected of doing restorative art, reconstructing John F. Kennedy's face on the afternoon of the assassination to create autopsy photographs designed to conceal the full measure of the President's wounds.

Liggett numbered among his accomplishments reattaching actress Jayne Mansfield's head after she had been decapitated in an automobile accident. Harrison discovered that Liggett had "died," only for his second wife to peer into his coffin and know: "It was not John." Liggett sought refuge in Las Vegas at Benny Binion's Horseshoe Casino. Harrison suggested to Horne that they co-write a true crime book about Liggett. When he added that Liggett "was so spooked by his JFK experience that he started murdering people," Horne drew back.

For the characters he found most provocative, Harrison created huge white vinyl binders filled with documents. Always he was skeptical about what he read. This passage about Liggett from one of Harrison's white binders reflects his associative thinking:

> He was charged with the "attempted murder" of the widow of Jay Bert Peck. When he left her house he was sure she was already gone from a beating and set her bed on fire. He took her car back to a bar where they had been drinking . . . Ohh, Jay Bert Peck (her husband) committed suicide a few years earlier. He was director of security for some guy named Clint Murchison, Sr. The brother also was under investigation for 5 other murders that all had the same MO. One of

them was a Dr. Mary Sherman in New Orleans. Dr. Sherman worked
with Dr. Alton Ochsner and a researcher on monkeys named David
Ferrie. ALL of the murders had the same MO and ALL had connections to an event that took place in Dallas back in 1963.

Harrison's euphemism for Las Vegas was "Lost Wages." "The Mortician's
ex-wife swears that she saw him 3 years ago in Lost Wages at Benny
Binion's," he asserted. "His brother [Liggett's] has ALL the earmarks of
working for a nameless company." The "nameless" company was, of course,
CIA. In 1988, Harrison was the first person to obtain President Kennedy's
death certificate from the Texas Bureau of Vital Statistics. It was twenty-five
years to the day after the assassination, the first moment that it became
available to the public.

As the years passed, several of Harrison's white vinyl binders chronicled
the life of Mac Wallace. "I don't think Wallace was in a shooting position," he
said. Wallace as a historical figure intrigued Harrison, not least because
Wallace had been convicted of murder with malice and yet had served no jail
time.

Some aspects of Wallace's history did not add up for J Harrison. Wallace
had had the temerity to write to J. Edgar Hoover himself, and had requested
the assistance of the FBI lab at his trial. Then, although Wallace had been
convicted of premeditated murder, he found a job with TEMCO, a major
defense contractor. Harrison was puzzled by Wallace's obtaining the SECRET
security clearance required. A friend on the Dallas Police Department's intelligence unit slipped Mac Wallace's classified Naval Intelligence file into
Harrison's hands, which is how it became available to the author.

He compiled genealogies of the Wallace family. He copied pages from the
Crusader, the Woodrow Wilson High School yearbook; and from the University
of Texas annual, the *Cactus*; and the divorce petitions and divorce decrees of
Mac and Andre Wallace. He received a copy of Mac Wallace's much-amended
death certificate. A separate file was devoted to Wallace's will and the unex-
plained appearance in probate court of Jerry Neal Wallace a second time, thirteen years after Wallace's death. One binder was devoted to the life of John
Douglas Kinser, complete with a genealogy. Harrison enjoyed the irony that
his own mother and Kinser resided in the same cemetery.

For eight years, Harrison attempted to pry Mac Wallace's FBI file from the
hands of the government. To his Freedom of Information Act (FOIA) request,
the Bureau finally replied on September 30, 1998, with a blizzard of paper.

Nearly half the writing was buried beneath heavy black redactions. Harrison imagined ominous revelations. Yet when Wallace's FBI file was reprocessed in 2014 and sent to the author unredacted, there were no "smoking guns." There are no references to Lyndon Johnson, except a note that Johnson was the employer of one of the Bureau's informants, Horace Busby.

Harrison also studied the testimony provided by Billie Sol Estes and Madeleine Brown, who had joined with Estes in his vendetta against Lyndon Johnson:

1. The party (if any took place) was at Clint Murchison Sr.'s house on the night of November 21, 1963. (Madeleine Brown's recounting of that party at which Lyndon Johnson revealed to her his foreknowledge of the Kennedy assassination did not strike J as valid.)
2. The host (if a party took place) was Clint Murchison Jr.
3. Murchison Sr. was in Athens, Texas, or at the Mexico ranch on that evening.
4. Murchison Sr. did not own the Dallas Cowboys; that was Murchison Jr.

Yet J Harrison took seriously Estes' accusations: "LBJ et al. were implicated in the multiple 'assassinations' by the Caddy/DOJ communications in August 1984," he wrote in one of his Wallace binders, "20 YEARS AGO ... AND accepted in the death of Henry Marshall, thereby changing his death from a suicide to a MURDER!" That Harrison had his doubts is reflected in the quotation marks around "assassinations." He did not name Mac Wallace, nor did he mention Wallace in connection with Marshall's death.

J Harrison remained perplexed by Wallace's death certificate, which was so replete with errors. Rumors wafted out of East Texas. Following the death on May 10, 1975, of her husband, Delmer Lee Akin, Andre had moved to a rental duplex in Georgetown, Texas. According to one of Harrison's sources in the Dallas Police Criminal Investigation Division (CID), "Mac Wallace" visited Andre right up to her death on June 5, 1980, at the age of fifty-six.

"I've got proof that Wallace survived the crash," Harrison told historian Walt Brown, author of several books about the JFK assassination, and with whom J was working closely.

Andre did welcome a dark-haired male visitor when she was suffering the final stages of breast cancer, and this man looked remarkably like Mac Wallace. It was their son, Michael, a dead ringer for his father, except that Michael wore glasses only for reading. His mother never mentioned seeing his father.

Michael Wallace is certain that she would have told him had Mac Wallace appeared on her doorstep after his "death."

Harrison took to sleeping with a gun under his pillow. When he went out, he took his gun. "You can't be too careful," he said. He began to carry copies of his most sensitive files in the trunk of his car. One day somebody broke into the car and stole the files. Normally self-contained, he was visibly shaken, according to his friend Malcolm Blunt, who talked to him right after it happened.

Harrison had made a living selling real estate. When the market crashed, he fell on hard times. For a while he lived in an old bread truck, and then a trailer. It was so overflowing with files that there was no room for a bed and he slept on the couch. He was a man with a cause, his days leavened by laughter at the absurdities he was uncovering. Growing old occasioned irony. "At age seventy-four some people forget things," he said. "Others remember things that never happened."

In the 1990s, Harrison had an investigative brainstorm. Born of the anomalies he discovered in the history of Mac Wallace, fueled by Billie Sol Estes' connecting Wallace to the Kennedy assassination, he looked into Wallace's whereabouts on November 22, 1963. Wallace putatively had been a protégé of Lyndon Johnson, the individual who profited most from the death of President Kennedy. Since Johnson was not known to have done favors for anyone without profiting substantially in return and Johnson's favors for Wallace may include Bob Long's desultory prosecution, the job at TEMCO, and the SECRET security clearance, might not Wallace have accomplished for him the ultimate favor?

There was that single fingerprint collected by the FBI from the sixth floor of the Texas School Book Depository on the day of the assassination that had never been identified. In the custody of the Warren Commission, it was designated as "Print 29" and had been lifted from "Box A," a carton sitting at the edge of the entrance to the sixth floor. Print 29 had been labeled "indistinct characteristics." Harrison contacted the National Archives in search of "Warren Commission Exhibit 656." This print was described as belonging to "an unknown person."

Harrison's plan was to obtain Mac Wallace's fingerprint card from the Austin Department of Public Safety, which had taken his prints when he was arrested for the murder of John Douglas Kinser. Then he would arrange for experts to compare it to Print 29. The fragility of a fingerprint on a carton meant that the latent had to have been created within ten days of the Kennedy assassination. After ten days, prints disappear from corrugated cartons, which are made of absorbent paper. The print most likely had been made within twenty-four hours of the murder of President Kennedy.

Even with Harrison's contacts in the Austin Police Department, it was not easy for him to obtain Wallace's prints. To gain access to public documents, the subject had to have been dead for twenty-five years. Mac Wallace had died on January 7, 1971. On the day before the twenty-fifth anniversary of Wallace's death, Harrison filed for the fingerprint card.

To Texas Attorney General Dan Morales, J Harrison described himself as "a person working on a statistical or research project." He included with his letter a copy of Mac Wallace's death certificate. On March 22, 1996, he met with Ben Kyser, manager of the Fingerprint and Records Services of the Texas Department of Public Safety. Unwilling to take responsibility, Kyser then turned Harrison's request over to Ron M. Pigott, assistant general counsel of the Texas Department of Public Safety.

Pigott was reluctant to authorize the release of the print because J Harrison was not the "estate representative" for Mac Wallace. He was concerned that "if the Department releases this information to people who do not have a special right of access to it, the criminal history record of information of Mr. Wallace will become public information open to inspection by all." Harrison then appealed to Craig Leavers, the open records investigator at the office of the Texas attorney general. He left messages at the attorney general's office on July 8, 10, 11, 12, and 22, 1996.

On July 26, Pigott sent Harrison a certified copy of the inked fingerprint card of Malcolm Everett Wallace that had been rolled on October 22, 1951. At least one other set of Wallace prints was in existence, those taken by the Navy at the time he joined the U.S. Marines. For those prints to be released, the person had to have left the service sixty-two years earlier. Wallace was discharged from the Marine Corps on August 28, 1940. Only in 2002 at the earliest could J Harrison have obtained Wallace's Navy fingerprints.

With the Austin prints and Warren Commission Exhibit 656, provided by the National Archives, in hand, Harrison approached a seasoned certified latent print examiner named Nathan Darby. Darby had worked for the Austin Police Department for years. He had begun in fingerprint analysis in 1942, when he was in military service. In 1948, he was awarded credentials by the International Association for Identification as a Certified Latent Print Examiner, the primary certifying organization that conferred authority on the examiner. In 1951, Wallace's fingerprints had come to Darby's attention in connection with the Kinser trial.

J Harrison requested of Darby that he compare Wallace's prints with the one discovered on the sixth floor of the Texas School Book Depository to determine whether they belonged to the same person. He did not mention the name "Mac Wallace" nor reveal to Darby that the task had anything to do with the Kennedy assassination. Darby said he would charge no fee.

Darby reported fourteen matching prints between the two sets of prints.

On March 9, 1998, Nathan Darby wrote an official letter to J Harrison. His letterhead described him as "Lieutenant Commander retired, Identification Criminal Records, Photography Laboratory, Austin Police Department":

> Dear Mr. J Harrison
>
> You provided me a photocopy of an inked fingerprint for comparison to a photocopy of a latent print. You also provided me with a photocopy of a standard fingerprint card with inked fingerprints on the card. The origin of the inked print, latent print, and the fingerprint card are unknown to me.
>
> I examined the inked print, now exhibit DAN #3, and the latent print, now exhibit DAN #4, and found identifying points.
>
> Based on my comparison, I concluded that the person who produced the inked fingerprint, exhibit DAN #3 also produced the latent fingerprint, exhibit DAN #4.
>
> I examined exhibit DAN #5 and found print #10 on exhibit #5 to be the same print as DAN #3. The position of the finger in space #10 on the fingerprint card represents the finger to be the left littler finger. Other spacings on exhibit DAN #5 were produced by the left little finger of the same person unknown to me.
>
> I can not testify to the origin or the source of any of the exhibits DAN #3, DAN #4, or DAN #5.
>
> Very truly yours,
> Nathan Darby

Three days later, Darby swore out a more detailed affidavit. He stated that the unknown person who provided the inked print of his left little finger for the Austin police was the same person who made the latent on the carton at the School Book Depository. He declared that he had discovered fourteen matching points, going with his original determination and aware that the FBI guideline was eight matches for a credible identification; the U.S. Courts preferred ten to twelve matches.

Still, Darby was not satisfied. He worked for another year, color-coding the latent supplied by the Archives in red, green, and blue. Because the subject had been sweating, and had been tense, Darby explained, moisture adhered to the Texas School Book Depository print. There was a black smudge, sharply defining the ridges and valleys. After the color-coding, Darby said he found thirty-four points of match. Only now was Darby informed of the identity of the person whose prints he had been examining.

One day, visiting the dentist, Darby ran into an acquaintance from the Austin police department. He remarked that he had been working on a finger-print identification that traced back to Mac Wallace. "Drop it! Leave it alone!" the police acquaintance said.

"It would be my dying declaration," said Darby, a small, vibrant grey-haired man, passionate in his convictions. "They match! They match!" he exclaimed on a video created by French journalist William Reymond. On that film Darby announces thirty points of match.

Cautious, Harrison sought a second opinion. He brought the prints to E. Harold Hoffmeister, who also claimed to be a certified latent print exam-iner and who worked for the Texas Department of Public Safety. Hoffmeister too had been certified by the International Association for Identification. He did accept a fee—a check for five hundred dollars from Barr McClellan, who was then working with J Harrison. Hoffmeister signed a "contract of employ-ment." He promised to "compare developed latent impressions with known impressions to establish identity."

At first, Hoffmeister concurred with Darby. He attested to the same points that Darby had claimed matched between the Warren Commission print and the Austin police print. Dated April 15, 1998, Hoffmeister's affidavit reads:

> It is my opinion that an unknown latent print I compared with the inked fingerprint impression of a subject unknown to me at this time matches the left little fingerprint of this subject.
>
> I concur with the marked exhibits of a latent print and rolled fingerprint given to me and done by an unknown CLPE.
>
> E. H. Hoffmeister
>
> I have examined the rolled inked impressions of Malcolm Everett Wallace & they match the rolled inked impressions I compared with the latent print.
>
> E. Hoffmeister. Mr. J. Harrison, 4-15-98.

Hoffmeister initialed his copy of the latent, along with fourteen matches pointing to the matching ridges he had identified. He initialed four pages of print impressions.

It seemed that as soon as he learned whose prints he had examined, and that the Kennedy assassination was involved, Hoffmeister recanted. The next day, he wrote:

> After Mr. Harrison left, I continued to analize [sic] the two prints (inked and latent) and the longer I looked at them the more questioned [sic] I became. Some points matched and they didn't. Then ALL points matched. Then NO points matched. I then realized that both the other CLPE and I were having to make mental decisions due to the fact that we were dealing with unknown generations of COPIES of the latent and NOT THE ORIGINAL.

Concluding that Hoffmeister had changed his mind out of fear, J Harrison forged ahead. He sent the Darby findings and exhibits to the homicide division of the Dallas police. They then turned the materials over to the FBI. Eighteen months later, the FBI responded with a telephone call. The print match was in error, they said. The Bureau sent no written documentation either to their Dallas field office or to the Dallas Police Department. If Bureau protocols demanded that their obligation was to contact Nathan Darby directly, outlining their reasons for deciding that the prints did not match, this time they were silent. Customarily the Bureau backed certified experts. On this occasion, with no explanation, they rejected the expert's findings.

J Harrison concealed Darby's name at the 1998 press conference announcing the identification of the print. In the spring of 2003, according to Austin lawyer Dawn Meredith, who had befriended Darby, his home was robbed. The security alarm was bypassed. The only item missing was a file relating to Mac Wallace's fingerprint that resided under Darby's bed.

"You could go to the bank with the I.D. of that print," Harrison told anyone who asked.

After the Darby fingerprint identification was announced, there were efforts to determine Mac Wallace's whereabouts on the day of the Kennedy assassination. He ought to have been in Anaheim, where he continued to work for Ling Electronics. Reporter William P. Barrett, writing for the *Dallas Times Herald,* says Mac Wallace was "untrackable" for the day of the assassination.

In California, Wallace was separated from his new wife, Virginia Ledgerwood, and living with his son. Michael recalls that almost certainly Wallace was home for dinner on November 22, 1963. Michael was fifteen years old; he was distressed that the President had been killed in Texas, that people were blaming Texas, which he considered still his home. Wallace attempted to console him, trying to make the distraught boy feel better.

Michael does not recall what time Wallace arrived home on the night of November 22, but he feels certain that he was there. "I would bet my paycheck," he told the author. Michael went on to a career in Southern California law enforcement, retiring after thirty years of service. His uprightness and his religious sensibility enhance his credibility. "We had the first discussion on the night of the assassination," Michael Wallace repeated to the author.

Despite his faith in the fingerprint identification, J Harrison never came to believe that Lyndon Johnson was behind the assassination. He never subscribed to Billie Sol Estes' accusation. "I never suspected Johnson and still don't," Harrison said. If anything, he added, Johnson was "in a very small pyramid that's inside the pyramid of who was actually involved." Even if Johnson had foreknowledge of the assassination—and Harrison was skeptical about Madeleine Brown's description of the party the night before at which the guest list seemed to be endlessly shifting—he was "not at the top of the pyramid."

There was something unnerving about the fingerprint identifications supplied by Darby and Hoffmeister. Even if their conclusions that the Austin and Warren Commission prints belong to the same person were correct, there remains the question of motive. A lifelong liberal, Mac Wallace would have had nothing against John F. Kennedy, no reason to harm him. Only his connection to Lyndon Johnson could conceivably have involved him in this crime.

This at once raises the issue of whether Johnson, ordinarily so careful about leaving footprints in his activities, would have enlisted someone who could easily be connected to him, and placed this person at the scene of the crime. The death of Sam Smithwick in his cell after summoning Coke Stevenson to confess what he knew about Box 13 and the credibility of the 1948 election for U.S. senator suggests that there were anonymous hit men, sheriffs, and deputy sheriffs aplenty lurking and on call in the sagebrush. It seems unlikely and illogical that Johnson would have sent Mac Wallace to implement the assassination of John F. Kennedy.

In May 2013, rendered uneasy by the fingerprint identification, I contacted an independent certified latent print examiner to verify the findings of Nathan Darby and Harold Hoffmeister. In all the books that used Wallace's presence at the Texas School Book Depository as evidence to implicate Lyndon Johnson in the assassination, no one had revisited the fingerprint analysis. Each book repeated, virtually by rote, what had been written before.

The certified latent print examiner I hired was Robert Garrett and he had enjoyed a long career in law enforcement in New Jersey, where he had been a senior crime scene analyst and "reconstructionist." He had been supervisor of the Middlesex County Prosecutor's Office crime scene unit.

Garrett had been trained in fingerprint analysis at FBI headquarters when they were located in downtown Washington, D.C., and then at the FBI laboratory at Quantico, Virginia. Now he was in charge of certification programs for the International Association for Identification, which still certifies all latent print examiners and is the singular accrediting institution.

I adopted J Harrison's approach and did not inform Garrett about whose print he would be examining. I did not mention that the Kennedy assassination was in any way connected to the fingerprint. When I handed him Harrison's Darby file, Garrett hesitated. He observed that Darby had worked from photocopies. Garrett insisted that he could not work with a photocopy of the latent, the Warren Commission exhibit. He required either a negative or a first-generation photograph of the latent print.

A photograph of the latent taken in 1963 by the FBI resided at the National Archives. It was of superior quality, and available to anyone who requested it.

Enough time had passed so that the Navy was willing to release Mac Wallace's military file from the National Archives in St. Louis. All I required were Wallace's military service number and his Social Security number, both of which J Harrison had included in his Wallace records. The Navy had produced a sharp, clear copy of Wallace's fingerprints that had been taken when he enlisted in the U.S. Marines in 1939.

From the documents in Harrison's files, the tracings, photocopies, and diagrams of the matches Nathan Darby had marked, it was apparent that Darby had relied on the old black-and-white model of fingerprint identification. Yet, without the gray scale, features were lost. What was required to determine whether it was Mac Wallace's print that had been discovered at the Texas School Book Depository was a first-generation photograph and the digital technology that had taken over the field of fingerprint identification. Garrett's methodology came under the heading of "digital forensics," a technology that had not yet been available in 1998 and could take into account multiple levels of gray.

At once Garrett noticed, as had Harold Hoffmeister, that there was a problem with the Austin fingerprints. These had been smudged because the roller used to make the inked print had not been thoroughly cleaned off after its use with the previous subject. Luckily, I was able to provide Garrett with the Navy prints, which are of a higher quality than those taken by local police departments.

Garrett determined that the prints taken by the Navy and those taken by the Austin police in 1951 at the time of the shooting of John Douglas Kinser belonged to the same person. But as for the print known as Warren Commission Exhibit 656, Print 29, of a left little finger, sent by the National Archives in high resolution, this print belonged to someone else entirely. I was as excited as J Harrison must have been when Nathan Darby told him there was a match. So my skepticism had been warranted.

The 256 levels of gray that Garrett discovered from his enhanced digital scan of the latent sent by the archives were not present in the image from which Nathan Darby drew his analysis. Based on these shadings, there were clear "discrepancies," the term Garrett used, between the two sets of Wallace prints and the unidentified print residing among the Warren Commission exhibits.

A "discrepancy," Garrett writes in his report, represents the friction ridge detail in one impression that does not exist in the corresponding area of another impression. In his "Analysis of Discrepancies," Garrett concludes:

Target feature: There is, in both the Wallace left little finger (#10) print and latent print CE 656, #29, a short ridge five ridge counts below the delta. This feature will be used to locate all other features or discrepancies between the two prints.

A. Four ridges up from the target feature in the latent is a ridge to the right. This is absent in the Wallace print.
B. Five ridges up from the target feature in the latent is a ridge ending to the right. This is absent in the Wallace print.
C. Two ridges up from the target feature in the latent is a ridge ending to the right. This is absent in the Wallace print.

D. Two ridges up from the target feature in the Wallace print is a
    ridge ending to the right. This is absent in the latent print.

E. Two ridges up from the target feature in the Wallace print is a
    ridge ending to the right. This is absent in the latent print.

F. Four ridges up from the target feature in the latent is a ridge
    ending to the right. This is absent in the Wallace print.

G. Seven ridges up from the target feature in the latent is a bifurca-
    tion to the left. This is absent in the Wallace print.

H. Eleven ridges up from the target feature in the latent is a ridge
    ending to the right. This is absent in the Wallace print.

Each of these discrepancies is sufficient to exclude Wallace number 10 as the
source of CE 656 number 29. Other discrepancies exist but have not been
documented in the image for the sake of clarity.

Garrett found the fingerprints released by the Austin Police Department all
but unusable. He wrote in his report, comparing the Austin print which
Darby and Hoffmeister used the latent:

> Although 14 minutiae are marked on both impressions, 2, 9, 10, 11,
> 12, 13 & 14 are indistinct on impression E. This may be due to copy
> artifacts, but nonetheless, they can't be used as reliable identifiable
> features. That leaves only 7 remaining features on which to rely.
> When these 7 features are plotted and plots compared, it is easy to
> see that the alignments are off. This can sometimes be attributed
> to distortion occurring at the time of deposition. However, there are
> no indicators of distortion in either D or E.

Garrett concluded, having determined that CE 656 number 29 was "a
developed latent fingerprint":

> These images, provided by the U.S. National Archives and Records
> Administration, are far superior to the copies of the image previ-
> ously provided. The images from the National Archives are of suffi-
> cient quality to be inserted into an automated fingerprint
> identification system (AFIS) and checked against existing finger-
> print databases. An examination of these high resolution images
> and a comparison to the recorded fingerprint record of Malcolm
> Everett (M. E.) Wallace from the United States Marine Corps, allows

me to conclude without any doubt that CE 656 number 29 was not made by the little finger (#10) of Malcolm Wallace.

Garrett took the additional step of comparing CE 656 number 29 to each of Mac Wallace's remaining nine fingers. None matched. None of his fingers could be the source of CE 656.

Whoever was up there on the sixth floor of the Texas School Book Depository wearing heavy, dark horn-rimmed glasses and observed by steel worker Richard Randolph Carr, who was standing on an adjacent scaffolding at Dealey Plaza, in an effort to apply for employment, there is no credible evidence that it was Mac Wallace. Carr had been on the construction elevator of the new Dallas County Courthouse, seven floors above the ground. He had observed two men run from behind the wooden fence where some shots came. One, a "dark complexioned white male about 5′ 8″, heavyset, [wore] dark rimmed glasses." Carr said he saw this man in "horn-rimmed glasses, in the second window of the top floor of the Texas School Book Depository." There is no credible evidence that it was Mac Wallace.

"It's obvious that these are not prints of the same person," Garrett said. "The unidentified print held in the Warren Commission exhibits did not belong to Mac Wallace. Darby and Hoffmeister were pointing out things that weren't there." Garrett added that he would have come to the same conclusion just by comparing the smudged Austin prints with the Warren Commission latent. Adding the Navy prints only confirmed his conclusion.

Garrett discovered that in 1998 Nathan Darby had not been a certified latent print examiner after all. He had perjured himself on his affidavit when he wrote: "I hold the designation of Certified Latent Fingerprint Examiner (#78–468), which is issued by the International Association for Identification." Darby's certification had expired on November 6, 1984. Darby had even written a letter to his own file stating that he did not intend to recertify. In 1998 he had not been a certified examiner for fourteen years.

Certifications were valid only for five years. Then, to recertify, continued work experience and education credits were required, along with passing a recertification examination. Darby had been grandfathered into the certification program in 1978, which meant that he had been awarded a certification based on his training and experience, but had not been required to pass a test. This practice had been abandoned after Darby's certification had expired. As for Harold Hoffmeister, his certification had lapsed on October 30, 1996, and he had made no effort to renew it.

In passing, I showed Bob Garrett the composite created by gas station attendant Nolan Griffin at the time of the murder of Henry Marshall. Garrett saw no particular resemblance between the man in horn-rimmed glasses with a round face and kinky hair and Mac Wallace. "It could have been anyone," Garrett said. In his accusations, Billie Sol Estes never mentioned Wallace as the figure in the composite. All he said was, "Some said the sketch resembled me, but I never had acne scars."

Griffin had noted scars on the man's face. Although Mac Wallace suffered a serious skin infection when he dropped out of the Columbia University School of Law, the Neal Douglass photographs taken of him at the Kinser trial reveal no facial scars. Neither Michael Wallace nor Nora Ann Carroll remember scars on Mac Wallace's face. They were not informed by me why scars were an issue.

Uneasy, J Harrison attempted under a 1998 FOIA request to obtain further Mac Wallace fingerprint filings, including the one from the U.S. Marine Corps. He sought fingerprints from the Dallas police, from the Office of Naval Intelligence, from Ling Electronics, from Luscombe Airplane Corporation, from the Department of Agriculture, and from the Department of State. None of these were forthcoming.

There is no credible evidence that Wallace had anything to do with the Kennedy assassination. Since the identification of Wallace's fingerprint has been the primary "evidentiary" basis for the contention that Lyndon Johnson was involved in the implementation of the assassination, there is no evidence that Johnson was a participant either.

Epilogue

"The truth is so often that which we do not say!"

—HOLLAND McCOMBS IN THE MIDST OF
HIS RESEARCH INTO THE LIFE OF LYNDON
JOHNSON FOR *LIFE* MAGAZINE

Billie Sol Estes' accusations could not have been embraced by anyone had they been entirely without foundation. Lyndon Johnson manifested a considerable dark side, one unequivocally expressed in his shocking response to the attack on the USS *Liberty*. Mac Wallace had committed a cold-blooded murder. Might he not then have gone on to kill again?

It may be logical to assume that Lyndon Johnson extracted significant favors from Wallace in exchange for Johnson's having gotten him his job at the Department of Agriculture, but the evidence is scant. Our understanding of Lyndon Johnson's role in the Kinser trial, if he had one, is limited by the fact that Robert (R. J.) Long's oral history was sanitized by the LBJ Library in 1984, 1985, and 1986. A 2013 appeal that the sanitized items be restored was ignored until 2016. Yet Henry Scarborough's anecdotal evidence that Lyndon Johnson traveled to Austin at the time of the Kinser trial and conferred with Long deserves consideration.

It is not known for certain whether Johnson procured for Wallace his job at TEMCO and the SECRET security clearance he required to keep it. The evidence that only someone with Johnson's power could have prevented the Office of Naval Intelligence from revoking and denying that clearance, as the Navy sought for over a decade to do, is circumstantial. What role the father of Floyd Stephens played, if any, in the murder of Henry Marshall has not emerged. Nor have facts surfaced regarding Billie Sol Estes' own participation in and knowledge of the murders that followed upon his fall from grace.

If Mac Wallace had been a serial killer in the pay of Lyndon Johnson, why had he died penniless? What accounts for the errors on Wallace's death certificate? How can the disappearance of his medical records from the hospital where he was taken after his fatal accident be explained? Where are the records from the Camp County sheriff's office for the evening that he died? Certainly the errors and the fact that important records inexplicably vanished suggest a cover-up of some force.

There is no credible evidence linking Lyndon Johnson to the murder of John F. Kennedy, that murder from which he so richly benefited. Johnson pursued politics that would not have been embraced by President Kennedy, but this reality suggests not that Johnson was a participant in the assassination, but the reverse, that he was kept distant from the crime, wreathed in plausible deniability.

Famously, U.S. Air Force Colonel L. Fletcher Prouty, the Pentagon's liaison to CIA, recounted that Lyndon Johnson had asked him, "Were they shooting at me?" Brigadier General Godfrey McHugh told of how on Air Force One, following the assassination, he discovered Lyndon Johnson "hiding in the toilet in the bedroom compartment, muttering 'conspiracy, conspiracy, they're after all of us.'" Physical cowardice or theatrics: Johnson was addicted to both.

In an untitled, unfinished video by French journalist William Reymond, Billie Sol Estes' ghostwriter Tom Bowden faces the camera and asserts that only Texans, Texas "families," were behind the Kennedy assassination. "Some guys that believed they were dealing out Texas justice," Bowden says. Bowden claims to have discovered "where the Billie Sol information came from," suggesting that Estes was used by people serving private agendas. A convicted felon and admitted liar, Estes enters history with little credibility.

Waiting to be treated at a veterans' hospital in Temple, Texas, in the mid-2000s, J Harrison heard the name "Billie Sol" called out. Harrison went over to Estes and asked in his easy way, "What are you doing now?" Estes said he was on the Texas county fair circuit, autographing two-dollar bills and charging five dollars.

"Are your problems behind you?" Harrison said.

"I've done a few things to cover myself," Estes said. He showed Harrison a photograph of several Mafia types at dinner. He received that photo in the mail in 1984, Estes said. One of the two women at the table was his sister. It was then, Estes claimed, that he decided not to talk to the FBI agents in Abilene. The Mafia had kept him silent.

J Harrison had made his copious files available to Barr McClellan, hoping that his research might see the light of day. When he read the manuscript of *Blood, Money and Power*, according to Walt Brown, he begged for revisions. J did not believe that Lyndon Johnson was behind the Kennedy assassination. When McClellan refused to make the changes, in frustration J wept. Brown reports that J discovered that although McClellan claimed to have had lunch with Mac Wallace, in fact he had only ridden down in the elevator from Ed Clark's office with Wallace once.

J came down with a virulent form of cancer. By May 2005, he was on his deathbed, in hospice care. One day the telephone rang. Did he want to talk to Barr? Walt asked. "No," J said, and turned away. J Harrison was an honest man. He had gone as far as he could in unraveling the story of Mac Wallace. The parameters of the Kennedy assassination eluded him, as they have many.

J Harrison died on May 25, 2005.

One day Billie Sol Estes revealed to William Reymond—with whom he was collaborating on a book and film that would never be completed—that he did not believe that Mac Wallace had committed that long list of murders on Lyndon Johnson's behalf of which Estes had previously accused him. Estes confided to Reymond that the murders were committed not by Mac Wallace, as he had claimed, but by a "Texas group." They had used the name "Mac Wallace" as an "alias." So Reymond revealed on the Education Forum, a Kennedy assassination Internet chat room: "Several times Billie said to us that he used Mac Wallace's name as an alias for somebody else. Though he said he didn't do that about the JFK's assassination but others [sic] murders."

In his 2005 memoir, Estes acknowledged: "We always used false names in communicating." Two decades after he had sent Douglas Caddy to the Justice Department with a list of murders supposedly committed by Mac Wallace, on behalf of Lyndon Johnson, Estes was spinning a tale of a "team" run by Wallace. "Some of the people had French names," Estes added.

We are left with the fact that a group of men were murdered over a period of a few years who had in common intimate knowledge of Estes' scams and swindles and Lyndon Johnson's connection to them. None of these murders was adjudicated. That Wallace admitted late in his life to having known Lyndon Johnson and his family suggests that he saw no reason to deny or conceal the acquaintance.

As Robertson County District Attorney John Paschall put it, "Mac Wallace makes a good scapegoat." It cannot be proven beyond a reasonable doubt that Wallace murdered anyone except John Douglas Kinser. In the absence of credible evidence, it seems fair to award Wallace's disappointed spirit what the law would have entitled to him in life: the presumption of innocence.

In the eighty-eighth year of her life, a widow once more, having been married three times, Nora Ann Carroll rejected the urban legend of Mac Wallace, certain that no part of it could be true. One night she dreamed of her college sweetheart. They were cuddling in the backseat of a small "coupe," her term, on an auto-train, traversing a California chasm to nowhere. There was no sex. It was all about offering each other the solace they had shared, if all too briefly, into eternity.

On February 11, 2013, I telephoned Billie Sol Estes to request, yet again, that he make available those incriminating tapes of Cliff Carter talking about Lyndon Johnson and Mac Wallace that had supposedly been made in 1961, 1963, and 1971. In December 1963, Estes supposedly had met with Carter and Wallace at the Driskill Hotel in Austin, for which there was, Estes claimed, an extant tape.

"I've turned down a million dollars for the tapes," Estes said. "They would send people to prison." He did not specify to whom he was referring. His targets, Carter, Wallace, and Johnson, had long been dead. Perhaps the only person in jeopardy was himself.

I ventured that there was no statute of limitations on murder.

"It would cost a hundred thousand dollars to hire a lawyer," Estes murmured, as if he were bored with the whole thing. The evidence of Lyndon Johnson's many collaborations with Billie Sol Estes remains as circumstantial in 2016 as it did in 1964 when Holland McCombs wandered through Texas during his investigation for *LIFE* magazine. Circumstantial evidence, however, is most certainly evidence.

Billie Sol Estes died on May 14, 2013, without producing the tapes. I asked his daughter, Pam, if I might pay her to listen to the tapes. They're being used for a documentary film, Pam said. Pamela Estes Padget died on June 28, 2014, without producing or releasing either the tapes or the film.

Despite the shoddy books accusing him of "masterminding" the Kennedy assassination, history has been more than kind to Lyndon Johnson. His biographers have granted him cover. Few Americans know of Johnson's role in the fate of the USS *Liberty*; the cover-up has survived intact over many decades. Johnson cannot be proven to have ordered the murder of Sam Smithwick, nor the murders of the Estes witnesses, let alone to have organized the Kennedy assassination and arranged to hire the President's killers, or even to have possessed foreknowledge of the assassination. Sufficient evidence isn't there. Loose ends, contradictory facts suggesting Lyndon Johnson's complicity, remain.

Yet a reassessment of Johnson's historical role seems to be in order. Lyndon Johnson was not elected to the United States Senate, and so should not have served there. His absence would have eliminated the widespread corruption and sale of political influence that characterized his activity as an elected official, "master of the Senate." He would not then have been in a position to be drafted as a Vice Presidential candidate, let alone been in place to ascend to the presidency upon the death of John F. Kennedy.

Rather, Johnson's financial corruption, his wholesale profiting from the sale of government contracts—as witnessed by his participation in the illegalities, scams, and maneuvers of Billie Sol Estes and Bobby Baker—might well have sent him to prison or at least sent him packing in ignominy back to Texas from Washington.

Johnson's voting record over his long career should have exposed his "Great Society" programs as a cynical ploy designed to provide him with a fresh persona, one fit for the historical moment, and exposing nothing so much as his insincerity. That these programs soon shriveled before the vast expenditures required by the Vietnam War suggest that they were not as important to Johnson as his rhetoric claimed. Most profoundly, Johnson's actions on June 8, 1967, when the USS *Liberty* was attacked, which are undisputed, offer the most telling and lucid glimpse into the quality of his public service and point to a moral culpability that lingers and casts a shadow over his historical role.

In a private call to Lyndon Johnson on November 23, 1963, J. Edgar Hoover noted that there wasn't much of a case against Oswald: "The evidence that they have at the present time is not very strong." If it cannot be demonstrated that Oswald was a shooter, firing from the sixth floor of D. H. Byrd's building, it certainly cannot be claimed that Mac Wallace was.

Mac Wallace, who re-created his life on a small scale after the murder of John Douglas Kinser, lived in the shadow of Johnson's will. He provides an object lesson for anyone who too carelessly might wander into a devil's bargain with a powerful and profoundly amoral public figure. His story, like the story of Billie Sol Estes, casts fresh and ample light on the dark side of Lyndon Johnson, whose many perfidies could not remain concealed forever.

Acknowledgments

I am grateful to Walt Brown, the historian who is custodian of the archives of former Dallas reserve police officer John Fraser ("J") Harrison, for so generously making Harrison's extensive files about Mac Wallace available to me. It is by examining J Harrison's trove of Office of Naval Intelligences files investigating Mac Wallace that I first became interested in this figure.

Heartfelt thanks go as well to my Freedom of Information Act lawyer, Daniel S. Alcorn, for his unstinting efforts, and to David M. Hardy of the FBI's Records Management Division for the reprocessing of the FBI file of Malcolm Everett Wallace. In June 2014, the Bureau sent us, free of charge, a virtually unredacted FBI file. My gratitude goes to the Bureau for this expression of transparency and encouragement of historical research.

In the spring, summer, and fall of 1964, as Lyndon Johnson was campaigning for the presidency against Barry Goldwater, *LIFE* magazine assigned a Texan researcher, Holland McCombs, to explore Johnson's life and political history. McCombs traveled deep into the Hill Country of Texas; to the urban centers of Houston, Dallas, and Austin; to San Antonio, to Corpus Christi, and to smaller towns like Abilene and Midland. He alighted in the tiny burg of Pecos, where Billie Sol Estes held sway. McCombs hit pay dirt in his research into Box 13—the disputed ballot box—in Jim Wells County. The full story of the senatorial election of 1948 has been told here for the first time, with the assistance of Holland McCombs' research notes.

McCombs deposited his research files at the University of Tennessee at Martin, a school that had been built on the site of its benefactors, the McCombs family. I am indebted to Sam Richardson and Karen Elmore, the archivists at the Paul Meek Library of the University of Tennessee at Martin, for their unflagging assistance and graciousness.

For sharing their memories of Malcolm Everett Wallace, I am grateful to

Michael Wallace, Meredithe Nix, Nora Ann Carroll, Virginia Princehouse, Joseph L. Schott, and William E. Carroll. The narrative of the whereabouts of Sam Houston Johnson in 1967 comes thanks to Houston attorney Douglas Caddy and Dr. Samuel D. Axelrad.

I should also like to thank Robert J. Garrett, Certified Latent Print Examiner, and Idman Forensics, for the scrupulous science that allowed me to reinvestigate the question of whether it was Mac Wallace's fingerprint that was discovered on the sixth floor of the Texas School Book Depository at the time of the Kennedy assassination. Special thanks go as well to Martha Wagner Murphy at the National Archives in College Park, Maryland, for organizing that pristine photograph of the unidentified latent fingerprint residing in the files of the Warren Commission. I appreciate as well the help of William Siebert at the National Archives in St. Louis.

Author Larry Hancock was exceptionally generous in sharing his research materials on Mac Wallace. Author Burton Hersh, author of *The Old Boys*, was always available and generous with his wide knowledge and bountiful wisdom.

Late in the writing of this book I learned the story of the USS *Liberty*. Most, I am indebted to Commander David Edwin Lewis, who was *Liberty*'s chief intelligence officer. Although he is a man who spent a lifetime in the covens of intelligence and secrecy, Dave Lewis was the most honest and forthright of witnesses.

For their help in bringing this too-little-known historical event to life, I am also grateful to these survivors of the attack on the USS *Liberty*: Pat Blue, widow of Allen Blue; Jim Cavanaugh; Jim Ennes; Ernie Gallo; Ron Grantski; Ron Kukal; Joe Lentini; Bryce Lockwood; Dave Lucas; Joe Meadors; Glenn Oliphant; Donald Pageler; Lloyd Painter; Bob Scarborough; Moe Shafer; Richard Sturman; and Phil Tourney.

Thanks go as well to Peter Flynn, MD. Dr. Anthony Wells's service in the field of intelligence did not keep him from solidarity with those who suffered in this attack. I appreciate the time he spent with me. Special thanks also to Tom Schaaf; Adlai Stevenson III; and Dr. Robert F. Kamansky.

I should also like to thank the following people who contributed to the research: John Armstrong; William P. Barrett; Rex Bradford; the late Billie Sol Estes; Guy Cade Fisher; Lauren Hamilton; Doug Horne; Mani Singh Kang; Tiffany Kelly; Alan Kent; Glenda Kinard; Peter Lemkin; Cindy McGovern; Dawn Meredith; Kevin Meyers; Linda Minor; Robert Morrow; Houston Old; the late Pamela Estes Padget; John Paschall; Connie Perdue; William Robert "Tosh" Plumlee; Laurel Pugliese; Rachel Rendish; Lyle Sardie;

and the late Ed Sherry. Special thanks to Page Cary for her hospitality in the state of Maine.

Among the librarians who were of particular help, special thanks go to Barbara Cline, Chris Banks, and Nicole Hadad at the Lyndon Baines Johnson Presidential Library in Austin; Daniel Alonzo at the Austin Public Library; Ann Serrano at the Dolph Briscoe Center for American History at the University of Texas at Austin; Lisa A. Fox at the University of North Texas at Denton; Ben Rogers formerly at the W. R. Poage Legislative Library at Baylor University in Waco, Texas; Clay Stalls, Department of Archives and Special Collections, William H. Hannon Library, Loyola Marymount University; and Karen Taylor-Ogren and Diane Miller at the Mercer County, New Jersey, Public Library, Hopewell Branch.

I am blessed by the generosity and friendship of Malcolm Blunt. For their extraordinary intelligence and consummate kindness, I express my appreciation once more to Ralph Schoenman, and to his brilliant wife, Mya Shone.

Audrey Szepinski was a shrewd, dedicated and tireless assistant. It is my good fortune to have made her acquaintance.

To Ellen Levine, a literary agent nonpareil, I am grateful beyond measure. I also owe a measure of gratitude to George Gibson, publisher at Bloomsbury and the editor of this book. My thanks go to George for his perspicacity, for his attention to detail and his sharing with me faith in the rule of law which Lyndon Johnson violated so flagrantly and so often.

The identification of a single fingerprint taken on November 22, 1963, from a carton at the Texas School Book Depository at Dealey Plaza as belonging to Mac Wallace was the single piece of evidence linking Lyndon Johnson to the Kennedy assassination. The following appendix provides forensic proof that the print in the custody of the Warren Commission did not in fact belong to Johnson acquaintance Mac Wallace.

Robert J. Garrett
Certified Senior Crime Scene Analyst
Certified Latent Print Examiner
Fellow, Fingerprint Society

4703 Gold Finch Drive
Denver, NC 28037
704-489-2186
rjgarrett@idman.com

Joan Mellen
PO Box 359
Pennington, NJ 08534

May 19, 2013

Re: Evaluation and Comparison of Fingerprints

Received from client, via FedEx on May 16, 2013, 7 pages of fingerprint images which have been labeled for reference in this report as follows:

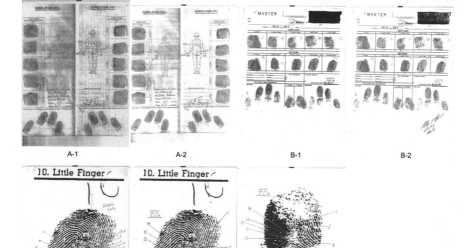

Client requests that examination and comparison involve only the left little finger (#10) of the provided fingerprint records (A-1, A-2, B-1 & B-2).

Each item was evaluated and the following observations were made:

A-1 & A-2 are copies of the same military identification record. Both the rolled and flat impressions of the left little finger (#10) are of value for identification purposes.

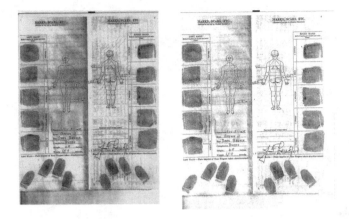

B-1 & B-2 are copies of the same fingerprint record. The flat impression of the left little finger (#10) is unusable for identification purposes. The rolled impression of the left little finger (#10) is of value for identification purposes though it contains a number of reproduction artifacts which may not truly represent the ridge characteristics of the known source.

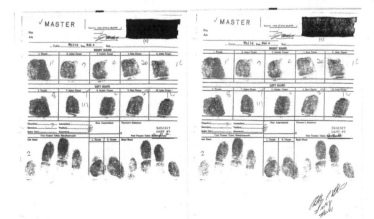

C is an enlargement of a left little finger (#10) rolled impression taken from the fingerprint record represented in B-1 & B-2. There are some artifacts which diminish the reliability of claimed identifying features. The sheet of paper is marked "working copy" and shows 35 features. Of these 35, 20 are ambiguous and can not be reliably determined to be actual reproducible identifying features.

D is an enlargement of a left little finger (#10) rolled impression taken from the fingerprint record represented in B-1 & B-2. There are some artifacts which diminish the reliability of claimed identifying features. The sheet of paper is marked "Exhibit Dan #3" and shows 14 features. Of these 14, 5 are ambiguous and can not be reliably determined to be actual reproducible identifying features.

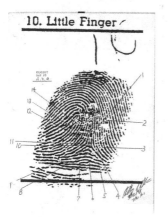

E shows an impression that may be a left slant loop, tented arch or whorl. The ridge flow indicates a delta area near the center of the impression. The identifying features occur above, at, below and to the right of the delta area as represented in the image. The reproduction quality of the print represented in E is poor. There are many artifacts attributable to the reproduction process. Although the copy provided, marked "Exhibit Dan #4," bears indicators claiming 14 ridge features, 7 of these features are indiscernible in the reproduction.

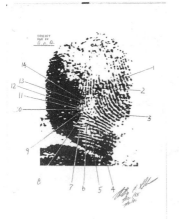

Comparison of **A** and **B** fingerprint records:

The fingerprint impressions appearing on the record in item **A** and the fingerprint impressions appearing on the record in item **B** were collected from the same source.

30 + Corresponding Minutiae   25 Corresponding Minutiae

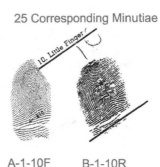

A-1-1R   B-1-1R   A-1-10F   B-1-10R

Comparison of A/B to E:

The poor reproduction quality of the print displayed in **E** required a tracing of the ridges to ensure consistent representation of the minutiae used for identification purposes.

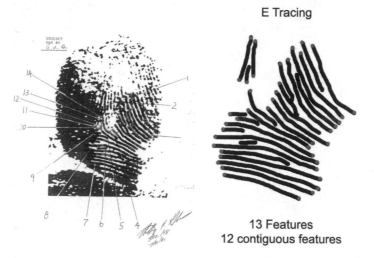

E Tracing

13 Features
12 contiguous features

The red dots indicate ambiguous features or end of ridge flow

Using the features established in the tracing, **E** was compared to the left little finger (#10) represented in the fingerprint records **A/B**. Six corresponding minutiae were plotted. However, three areas of discrepancy were noted:

D1: There is an ending ridge or bifurcation present in **E**. This feature is not present in the rolled impression of the left little finger (#10) from **A-1**.

D2: There are two ending ridges or a bifurcation and ending ridge present in the rolled impression of the left little finger (#10) from **A-1**. This feature is not present in **E**.

D3: There is an ending ridge or bifurcation present in **E**. This feature is not present in the rolled impression of the left little finger (#10) from **A-1**.

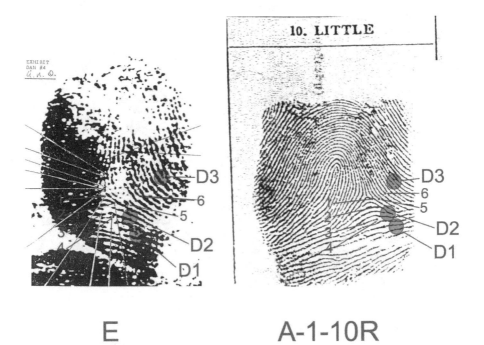

E   A-1-10R

Evaluation of previous comparison **D** to **E**:

Although 14 minutiae are marked on both impressions, points 2,9,10,11,12,13 & 14 are indistinct on impression E. This may be due to copy artifacts, but nonetheless, they can't be used as reliable identifiable features. That leaves only 7 remaining features on which to rely. When these 7 features are plotted and the plots compared, it is easy to see that the alignments are off. This can sometimes be attributed to distortion occurring at the time of deposition. However, there are no indicators of distortion in either **D** or **E**.

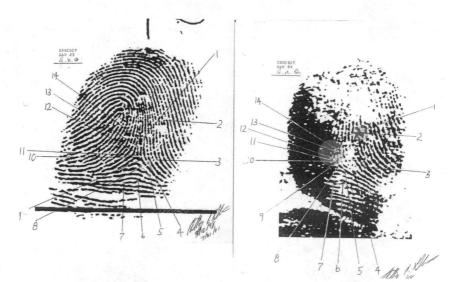

The yellow areas highlight regions of ambiguity due to poor reproduction

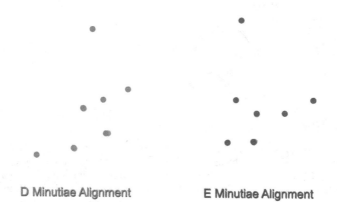

D Minutiae Alignment   E Minutiae Alignment

Plot of minutiae as observed in D and E

Conclusions

The fingerprint records replicated in items **A-1/A-2 and B-1/B-2** share a common source and were collected from the same individual.

The fingerprint represented in item **E** is of poor quality. Reproduction anomalies may be responsible for the presence or absence of identifying minutiae. Although I have pointed out areas of discrepancy, these may be overcome by an overwhelming number of identifying minutiae in correspondence based on current statistical research. However, having identified only six corresponding minutiae, this falls well below the statistical threshold. There is insufficient corresponding data present in the **E** document that would allow me to conclude that **E** shares a common source with **A** or **B**.

Question regarding a numerical standard for establishing identity

There is currently no numerical standard, a specific number of corresponding features, necessary for establishing identity with regard to fingerprints in any court of the United States or its political subdivisions. All conclusions are opinions of the examiner. Generally, high quality prints which display individualizing features other than ridge events (minutiae) will require fewer corresponding minutiae for a conclusion of identification than poor quality prints displaying minutiae only.

Robert J. Garrett
IDMAN Forensics, LLC
Certified Latent Print Examiner
Certified Senior Crime Scene Analyst
Fellow, Fingerprint Society

Robert J. Garrett
Certified Senior Crime Scene Analyst
Certified Latent Print Examiner
Fellow, Fingerprint Society

4703 Gold Finch Drive
Denver, NC 28037
704-489-2186
rjgarrett@idman.com

Joan Mellen
PO Box 359
Pennington, NJ 08534

June 19, 2013

Re: Wallace Fingerprint Examination

On this date I received, via FedEx, a CD containing high resolution digital images of the Warren Commission exhibit CE 656 number 29, a developed latent fingerprint. These images, provided by the U.S. National Archives and Records Administration, are far superior to the copies of the image previously provided. The images from the National Archives are of sufficient quality to be entered in to an automated fingerprint identification system (AFIS) and checked against existing fingerprint databases.

An examination of these high resolution images and a comparison to the recorded fingerprint record of Malcolm Everett (M.E.) Wallace from the United States Marine Corps, allows me to conclude without any doubt that CE 656 number 29 was not made by the left little finger (#10) of Malcolm Wallace. Additionally, I compared CE 656 number 29 to Wallace's remaining nine fingers. None of the remaining fingers could be the source of CE656 number 29.

Robert J. Garrett
IDMAN Forensics, LLC
Certified Latent Print Examiner
Certified Senior Crime Scene Analyst
Fellow, Fingerprint Society

Wallace # 10

CE 656 #29

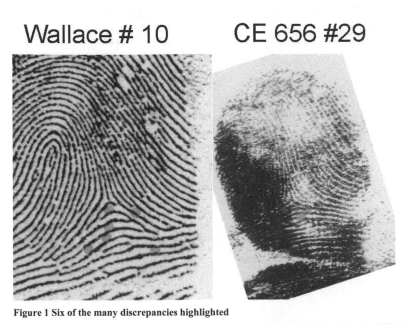

Figure 1 Six of the many discrepancies highlighted

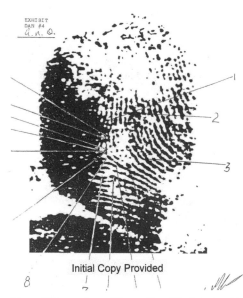

Initial Copy Provided

National Archive Image CE 656 #29

Figure 2 Comparison of the quality of the latent as seen in the initial copy and the National Archives Image

Wallace Fingerprint Examination

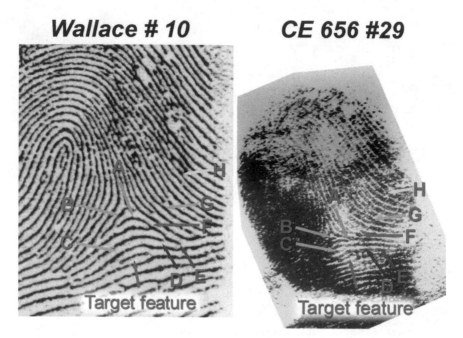

Figure 3 Analysis of discrepancies

Analysis of Discrepancies

Target feature: There is, in both the Wallace left little finger (#10) print and latent print CE 656 #29, a short ridge five ridge counts below the delta, This feature will be used to locate all other features or discrepancies between the two prints.

A: four ridges up from the target feature in the latent is a ridge ending to the right. This is absent in the Wallace print

B: five ridges up from the target feature in the latent is a ridge ending to the right. This is absent in the Wallace print

C: Two ridges up from the target feature in the latent is a ridge ending to the right. This is absent in the Wallace print

D: Two ridges up from the target feature in the Wallace print is a ridge ending to the right. This is absent in the latent print

Wallace Fingerprint Examination

E: Two ridges up from the target feature in the Wallace print is a ridge ending to the right. This is absent in the latent print

F: four ridges up from the target feature in the latent is a ridge ending to the right. This is absent in the Wallace print

G: seven ridges up from the target feature in the latent is a bifurcation to the left. This is absent in the Wallace print

H: eleven ridges up from the target feature in the latent is a ridge ending to the right. This is absent in the Wallace print

Each of these discrepancies is sufficient to exclude Wallace #10 as the source of CE 656 #29. Other discrepancies exist but have not been documented in the image for the sake of clarity. [1]

Terminology

Discrepancy: The presence of friction ridge detail in one impression that does not exist in the corresponding area of another impression

Features: Distinctive details of the friction ridges, including Level 1, 2, and 3 details (also known as characteristics).

Bifurcation: The point at which one friction ridge divides into two friction ridges.

Delta: The point on a friction ridge at or nearest to the point of divergence of two type lines, and located at or directly in front of the point of divergence.

Ending ridge: A single friction ridge that terminates within the friction ridge structure.

Short ridge: A single friction ridge beginning, traveling a short distance, and then ending.

Exclusion: is the decision by an examiner that there are sufficient features in disagreement to conclude that two friction ridge impressions originated from different sources. Exclusion implies that the likelihood of observing these features in disagreement, if the impressions are coming from the same source, is so remote that it is considered as a practical impossibility. [2]

---

[1] SWGFAST Document #10 "Standards for Examining Friction Ridge Impressions and Resulting Conclusions ver. 2.0"

[2] SWGFAST Document #19 "Standard Terminology of Friction Ridge Examination ver. 4.1"

Wallace Fingerprint Examination

Notes

Introduction

xxii: Biographer Robert Caro, nonetheless, insists upon Johnson's sincerity: *Robert A. Caro, The Years of Lyndon Johnson: The Passage of Power* (New York: Alfred A. Knopf, 2012), p. 486.

xxiii: a full-court press designed to restore Lyndon Johnson's credibility: The *Washington Post* published a five-part series about Lyndon Johnson that concluded on May 22, 2014, with an article asserting that Johnson was, in fact, not truly a Texan, but a resident of Washington, D.C., and should be seen as such. See Karen Tumulty, "The Great Society at Fifty," *Washington Post*, May 18, 2014. The subtitle of this article was "LBJ's unprecedented and ambitious domestic vision changed the nation. Half a century later, it continues to define politics and power in America." See also Michael A. Fletcher, "Great Society at 50: Prince George's Illustrates Programs' Transformative Legacy—and Limits," *Washington Post*, May 19, 2014; and David A. Fahrenthold, "Great Society at 50: LBJ's Job Corps Will Cost Taxpayers $1.7 Billion This Year. Does It Work?" *Washington Post*, May 20, 2014.

xxiii: "Nobody wanted that war less than Lyndon Johnson": "Rescuing a Vietnam Casualty: Johnson's Legacy," *New York Times*, February 16, 2014, p. 1. Her sister, Lynda Bird, had already declared in a 2004 interview broadcast on C-Span 3, "He was struggling to fulfill our commitment to these people." Both statements were presented unchallenged by historians.

xxiii: On Robert A. Caro not mentioning either Billie Sol Estes or Mac Wallace: "Do you plan to cover the role of Mac Wallace in your forthcoming work on LBJ?" Douglas Caddy asked Caro at a University of Houston lecture. According to Caddy, Caro looked startled, grabbed the lapels of his suit and asked who he was. He said he wanted to talk to Caddy further. Caddy gave Caro his card but never heard anything further from him. Billie Sol Estes, Caddy relates, in the mid-1980s told him that Caro and J. Evetts Haley came to visit him but that he refused to see them. Caddy related this anecdote on EducationForum.com on March 3, 2012. E-mail, Lyle Sardie to Joan Mellen, July 19, 2012.

1: Texans

1: "Who is to give Texas character?": Quoted in Marshall De Bruhl, *Sword of San Jacinto: A Life of Sam Houston* (New York: Random House, 1993), p. 258.

1:     "habitual liars": Joseph William Schmitz, *Texas Culture in the Days of the Republic, 1836–1846* (San Antonio: Naylor Company, 1960), p. 7.

1:     "rude, boastful and vulgar": Ibid., p. 3.

1:     "the avarice of selfish and dishonest men": John Henry Brown, *History of Texas from 1685 to 1892.* 2 vols. (Austin and New York: Pemberton Press, 1970). Vol. 1, p. 131.

1:     a distinct Texan character: Stanley Siegel, *A Political History of the Texas Republic, 1836–1845* (Austin: University of Texas Press, 1956), p. viii.

2:     born in a log cabin: DPR Collect, Will Lang, *LIFE* magazine, Time and Life Bldg. From Holland McCombs, December 2, 1963. Holland McCombs Papers: "No need do any more checking on log cabin 'birthplace.' The President was not born there. That log cabin was built by his grandfather and great-uncles to use as a sort of camp place and headquarters for their big trail driving operations in seventies and eighties. House where Lyndon and his two older sisters born on Johnson Ranch is neat but modest low-roofed and part-pillared little ranch house."

2:     "small shack": See Robert A. Caro, *The Years of Lyndon Johnson: The Path to Power* (New York: Alfred A. Knopf, 1982), p. 52.

3:     "provoked with that man": Holland McCombs to William Lambert and Keith Wheeler, April 1, 1964. Holland McCombs Papers, Box 146, File 5. This anecdote is included in McCombs' report, "LBJ and the Political Power Structure of Texas." Available in Holland McCombs Papers at the University of Tennessee at Martin.

3:     locked him into an icebox: Holland McCombs to William Lambert and Keith Wheeler, April 1, 1964.

3:     stole his first election: Caro, *The Path to Power*, p. 140.

3:     "Hitlerized": Ibid., pp. 190–91.

4:     For a discussion of the role of Roy Miller, see John E. Lyle Jr., Oral History Interview, transcript April 13, 1984. LBJ Library.

4:     Alice Gertrudis King Kleberg takes a dislike to Lyndon Johnson and advises her son not to hire him: Author's conversation in Miami with Helen Kleberg Groves, daughter of Robert M. Kleberg Jr., November 2013.

4:     Lyndon Johnson and the Citizens' League: J. Evetts Haley, *A Texan Looks at Lyndon: A Study in Illegitimate Power* (Canyon, TX: Palo Duro Press, 1964), p. 11. Helen Kleberg Groves told me that the Citizens' League incident occurred during a later campaign, not Richard M. Kleberg's first campaign for Congress.

5:     "help Lyndon get to know his way around": Holland McCombs to William Lambert and Keith Wheeler, April 1, 1964. Holland McCombs Papers, Box 146, File 5.

6:     "sexual liaison" in the Klebergs' office after Sam Houston Johnson took over: Robert A. Caro, *The Years of Lyndon Johnson: Master of the Senate* (New York: Vintage Books, 2003), p. 434. Caro writes that the details have been lost.

6:     "He'll climb over you": McCombs to Lambert and Wheeler.

6:     Franklin Roosevelt arranges for Lyndon Johnson to be on the House Naval Affairs Committee even before Johnson arrives in Washington: Holland McCombs, Rough Draft, Third Take. April 16, 1964. To: William Lambert and Keith Wheeler. Holland McCombs. "Box 13." Holland McCombs Papers, Box 146, File 11.

6:     "a great help on naval affairs": quoted by Robert Dallek, *Lone Star Rising: Lyndon Johnson and His Times, 1908–1960*, vol. 1. (New York: Oxford University Press, 1991), pp. 164–65.

6:     "as cold a cutter as you ever saw": Holland McCombs Papers, Max Brooks Story, June 8, 1964.

7:     The Marshall Ford Dam: See Holland McCombs to William Lambert, reporting on his interview with R. M. Dixon, July 29, 1964. Holland McCombs Papers, Box 146, File 6.

7:     Lyndon Johnson is "the same as a major stockholder": Holland McCombs to William Lambert, June 10, 1964. Holland McCombs Papers.

7:     details of the Marshall Ford Dam contract: See phone call from James Rowe, *Corpus Christi Caller-Times*, to Holland McCombs, July 9, 1964. Holland McCombs Papers, Box 148, File 14.

7:     "You never find his name anywhere": Holland McCombs to William Lambert, June 15, 1964: "ADD: BROWN & ROOT, MARSHALL FORD DAM AND HIGHLAND LAKES COUNTRY, WORLD-WIDE CONTRACTS, THE BEGINNINGS AND WORKS OF THE ESTABLISHMENT." Box 146, File 6.

8:     Richard Kleberg and Lyndon Johnson "actively collaborated" to ensure that Brown & Root be awarded the contract for the Corpus Christi Naval Station: Joseph A. Pratt and Christopher J. Castaneda, *Builders: Herman and George R. Brown* (College Station, TX: Texas A & M University Press, 1999), p. 69.

8:     George Brown bluffs Henry Kaiser on the contract for the Corpus Christi Naval Air Station: Pratt and Castaneda, *Builders*, pp. 71–72.

9:     Odessa would not get the housing funds: John Sliney to Holland McCombs, April 21, 1964. Holland McCombs Papers, Box 149, File 8. The column appeared on June 25, 1941, and was called "Kicking Around the Basin." The paper may have been named the *Odessa News Times* then.

9–10: "we do reserve the right to do our own thinking": John Sliney to Holland McCombs, April 21, 1964. Holland McCombs Papers, Box 149, File 8.

10:    "What the hell are YOU doing here?" Holland McCombs to William Lambert, Mike Silva, and Keith Wheeler, April 15, 1964, "LBJ and the Political Power Structure of Texas." ADD #1 –INSERT V – TO BE ATTACHED SECOND TAKE PAGE 40 AFTER END OF SECOND PARAGRAPH. Holland McCombs Papers.

10:    "I guess I'll just pass the biscuits": quoted by Holland McCombs, "LBJ and the Political Power Structure of Texas," to William Lambert and Keith Wheeler, April 6, 1964. Rough Draft, Second Take, p. 43.

10:    On Herman Brown's contributions to Lyndon Johnson's 1941 campaign for the U.S. Senate, see Robert A. Caro, *The Years of Lyndon Johnson: Means of Ascent* (New York: Alfred A. Knopf, 1990), pp. 16, 180; and Haley, *A Texan Looks at Lyndon*, pp. 86–89.

10:    Frank Scofield: The Scofield story is told in Haley, *A Texan Looks at Lyndon*, pp. 84–92. See also Billie Sol Estes, *Billie Sol Estes: A Texas Legend* (Granbury, TX: BS Productions, 2005), pp. 88–91.

10:    "Roosevelt called in Assistant Secretary of the Treasury Elmer Irey": Haley, p. 84.

11:    Robert Caro discusses Lyndon Johnson's activities leading up to his receiving a Silver Star from General Douglas MacArthur in "All Quiet on the Western Front" and "In the Pacific" in *Means of Ascent*, pp. 19–53.

12:    how Lyndon Johnson bought KTBC: See Holland McCombs, notes on a telephone conversation with Mike Silva, April 17, 1964. Holland McCombs Papers.

12:    For a discussion of how Lyndon Johnson acquired KTBC, see Haley, pp. 55–82. Haley was general ranch manager for J. M. West, who first bought KTBC radio in Austin for $87,000. West had purchased the station from a Dr. Ulmer only to find the FCC lagging in approving the transaction. Ulmer offered Alvin J. Wirtz, a Johnson lawyer and power broker, $10,000 only for West to evade him. When West died in 1942, LBJ and Lady Bird bought the station for $15,000, alternately $17,500. Johnson claimed the station belonged to his wife. Johnson associate Jesse Kellam, Johnson aide Walter Jenkins, Lynda Bird, and Luci Baines: everyone owned shares but

LBJ himself. Before long the Johnsons expanded to Waco and other places, creating a mega-communications network. It was Jesse Killam who came to be known as Johnson's "hatchet man." Haley also covers how Brown & Root fraudulently made campaign contributions to Johnson's 1941 campaign for the U.S. Senate. Along the way, Johnson and his cohort saw to the ruin of Frank Scofield, the Collector of Internal Revenue for the First District of Texas who uncovered the Brown & Root fraud. Scofield by the end resigned and his post was filled by a Johnson crony named Robert W. Phinney. Phinney shifted Scofield's records to a Quonset hut in South Austin which burned to the ground turning the Brown & Root records to ashes. Kathleen Yellott, President of an organization of Texas Nursing Home Operators, who had knowledge of who set the fire, was falsely charged by a federal grand jury. Although her tax record was so impeccable that the jury found "no bill," the cost of defending the case ruined her.

In 1964, the issue arose as to whether the Johnson family television station should be permitted to buy into Capital Cable: "Johnsons' Austin TV Firm Might Be Denied New Role," *Dallas Times Herald*, May 3, 1964. See also Raymond J. Crowley, "Johnsons Know How to Earn Dollar," *Dallas Morning News*, June 10, 1964; and "*LIFE* Reports 'Difference' in LBJ's Wealth," *Dallas Times Herald*, August 18, 1964. Johnson crony A. W. Moursund reported that Johnson was worth four million dollars in 1964, only for *LIFE* to report that a more accurate figure was fourteen million dollars.

2: A Man of Good Character

13: Walter Jenkins: "Jenkins Joined LBJ 25 Years Ago," *Dallas Morning News*, October 16, 1964.

13: "Ronnie's not our kind of guy": *The Rag Blog;* "LBJ, *The Texas Observer* and Me," blog entry by Ronnie Dugger, August 23, 2008. Also per author's conversation with Ronnie Dugger in Dallas, November 24, 2013.

13: "fair and accurate book": E-mail from Ronnie Dugger to Joan Mellen, January 10, 2014. Dugger sent the message to Johnson through George Christian: "Tell the President no deal." Dugger's biography of Johnson appeared in 1982, two years before the accusations of Billie Sol Estes against Lyndon Johnson.

14: "sucked it right out like a vampire": Quoted in Robert A. Caro, *The Years of Lyndon Johnson: The Passage of Power*, (New York: Alred A. Knopf, 2012), p. 410.

14: "that was the way his leader, Lyndon Johnson, talked most of the time": Eric F. Goldman, *The Tragedy of Lyndon Johnson* (New York: Alfred A. Knopf, 1969), p. 124.

14: "forget their private lives in his interests": George Reedy, *Lyndon B. Johnson: A Memoir* (New York: Andrews McMeel, 1985), p. xvi.

15: the Wallaces played dominoes: Author interview with Connie Perdue, January 9, 2013. Connie Perdue, the daughter of Jerry Neal Wallace, is Mac Wallace's niece.

15: "We're going to fight this guy until he agrees to leave us alone": Author interview with Mac Wallace's son, Michael Wallace, December 11, 2012.

15: the Woodrow Wilson High School football team and Mac Wallace's vivid classmates: Files of John Fraser Harrison.

15: "CIA" is rendered without the definite article "the" in keeping with the agency's own method of referring to itself.

15: Eugene Noblitt identifies the man in CIA's Mexico City photograph of "Lee Harvey Oswald" as Ralph Geb, his classmate at Woodrow Wilson High School. See Glen Sample and Mark

Collom, *The Men on the Sixth Floor*. Self-published (Garden Grove, CA: Semple Graphics, 2003), pp. 97–107.

David Atlee Phillips concocted the scenario in Mexico City of Oswald's efforts to obtain a visa to Cuba as a disinformation scheme. Phillips came to be known as CIA's propaganda genius: Presentation of Antonio Veciana, whose CIA handler was Phillips, at the Lesar Conference commemorating the fiftieth anniversary of the publication of the Warren Report, "The Warren Report and the JFK Assassination: Five Decades of Significant Disclosures," Bethesda, Maryland, September 26, 2014. Veciana on this occasion also confirmed that he had witnessed Phillips and Oswald together in Dallas shortly before the Kennedy assassination. It was clear to Veciana that Phillips was Oswald's handler, a view previously suspected, but here established unequivocally.

15:    Insall B. Hale, later an FBI agent and Director of Security at Convair in Fort Worth, born September 9, 1915, was also a Wallace classmate: Research into the later lives of Mac Wallace's Woodrow Wilson High School classmates is courtesy of Walt Brown and John Fraser Harrison. Files of John Fraser Harrison.

15:    Russell Douglas Matthews a "stalker": E-mail from Robert Plumlee, May 1, 2013, to Joan Mellen. "R.D. used to work for LBJ and was a 'stalker,' whatever that means. That is what my stepfather, Clarence M. Morgan, used to call him and others that hung around Knox Street and the Highland Park Pharmacy at Knox and Travis Street. At one point in the early fifties some of those people who traveled with Wallace and Estes knew Clarence and sometimes came over to the house in Highland Park on Lexington Street, for what reasons I never knew. I think but am not sure Matthews was one of those . . . I am not sure how R.D. would be played but he was in the Dallas Mix and rumored to be KKK, as per Jay [sic] Harrison."

16:    Mac Wallace enlists in the U.S. Marines: National Personnel Records Center, Military Personnel Records, St. Louis, Missouri. See also Navy Department, Bureau of Naval Personnel, Washington 25, D. C. February 16, 1949. From Chief of Naval Personnel (H. N. Levy) to Director of Personnel, Marine Corps (Enlisted Performance Division). Washington 25, D.C. Subj: USS Lexington: Information concerning Mac Wallace's military file is available from the Military Personnel Records archive at St. Louis.

16:    the Wallaces did not own guns and did not hunt: Author interview with Connie Perdue, January 9, 2013.

17:    "It hurt like hell!": Author interview with Nora Ann Carroll Stevenson, January 2, 2013.

17:    "This man may eventually need another spinal fusion": From Mac Wallace's military file.

17:    Mac Wallace attempts to re-enlist in the Marine Corps: To Major General Commandant, U.S.M.C. from Malcolm Everett Wallace. Subject: Re-enlistment Despite Medical Discharge, December 13, 1941. From Mac Wallace's military file.

17:    "It is a policy of the Marine Corps": From W. E. Burke, Lt. Col., U.S. Marine Corps, Division of Recruiting. Headquarters, U.S. Marine Corps, Washington, D.C., October 22, 1942, to Mr. Malcolm E. Wallace, 2703 Speedway, Austin, Texas. See also From W. E. Burke, Major, U.S. Marine Corps, to My dear Mr. Wallace, February 10, 1942. From Mac Wallace's military file.

18:    Mac Wallace resided at rooming houses and co-ops: FBI file of Malcolm Everett Wallace: 121-20798.

18:    sleeping porch: Author interview with Joseph Louis Schott, February 12, 2013. When Schott retired from the FBI at the age of fifty, he discussed his involvement in the investigation of the Kennedy assassination, but didn't mention his acquaintance with Mac Wallace. Schott's focus was on his having written several novels and "some fifty magazine articles." He served twenty-three years as Special Agent for the FBI.

18–19: jobs held by Mac Wallace during his years at the University of Texas: See Reprocessed FBI file of Malcolm Everett Wallace. 323 342 A. 121-20798. Fingerprints were provided to the Bureau from each of these employers. Courtesy of the Federal Bureau of Investigation.

19:     lost her virginity: Author interviews with Nora Ann Carroll Stevenson. See also Enid (Ewing) Cary to My dear Nora Ann: March 17, 1943. Courtesy of Nora Ann Carroll Stevenson.

19:     "Pi Phi Seniors Will Pins, A's, False Tooth to Undergrads." Clipping, Winter 1944. Courtesy of Nora Ann Carroll Stevenson.

19:     "leader of the revolutionary socialistic movement": Author interview with Nora Ann Carroll Stevenson.

20:     Nora Ann Carroll records her meeting with Mac Wallace, who at once eclipses Ted Cary: Sas to Dearest Mother, September 25, 1943. Courtesy of Nora Ann Carroll Stevenson.

20:     "We just clicked": Author telephone interview with Nora Ann Carroll Stevenson.

20:     Nora Ann Carroll gives Mac Wallace money out of her allowance: E-mail from William E. Carroll to Joan Mellen, June 28, 2013.

20:     A description of Clarence Ayres appears in Ronnie Dugger, Our Invaded Universities: Form, Reform, and New Starts (New York: W. W. Norton, 1974), p. 119.

20:     Hazen Suppers: "Christianity and Block Voting: One of Unique Hazen Topics," Daily Texan, Fall 1943 (undated).

21:     "For there is no God": Malcolm Everett Wallace to Nora Ann Carroll dearest, March 16, 1945. Letter provided by Nora Ann Carroll Stevenson.

21:     No one at college thought of him as someone who drank more than anyone else: Author interview with Nora Ann Carroll Stevenson, January 2, 2013.

21:     Mac Wallace plays football for the Tejas Club team: Speed Taylor, "Unbeaten Tejas Wallops Dragons," Daily Texan, December 5, 1943.

21–22: Mac Wallace outlines the Christmas presents he has bought for his family: Mac Wallace to Nora Ann, dearest, Friday afternoon, December 24, 1943. Courtesy of Meredithe Nix. Nora Ann Carroll Stevenson does not remember what gift Mac Wallace gave her at Christmas 1943.

23:     "A lovely little dark-eyed nymph": Poem by Mac Wallace, courtesy of Nora Ann Carroll Stevenson and William E. Carroll.

3: "HE MUST BE A REAL LEADER"

24:     "It might be said that this was an early manifestation of the student protest concept": Homer P. Rainey, The Tower and the Dome (Boulder, CO: Pruett Press, 1971), p. 13.

24:     it fired Mac's healthy competitive instincts to defeat Hill: This is the view of Nora Ann Carroll Stevenson: Nora Ann (Carroll) Stevenson to Bill Adler, May 4, 1986. Courtesy of William E. Carroll.

25:     "Communists had no control in [the] organization": FBI Confidential Report on Mac Wallace, San Antonio, December 13, 1949. Character of Case: Loyalty of Government Employees. The FBI was to find that although "some Communist Party members were alleged to have joined the [Common Sense Club]," Mac Wallace "was not a member of the Communist Party and did not adhere to their principles nor was he friendly towards their organization."

25:     He was someone who looked out for the underdog: Mary C. Bounds, "Accused Man's Relatives Dispute Estes' Story," Dallas Morning News, March 29, 1984.

25:   "liberal views on labor and the racial question": Reprocessed FBI file of Malcolm Everett
       Wallace, 121-1888-jah. December 19, 1949. John O. Markward, interview by J. Joseph Tamsey.
       The reference is FBI file 121-20798. Courtesy of the Federal Bureau of Investigation.

25:   "What shall I do when I get my degree in March?" Nora Ann Carroll to her father, September
       2, 1943; "I am tempted to stay here after graduation": Nora Ann Carroll had written to her
       mother, Lelia Carroll, on August 8, 1943.

25:   Mac Wallace writes to Governor Coke Stevenson, April 22, 1944: Records of the Students'
       Association of the University of Texas, 1944–45, Dolph Briscoe Center for American History,
       University of Texas at Austin. Stevenson's reply is dated three days later. He speaks of "any
       measure affecting the welfare of the University": Coke Stevenson to Malcolm Everett Wallace,
       April 25, 1944. Records of the Students' Association of the University of Texas.

25:   Mac Wallace requested a "personal conference" with the governor: Malcolm Everett Wallace
       to Governor Coke Stevenson, May 1, 1944. Records of the Students' Association.

25:   again the Regents declined to meet with the students: See Edward B. Tucker to Mr. Malcolm
       E. Wallace, January 19, 1945; and Ernest E. Kirkpatrick to Malcolm E. Wallace, January 22,
       1945. Kirkpatrick writes: "Pending confirmation of my appointment as Regent, I deem it
       unwise for me to take any part in any meeting pertaining to the University situation." Dudley
       Woodward also declined, despite Mac Wallace's assurance that he would "have absolute
       freedom to tell the students whatever you wish." Mac had written that Woodward's accep-
       tance would be a "democratic gesture." Woodward replied that he had the "definite impres-
       sion that the student body is earnestly convinced that the welfare of the University requires
       the election of Dr. Rainey to the Presidency": Dudley Woodward to Malcolm E. Wallace,
       January 15, 1945. Records of the Students' Association.

26:   "I detest hero-worship . . . but I sure as hell admire Wallace": Malcolm Everett Wallace to
       Nora Ann Carroll, July 28, 1944. Courtesy of Nora Ann Carroll Stevenson.

26:   "a beautiful skin stretched around a framework of secure private practices": Malcolm Everett
       Wallace to Nora Ann Carroll, July 11, 1944. Courtesy of Nora Ann Carroll Stevenson.

27:   "speaking to a gathering of our campus citizens": Malcolm Everett Wallace to Mr. Edward
       Clark, July 26, 1944. Records of the Students' Association of the University of Texas, 1944–45.

27:   Edward A. Clark on his first impressions of Lyndon Johnson: Robert A. Caro, *The Years of
       Lyndon Johnson: The Path to Power* (New York: Alfred A. Knopf, 1982), p. 363.

27:   Clark went on to become Johnson's principal attorney and "principal operative in Texas":
       Caro, *The Years of Lyndon Johnson: Master of the Senate* (New York: Vintage Books,: 2003),
       p. 120.

27:   Wallace's suggestion for the topic of Johnson's speech: Records of the Students' Association
       of the University of Texas, 1944–45, Briscoe Center, University of Texas at Austin.

28:   a conflict between "reactionary nouveau riche capitalism and the concepts of a liberal democ-
       racy": Homer P. Rainey, *The Tower and the Dome*, pp. 21, 30.

29:   Karl Hoblitzelle: After Hoblitzelle's death, his foundation would be administered by the
       Republic National Bank of Dallas, where it disbursed funds to CIA operations, CIA-funded
       groups, and CIA-friendly propagandists. See Frances Stonor Saunders, *Who Paid The Piper?
       The CIA and the Cultural Cold War* (London: Granta Books, 1999), pp. 135, 219, 274, 341, 354,
       355; and Hugh Wilford, *The Mighty Wurlitzer: How the CIA Played America* (Cambridge, MA:
       Harvard University Press, 2008), p. 108.

29:   "organized labor was the object of particular and consistent condemnation": *Dallas Morning
       News,* March 23, 1944.

29:   Herman Brown employed three lobbyists: See Joseph A. Pratt and Christopher J. Castaneda,
       Builders: Herman and George R. Brown (College Station, TX: Texas A & M University Press,

1999). See Albert Maverick, interview by Christopher Castaneda and Joseph Pratt, October 21, 1990, Fondren Library, Rice University, Houston; and Frank C. Oltorf, interview by Joseph Pratt, July 7, 1995, Fondren Library.

29: Johnson did not hire union labor [at his Austin radio station] never had a union in our radio and TV business": interview Lady Bird Johnson, interview by Christopher J. Castaneda, Fondren Library, Rice University, Houston.

30: "we just don't like what they're teaching": Jim Nicar, "Academic Freedom," *Texas Alcalde*, November/December 1994.

30: "What's that got to do with anything?": Homer P. Rainey, interview by Dr. Kendall Cochran, August 1967. North Texas State University Oral History Collection, Number 11. February 5, 1968.

31: "small wealthy clique": Nora Ann (Carroll) Stevenson to Bill Adler, May 4, 1986. In this three-and-a-half-page single-spaced letter, Nora Ann recalls her time at the University of Texas and her relationship with Mac Wallace.

31: "a spirit of loyalty to the ideals fostered by the University of Texas": Mac Wallace to members of the campus United Chest Appeals, September 30, 1944. Records of the Students' Association of the University of Texas, 1944–45.

31: "Ministers and mothers of Texas": Rainey, p. 65.

31: "the boys who would face a post-war era": Henry Nash Smith, "The Controversy at the University of Texas, 1939–1945." A Paper Read at the Request of the Student Committee for Academic Freedom, August 13, 1945. Published by the Student Committee for Academic Freedom, Students' Association of the University of Texas.

31: Rainey and his followers were accused of glorifying the two anarchists as "Communist murderers": S. Raymond Brooks, "Med Prof Charges Dr. Rainey Violated 'Tenure'," *Austin American*, November 28, 1944.

32: Rainey would talk of "undue political interference": Rainey, *The Tower and the Dome*, p. 53.

32: "a cause much bigger than himself": Ibid., Rainey's report, "The Future Development of the University of Texas," is available at the Briscoe Center, University of Texas at Austin, in the Records of the Students' Association. "A Resolution," by Mac Wallace, is also available at the Briscoe Center.

32: coffee pot: quoted by Bill Nicar, "Academic Freedom," *Texas Alcalde*, November/December 1994. In his response to the Regents' firing of University of Texas President Homer Rainey, Governor Coke Stevenson hardly lives up to the idealized portrait presented by Robert A. Caro in *The Years of Lyndon Johnson: Means of Ascent* (Alfred A. Knopf: New York, 1990), p. 170. Caro justifies Stevenson's acquiescence in the firing of Rainey: "His lack of formal education hurt most after the O'Daniel-dominated Board of Regents of the University of Texas dismissed liberal university president Homer Rainey. The Rainey dismissal caused lasting damage to the concept of academic freedom at the state university, and Stevenson's refusal to intervene in this controversy revealed that he did not adequately grasp that concept." That Mac Wallace explored the issue of academic freedom with Stevenson suggests that the governor was not entirely uninformed. But the name "Mac Wallace" appears in none of Caro's four volumes about Johnson, a significant omission.

32: Mac Wallace worked closely with Homer Rainey: See Homer P. Rainey to Dean C. T. McCormick. July 22, 1944. Records of the Students' Association of the University of Texas, 1944–45, Briscoe Center, University of Texas at Austin. See also Malcolm E. Wallace to Dr. Homer P. Rainey, August 1, 1944.

32: For Regent Bullington's "diatribe," see "Bullington Denies Rainey Charges," *Austin American*, November 12, 1944. Bullington's diatribe was thirty pages long. Bullington was charged with smearing the university: See "Bullington Charges Austin Papers Did UT Most Injury by Printing His Testimony, *Austin American*, November 28, 1944. See also Raymond Brooks and Margaret Mayer, "Bullington Threat Against Rainey Bared," *Austin American*, November 22, 1944. Bullington called UT a "nest of homosexuality": Brooks and Mayer, "Charges, Accusations and Denials Fly in Long Probe Before Senators," *Austin American*, November 18, 1944.

32:    "I am speaking for the seven thousand students": See Marcy Townsley, "Meeting Asks Regents to Appear Here," *Austin American*, November 3, 1944.

32:    Homer Rainey was fired by the Regents: Gordon Fulcher, "Multi-Millionaire Regents Fire Rainey," *Austin American*, November 2, 1944.

33:    "They made the decision. . . .": Notes among Records of the Students' Association of the University of Texas, Briscoe Center.

33:    Dr. Chauncey D. Leake: "Med Students' President Backs Move Resolution," *Austin American*, November 16, 1944. Leake protested against the idea of his becoming president of the University of Texas, saying, "I'm a medical educator."

33:    Stevenson knew nothing about the rumor: "Coke Says He Doesn't Know Of Proposal," *The Austin American*, November 10, 1944.

33:    the Reverend Blake Smith addressed the student body: Marcy Townsley, "Meeting Asks Regents to Appear Here," *Austin American*, November 3, 1944.

34:    Rainey singled out Mac Wallace "for your fine leadership": Rainey does not mention Mac Wallace's name in *The Tower and The Dome*, his account of the controversy at the University of Texas published by Pruett Press in 1971, two decades after the murder of John Douglas Kinser.

34:    "gutter reds and parlor pinks": Quoted in Jim Nicar, "Academic Freedom," *Texas Alcalde*, November/December 1994.

36:    97 percent of the student body participate in the November 3 demonstration in support of Homer Rainey: TO: Director, FBI. FROM: SAC, San Antonio. 100-336244-25.

36:    Mac Wallace addresses Nora Ann Carroll from the podium at Gregory Gymnasium: Author interview with Nora Ann Carroll Stevenson, Bangor, Maine, June 2013.

36:    the faculty resolution commends the students for their orderly behavior: Raymond Brooks, "Faculty Requests Return of Rainey; AAUP Asserts Ouster Bodes Ill," *Austin American*, November 4, 1944.

37:    For the description of the Texas-SMU football game: "Football Crowd Pays Rainey Silent Tribute," *Austin American*, November 5, 1944. Author interviews with Nora Ann Carroll Stevenson and with William E. Carroll.

37:    moment of silence seemed to last forever: Conversation with Nora Ann Carroll Stevenson, June 25, 2013.

37:    "absolute perfection": Author interview with Nora Ann Carroll Stevenson, December 13, 2012.

38:    "He must be a real leader": Quoted in "Football Crowd Pays Rainey Silent Tribute," *Austin American*, November 5, 1944. See also "Throughout the whole sorry episode": R. O. Zollinger, "University Must Be Freed of Shackles," *Austin American*, n.d.

38:    "native fascists": Rainey, *The Tower and the Dome*, p. 3.

38:    Rainey was accused of friendliness to Negroes: Rainey, *The Tower and the Dome*, pp. 83–84. J. Evetts Haley wrote an attack on the movement in support of Homer Rainey. It was titled "The University of Texas and the Issue," n.d., pp. 1–31.

38:    A costume party birthday party: Author interviews with Nora Ann Carroll Stevenson, Skowhegan, Maine, May 10–13, 2013.

39:    "I was a snob": Author interview with Nora Ann Carroll Stevenson, January 16, 2013.

39: "What about you?": Author interview with Nora Ann Carroll Stevenson, December 13, 2012. These words of Mac Wallace's would remain with Nora Ann for the rest of her life, the moment when Mac seemed to have revealed himself to have been the lesser man. We reviewed the incident during our meetings in May 2013.

40: "depending on whether I get a husband": Nora Ann considered traveling on her own "unless marriage interferes": Nora Ann Carroll to Darling Dad. October 1944.

40: an Army colonel: Lieutenant Colonel Orr to Mac Wallace, November 10, 1944. Wallace's reply is undated. Records of the Students' Association of the University of Texas, Briscoe Center, University of Texas at Austin.

40: "no one had dictated their movements or demonstrations": See "Mac Wallace Called To Stand," *Daily Texan*, November 22, 1944. See also: Margaret Mayer, "Senate Investigation Goes Into Dispelling Rumors On Rainey," *Austin American*, November 17, 1944. See also, Raymond Brooks and Margaret Mayer, "Charges, Accusations and Denials Fly In Long Probe Before Senators," *Austin American*, November 18, 1944.

See also: "business executives and attorneys": "Big Business Plot To Rule Schools Told," *Austin American*, November 29, 1944. Robert Lee Bobbitt, a former Texas attorney general, then testified that a conspiracy to limit academic freedom at state institutions by securing control of governing boards had been organized. Among the men "with reactionary ideas and strong wills" placed on the governing boards by Governor O'Daniel were D. F. Strickland and his employer, Karl Hoblitzelle. "O'Daniel and Several Of Backers Started Move," Bobbitt Says," *Austin American*, November 29, 1944. Only a year after Rainey had taken office, he had been targeted by this group.

41: The FBI investigated Mac Wallace. See: FBI. To: Director, FBI. From: SAC, San Antonio. Subject: Redacted. Internal Security R. FBI File of Mac Wallace 100-336244. The date of the document is nearly illegible but seems to be July 6, 1945. One of his classmates told the FBI that Mac was "completely uninformed on Communism."

41: "the real danger is not Communism," Rainey asserted: "Rainey Prefers UT Post to Any in World," *Austin American*, November 29, 1944.

41: "we will ruin you": Rainey, *The Tower and the Dome*, p. 14.

41: indefinite probation: "UT on Probation," *Austin American*, July 23, 1945.

42: help Ted with his research: Nora Ann Carroll to Dearest Dad, July 29, 1944. This declaration came on the heels of a 24-page letter from Ted Cary.

42: "It is imperative": Nora Ann Carroll to Lelia Carroll, ca. December 15, 1944.

42: "Nora Ann, darling": Mac Wallace to Nora Ann Carroll, Tuesday night, March 7, 1945. "The dead can mourn its own."

42: he was resigning to continue his studies, Mac said, in effect, as he made plans to move to New York: Mac Wallace FBI file.

42: "I leave Mac Wallace": annotation on letter, Nora Ann Carroll, July 27, 1944. Partial copy. Letter Edward A. Cary to Nora Ann Carroll. The annotation was obviously written in the early spring of 1945.

4: LYNDON JOHNSON BETRAYS RICHARD M. KLEBERG AND GEORGE PARR WORKS HIS MAGIC

44: "everything in political bossmanship": Holland McCombs, Rough Draft, Third Take. "Box 13." William Lambert and Keith Wheeler, from Holland McCombs, April 16, 1964, p. 47. Holland McCombs Papers, Box 146, File 11.

43–44: Holland McCombs' description of George Parr: "LBJ and the Political Power Structure of Texas," April 1964, p. 48. Holland McCombs Papers.

44–45: George Parr and his father visit Robert J. Kleberg Jr.: See Joan Mellen, *The Great Game in Cuba: How the CIA Sabotaged Its Own Plot to Unseat Fidel Castro* (New York: Skyhorse Publishing, 2013). This scene is much more apt in this context of Lyndon Johnson's rampages in Texas, here evidenced in the alliance between Johnson and the infamous czar of Duval County. More is to come. For Robert J. Kleberg Jr.'s relationships with J. Edgar Hoover and Allen Dulles, see *The Great Game in Cuba*.

45: "You're crucifying my father!": This scene was reported by journalist James Rowe to Holland McCombs. April 9, 1964. Holland McCombs Papers, Box 148, File 25. James Rowe was a reporter for the *Corpus Christi Caller-Times*. Holland McCombs Papers.

45: "honest and fearless man": Holland McCombs to William Lambert, June 12, 1964. Holland McCombs Papers. McCombs served as the researcher on Tom Lea's two-volume biography of King Ranch and was close to the Kleberg family, hence Dick Reynolds' agreeing to talk to him about his father-in-law.

45: Comments of Dick Reynolds, Richard Kleberg's son-in-law, about Lyndon Johnson come from an interview with Reynolds by Holland McCombs. Holland McCombs Papers, Box 148, File 5.

45: John Lyle runs against Richard M. Kleberg for the U.S. Congress: See John E. Lyle Jr., Oral History Interview, April 13, 1984, by Michael L. Gillette, LBJ Library Online: MillerCenter.org.

45: Lyndon Johnson and John Lyle became friends in 1934 or 1935: See John E. Lyle Jr., Oral History Interview, April 13, 1984.

46: "close personal friends": Ibid.

46: Johnson enlisted Lyle as his intermediary when he wanted to communicate with George Parr: Ibid.

46: "without making a speech or shaking a hand": James Rowe to Holland McCombs, April 9, 1964. Holland McCombs Papers, Box 148, File 25.

47: "I don't think you'd be interested in my opinion of Mr. Johnson": Ronnie Dugger, *The Politician: The Life and Times of Lyndon Johnson* (New York: W. W. Norton, 1982), p. 432n.

48: Lyndon Johnson writes to Herman and Margaret Brown about his visit to Fort Clark: Joseph A. Pratt and Christopher J. Castaneda, *Builders: Herman and George R. Brown* (College Station, TX: Texas A & M University Press, 1999), p. 173.

48: Johnson makes a personal trip to Texas to call on George Parr: Holland McCombs, Rough Draft, Third Take, April 16, 1964. Holland McCombs Papers. To: William Lambert and Keith Wheeler. Holland McCombs Papers, Box 146, File 11.

48: Billie Sol Estes contended that Lyndon Johnson attempted to recruit every member of the University of Texas's elite Friars' Society: Billie Sol Estes, *Billie Sol Estes: A Texas Legend* (Granbury, TX: BS Productions, 2005), p. 54.

48: Johnson got John Connally a job with the NYA to help him finance his education: Holland McCombs, Rough Draft, Insert II. No page number. Holland McCombs Papers.

49: "big labor leaders": Holland McCombs, Rough Draft, p. 57–58. Ibid.

49: Coke Stevenson refuses to appoint a Parr favorite as district attorney and George Parr breaks with Stevenson: James Rowe to Dear Holland, April 9, 1964. Holland McCombs Papers, Box 148, Folder 25.

50: "had done them some money-saving favor": Holland McCombs Papers, Box 149, File 3.

50: "before the election began, Johnson had a 25,000-vote head start": See Robert A. Caro, *The Years of Lyndon Johnson: Means of Ascent* (New York: Alfred A. Knopf, 1990), p. 191. See for a detailed description of the events leading up to the 1948 campaign.

50: Johnson together with John Connally pays a pre-campaign visit to George Parr: Holland McCombs, "Box 13," and Holland McCombs, "LBJ and the Political Power Structure of Texas," Box 146, File 11, Holland McCombs Papers, p. 50. McCombs' source was James M. Rowe, a reporter for the *Corpus Christi Caller-Times*, who helped him with his research. Rowe recounted that George Parr himself had told Rowe this was the reason he broke with Stevenson. The letter from Rowe to McCombs is in Box 148, File 25. Rowe also did research for McCombs about John Lyle. Rowe wrote: "I know that in 1948, Johnson, accompanied by John Connally, came to South Texas, and visited with George Parr before he had made up his mind that he would run for the U.S. Senate. I am reasonably sure that Parr promised him his support, because Parr was mad with Stevenson who had refused to appoint a district attorney nominee whom Parr supported in Webb County—Parr told me this was the reason he broke with Stevenson."

50: Parr was assisted in the 1948 campaign by a lawyer named Polk Shelton: "1948 Election," Handwritten memo pad. Holland McCombs Papers, Box 148, File 5.

50: Lyndon Baines Johnson and Polk Shelton: Ibid. See also Polk Shelton, Oral History Interview, February 28, 1978, LBJ Library. Online: MillerCenter.org.

50: "strong for him ever since then": Emmett Shelton, Oral History Interview, June 15, 1982, by Michael L. Gillette, LBJ Library., Online: MillerCenter.org.

51: Number of ballots issued: Holland McCombs, "Box 13." Holland McCombs Papers, Box 146, File 11.

51: "TOO raw—even for George": See Leslie H. Whitten, "Research Helps Clear Issue of Warrior Kin," *San Antonio Light* (date obliterated).

52: John Lyle's interview for the LBJ Library on August 25, 1986. His denial that Johnson had gone to South Texas before he decided to run for the Senate in 1948 appears on p. 25.

52: A sense of loyalty to the man who had done so much for him led John Lyle to defend Lyndon Johnson after Johnson's death. "One reads such cruel things about President Johnson now," he said plaintively," as he argued in his oral history for the LBJ Library that Johnson "was never able to get the public to fully appreciate the real Lyndon Johnson . . . Johnson was a sincere [man], much more able than people realize." With Johnson's misuse of office on the record, Lyle's paean to Johnson seems embarrassing.

52: Lyndon Johnson telephoned George Parr every day: this was a scoop accomplished by Holland McCombs based on the notes of his interviews with J. B. Donohoe. Available in Holland McCombs Papers.

52: he had done all he could in Duval County: Interview of J. B. Donohoe: "Box 13": Box 146, File 6. See also File 11: William Lambert; Keith Wheeler; Holland McCombs. April 16, 1964. Rough Draft, Third Take: "Box 13."

53: Stevenson was trying to get the ballot box and record of Precinct 13 open: Caro, *Means of Ascent*, pp. 334ff.

53: Johnson affected indifference: See Holland McCombs, "Box 13," April 16, 1964. Box 146, File 5.

53: Box 13: Robert Caro treats the Jim Wells County Box 13 fraud as if it were a research discovery of his own. This was far from the case. Holland McCombs, for example, did a thorough exploration of the issue using sources unknown to Caro two decades after the event in the spring and summer of 1964. See Caro, *Means of Ascent*, pp. 303–401.

53: "stem-winding, arm-waving school of courthouse lawyers": Caro, *Means of Ascent*, p. 347.

110: John Cofer: "gaunt, six foot four inches tall and cadaverous": Holland McCombs to William Lambert. June 11, 1965. "ADD: SUGGESTIONS, IDEAS . . . SECOND DRAFT."

54:    Holland McCombs worked as the principal researcher for Tom Lea, *King Ranch*. 2 vols. (Boston: Little, Brown, 1957).

54:    Donohue had been sitting in Parr's office when many calls from Lyndon Johnson came in. See: Holland McCombs interviews with J. B. Donohoe, Holland McCombs Papers, "Box 13," Box 146, files 5 and 6.

54:    "How many would it take?" Holland McCombs to William Lambert, June 8, 1964. McCombs had interviewed a man named Dick Craig.

55:    "Lyndon was very worried about what George did AFTER he had stolen the election for him": Holland McCombs to William Lambert, June 8, 1964.

57:    "slipping off his bed": Caro, *Means of Ascent*, p. 385.

57:    On the Smithwick murder: See Clayton Hickerson, "Sam Smithwick Death Raised by Dougherty," *Victoria Advocate*, June 20, 1954.

57:    Stevenson sees a line from George Parr to Chicago to Dallas: Harry Benge Crozier to Holland McCombs, July 1, 1964. The Holland McCombs Papers.

57:    "Shivers said I was a *murderer*": Johnson accuses Governor Allan Shivers of accusing him of being a murderer: Ronnie Dugger, *The Politician*, pp. 340–341, 465.

5: SENATOR LYNDON JOHNSON

58:    "We know just about the worst about Lyndon": Holland McCombs to William Lambert, June 17, 1964.

58:    Johnson pays a call on Clint Murchison Sr.: Holland McCombs to William Lambert, June 17, 1964. Holland McCombs Papers.

58:    Johnson requests the position of chairman of a subcommittee: Robert A. Caro, *The Years of Lyndon Johnson: Master of the Senate* (New York: Alfred A. Knopf, 2002), p. 248.

58:    Caro explores in considerable detail how Lyndon Johnson had Leland Olds removed: "Lyndon Johnson and the Liberal" and "The Hearing" in Caro, *Master of the Senate*, pp. 232–291.

58:    "He has reserved his applause for Lenin": Dugger, *The Life and Times of Lyndon Johnson*, p. 35

59:    "here comes Melvin rushing back in the contracting business": Holland McCombs memo to Lambert, June 12, 1964. Holland McCombs Papers.

59:    "half a million in a tax deficiency case": Holland McCombs to William Lambert, June 10, 1964. "ADD LAMAR SAVINGS AND HUGH WOLFE." Holland McCombs Papers.

60:    Jake Jacobson for national banks: Holland McCombs to William Lambert, June 11, 1964. "ADD: SUGGESTIONS, IDEAS ... SECOND DRAFT."

60:    Bob Phinney, Jake Jacobson, Ed Clark: Holland McCombs to William Lambert, June 11, 1964. "ADD: SUGGESTIONS, IDEAS ... SECOND DRAFT."

60:    Emmett Shelton discusses Lyndon Johnson's relationship with Bob Phinney on pp. 14–15 of "BOX 13: ROUGH DRAFT – THIRD TAKE," To: William Lambert and Keith Wheeler, April 16, 1964. Holland McCombs Papers, Box 146, File 11.

61:    On Pat Zachry, see Holland McCombs to Audrey Jewett, New York, July 15, 1964. "ADD H. B. ZACHRY, H. B. ZACHRY CO., LYNDON'S WAY, PLANE CRASH, ETC." Holland McCombs Papers.

61:    Zachry and the substandard rock: Holland McCombs to William Lambert, May 15, 1964.

61:    On the Kwajalein housekeeping contract: See Herbert Solow, "How Not to Award a Navy Contract," *Fortune*, December 1960, p. 15ff.

62:   The redesign of LAX was contracted to Pereira & Luckman, the firm Charles Luckman was then with. In 1959, he went out on his own. LBJ dedicated the new Los Angeles International Airport and was photographed with Charles Luckman in 1961. The photograph is available in the Charles Luckman Papers, Box 6, Folder 8, William H. Hannon Library, Loyola Marymount University.

63:   James D. Fowler does not receive engineering work on the Bergstrom Air Force Base: Holland McCombs for Audrey Jewett. Via Will Lang. LIFE magazine. July 9, 1964. Holland McCombs Papers, Box 146, File 6. See also interview of McCombs with Fowler, May 11, 1964. Holland McCombs Papers, Box 148, File 19.

63:   James D. Fowler allows his name to be used: Holland McCombs for Audrey Jewett. Will Lang/LIFE magazine. July 9, 1964. Holland McCombs Papers.

63:   "Lyndon feeds his friends, and beats his enemies": Holland McCombs, "ADD LAMAR SAVINGS AND HUGH WOLFE." June 10, 1964. See also McCombs to William Lambert, May 13, 1964; and Memo to Lambert, June 12, 1964.

63:   "you never find his name anywhere": Holland McCombs conducted several interviews with R. M. Dixon. See: Holland McCombs to William Lambert, June 15, 1964. "ADD: BROWN & ROOT, MARSHALL FORD DAM AND HIGHLAND LAKES COUNTRY, WORLD-WIDE CONTRACTS, THE BEGINNINGS AND WORKS OF THE ESTABLISHMENT." Box 146, File 6.

63:   On Lyndon Johnson and his father-in-law, Thomas Jefferson Taylor: See Holland McCombs to William Lambert, June 8, 1964, "ADD T. J. TAYLOR;" Holland McCombs to William Lambert, June 12, 1964. "ADD T. J. TAYLOR;" and Holland McCombs to William Lambert, May 12, 1964. Box 146, File 8.

64:   in 1956 Johnson earns $1,029,531 from his radio station: J. Evetts Haley, A Texan Looks at Lyndon, (Canyon, TX: Palo Duro Press, 1964), p. 72.

64:   Jaques Power Saw: Holland McCombs notes (typed), April 3, 1964. Box 149, File 15.

64:   McCombs discovered that the stocks in Lamar Savings were purchased in the name of KTBC: Lamar Savings. Holland McCombs to William Lambert – LIFE – NEW YORK. June 24, 1964.

64:   Brazos-Tenth Corporation: Holland McCombs Papers, "Box 13, Second Take," p. 52.

64:   the LBJ Company and its holdings: See Parade, March 22, 1964. Questions and answers: Ann E. Bradley of Terre Haute, Indiana, asked: "I would like to find out something about the LBJ Company, owned by President Johnson's family. I know the company owns the only TV station in Austin, Texas, but does it have any other assets?"

65:   "a lot of buying money": Holland McCombs notes, April 3, 1964. Box 149, File 15.

65:   Lyndon buys the ranch(es) and the radio station: See William Lambert–LIFE–NEW YORK. June 11, 1964.

65:   purchase of the LBJ Ranch: Will Lang for Don Underwood to LIFE—New York; Holland McCombs—Dallas. December 16, 1963.

65:   the list of ranches LBJ accumulated seems to be of the time he became President of the United States: Day Press Collection for LIFE Only. To: William Lambert, July 20, 1964. This letter is marked "DO NOT DITTO." Talking to Holland McCombs, Moursund said that "LIFE has spent by far the most of the time with Lyndon's oppositionists and getting their story and spending far too little time with Lyndon's protagonists and close associates. He says that in all fairness he believes that LIFE should check these matters with the President who would be chiefly concerned as well as best informed." In his interview with George Brown, McCombs received a similar response: "George Brown feels that LIFE has gone to Lyndon's enemies for most of the material, and feels that Lyndon's friends and associates should have a chance to present LBJ's side of the case."

66: "government contractors, lawyers, bureaucrats": Holland McCombs to William Lambert – LIFE—NEW YORK. June 15, 1964. "ADD: BROWN & ROOT, MARSHALL FORD DAM AND HIGHLAND LAKES COUNTRY, WORLD-WIDE CONTRACTS, THE BEGINNINGS AND WORKS OF THE ESTABLISHMENT."

66: "full of paradoxes": Holland McCombs to Bill Lambert, March 9, 1964: "Politics and the Power Structure of Texas." Box 147, File 1.

66: "We have a great journalistic opportunity": Holland McCombs to William Lambert. June 11, 1964. "Suggestions, Ideas, and Up-Comings for Possible Inclusion in Second Draft and for Info in Presenting First Draft."

66: Johnson was equally close to CIA: With his ally Senator Richard Russell of Georgia, Johnson saw to it that CIA operations would remain exempt from congressional oversight, which had been granted to the Senate Armed Services Committee. Over the years, this committee was dominated by Russell. Johnson himself served on a subcommittee on the Central Intelligence Agency, the first Joint Committee on Foreign Intelligence. Johnson appointed Russell to its subcommittee on the Central Intelligence Agency. See: CIA. Proposed Legislation to Establish a Joint Committee on Foreign Intelligence. 1/6/1956.

67: Herman and George Brown were CIA assets: CIA. Record Number: 104-10117-10203. Record Series: JFK. Agency file number: 80T01357A. From: Hall, Sarah K. To: Chief, LEOB/SRS (Liaison External Operation Branch/Security Research Staff). Title: Memo: December 1967 "Ramparts" Article Entitled: "The CIA's 'Brown and Root Dimensions:'" Date: 12/20/67. Pages: 8. Subjects: "Ramparts" "Brown and Root." JFK42:D12 1994.03.21.14:46:56:680028: NARA (National Archives and Records Administration).

6: MAC WALLACE GOES TO WASHINGTON UNDER THE AUSPICES OF LYNDON JOHNSON

68: "Shall he go, or come?" Johann Wolfgang von Goethe, *Faust*, trans. Bayard Taylor (New York: Modern Library, 1950), p. 238.

68: Mac Wallace lives on Riverside Drive and writes a five-page single-spaced letter to Nora Ann Carroll in New Orleans: Malcolm Everett Wallace to Nora Ann Carroll, March 16, 1945. Courtesy of William E. Carroll.

69–70: "Where do we go from here?" Mac Wallace to Nora Ann, my lovely one, May 25, 1945.

70: Newtex Steamship Corporation . . . Jefferson School . . . Bertrand Russell: Malcolm Everett Wallace to Nora Ann Carroll, 25 May 1945.

70: "extremely interesting and fairly remunerative": Mac Wallace to Nora Ann, my lovely one, May 25, 1945.

70: Mac Wallace describes his courses in New York: Mac Wallace to Nora Ann Carroll, May 25, 1945. This letter was written on Newtex Steamship Corporation letterhead.

70: "reasons of ill health": FBI file of Malcolm Everett Wallace 121-8452. New York field office report.

72: "the big liberals, passing out money": Transcript, Horace Richard Busby Oral History Interview IV, July 29, 1988, by Michael L. Gillette, p. 19, LBJ Library.

72: "the real political dregs": Mac Wallace to My Dear Nora Ann, July 16, 1946.

72: Mac encounters Josefa Johnson now that he is back at the University of Texas: According to Horace Busby, who knew Mac during this period, and worked with Wallace on the Rainey gubernatorial campaign, Mac Wallace "dated" Josefa Johnson while he was a student at the

University of Texas. Horace Busby revealed this to journalist Bill Adler, "The Killing of Henry Marshall," *Texas Observer* (November 7, 1986).

72: "political connotations": Mac Wallace to My Dear Nora Ann, July 16, 1946.

73: Joseph Louis Schott presents Mac Wallace with a .25 caliber Schmeisser pistol: there are three sources for this scene: Nora Ann Carroll; Joseph Louis Schott; and, from hearsay, William Carroll, Nora Ann's brother.

73: "I've had my gut full of the war": Author interview with Joseph Louis Schott, February 2, 2013.

73: a slit of skin was torn off the index finger: Author interview with Joseph Louis Schott. February 12, 2013.

74: Andre had dated the son of Clarence E. Ayres: Reprocessed FBI file of Malcolm Everett Wallace, Interview with Dr. Clarence E. Ayres as part of the FBI's loyalty investigation into Mac Wallace. NY 121-8452.

74: Mac Wallace and Mary Andre Dubose Barton are married: Travis County [Texas] Marriages, vol. 49, p. 125, #1267.

74: "damn fool in his emotional life . . . suffered for it the rest of his life": Author interview with Nora Ann Carroll, January 2, 2013.

74: "nice young couple": comments of the neighbors at 311 West 100th Street appear in Mac Wallace's FBI file. The same is true for the comment of one of Mac Wallace's students at Long Island University, "one of the best instructors I ever had" and "a fine man." The FBI does not include the names of its informants.

75: sent her home to her mother: Divorce Action Filed in 98th District Court, vol. 49, p. 463. Cause #81,189. Filed in Austin, Travis County, Texas, Judge Charles O. Betts.

75: "shaping": Conversation with Nora Ann Carroll, June 19, 2013.

76: "a lover of argument": Quotations from Mac Wallace's colleagues at North Carolina State are from his FBI file. These were comments they provided in interviews with FBI agents.

77: one winter day in 1949 Mac Wallace and Nora Ann meet in New York: The source of this anecdote is Nora Ann Carroll Stevenson.

77: a member of the Episcopal faith: Mac Wallace, RÉSUMÉ. 1 March 1960. Courtesy of William E. Carroll.

77: Communist Russia: Henry Scarborough to William E. Carroll, June 9, 1997. Courtesy of William E. Carroll.

77: Busby was employed in the office of Senator Lyndon Johnson: the source of this detail is the unredacted FBI file of Mac Wallace.

77: FBI interview with Horace Busby is taken from the reprocessed FBI file of Malcolm Everett Wallace: "Results of Investigation," dated February 20, 1950. Busby's name is redacted, but it is clearly he, working as an aide in the office of Senator Lyndon Johnson. See also: Confidential. By Special Messenger. March 2, 1950. To: Mr. James E. Hatcher, Chief, Investigations Division, U.S. Civil Service Commission From: J. Edgar Hoover, Director, Federal Bureau of Investigation. Subject: Malcolm Everett Wallace. NY 121-8452. For Nowotny's revision: See Administrative Page (no date or number).

77: Horace Busby's statement to the FBI, February 20, 1950; FOIPA Request No. 1206789-001. Subject: Wallace, Malcolm Everett, Appeal No. AP-2013-00247. Release No. 266688. June 12, 2014. This document is the product of an appeal to the FBI to release the unredacted file, which they did.

78: "fired with bitterness": Federal Bureau of Investigation. Report made at Washington, D.C. 2/20/50. File No. 121-13126. 121-20798-33. Report dated December 22, 1949. The informant's name is redacted.

78: "supposed to help others get loans for small businesses if they can arrange to buy or get a piece of it": Holland McCombs to William Lambert, April 6, 1964, pp. 22–23.

78: Emmett Shelton recounts to Holland McCombs how Mack [sic] Wallace was used by Lyndon Johnson: Holland McCombs "LBJ AND THE POLITICAL POWER STRUCTURE OF TEXAS: ROUGH DRAFT – SECOND TAKE." To: William Lambert and Keith Wheeler. April 6, 1964. p. 23.

78: Mac Wallace called a "hatchet man": See Holland McCombs: To Bill Lambert from Holland McCombs, March 9, 1964. Office Memorandum. Not turned in. In the notes for his essay "Politics and the Power Structure of Texas," McCombs writes: "Mack [sic] Wallace sent from Ag. Dept. hatchet man." No source is attached. There is no date. Box 147, File 2. See also Box 147, File 3; and Box 146, File 11.

79: "scholastic background and teaching record": FBI. "Results of Investigation." FBI 1949–50 investigation of Mac Wallace for clearance for government employment. As a new government employee, Wallace was subjected to a full security check by the Bureau.

79: "numerous panel discussions": Reprocessed FBI file of Malcolm Everett Wallace: WFO 121-13126. Results of Investigation, December 19, 1949. Loyalty of Government Employees.

79: Josefa Johnson and Mac Wallace enjoy a dalliance in Virginia: Stephen Pegues, "Texas Mafia," p. 30. A caveat: The unpublished Pegues manuscript, which was made available to the author from J Harrison's files, is characterized by exaggeration. Another source for Wallace's affair with Josefa Johnson is Horace Busby, who confided this information to journalist William P. Barrett of the *Dallas Times Herald*.

79: Hitler's linen and silver: See "Texan Bags Hitler's Own Linen, Silver," *San Antonio Express*, July 31, 1945.

79: "stable of high class prostitutes" See Mona D. Sizer, *Outrageous Texas: Tales of the Rich and Infamous* (Boulder, CO: Taylor Trade Publishing, 2008).

80: hospital wards for alcoholics: Caro, *Master of the Senate*, p. 433.

81: Lady Bird Johnson and Weslaco radio: the sources are Holland McCombs, and J. Evetts Haley, "Lady Bird's Business," in *A Texan Looks at Lyndon: A Study in Illegitimate Power* (Canyon, TX: Palo Duro Press, 1964), pp. 55–82. Haley is particularly detailed and knowledgeable about the LBJ radio station and its subsidiaries since he worked for Jim West, who had intended to purchase KTBC.

81: a reference to Mac Wallace in McCombs' notebooks: Box 147, File 3: Reporter's pad. No page numbers.

81: a physical altercation: The source is the notes of Onis Doherty, chief investigator for Travis County District Attorney Bob Long. Doherty's assistant, Trueman O'Quinn, obtained a photostatic copy of the hospital record describing Andre's treatment. Doherty's notes are in the Office of Naval Intelligence files.

82: Kinser family details courtesy of the files of John Fraser Harrison. Courtesy of Walt Brown.

82: For a description of the Butler Pitch & Putt Golf Course, see Dianne King Akers, "Staying the Course: For 50 Years, Winston Kinser Has Given His All to a Golf Range That's Taken Much from Him. You Couldn't Pay Him to Leave," *Austin American Statesman*, June 19, 2000.

82: Josefa Johnson is escorted to a party by John Douglas Kinser: Stephen Pegues, "Texas Mafia," unpublished manuscript, p. 19. Pegues died prematurely one night at the age of forty-six, leaving the manuscript with no source notes, nothing substantiated.

82: Kinser liked to spank and be spanked: Pegues, "Texas Mafia," p. 30.

82: Andre files another divorce action against Mac Wallace: Mrs. Mary Andre Barton Wallace vs. Malcolm Everett Wallace, filed in 126th District Court. Cause #87,305 filed in Austin, Travis County, Texas. vol. 117, p. 157.

82: Josefa meets Kinser at roadhouses: these anecdotes derive from the notes of Onis Doherty, who was investigating the Kinser murder. The notes appear in the files of the Austin police. They also appear in the Office of Naval Intelligence file.

83: Elgin Williams writes to Mac Wallace about Andre and "a man": R. J. Long oral history (1972). LBJ library. Donated by his sister, Edith C. Long, February 17, 1983. The interviewer was Joe B. Frantz and the interview took place at Dr. Frantz's office at the University of Texas at Austin on April 19, 1972. The LBJ Library, more devoted to concealing the truth about Johnson than to functioning as a branch of the National Archives that it purports to be, sanitized the Long interview in 1984; re-reviewed it and upheld the sanitizing in 1985; and confirmed the sanitizing again in 1986. See Withdrawal sheets, Presidential libraries, Oral History Collection. In 2016 the LBJ Library released a "mostly" unredacted version of the Long oral history.

83: "bash his face in": Notes of Onis Doherty. Doherty's testimony appears in the 1961 report on Mac Wallace by the Office of Naval Intelligence. United States Government Memorandum. United States Naval Intelligence. 20 July, 1961. 19 pages. RE: Malcolm Everett Wallace. CONFIDENTIAL.

83: "I'll bash his face in": Police file. Andre spoke freely to the investigators of the Kinser murder. She is obviously the source.

84: a "homosexual and a whore": James M. Day, *Captain Clint Peoples, Texas Ranger: Fifty Years a Lawman* (Waco: Texian Press, 1980), p. 8. Clint Peoples investigated Mac Wallace and Mary Andre Wallace for Bob (Robert J.) Long as part of the prosecution team in the Kinser case.

7: THE KILLING OF JOHN DOUGLAS KINSER

85: Mac Wallace told Roberta Barton that he wanted a divorce: The statements from Roberta Barton's point of view come from her interviews with R. V. Long's investigators after the killing of John Douglas Kinser. They are included in Mac Wallace's Office of Naval Intelligence file.

86: "I shot a thirty today": This quote and other details are from the Austin Police Department file on the murder of John Douglas Kinser.

86: juggling his various creditors: Stephen Pegues, "Texas Mafia," unpublished manuscript, p. 32.

86: Mac Wallace shoots John Douglas Kinser: Case Number 78693. Offense Report. Police Dept, City of Austin. Offense Reported: Murder. Person Reporting Offense: J. E. White, Hark Fuller, Pete Edgar, Ted Unger. Time and Date of Occurence: About 3:00, 10-22-51. The sharpest reporting on the Kinser murder was done by Leonard Mohrmann for the *Austin American* newspaper. See, for example, "Suspect Held in Gun Death of Doug Kinser," October 23, 1951; "Court Overrules Wallace in Challenge of Evidence," February 21, 1952.

86: one bullet penetrated two arteries of the heart: See: Follow-up Report, Austin Police Department, 10-23-51.

86: Mac emerged from the clubhouse with the pistol in his hand: James M. Day, *Captain Clint Peoples, Texas Ranger: Fifty Years a Lawman* (Waco: Texian Press, 1980), p. 80. See also Marjorie Clapp, "Wallace Out on Bail; Still No Motive Clue," *Daily Texan*, October 26, 1951.

86: "fast rate of speed": Testimony of Ted Ungar. Austin Police file on the murder of John Douglas Kinser.

86: the police retrieved three "hulls": Follow-up Report. Austin Police Department. Date: 10-23-51. Offense # 78693. Date of Offense: 10-22-51.

87: Mac hid the Schmeisser pistol inside a tree stump: So Mac Wallace told his children one day when they were taking a car trip into the Hill Country: Author interview with Meredithe Wallace Nix, November 22, 2013, Dallas.

87: a live Peters cartridge: Follow-up Report, Austin Police Department. 10-23-51. Offense #78693. Re: Malcolm Everett Wallace. Confidential.

87: wrinkled, bloodied shirt: These details may be found in United States Government Memorandum. United States Naval Intelligence. July 20, 1961. RE: Malcolm Everett Wallace. Confidential.

87: "I work for Johnson": See "Alleged Triggerman Told Police He Worked for LBJ, Ex-Cop Says," Sherman, Texas, newspaper. April 5, 1984. See also William P. Barrett, "Retired Officer Links Estes 'Gunman' to LBJ," *Dallas Times Herald*, April 6, 1984.

88: fired a gun: See Leonard Mohrmann, "State Rests Testimony in Mac Wallace Hearing," *Austin American*, February 25, 1952.

88: William E. (Bill) Carroll: Bill Carroll would in 1959 become District Attorney of the First Judicial District of Texas—Jasper, Newton, Sabine, and San Augustine counties.

88: news flash over his car radio: E-mail from William E. Carroll to Joan Mellen, December 21, 2012.

89: "Have you ever hunted with Wallace?" This account of Bill Carroll's efforts for Mac Wallace and the *habeas corpus* hearing is derived from William E. Carroll, "The Life and Times of an East Texas Lawyer," unpublished. Courtesy of Mr. Carroll.

89: Bill Carroll shakes his finger in Bob Long's face and tells him he has just made the biggest mistake of his life: E-mail from William E. Carroll to Joan Mellen, June 27, 2013.

89: Judge Charles O. Betts grants the writ of *habeas corpus* and releases Mac Wallace after he spends one night in jail: Request Granted for Writ of *Habeas Corpus* for Malcolm Everett Wallace, October 23, 1951. The State of Texas. To: R. D. Thorp, Chief of Police of Austin, Texas. Signed by Chas. O. Betts. Files of John Fraser Harrison.

89: "if a man could love a man": Polk Shelton, Oral History Interview, February 28, 1978, LBJ Library.

90: a minute and a half of freedom: Leonard Mohrmann, "Mac Wallace Charged in Shooting of Kinser," *Austin American*, October 24, 1951. See also "Wallace Hearing Is Set for Today," *Daily Texan*, October 25, 1951.

90: Andre's conversation is taken from the investigative notes of Onis Doherty. Available in Mac Wallace's Office of Naval Intelligence file.

91: Mac would return to Washington, D.C., with his family: Leonard Mohrmann, "Wallace's Side of Case Nears," *Austin American*, February 25, 1952. This statement, repeated over the years by authors without verification, occasioned many future errors. It was not true.

91: bond is reduced to $10,000: Leonard Mohrmann, "Mac Wallace Bound Over; Bond Placed at $10,000," *Austin American*, October 25, 1951.

91: Mac Wallace holds a press conference: Leonard Mohrmann, "Jury Selection in Kinser Case Begins Today," *Austin American*, February 19, 1952.

91: "very mild mannered": Office of Naval Intelligence, July 20, 1961, report on Mac Wallace.

91: The interview of Joseph Louis Schott by Special Agent R. W. Newby was redacted in its entirety in Mac Wallace's FBI file as it was released in the late 1990s. It appears in full in the "reprocessed" file released to the author in 2014.

91:   Mac Wallace telephones Alex Rosen at FBI headquarters: Rosen's memo of his telephone conversation with Mac Wallace is dated January 28, 1952. See Mac Wallace FBI file 121-20798-37.

92:   "in a very intelligent manner and without any indication of any emotional disturbance": Alex Rosen's description of Mac Wallace's telephone call, January 28, 1952.

92:   "may have used a pistol": FBI. 11-14-51. To: Director, FBI. From: SAC (Special Agent in Charge), Dallas. Attention: Inspector Mohr.

92:   "appear as requested": Teletype. November 5, 1951. FBI. Dallas. 11-5-51. Director. Urgent. FBI file 121-20798. Mac Wallace.

92:   took Schott by surprise: Author Interview with Joseph L. Schott.

92:   terse letter: See Nora Stevenson to Bill Adler, May 4, 1986 (letter).

93:   Mac Wallace writes to J. Edgar Hoover. January 30, 1952. Mac Wallace to Mr. John Edgar Hoover. FBI file of Mac Wallace: 121209838. FOIPA Request No. 1206789-001. Subject: Wallace, Malcolm Everett. Appeal No. AP-2013-02247. Release No. 266688. Hoover's reply, also included in Mac Wallace's FBI file, is dated February 6, 1952.

93:   "the latest dirt with the President": E-mail from Burton Hersh to Joan Mellen, February 9, 2014.

93–94: Alice Marie Riddle Wallace was suffering from a brain tumor: Author interview with Connie Perdue, January 9, 2013. I had no means of verifying this statement. No one else mentioned a brain tumor.

94:   "You better not do this to me": Author interview with Joseph L. Schott, February 12, 2013.

94:   "It's a touchy case": Quoted by Stephen Pegues, "Texas Mafia," pp. 36–37.

94:   "fooling with this Johnson gal": Clint Peoples, Oral History Interview VII, November 21, 1984, Dallas Public Library.

95:   "off base": Author interview with Joseph L. Schott, February 12, 2013.

95:   Andre's homosexuality: See "Alleged Homosexuality and Associates of Andrea [sic] Barton Wallace": Jim Boutwell, Internal Security Section of the Department of Public Safety, to Clint Peoples, February 18, 1952.

95:   "the big question in the trial": Leonard Mohrmann, "Wallace's Side of Case Nears," *Austin American*, February 25, 1952.

95:   Stuart Chamberlin thought "the shooting was over Andre": Notes of the investigation of Onis Doherty. Doherty's testimony appears in the 1961 report on Mac Wallace by the Office of Naval Intelligence. July 20, 1961. 19 pages.

95:   Bob Long is approached by a local dentist: See Oral History with R. J. Long, Oral History Interview, April 19, 1972, by Joe B. Frantz, page 38, LBJ Library NARA. p. 38. The name of the dentist has never been made public. Long says: "Can't remember his name—a doctor, a dentist, who was stationed at Bergstrom . . ."

95:   "grandstand play": Leonard Mohrmann, "DA Offers Full Freedom for Wallace If Innocence Indicated by Lie Detector," *Austin American*, vol. 38, no. 148. Undated.

8: TEXAS JUSTICE

96:   "And, in spite of the sense of struggle and tragedy in the minds of many": Theodore Dreiser, *An American Tragedy* (New York: The Laurel Dreiser, 1959), p. 669.

96:   Polk Shelton hires John Cofer: Undated notes of William E. Carroll. Carroll describes Shelton's summoning of Cofer as Shelton's own idea.

96: "nothing to do with our firm being employed in the Wallace case": Hume Cofer to William E. Carroll, December 28, 1995. Courtesy of Mr. Carroll. In listing the cases in which his father was involved and that concerned Lyndon Johnson, Judge Cofer neglects to mention the Billie Sol Estes trials.

96: Hume Cofer, alive at this writing, has chosen to remain silent.

97: Mac Wallace reads the newspaper: Leonard Mohrmann, "Wallace Trial Lines Up Kin on Opposite Sides," *Austin American*, February 21, 1952.

97: "comely brunette": Leonard Mohrmann, "Spotlight Hits Major Witness," *Austin American*, February 20, 1952.

97: "Paramour statute": The Texas statute, Penal Code, article 1220: "Homicide is justifiable when committed by the husband upon the person of any one taken in the act of adultery with the wife, providing the killing take place before the parties in the act of adultery have separated." In practice, circumstantial evidence had to be admitted by the court since it was unlikely and unreasonable to expect to catch the guilty lovers in the act of sexual congress. Adultery was considered to be an "ecclesiastical crime" in early Texas. Alienation of affection laws dated from 1840 and the Congress of the Republic of Texas. Only in 1973 did the Texas legislature repeal the paramour statute

97: Gideon K. "Legs" Lewis is murdered and the perpetrator, his lover's doctor husband, is not tried for the crime: See Joan Mellen, *The Great Game in Cuba: How the CIA Sabotaged Its Own Plot to Unseat Fidel Castro* (New York: Skyhorse Publishing, 2013), p. 11.

97: the "paramour defense" or "paramour statute": See Anthony Price v. The State. No. 3581. COURT OF APPEALS OF TEXAS, 18 Tex. Ct. App. 474: 1885. Tex. Crim. App. LEXIS 134, June 13, 1885, Delivered. PRIOR HISTORY: Appeal from the District Court of Travis. Tried below before the Hon. A. S. Walker. See also: Interviews with William E. Carroll.

98: Mac Wallace almost certainly would have been acquitted: Interview with William E. Carroll. Of course he had to have pleaded guilty.

98: the jurors were middle-aged Caucasian men: Leonard Mohrmann, "Jury List Complete for Wallace's Trial," *Austin American*, February 20, 1952.

98: "Juror Number One": Leonard Mohrmann, "5 chosen as Jurymen in Mac Wallace Trial," *Austin American*, February 19, 1952.

98: Gus Lanier knew Mac Wallace's uncle by marriage, Harold Barrow, in Leon County: E-mail from James Eldon Wallace to William E. Carroll, August 5, 1993.

98: "They let this guy on the jury know . . . that Lanier was a friend of Wallace's": Oral history interview of R. J. Long. The interview took place at Dr. Joe B. Frantz's office at the University of Texas at Austin.

99: Gus Lanier says he "knew Mac Wallace in school and is acquainted with the defendant's family": Leonard Mohrmann, "Court Overrules Wallace in Challenge of Evidence," *Austin American*, February 21, 1952.

99: three-year-old Michael rushes out to hug his father: Author interview with Nora Ann Carroll, May 12, 2013.

99: "rife with the unusual": Leonard Mohrmann, "Jury Selection in Kinser Case Begins Today," *Austin American*, February 19, 1952.

99: modus operandi of Polk Shelton: Polk Shelton's standard operational procedure was to apply at the start of every trial for a suspended sentence: Author telephone interview with William E. Carroll.

99: "cigarettes": Leonard Mohrmann, "Wallace Case Nearing Jury as Defense Abruptly Rests," *Austin American*, February 26, 1952.

101: "smeared their hands with several of these substances": Henry Scarborough to William E. Carroll. Letter, June 13, 1997. Courtesy of Mr. Carroll.

101: so intelligent a man: Ibid.

101: Henry Scarborough describes how Mac Wallace asked him to be an expert witness and his experiences at the trial: Henry Scarborough to Nora Ann Carroll Stevenson, September 1, 2003; Henry Scarborough to William E. Carroll, June 13, 1997. Letters. Carroll at the time was considering writing a book about the Kinser trial.

101: Mac Wallace asks Scarborough to sit at a table on the other side of which were the district attorney and his assistant: Henry Scarborough to William E. Carroll, June 13, 1997.

101: Henry Scarborough attends the Kinser trial and trips on a metal spittoon: Henry Scarborough to Nora Ann Carroll Stevenson, September 1, 2003. Courtesy of Mrs. Stevenson.

102: FBI agents laughed at the idea that nitrate particles could be deposited by a rusty beer can opener: FBI. TO: DIRECTOR, FBI. FROM: SAC, DALLAS. 3-3-52.

102: "it might be injurious for her" Leonard Mohrmann, "Spotlight Hits Major Witness," *Austin American*, February 20, 1952.

102: Cofer's defense: See Leonard Mohrmann, "Wallace Case Issues Rounded Up for Jury," *Austin American*, February 26, 1952.

102: "the jury would convict you sure as hell": R. J. Long Interview with Joe B. Franz, April 19, 1972. LBJ Library.

103: "Our best witness is buried six feet under the ground": See Leonard Mohrmann, "Verdict Probably Today in Mac Wallace's Trial," *Austin American*, February 27, 1952. See also Leonard Mohrmann, "Jury Agrees on Murder with Malice," *Austin American*, February 28, 1952.

104: Johnson had persuaded one other juror: R. J. Long Interview with Joe B. Frantz, April 19, 1972. LBJ Library. ("This fellow Johnson talked another juror into going with him; but now, if Johnson hadn't been on there though, I'd have gotten a conviction. I got a conviction, but it wasn't worth a damn.")

104: Long races for the exit before the verdict is read: As reported by Leonard Mohrmann in the *Austin American*, February 28, 1952. A decade later, J. Evetts Haley in *A Texan Looks At Lyndon: A Study in Illegitimate Power* (Canyon, TX: Palo Duro Press, 1964), would write: "Long was on his way out of the courtroom while the verdict was being read" (p. 108).

104: "faint smile": Wray Weddell Jr., "Wallace Gets 5-Year Suspended Sentence, 9 Busy Courtroom Days Climaxed by Quiet Finish," *Austin American*, February 27, 1952.

104: remanded to jail: From the Court Records. Files of John Fraser Harrison.

104: Mac Wallace released from custody: Leonard Mohrmann, "Five-Year Suspended Term Given Wallace," *Austin American*, February 28, 1952.

104: Mac borrowed "something over $1500" from his brother James Eldon Wallace: E-mail from Jim Wallace to William E. Carroll, August 6, 2003. Courtesy of William E. Carroll. Cofer, of course, could not have been charging his normal fee.

104: "fair and accurate": Quoted in Wray Weddell Jr., "Wallace Gets 5-Year Suspended Sentence."

105: Polk Shelton polls the jurors: E-mail from William E. Carroll to Joan Mellen. January 12, 2013. Nora Ann Carroll's mother called the trial "such a brief tragic moment": Mrs. Lelia Carroll to Nora Ann Carroll, October 27, 1951.

105: Nora Ann thanked her "lucky stars" that she hadn't been "taken in by his handsome figure . . .": Author interview with Nora Ann Carroll Stevenson, May 2013.

105: Johnson had flown to Austin secretly: Henry Scarborough to William E. Carroll, June 13, 1997.

105: "too bad the jury did not do the right thing": Henry Scarborough to William E. Carroll, June 13, 1997.

106: jurors apologize to Kinser's parents: Bill Adler, "The Killing of Henry Marshall," *Texas Observer* (November 7, 1986).

106: "Would he have been tried again?" This incident is recounted in R. J. Long's oral history for the LBJ library, April 19, 1972.

106: Senator Ralph Yarborough speaks to author Stephen Pegues: Recounted in "Texas Mafia," Pegues's unpublished manuscript. While no date is offered for the interview with Yarborough, it appears to be genuine.

106: Long writes to Ben Kaplan: This letter appears in the Office of Naval Intelligence Report of July 20, 1961. The Navy notes that there was "no letter of reply from Mr. Ben Kaplan in Subject's dossier."

106: Long states that he had no contact with Lyndon Johnson during the Kinser trial: R. J. Long oral history interview for the LBJ library.

106–7: R. J. (Bob) Long discusses his acquaintance with LBJ in his oral history interview for the LBJ library, April 19, 1972. The interviewer is Joe B. Frantz.

107: "polish and class," "second-rate lawyer": William E. Carroll, "The Life and Times of An East Texas Lawyer."

107: "alcoholism, cruelty, belligerence . . ." Mac Wallace files for divorce on May 1: Cause #65313-F/J. Dallas County, Texas. Mac Wallace was granted a divorce on June 6, 1952: vol. G. pp. 451–2. Juvenile Court of Dallas County, Texas.

107–108: For a description of Jonco Aircraft Corporation, see *Resourceful Oklahoma* 3, no. 5 (May 1952), p. 2.

108: David Harold Byrd: See: David Harold ("Dry Hole") Byrd, *I'm an Endangered Species: The Autobiography of a Free Enterpriser* (Houston: Pacesetter Press, 1978). This book was clearly self-published.

108: Wallace and Mary Andre Dubose Barton Wallace remarry: Dallas County Marriages, vol. 119, p. 572. ("Mrs. Mary Andre Wallace and Malcolm Everett Wallace.")

108: The Texas School Book Depository building belonged to D. H. Byrd: See Matthew Hayes Nall, "Texas School Book Depository," in *Handbook of Texas Online*. Published by the Texas State Historical Association.

109: "Texas is still the land of great opportunity": D. H. Byrd to Mr. Henry R. Luce, April 23, 1948. Corbitt Special Collections, University Archives, University of Tennessee at Martin. Byrd was responding to two articles, one in *Fortune* magazine, "The Land of the Big Rich," and the other in *LIFE* titled "The Southwest Has a New Crop of Super Rich."

109: Byrd would run fifty-two companies: See Byrd, *I'm an Endangered Species*, "Introduction," p. 2.

109: a rapport with "the politicians who ran things": See Byrd, *I'm an Endangered Species*, pp. 37–38.

109: "Where you have capitalism, you have capitalists": D. H. Byrd to Mr. Henry R. Luce, April 23, 1948. Corbitt Special Collections, University Archives, University of Tennessee at Martin.

109: "men I could go to any time that I wanted action": Byrd, *I'm an Endangered Species*, pp. 37–38.

109: Corvus Weapon System program: See Mac Wallace, Résumé, March 1, 1960. Courtesy of William E. Carroll.

109: "You've done so much to be helpful to me": Lyndon Baines Johnson to D. H. Byrd, June 25, 1960. Senate Papers, Masters Files 1953–61, 1960. LBJ Library.

109: Lyndon Johnson supports D. H. Byrd's Civil Air Patrol: Lyndon B. Johnson to Colonel D. H. Byrd, Vice Chairman, Executive Board, Civil Air Patrol, February 2, 1954. LBJ Library.

109–110: Byrd's connection to Lyndon Johnson: Byrd calls himself "a friend of Lyndon Johnson": D. H. Byrd to Mr. Richard Maguire, Treasurer, Democratic National Committee, March 26, 1965. Byrd's correspondence with Lyndon Johnson is available in the LBJ Library in Senate Papers, Masters Files 1953–61, Box 28. See also Lyndon B. Johnson to Colonel D. H. Byrd, July 15, 1953; Lyndon Johnson to D. H. Byrd, April 13, 1953; Lyndon B. Johnson to Mr. D. H. Byrd, May 17, 1955; Lyndon B. Johnson to D. H. Byrd, September 2, 1956; Lyndon B. Johnson to D. H. Byrd, May 31, 1956; Lyndon B. Johnson to D. H. Byrd, March 9, 1956; Lyndon B. Johnson to D. H. Byrd, August 9, 1958; and Lyndon B. Johnson to D. H. Byrd, June 25, 1960.

109–10: these thank-you notes reside at the LBJ library in the Johnson-Byrd correspondence, Senate Papers. Intervened personally: See September 17, 1959.

111: Byrd at TEMCO also employs Raymond Fehmer, the father of Johnson's personal secretary: Historian Bruce Adamson is responsible for this discovery.

111: "Mac Wallace never worked for Byrd": Author interview with Billie Sol Estes, Granbury, Texas, June 15, 2010.

9: Two Faustian Bargains: Little Lyndon and Billie Sol

112: William Miller quoted in Michael Beschloss, *Reaching for Glory: Lyndon Johnson's Secret White House Tapes, 1964–1965* (New York: Simon & Schuster, 2001), p. 29. Beschloss points out that "let us continue" was a reference to Johnson's speech to Congress on November 27, 1963, less than a week after the Kennedy assassination.

112: "his drinking habits, his sex habits, his intellectual capacity": Robert Dallek offers this description of how Johnson rose to power in the U.S. Senate, as conveyed by John Kenneth Galbraith based on an interview with historian Arthur Schlesinger. See Dallek, *Lone Star Rising: Lyndon Johnson and His Times, 1908–1960* (New York: Oxford University Press, 1991), p. 352.

112: Johnson confronts Senator Harry Byrd: Dallek, p. 353.

112: "first big move to the leadership": Dallek, p. 353.

112: "I want to know who's the power over there": Dallek, *Lone Star Rising*, p. 378.

113: Joseph McCarthy and Drew Pearson and Lyndon Johnson: Dallek, Ibid., p. 432.

113: "Saw L. Johnson": Dallek, Ibid., p. 423.

113: "Lyndon Johnson represents Lyndon Johnson": quoted in Robert A. Caro, *The Years of Lyndon Johnson: Master of the Senate* (New York: Alfred A. Knopf, 2002), p. 557.

113: shedding his knickers for a black suit: "That High-Living Baker Boy Scandalizes the Capital," *LIFE* magazine, "The Bobby Baker Bombshell," cover story, November 8, 1963, p. 35. The research for these stones was done by Holland McCombs, according to Karen Elmore at the Paul Meek Library, University of Tennessee at Martin.

113: "I understand you know where the bodies are buried in the Senate": Bobby Baker, *Wheeling and Dealing: Confessions of a Capitol Hill Operator* (New York: W. W. Norton, 1978), p. 34.

113: Bobby Baker is elected Assistant Secretary of the Senate minority: Baker, *Wheeling and Dealing*, p. 34.

114: Lyndon Johnson as majority leader controlled the election of Bobby Baker as Secretary to the Majority: Robert G. Baker, Oral History Interview VI, July 24, 1984, by Michael L. Gillette, p. 239, LBJ Library. See also Robert G. Baker, Oral History Interview III, p. 8, December 9, 1983. Interviewer: Michael L. Gillette. Both are available at the website of the Miller Center at the University of Virginia.

114:    "He seemed to *sense* each man's individual price": Baker (with Larry L. King),*Wheeling and Dealing*, p. 87.

114:    "The Leader would like to know what your position is": Robert G. Baker, Oral History Interview V, May 2, 1984, by Michael L. Gillette p. 30, LBJ Library.

114:    an "Interparliamentary Union" and free trips for senators and congressmen: Robert G. Baker, Oral History Interview VII, October 11, 1984, by Michael L. Gillette, pp. 12–14, LBJ Library.

114:    "a severe whiskey problem and a woman problem": Robert G. Baker, Oral History Interview IV, February 29, 1984, by Michael L. Gillette.

114:    Styles Bridges receives five thousand dollars in cash: Caro, *Master of the Senate*, p. 664.

114:    "You never knew when he'd call up": Robert G. Baker, Oral History Interview I, October 23, 1974, by Michael L. Gillette, p. 16, LBJ Library.

115:    "You're closer to me": Ibid., p. 17.

115:    "How unfair for this person not to have a son": Lynda Bird Johnson, Oral History Interview, August 23, 2004, LBJ library. Broadcast on C-Span3 American History Television, February 20, 2014.

115:    "one of the outstanding Americans": Baker, *Wheeling and Dealing*, p. 28.

115:    "didn't move fast enough": This incident is recounted by Caro in *Master of the Senate*, p. 594.

115:    Baker noted that "a lot of newspapers would call me 'Little Lyndon' or his alter ego . . .": Robert G. Baker, Oral History Interview II, October 31, 1974, by Michael L. Gillette, p. 4, LBJ Library. Baker also writes in his memoir, *Wheeling and Dealing*, that "the press often referred to me as 'Little Lyndon'" (p. 73).

115:    "the Mole": See G. R. Schreiber, *The Bobby Baker Affair: How to Make Millions in Washington* (Chicago: Henry Regnery, 1964), p. 9.

115:    "most trusted, most loyal": *The Daily Morning News*, November 15, 1963.

115:    Baker called Lyndon Johnson "the Leader": Robert G. Baker, Oral History Interview II, October 31, 1974, p. 15.

115:    On the contention between Johnson and Yarborough: John Connally replied that LBJ had made it clear that if they "didn't stop and discredit Yarborough he eventually would take over control of Texas politics": Interview with Ralph Yarborough, July 29, 1978, p. 6, House Select Committee on Assassination (HSCA) 010459. HSCA Papers. National Archives and Records Administration (NARA).

115:    "the poor, underprivileged, and exploited Americans": p. 1. House Select Committee on Assassinations, July 29, 1978. Interview with Ralph Yarborough. Austin, Texas.

115–116: "Lyndon would like to break his neck": Holland McCombs to William Lambert, June 17, 1964. Holland McCombs Papers. See also "Lyndon would like to break his neck": Billie Sol Estes speaking to Holland McCombs, May 15, 1964, Box 149, File 18. Holland McCombs Papers.

116:    the reasons Johnson came to back Yarborough: Holland McCombs to William Lambert, June 11, 1964. "ADD: SUGGESTIONS, IDEAS . . . SECOND DRAFT."

116:    For Lyndon Johnson's harassment of Senator Ralph Yarborough, see Interview with Ralph Yarborough, July 29–August 1, 1978, by Lee Matthew, HSCA 010459. HSCA Papers. NARA.

116:    they split up the patronage: Interview with Byron Skelton. September 14, 1964. JFK collection, NARA. Skelton was a Democratic National Committeeman.

116:    Ralph Yarborough explains how he traded off patronage with Lyndon Johnson: Select Committee On Assassinations. Interview with Ralph Yarborough. July 29, 1978: 010459. NARA.

116:    Kennedy gives LBJ patronage over Texas: Baker, *Wheeling and Dealing*, p. 146.

116:    Ralph Yarborough is not invited to an event in honor of JFK: Select Committee On Assassinations. Interview with Ralph Yarborough. July 29, 1978: 010459. NARA.

117: Connally says that much of his trouble with Yarborough stemmed from Lyndon Johnson's trouble with Yarborough: Confidential interview with Governor John Connally, September 16, 1964. JFK collection. NARA.

117: Bill Moyers sums up the relationship between Connally, Johnson, and Yarborough: Deposition of Bill D. Moyers, House Select Committee on Assassinations, August 16, 1979. HSCA Papers. NARA. Moyers explains that Yarborough represented the liberal Democrats and Connally the regular and conservative Democratic forces.

117: "a whore: he was for hire": Robert G. Baker, Oral History Interview IV, February 29, 1984, by Michael L. Gillette, LBJ Library.

117: "I'll have them niggers voting Democratic": Ronald Kessler, *Inside The White House: The Hidden Lives of the Modern Presidents and the Secrets of the World's Most Powerful Institution* (Simon and Schuster: New York, 1995), pp. 33–34.

117: "all hell had broken loose": Robert G. Baker, Oral History Interview IV, May 12, 1999, LBJ Library.

117: "very very pro-military": Ibid., p. 9.

117: "Machiavellian mind": Robert G. Baker, Oral History Interview IV, February 29, 1984. Interviewed by Michael L. Gillette for the LBJ Library, p. 17.

117: "He dealt in everything": J. Evetts Haley, *A Texan Looks at Lyndon: A Study in Illegitimate Power* (Canyon, TX: Palo Duro Press, 1964), p. 72.

118: the Quorum Club: See Holland McCombs to William Lambert c/o Audrey Jewett, November 4, 1963: "ADD BOBBY BAKER." Holland McCombs Papers.

118: "top-level aides to President Lyndon Johnson": Baker, *Wheeling and Dealing*, p. 108.

118: Serv-U vending machines manufactured by a Chicago-based corporation secretly owned by Tony Accardo, Paul Ricca, Gus Alex, and Sam Giancana and others: See John William Tuohy, "Mob Story: The Vice President," AmericanMafia.com, July 2002. Available online.

118: Baker and the InterContinental Hotel: See Schreiber, *The Bobby Baker Affair*, p. 133. They did not attend the casino opening. Ibid., pp. 130–143.

118: Bobby Baker's kickbacks from HAMPCO: See Schreiber, *The Bobby Baker Affair*, p. 118–19. The text of the agreement between HAMPCO and Tucker and Baker is on p. 123 in "Meat for the Poor People."

119: "ground up to make sausages": Ibid., p. 129.

119: I. I. Davidson and the HAMPCO meat trajectory: Ibid., p. 121. Schreiber mistakenly calls I. I. (Isadore Irving) Davidson "Irwin."

119: Alfred Novak: See Baker, *Wheeling and Dealing*, p. 47–48.

119: Baker, the Novaks, and the Carousel Motel: See Schreiber, *The Bobby Baker Affair*, pp. 51–66.

120: a "sort of black market": Clark Tabor was interviewed by Holland McCombs. Holland McCombs Papers.

120: Cliff Carter encouraged Estes to purchase old barracks: Billie Sol Estes, *Billie Sol Estes: A Texas Legend* (Granbury, TX: BS Productions, 2005), p. 25.

120: taking back mortgages, Ibid., p. 26.

120: strict acreage controls: James M. Day, *Captain Clint Peoples, Texas Ranger: Fifty Years a Lawman* (Waco: Texian Press, 1980), p. 132.

121: "Lyndon could trust him to pick up the money": Bill Adler, "The Killing of Henry Marshall," *Texas Observer* (November 7, 1986).

121: "I'll get a-hold of Lyndon": Holland McCombs interview with Frank Cain. Holland McCombs Papers.

121: Estes takes members of the staffs of Ralph Yarborough and Lyndon Johnson to dinner: Ibid., "ADD LBJ STORY— BILLIE SOL ESTES."

121–122:   Frank Cain tells McCombs about Estes' calls to Lyndon Johnson: Holland McCombs to
           Audrey Jewett, *LIFE*, New York. July 23, 1964. "ADD LBJ STORY—BILLIE SOL ESTES."
           Holland McCombs Papers.

122:       the plan was to use the income from grain storage: Ibid., p. 82.

122:       an annual income of between five and seven million dollars from grain storage: Haley, *A
           Texan Looks at Lyndon*, p. 122.

122:       Estes is storing 23,107,000 million bushels of grain: TO: Patricia Hough – FORTUNE.
           FROM: Holland McCombs. DATE: May 19, 1969. FOURTH TAKE. Box 245, file 3.
           McCombs' sources is J. H. Pierce, a former Estes employee.

122:       Lyndon Johnson had a controlling interest in how government grain was shipped: Holland
           McCombs small notebook, Holland McCombs Papers, Box 149, File 16.

122:       William E. Morris . . . "the S.S. Pecos Trader": See Adler, "The Killing of Henry Marshall."

123:       Ralph Yarborough was a beneficiary of Estes' largesse: See *Dallas Morning News*, June 7, 1964.

123:       Estes claimed to have funded LBJ's campaign in the 1960 Democratic Party primary: Estes,
           Billie Sol Estes, p. 65.

123:       at a barbecue in honor of Ralph Yarborough: Billie Sol Estes supposedly handed cash over to
           Senator Yarborough: Jimmy Banks, "$50,000 Question Remains: Did Senator Get That
           Sum?" *Dallas Morning News*, June 7, 1964.

123:       Clifton Crawford Carter collects campaign contributions in perpetuity: See Clifton C. Carter
           Oral History Interview, October 1, 9, 15, and 30, 1968, and March 25, 1969, by Dorothy L.
           Pierce, LBJ Library. You have to read between the lines, but see pp. 145–60.

123:       "bag man . . . Lyndon could trust him to pick up the money and keep his mouth shut": Bill
           Adler, "The Killing of Henry Marshall," *Texas Observer* (November 7, 1986).

124:       "If Billie Sol builds the storage facilities": So Estes writes in his memoir, *Billie Sol Estes*, p. 34.

124:       "just to call Lyndon Johnson": Evan Moore, "The Secrets of Billie Sol," *Houston Chronicle*,
           June 23, 1996, p. 10. See also "I would call Lyndon" in Estes, *Billie Sol Estes*, pp. 80–81. Also:
           And "I will get Lyndon Johnson on the phone."

124:       Estes made his private airplanes available: This was reported by Drew Pearson, who wrote
           that Texans received calls from Billie Sol Estes inviting them to fly to Washington in his
           private plane: Pearson, "How Estes Succeeded: Money Talks in U.S," May 19, 1962.
           Syndicated column.

124:       Billie Sol's hero is Harry S. Truman: Billie Sol Estes quoted in Pam Estes, *Billie Sol: King of
           Texas Wheeler-Dealers* (Granbury, TX: Pamelaco Productions, 1983), p. 45.

124:       "I have always worshipped money": Ibid., p. 45.

125:       Billie Sol Estes claims to have passed $10 million in bribes to Lyndon Johnson: Burton
           Hersh, *Bobby and J. Edgar: The Historic Face-Off Between the Kennedys and J. Edgar Hoover that
           Transformed America* (New York: Basic Books, 2007), p. 406.

125:       $35 million in tax liens: William P. Barrett, "Dealer's Choice: Billie Sol Estes Still Isn't
           Showing His Cards," *Dallas Times Herald*, May 13, 1984.

10: ENTER THE OFFICE OF NAVAL INTELLIGENCE

126:       For some insight into how the various components of the intelligence services handled secu-
           rity clearances, see CIA. Memorandum for: Director of Central Intelligence. Subject: Final
           Report of Working Group on Organization and Activities. April 6, 1962. 35 pages. No riff
           (explanatory cover sheet) available. National Archives and Records Administration (NARA).

126: Walter Jenkins's "Q" clearance: Mike Quinn, "LBJ Probe Clears Jenkins of Any Security Violations," *Dallas Morning News*, October 23, 1964. Jenkins was arrested on October 7, 1964. Johnson not only fired him, but ordered an FBI investigation in an effort (for public consumption) to clear his administration of having "compromised the security" of the United States.

127: peripatetic life: See: Paul Shankman and Angela Thieman Dino, "The FBI File of Leslie A. White," *American Anthropologist*, New Series, 103, no. 1 (March 2001), pp. 161–64.

127: "something to fight *for*": Elgin Williams, "The Left and the American Way of Life," *Monthly Review* 2, no. 8 (December 1950), pp. 391–93.

127: A Reed College spokesman insisted to the author that Williams was not fired by Reed for his left-wing politics, but as a result of a drop in student enrollment at the time of the Korean War. In 1954, however, Reed fired Stanley Moore, a professor of philosophy, for invoking his Fifth Amendment privilege at a hearing before the House Un-American Activities Committee (HUAC). Moore was fired by Reed's board of trustees. See Ellen W. Schrecker, *No Ivory Tower: McCarthyism and the Universities* (New York: Oxford University Press, 1986), pp. 236–37.

127: Elgin Williams taught at Mexico City College in the summer of 1951. He took up archaeology and was appointed a trustee at the *Instituto Interamericano*.

127: "with a thirst for knowledge concerning non-literature and prehistoric cultures": See: Shankman and Dino, Op. Cit.

127: Elgin Williams dies during shock therapy treatment: Author interview with Nora Ann Carroll, January 2, 2013. See Elgin Williams obituary, *New World Antiquity* 3, no. 10 (October 1956), p. 160.

127: Mac Wallace appears before Judge Betts in February 1957: "Mac Wallace Case Closed," *Austin American*, February 28, 1957. See also Court Records, Travis County, Texas.

128: "I am not sure that we still have a conviction": The Office of Naval Intelligence (ONI)'s 1957 investigation of Mac Wallace is dated July 12. P. T. Smith was the special agent handling the investigation for the Eighth Naval District, San Antonio, Texas. It was a "special Investigation—Local Inquiry." Confidential Naval Intelligence Report. Re: Malcolm Everett Wallace, July 12, 1957.

128: Mac read bedtime stories to his children from Greek mythology: Joan Mellen telephone conversation with Meredithe Nix, June 2012.

129: "When you have a guest, whatever they want, it's theirs:" Author interview with Michael Wallace, December 6, 2012.

129: death of Alice Marie Riddle Wallace: Vital Records #31351. 9 September 1959. Terrell State Hospital, Terrell, Kaufman County, Texas.

129: "I bet you can't guess what I threw out the car window": Author interview with Meredithe Nix, November 22, 2013, Dallas.

130: Mac and Andre are remarried on New Year's Eve: Dallas County Marriages, Dallas, Texas, vol. 147, p.7.

130: the incest: "It happened": Author interviews with Meredithe Nix, July 10, 2013, and November 22, 2013, Dallas.

131: "when Elaine was molested": Author interview with Meredithe Nix, November 22, 2013, Dallas.

131: Control Supervisor: So the files of the ONI reveal. See Naval Intelligence Report, December 27, 1962. See also: MEMORANDUM FOR THE DIRECTOR, OIPAAR. FROM: SCREENING BOARD, PANEL NO. 1. September 27, 1962. SUBJECT: WALLACE, MALCOLM E. 62–340 TWO PAGES.

131: "up-to-date" investigation of Malcolm E. Wallace: U.S. Naval Intelligence Report. RE: Malcolm Everett Wallace. August 15, 1959. A. C. Sullivan, Special Agent, Dallas.

131:   On the ONI investigations of Mac Wallace: These records passed through the hands of Texas
       Ranger and later U.S. Marshall Clint Peoples, who in turn shared them with the Dallas
       police. The police made them available to former Dallas police officer John Fraser Harrison,
       who was investigating the life of Mac Wallace.

132:   no new evidence: See U.S. Naval Intelligence Report. Re: Malcolm Everett Wallace. April 25,
       1960.

132:   filed for divorce: Cause #60-6781. Dallas County, Texas. November 17, 1960. Filed by Mary
       Andre Wallace.

132:   "his breath was strong of alcohol": Dallas City Corporation Court #2, Cause #J-22861.

132:   "regroup his life": Mary C. Bounds, "Accused Man's Relatives Dispute Estes' Story," *Dallas
       Morning News*, March 29, 1984.

132:   Ling Electronics: Ling-TEMCO-Vought: In 1961 as well, D. H. Byrd created a defense elec-
       tronics firm called E-Systems, later renamed Raytheon. Run by former CIA and FBI officers,
       Raytheon worked closely with CIA. In 1975, Raytheon would purchase a CIA proprietary
       (front company) called Air Asia and would go on to become a major National Security
       Agency contractor into the twenty-first century.

132:   James Ling is friendly with Lyndon Johnson: Bill Adler, "The Killing of Henry Marshall,"
       Texas Observer (November 7, 1986), p. 19.

133:   Ling contributes a quarter of a million dollars: "Odds and Ends Combed Out of Some Will
       Wilson Interviews," June 12, 1964. Holland McCombs Papers.

133:   "the recipient of more and more generous government contracts": Holland McCombs to
       William Lambert. June 11, 1964: "ADD: SUGGESTIONS, IDEAS . . . SECOND DRAFT."
       Holland McCombs Papers.

133:   the most comprehensive investigation of Mac Wallace to date: Naval Intelligence Document
       #3927 is dated July 20, 1961. 19 pages. Although reports were received on November 9, 1961,
       the completed document itself was backdated to July 20, 1961.

133:   "the possibility of a 'triangle'": United States Government Memorandum. United States
       Naval Intelligence. July 20, 1961.

134:   "the recipient of valuable property in the city of Austin": United States Government
       Memorandum. United States Naval Intelligence. July 20, 1961, apparently misdated since
       subsequent events later in the year 1961 appear in this memorandum.

135:   "radical": Nowotny was interviewed years later on the subject of Mac Wallace's political views
       when he was president of the student body at the University of Texas by the Office of Naval
       Intelligence: United States Government Memorandum. United States Naval Intelligence.
       July 20, 1961. The file on Wallace compiled by the ONI is contained in the papers of John
       Fraser Harrison. The source of this classified file was Marshal Clint Peoples, who aided the
       Navy in its investigation of Wallace and procured copies of the file after Wallace's death.
       Courtesy of Walt Brown.

136:   "How in the world could . . . Wallace, an obvious security risk": Sullivan is quoted in David
       Hanners, "Files on Wallace Missing, Officials Say," *Dallas Morning News*, May 13, 1984. In
       1984, Hanners located Sullivan working in Dallas.

11: SOME FAUSTIAN BARGAINS COME DUE: THE FALLS OF BILLIE SOL
ESTES AND BOBBY BAKER

137:   on Johnson's political aspirations: Robert A. Caro, in *The Years of Lyndon Johnson: The Path to
       Power* (New York, Alfred A. Knopf, 1982), pp. 76–77, contrasts Johnson's large-size political

aspirations with the local focus of his father, Sam Ealy Johnson. Johnson professed to want to be President of the United States: Caro, *The Path to Power*, pp. 134–35.

137–138: Joseph P. Kennedy offers Lyndon Johnson a million dollars to run as John F. Kennedy's Vice President: Burton Hersh, *Bobby and J. Edgar: The Historic Face-Off Between the Kennedys and J. Edgar Hoover that Transformed America* (New York: Basic Books, 2007), p. 14. "It was the old man who wanted me," Lyndon Johnson later said. Ibid., p. 16.

138: "Who told him he could do that?" Joseph A. Pratt and Christopher J. Castaneda, *Builders: Herman and George R. Brown* (College Station, TX: Texas A & M University Press, 1999), p. 185.

138: a tunnel to the Vatican . . . built by Brown & Root: Holland McCombs to Will Lang, *LIFE* magazine, for Audrey Jewett. Undated. Holland McCombs Papers.

138: Abe Fortas argues for a writ before the U.S. Supreme Court: John E. Clark, *The Fall of the Duke of Duval: A Prosecutor's Journal* (Austin, TX: Eakin Press, 1999), p. 82.

138: "as evidence he had invested the county's money wisely": Clark, *Duke of Duval*, p. 85. Clark points out that George Parr still had "tax liens and civil claims to contend with, he was in bankruptcy, the Old Party was largely out of power and the federal tax evasion indictment against him was still pending—but at least he wasn't going to prison any time soon."

139: two years, ten months, and two days: Reflects a plaque Jacqueline Kennedy had placed in the Lincoln Bedroom of the White House: "In this room lived John Fitzgerald Kennedy with his wife Jacqueline during the two years, ten months and two days he was President of the United States."

139: "get up here right away": Holland McCombs records. McCombs interviewed the families of the deceased pilots. He also traced the insurance history and ownership records of the plane and so knew that when Johnson claimed the plane had been "chartered" this was not true. There was also a discrepancy between the date that appeared on the bill of sale to the LBJ Company, March 29, 1960, and the date the sale was recorded, February 1, 1961. McCombs found that the delay in Brazos-Tenth Street registering the plane could not be explained.

139: Lyndon Johnson finds $250,000 to pay off the families of the dead pilots: Holland McCombs, "ROUGH DRAFT."

140: "It's those dern, crooked politicians" Pam Estes, *Billie Sol: King of Texas Wheeler-Dealers* (Granbury, TX: Pamelaco Productions, 1983, revised 2004), p. 40.

140: the gift of some roses: LBJ's thank-you notes to Billie Sol Estes are available at the LBJ Library.

140: "Call on me in the Vice-President's office": quoted in Bill Adler, "The Killing of Henry Marshall," *Texas Observer* (November 7, 1986). For the LBJ–Estes correspondence, see LBJ Library.

140: Estes' empire begins to crumble: CQ Almanac Online Edition, 1962. http://library.cqpress/cqalmanac/document.php?id=cqal62-878

140: unsecured seven-million-dollar loan: Stephen Pegues, "Texas Mafia," unpublished manuscript, p. 93.

140: Frank Cain commented on the absence of references to LBJ in the Estes depositions and court records: Holland McCombs interview with Frank Cain, July 23, 1964.

141: "We don't have it," Orr said: Holland McCombs records.

142: A. B. Foster calls the new regulations "unreasonable": Quoted in Adler, "The Killing of Henry Marshall."

142: Henry Marshall offered a promotion in the Department of Agriculture: Clint Peoples, Oral History Interview VII, November 21, 1984, p. 257, Dallas Public Library.

142:   Lyndon Johnson meets with Ward Jackson: J. Evetts Haley, *A Texan Looks at Lyndon: A Study in Illegitimate Power* (Canyon, TX: Palo Duro Press, 1964), p. 116.

142:   There was a rumor that Mrs. Johnson was a heavy investor in Commercial Solvents: Ibid. Haley's book was distributed by the Liberty Lobby bookstore. Haley himself had been a participant in the negotiations that brought the KTBC radio station to Lyndon Johnson. He had worked for the West ranch. West had gone to the FCC to get help, which was how Lyndon Johnson learned that the station was in trouble and moved in.

142:   "if I can again assist you": See Ibid., p. 118.

143:   there was a witness to the plane being there: *Billie Sol Estes, A Texas Legend* (Billie Sol Estes: BS Productions (Granbury Texas: 2005), p. 102. All further references to "Estes" are to Billie Sol, not Pam.

143:   Marshall got out of his truck: For the details of the attack on Henry Marshall, see Adler, "The Killing of Henry Marshall." There are also details in "Texas Mafia," the unpublished manuscript of Stephen Pegues, which obviously derive from Pegues's interviews with Billie Sol Estes. See also Billie Sol Estes, *Billie Sol Estes: A Texas Legend* (Granbury, TX: BS Productions, 2005), ch. 11; and news reports of the 1962 grand jury inquiry into Marshall's death.

143:   the rifle would have to be pumped each time to eject the shell: Adler, "The Killing of Henry Marshall," pp. 10–11.

144:   the sun was going to come up in the west: Author interview with John Paschall, July 13, 2012. Billie Sol Estes too notes that the sheriff controlled local politics: Estes, *Billie Sol Estes*, p. 49.

144:   "I'll ride a jackass to the moon": Bartee Haile, "Absurd Suicide Finally Ruled to Be a Murder," *Sulphur Springs (Texas) News Telegraph*, August 25, 1984.

144:   Josefa Johnson dies on Christmas morning, 25 December, 1961, Texas: Vital Records #70698.

145:   "Josefa died?" Holland McCombs to William Lambert at *LIFE* magazine, June 25, 1964; and Holland McCombs to William Lambert, June 29, 1964. Holland McCombs Papers.

145:   Josefa was in bad health: Author interview with William P. Barrett, May 30, 2012.

145:   Estes gives Walter Jenkins $145,015: Estes, *Billie Sol Estes*, p. 77.

145:   "we know you've been giving a lot of money to Lyndon": Ibid., p. 83.

145:   Estes gives Cliff Carter tickets to a Democratic Party fund-raising dinner: Testimony of William E. Morris, a former Agriculture Department employee before the House Intergovernmental Regulations Subcommittee hearings held May 28 to September 13, 1962. Transcript available at the LBJ Library, Austin.

146:   "I can stop all that": Quoted in the San Angelo *Standard-Times*, April 21, 1962.

146:   Estes calls an unlisted White House Number: A UPI release of June 23, 1962, reveals that a Texas assistant attorney general scrutinized telephone company records relating to Billie Sol Estes. He testified that calls were made from Billie Sol Estes' telephones to a member of Vice President Johnson's staff. Between September 1960 and March 1962, there were thirty-eight calls to Ralph Yarborough. Two were made on March 29, 1962, the day Estes was arrested. Three were to Cliff Carter Three went to the unlisted White House number. A call went to a "Mr. Carter" at Arlington, Virginia, on March 28 when Estes was at the Statler Hilton in Dallas conferring with finance company representatives about mortgages totaling more than $20 million on fertilizer tanks. At 9:02 P.M. Estes talked to Carter for six minutes, a desperation call.

146:   the FBI's investigation into Estes was called off in November 1961: Holland McCombs to Audrey Jewett, *LIFE*, New York, July 23, 1964. Holland McCombs Papers.

146:   Oscar Griffin: See Douglas Martin, "Oscar Griffin Jr., 78, Pulitzer Prize Winner Who Brought Down Scheming Texas Tycoon, Dies," *The New York Times*, December 10, 2011.

147: Johnson asks Hoover to intervene in the matter of the articles in the *Independent:* Athan G. Theoharis and John Stuart Cox, *The Boss: J. Edgar Hoover and the Great American Inquisition* (Philadelphia: Temple University Press, 1988), p. 346.

147: Hoover promised to "get on it right away": Ibid., p. 346. See also Mark North, *Act of Treason: The Role of J. Edgar Hoover in the Assassination of President Kennedy* (New York: Skyhorse Publishing, 2011), p. 77.

147: "would have Walter Jenkins get in touch with Mr. DeLoach": North, *Act of Treason*, p.129.

147: Johnson enlists the FBI to silence Bill Cramer: Ibid.

147: "want to be of every possible assistance to the Vice President": Ibid., p. 142.

147: the IRS conducts an investigation of Billie Sol Estes: See Pam Estes, *Billie Sol*, pp. 76–80.

148: "I'll never go to jail": "DPR COLLEGE." Miguel Acoca, *LIFE* magazine, December 1, 1964. Holland McCombs Papers.

148: "transporting bogus tank mortgages across state lines": Bill Adler, "The Killing of Henry Marshall," p. 7.

148: Mary Kimbrough Jones: Haley, *A Texan Looks at Lyndon*, p. 133. See also *Time* magazine cover story, "The Billie Sol Estes Scandal," May 1962. Senator Williams, "railroaded" into a mental institution: quoted in the CQ Almanac Online Edition for 1962.

148: Cliff Carter tells Billie Sol that everything would be all right: Billie Sol Estes, *Billie Sol Estes*, p. 83.

149: a list of every government passenger: Amarillo *Globe-Times*, May 15, 1962.

149: "ever contributed to any of your political campaigns": Memorandum, June 14, 1962. To: Vice President Johnson. From: Warren Woodward. LBJ Library. Vice-Presidential Papers. Johnson was fickle. When Jenkins was arrested in October 1964 on a morals charge, having been discovered in a "compromising situation" in a YMCA toilet, the second time in this place, the first having been in 1959, Johnson fired him.

150: "I put a private detective on the Potter case . . . I regret we were not successful": Owen W. Kilday, Sheriff, Bexar County, Texas, to Vice President Lyndon Johnson, May 22, 1962. Vice-Presidential Papers. LBJ Library. A diligent reporter named Mike Cox discovered this document at the LBJ Library. Cox's article "Johnson May Have Ordered Hotel Bugging" was published in the *Austin American Statesman*, April 13, 1984. See also William P. Barrett, "Papers Indicate LBJ Tried to Tape Estes Meeting," *Dallas Times Herald*, April 20, 1984. In his memoir, Billie Sol Estes acknowledges that he was scheduled to meet with Potter: Estes, *Billie Sol Estes*, p. 103. Estes also reveals that Sheriff Owen Kilday was a Johnson operative (p. 55).

Under "Confidential Investigation," Kilday's letter and the bill for the services of Charles S. Bond were discovered among Johnson's Vice-Presidential papers by Cox. Earlier, Cox had uncovered a transcript of a conversation between Johnson and Orville Freeman, the agriculture secretary, in which Johnson said that he had met Estes only once and knew nothing of his business. At a January dinner with Senator Ralph Yarborough, Johnson said, "I don't know anything about the man's [Estes'] business transactions." These were fabrications.

151: "dead before nightfall": Billie Sol Estes, *Billie Sol Estes*, p. 102.

151: Will Wilson files an anti-trust suit on behalf of the State of Texas: See "Texan Says Estes, Firm in Collusion, *Waco Times-Herald*, June 14, 1962, p. 1; "Estes Tumble Surprised Fertilizer Firm Officials," *Houston Post*, June 15, 1962; Richard M. Morehead, "Trust Suit Planned in Estes Case," *Dallas Morning News*, May 11, 1962, section 1, p. 14; John Mashek, "Ike Cites 'Teapot Dome' Case as Pattern for JFK on Estes," *Dallas Morning News*, May 11, 1962, section 1, p. 14. In none of these articles is Lyndon Johnson's name mentioned.

151: Billie Sol Estes shelters under his Fifth Amendment privilege seventy-five times: So says Stephen Pegues, "Texas Mafia," p. 138.

151: three other grand jurors were kin to the Stegalls: Stephen Pegues interview with Donald Marshall, son of Henry Marshall. Ibid., p. 134.

151: Lyndon Johnson appoints Barefoot Sanders as U.S. Attorney for the Northern District of Texas: Clint Carter, Oral History Interview, Op. Cit., LBJ Library, p. 520 of Notes.

151: Estes said the figure paid to Cofer was $85,000. He told this to the author although it does not appear in his memoir. Nor does his daughter Pam Estes mention this figure in her memoir, *Billie Sol*, although she writes that she believes Cofer mishandled Estes' case in his effort to protect Lyndon Johnson from being exposed (pp. 65–66).

152: on the composite: Harley Pershing, "Marshall's Estes Check Believed Death Motive," *Fort Worth Star-Telegram*, July 20, 1962, p. 1. See also Ken Lanterman and Rebecca Pflugfelder, "Peoples: More Deaths May Be Tied to Estes," *Bryan (Texas) College-Station Eagle*, March 24, 1984. Author interview with Bryan County District Attorney John Paschall. The suspect is positively identified by Griffin: Adler, "The Killing of Henry Marshall," p. 14.

152: He ordered Griffin to "back off": Author interview with John Paschall, July 13, 2012.

152: the grand jury hearing is halted "abruptly": George Kuempe, "Grand Jurors Say Probe into 1962 Death Halted Abruptly," *Dallas Morning News*, May 20, 1984.

152: Judge Barron revealed that Robert F. Kennedy had telephoned him every day: Judge Barron offered these details to journalist Bill Adler in 1986 for his *Texas Observer* article, "The Killing of Henry Marshall," p. 14.

153: "LBJ, Yarborough Linked with Estes, *McAllen (Texas) Valley Evening Monitor*, June 24, 1962, p. 1.

153: it was Holleman: "Odds and Ends Combed Out of Some Will Wilson Interviews," June 12, 1964. Holland McCombs Papers.

153: "he'd run up a telephone bill": To: Patricia Hough, *Fortune*, from Holland McCombs. May 29, 1962. Holland McCombs Papers, Box 245, File 1.

154: "Why haven't they found out and exposed everyone": See Holland McCombs Papers, Box 149, File 13 and Box 245, File 1.

155: "I'll call Jack": Oscar Griffin Jr., "How We Exposed Billie Sol Estes," in the *Pecos Independent*.

155: Billie Sol Estes approaches Barry Goldwater: Mike Durham, *LIFE*, Miami, from Holland McCombs, Dallas. October 19, 1964. Holland McCombs Papers, Box 14, File 3. See also McCombs, March 12, 1965. Hal Winger and Don Cravens, *LIFE*, Beverly Hills, CA, Box 14, File 3.

155: "Do you know who Henry Marshall was"? CQ Almanac Online Edition. Wilson C. Tucker relayed this conversation he had with Estes and his lawyer on October 18, 1961. Tucker worked for the Agricultural Stabilization and Conservation Services. Op. Cit.

155: "not a single fertilizer tank payment was past due": Billie Sol Estes, *Billie Sol Estes*, p. 109.

156: John Cofer refuses to confer with Estes or listen to his suggestions: Pam Estes, *Billie Sol*, p. 87.

156: "one of the most gigantic swindles": "Partial Text of Remarks Given in Estes Sentencing," *Dallas Morning News*, April 16, 1963.

156: "he would have gone to prison and I would have gotten immunity": "Estes Says He Could Have Sent LBJ to Jail," *Lubbock (Texas) Avalanche Journal*, November 18, 1983.

157: tools scattered about his garage: Pegues, "Texas Mafia," pp. 158–59.

158: "he might meet with an unfortunate—and probably fatal—accident": Phil Brennan, "Some Relevant Facts About the JFK Assassination," online. November 19, 2003.

158: "to assist in securing defense contracts": Robert A. Caro, *The Years of Lyndon Johnson: The Passage of Power* (New York: Alfred A. Knopf, 2012), p. 277.

158:   Sarah McClendon's story: See Caro, *Passage of Power*, pp. 278–81.

159:   Bobby Baker is under FBI surveillance 24 hours a day … "he and Lyndon are on the telephone about 30 minutes a day": Drew Pearson Diary, Wednesday, November 6, 1963. Personal Papers of Drew Pearson. LBJ Library. Available at NARA. Pearson protected Johnson in his columns. So he wrote in his Diary: "I'm beginning to wonder whether I shouldn't have persued [sic] the Bobby Baker story myself instead of turning it over to Jack [Anderson], when we first heard about it approximately a year ago." Baker behaved as if he were invisible, his operations indecipherable. This was not the case.

159:   Hoover refuses to bug Bobby Baker and so the Narcotics Bureau is called in to do it: Diary of Drew Pearson, January 13, 1967.

159:   "during the McCarthy era when he refused to stand up and fight": Diary of Drew Pearson, November 27, 1963.

159:   *LIFE* magazine: Keith Wheeler, "Scandal Grows and Grows in Washington." *LIFE* (November 8, 1963). The issue featured "The Bobby Baker Bombshell" and pictured Bobby Baker on the cover.

160:   eighteen banks in eight states … $2,784,520: G. R. Schreiber, *The Bobby Baker Affair: How to Make Millions in Washington* (Chicago: Henry Regnery, 1964), p. 176. For one set of figures pertaining to Baker's finances, see Schreiber, *Bobby Baker Affair*, pp. 176–77. For another, see Bobby Baker, *Wheeling and Dealing: Confessions of a Capitol Hill Operator* (New York: W. W. Norton, 1978), p. 156.

160:   Abe Fortas defends Bobby Baker at the suggestion of Lyndon Johnson: "Lyndon helped him get a very fine attorney, Abe Fortas." Diary of Drew Pearson, Thursday, November 22, 1967. Personal Papers of Drew Pearson. LBJ Library.

160:   "high up there with Lyndon and Kerr": Will Lang for Sackett, November 11, 1963. Holland McCombs Papers.

160:   Baker's relationship to Senator Robert Kerr: See Schreiber, *Bobby Baker Affair*, p. 28. Schreiber suggests that Kerr bankrolled several of Baker's projects.

160:   "his Lyndon involvements": McCombs could not find anything "they can pin down … in either Billie Sol or Bobby Baker": Holland McCombs Papers, Box 146, File 11.

160:   Ralph Hill introduced Don Reynolds to Senator John Williams: Robert G. Baker, Oral History Interview VII, October 11, 1984, by Michael L. Gillette, p. 37, LBJ Library.

161:   Walter Jenkins browbeats Don Reynolds into buying air time on Lyndon Johnson's station: "Jenkins Faces Call by Baker Probers," *Dallas Morning News*, January 15, 1965.

162:   "The S.O.B. will never live out his term": See Edward J. Epstein, "Who's Afraid of the Warren Report?" *Esquire* magazine, December 1966.

162:   Johnson takes a $100,000 payoff for the TFX fighter plane contract: See Victor Lasky, *It Didn't Start with Watergate* (New York: Dial Press, 1977), p. 131.

162:   General Curtis LeMay is dumbfounded: See General Curtis LeMay, Oral History Interview, June 28, 1971, by Joe B. Frantz, p. 17, LBJ Library. "The first evaluation, Boeing won by a mile … after four evaluations Boeing still won by an overwhelming margin."

163:   "I'm sure it was a political decision": Ibid., p. 18. General Dynamics was close to bankruptcy: So said Richard Austin Smith in *Fortune* magazine. Smith wrote that "unless it gets the contract for the joint Navy-Air Force fighter (TFX), the company was down the road to receivership." "The 7-Billion Dollar Contract …" *Fortune*, March 1963. Smith wrote that General Dynamics was "close to bankruptcy."

163:   Reynolds's FBI file is turned over to Lyndon Johnson: See "Baker Probe Witness Thinks File Was Pulled Out of FBI," *Dallas Morning News*, February 9, 1964, section 1, p. 8.

163: Fred Black was a close friend of mobster Johnny Rosselli: See Larry Hancock, *Someone Would Have Talked* (Southlake, TX: JFK Lancer Productions, 2010).

164: "Lyndon and I just want you to know we love you": Baker, *Wheeling and Dealing*, p. 274.

164: Lynda Bird terms her parents' marriage "a little oppressive": Interview with Lynda Bird Johnson broadcast on the History Channel, February 23, 2014. These comments derive from Lynda Bird Johnson's oral history for the LBJ Library, August 23, 2004.

164: In one day it sold 8,000 copies: See "Anti-LBJ Book Selling Fast," *San Antonio Light*, July 21, 1964.

165: visited by two IRS agents: Author interview with Douglas Caddy, December 18, 2013; e-mail from Caddy, January 8, 2014.

165: Lyndon Johnson arranges a loan . . . Kerr had "carried the ball": Drew Pearson *Diary*, January 20, 1967. LBJ Library.

165: Drew Pearson and Jack Anderson: *The Case Against Congress* was published by Simon & Schuster in 1968.

165: "had done his best to delay and avoid trial": Evan Thomas, *The Man to See* (New York: Simon & Schuster, 2012), p. 214. There is an excellent description of Bobby Baker's trial in this biography of his attorney, Edward Bennett Williams.

165: Baker had lied on the stand: Ibid., p. 222.

165: "Bittman suspected Justice steered the ultimate indictment": Ibid., p. 218.

166: "a generally corrupt system": Michael Tigar quoted in Bobby Baker, *Wheeling and Dealing*, pp. 216–217.

166: Carlos Marcello offers Bobby Baker a million dollars: Bobby Baker, interviewed by Burton Hersh, May 30, 2005. Quoted in Hersh, *Bobby and J. Edgar*, p. 272. E-mail to Joan Mellen from Burton Hersh, January 15, 2015.

166: "your dear, great friend": Hersh, *Bobby and J. Edgar*, p. 272.

12: MAC WALLACE IN CALIFORNIA

167: Mary Andre marries Delmer Lee Akin: Dallas County (Texas) Marriage Records, vol. 154, p. 450.

167: Andre tells the Navy investigators that Mac committed incest with his nine-year-old daughter: See Memorandum for the Director, OIPAAR. September 27, 1962. From: Screening Board, Panel No. 1. Subject: Wallace, Malcolm E. 62-340, Signed by John Owen, Capt USN, Chairman; Harris J. North, Lt. Col, USA; David E. Henretta, USAF, Member. Also: Author telephone interviews with Michael Alvin Wallace.

167–168: Andre outlines the incest charge to Navy investigators: The interview took place in Timpson, Texas, e-mail from A. Meredithe Nix to William E. Carroll, August 3, 2003. Courtesy of William E. Carroll.

168: The Screening Board summarized Wise's investigation: Memorandum to the Director, Office of Industrial Personnel Access Authorization Review. From: Screening Board, Panel No. 1. August 4, 1964. One page. The Statement of Reasons is Memorandum for the Director of Naval Intelligence, Department of the Navy. Re: Malcolm Everett Wallace. September 18, 1964.

169–170: he regretted some things that had happened: "I've been in the newspapers twice." Author interview with Virginia Princehouse, December 10, 2012.

171: Pat Elliott had herself kept in touch with Mac Wallace over the years: Nora Ann Carroll Stevenson to Marjorie Turner, February 8, 2008. Letter.

171: he met her at the airport in Los Angeles: Nora Ann Carroll Stevenson recounted the details of the time she spent with Mac Wallace in California during the summer of 1963. Author interviews, May 10–13, 2013.

172: "he has changed so much": Nora Ann Cary to Lelia Carroll, July 25, 1963. Letter courtesy of Nora Ann Carroll Stevenson.

172: "God in the form of a roving street-photographer": Nora Ann Carroll to Marjorie Turner. Undated letter.

172: "a sense of deep remorse": Nora Ann Carroll Stevenson to Bill Adler, May 4, 1986.

172: taken advantage of Andre: Mac explained how he had felt about Kinser and Andre to Nora Ann Carroll some years later: Nora Ann Carroll Stevenson to Bill Adler, May 4, 1986. Courtesy of William E. Carroll.

172: "it was the only night we ever had": Nora Ann Carroll to Marjorie Turner. Undated.

174: All passion had been spent: Author interview with Nora Ann Carroll Stevenson, January 3, 2013.

174: Mac Wallace frolics in the Holiday Inn swimming pool with Page Cary and her friend, Jill: Joan Mellen conversation with Page Cary, May 10, 2013.

175: Mac Wallace liked to play the devil's advocate: Author interview with Meredithe Nix, November 22, 2013.

175: the "charge involving the daughter": Memorandum for the Director. OIPAAR/Re: Malcolm E. Wallace. August 27, 1964.

176: "Director of Purchasing and Subcontracts": "Résumé for M. E. Wallace." 1970.

176: Joe Bloomberg works under Mac: Joe Bloomberg was interviewed by author Glen Sample. See Glen Sample and Mark Collom, *The Men on the Sixth Floor* (Sample Graphics, 2003), p. 212. There seems no reason to doubt the validity of this interview, although the book itself is deeply flawed, the story of Loy Factor and his recruitment by Mac Wallace and his placing Wallace on the sixth floor of the Texas School Book Depository on November 22, 1963, unconvincing.

13: PRESIDENT LYNDON JOHNSON, PART I

178: "Are we to teach our children that rough and ruthless politics as practiced by Lyndon is a virtue": Holland McCombs to William Lambert, June 11, 1964. Holland McCombs Papers.

178: "tapes and memoranda documenting some of Johnson's own questionable activities": Curt Gentry, *J. Edgar Hoover: The Man and the Secrets* (New York: W. W. Norton, 1991), p. 558.

178: Lyndon Johnson maps out the "Great Society" at four A.M. on November 23, 1963: Jack Valenti, "Lyndon Johnson: An Awesome Engine of a Man," in Thomas W. Cowger and Sherwin J. Markman, eds., *Lyndon Johnson Remembered: An Intimate Portrait of a Presidency* (Oxford, UK: Rowman & Littlefield, 2003), p. 37.

302: baby face: So Madeleine Brown describes herself in *Texas in the Morning: The Love Story of Madeleine Brown and President Lyndon Baines Johnson* (Baltimore: Conservatory Press, 1997), p. 5. According to Brown, she "fell deeply in love" with Lyndon Johnson and was "uncontrollably excited, sexually aroused by this powerful man." See *The Men Who Killed Kennedy: The Guilty Men* produced for the History Channel by Nigel Turner, 2003. This was the final episode of the series. Brown refers to Mac Wallace as "the crazy South Texas Killer" (p. 83) and claims that it was "Mac Wallace who fired the gun" (p. 170). Her evidence seems largely that she saw Lyndon Johnson and Mac Wallace together at Johnson's radio station (p. 146).

Brown also claimed that there was a Wallace Plumbing Truck at the scene of the assassination (p. 85).

178: Robert A. Caro, Lyndon Johnson's biographer, ignores the existence of both Billie Sol Estes and Madeleine Brown. Letters to Brown from Johnson lawyers prove inescapably, however, that Johnson paid Brown's expenses and that she bore Johnson a son, Steven. Six feet four inches tall, with big floppy ears, Steven closely resembled Lyndon Johnson. "You have my personal assurance that I will continue with the financial arrangements that Lyndon provided for you and Steve throughout the past," lawyer Jerome T. Ragsdale wrote to Brown on May 18, 1973, shortly after Johnson's death.

179: "I'm going to get Kennedy's tax cut out of the Senate Finance Committee": Quoted in Julian F. Zelizer, *The Fierce Urgency of Now: Lyndon Johnson, Congress, and the Battle for the Great Society* (New York: Penguin, 2015), pp. 1–2. Zelizer does not notice the anomaly of how Johnson could have organized his entire legislative program less than twenty-four hours after the death of President Kennedy.

179: Lyndon Johnson is briefed on November 23, 1963, by DCI John McCone: The source is an essay by John Helgerson, a former deputy director for intelligence of CIA, that was published by CIA's Center for the Study of Intelligence. Its title is "The Transition to President Johnson." The location was the White House.

179: "a hardening up of President Kennedy's November 18 statement": Memorandum for Mr. Bundy. December 23, 1963. Subject: Presidential Statement on Cuba. From: Gordon Chase. NSC. 145-10001-10075. Number: 89. National Archives and Records Administration (NARA). The text of President Kennedy's speech before the Inter American Press Association in Miami Beach is available in the Papers of John F. Kennedy. Presidential Papers. President's Office Files. Speech Files. Address to Inter American Press Association. Miami, Florida. November 18, 1963. JFK Library.

180: John F. Kennedy instructs CIA to share the agency's presidential briefing statements (President's intelligence checklist) "under no circumstances" with Vice President Johnson: CIA director John Brennan mentioned this fact in his address at the LBJ Library on the occasion of CIA's release of the Presidential Briefing Statements for Presidents Kennedy and Johnson on September 16, 2015. Among those present representing the agency were Brennan, CIA director; David Robarge, the chief CIA historian; Admiral Bobby Inman; and Joe Lambert, the director for information management services. James R. Clapper, the director of national intelligence, was also present, among others.

Bromley Smith, the deputy under JFK's National Security Council adviser, McGeorge Bundy, told this to CIA's Richard Lehman, who developed the President's intelligence checklist, and who recounted the story in an interview with Richard Kovar: "Johnson really was not that much of a reader; the thing didn't appeal to him the way it did to Kennedy. We finally settled by broadening dissemination so that we sent it to Rusk and McNamara and . . . after it had been in business for a couple of months, I had innocently asked the question, 'What about the Vice President?' and Bromley said, 'Under no circumstances.'

180: Fourteen-minute gap: That Johnson knew no limits in covering up facts that were inconvenient to his political well-being is also apparent. We may pause briefly before an incident that occurred shortly after the Kennedy assassination. Most of the time Lyndon Johnson kept his name off documents that might reveal his complicity in a crime or misdemeanor. In the Johnson Presidential tapes, there is an extraordinary erasure, a fourteen-minute gap, for November 23, obliterating a telephone call of that date between Johnson and J. Edgar Hoover.

"We have a problem," Hoover told Johnson. The man calling himself Oswald in Mexico City did not have the voice, nor was he the same man arrested in Dallas.

The call was preserved in a transcript and included Hoover's disclosure that Lee Harvey Oswald had been impersonated weeks earlier in Mexico City. Then the recording of that call had disappeared from the magnetic belt on which it was originally recorded. This research was accomplished by Rex E. Bradford. That there was an erasure can be confirmed at the LBJ Library, which took custody of the Johnson records. Hoover would not conceivably have made such a call had Lyndon Johnson been the organizer of the Kennedy assassination. A good part of Johnson's prodigious energy was committed to cultivating disinformation and falsifying history. For the erasure from the Johnson Presidential tapes, see "The Fourteen Minute Gap: An Update" by Rex E. Bradford. September 8, 2002, at www.historymatters .com/essays/frameup/FourteenMinuteGap. Bradford reports that the LBJ Library in a memo confirmed to him the erasure of the Johnson-Hoover phone call. Johnson subsequently ordered that all assassination evidence collected by federal agents be put under lock and key for seventy-five years.

180:    "a Roosevelt New Dealer": from Johnson's first address to a joint session of Congress on November 27, 1963. See also Robert A. Caro, *The Years of Lyndon Johnson: The Passage of Power* (New York: Alfred A. Knopf, 2012), p. 397.

181:    "A Texan, an acute and ruthless 'politician'": Christopher Sandford, *Harold and Jack: The Remarkable Friendship of Prime Minister Macmillan and President Kennedy* (Amherst, NY: Prometheus Books, 2014), p. 28.

181:    "I wanted to help commit LBJ to carrying on Kennedy's program": Caro, *Passage of Power*, p. 413.

181:    "gonna support them all": Ibid. p. 408.

181:    "I need you more than President Kennedy needed you": Ibid., p. 410.

181:    "the education, culture and understanding that President Kennedy had": Ibid., p. 411.

181:    "By all rights, you, Adlai, should be sitting here": E-mail from Adlai Stevenson III, to Joan Mellen, February 16, 2015.

182:    "a posthumous repudiation of John F. Kennedy": Caro, *Passage of Power*, p. 425.

182:    "we could have beaten Kennedy": Ibid., p. 465.

182:    the passage of the 1964 Civil Rights Act: "We did give him regular reports," quoted in Clay Risen, "The Shrinking of Lyndon Johnson" *New Republic*, February 9, 2014. Risen writes of Johnson: "He wasn't the arm-twisting, indomitable genius of Robert Caro's imagination."

182:    "we can say to the Mexican": Caro, *Passage of Power*, p. 486.

182:    "Scrub 'em up": Johnson told all this to Dick West, an editor at the *Dallas Morning News*. The quotation comes from a taped conversation. See David A. Fahrenthold, "Great Society at 50: LBJ's Job Corps Will Cost Taxpayers $1.7 Billion This Year. Does It Work?" *Washington Post*, May 20, 2014, p. A1.

183:    driving black children out of a swimming hole: D. Jablow Hershman, *Power Beyond Reason: The Mental Collapse of Lyndon Johnson*. (Fort Lee, NJ: Barricade, 2002), p. 30.

183:    Lyndon Johnson puts snakes in the trunk of his car to frighten African-American gas station attendant: Robert A. Caro, *The Years of Lyndon Johnson: Master of the Senate* (New York: Alfred A. Knopf, 2002), p. 715.

183:    "Niggers": Warren Trammell to Robert Morrow. E-mail, August 28, 2013. Trammell's father, Seymour Trammell, was a George Wallace adviser. His son is recounting a meeting Wallace had with Lyndon Johnson in the Oval Office that was attended by his father. Courtesy of Mr. Morrow.

183:    "I am G-damned tired of hearing 'bout those g-damned niggers": E-mail from Warren Trammell, son of Seymour Trammell, who attended the 1965 meeting, to Robert Morrow,

August 29, 2013. Trammell, from Alabama, was an adviser to Wallace. The meeting took place on March 13, 1965.

183: "positive self-identity": Quoted in Tavis Smiley with David Ritz, *Death of a King: The Real Story of Dr. Martin Luther King's Final Year* (New York: Little, Brown, 2014), p. 82.

183: "shot down on the battlefields of Vietnam": Ibid., p. 42.

183: "a martyr's cause": Caro, *The Passage of Power*, p. 600.

183: in 1964, Johnson visits Ted Kennedy in hospital to garner his support for the Voting Rights Act: E-mail to Joan Mellen from Burton Hersh, biographer of Edward M. Kennedy. January 27, 2015.

184: Stephen Currier was the son-in-law of Ambassador David K. E. Bruce. He and his wife, Bruce's daughter Audrey, granddaughter and heir of industrialist Andrew Mellon, created the Taconic Foundation dedicated to civil rights issues, among them voting rights. They sponsored a voter education project in Mississippi. Harold Fleming confirmed to me in an interview in 1979 that Stephen Currier worked long into the nights authoring Johnson's voting rights bill. Currier became another young man enlisted by Lyndon Johnson to his causes.

184: President Kennedy withstands pressure to send ground troops to Vietnam virtually on a daily basis: For chapter and verse, see Gordon M. Goldstein, *Lessons in Disaster: McGeorge Bundy and the Path to War in Vietnam* (New York: Henry Holt, 2008). This is the autobiography of McGeorge Bundy, completed after his death by his assistant, Gordon M. Goldstein. Kennedy's conviction that the United States must not send combat troops, "boots on the ground," to Vietnam was firm and undeniable.

184: General MacArthur tells JFK that a land war in Asia would be a "mistake": Kennedy recorded MacArthur's statement to him in an "aide-memoire," something he rarely did. The source is Arthur Schlesinger Jr., "What Would He Have Done?" *New York Times*, March 29, 1992. Review of *JFK and Vietnam* by John M. Newman.

184: "used every dirty trick in the bag": Quoted in *Mr. Conservative: Goldwater on Goldwater*. HBO documentary film.

184–185: November 24, 1963, three P.M. meeting at the Executive Office Building on South Vietnam: Memorandum for the Record. November 25, 1963. Subject: South Vietnam Situation. Attendance: The President, Secretaries Rusk, McNamara, Ball, Messrs. Bundy and McCone, Ambassador Lodge. The subject was "the military situation in South Vietnam." 3 pages. Release of the Historical Review Program of CIA in Full, 1998. See also: President Kennedy and the real politick of Vietnam: CIA. Memorandum for the Record. Subject: Presidential meeting on Vietnam, September 10, 1963. From: Colby, Wm. E. C/Far East Division. Date: 09/12/63. Pages: 5. Subjects: Phillips, Rufus, JFK. Mtg on SVN. 104-10310-10224. JFK-Misc. CIA-DDP-FILES.

185: "We cannot retreat": Drew Pearson Diary, January 19, 1967. LBJ Library.

185: "a flamboyant American Legion–type of speech": Drew Pearson Diary, February 11, 1967. Pearson sees Rusk as militaristic, nationalistic, and warmongering, as did many at that time.

185: "kill a bunch of people": Quoted in *LBJ and Vietnam: In the Eye of the Storm*. Broadcast on the Military History channel, May 10, 2014.

185: "Just let me get elected. . . .": Quoted in Stanley Karnow, *Vietnam: A History* (New York: Penguin, 1984), p. 342.

185: "deeper military plunge": Ibid., p. 343.

185: D. H. Byrd receives a contract from the government to build a jet bomber in January 1964: This information was developed by author and former Canadian diplomat Peter Dale Scott.

185: A-7 Corsair II: John Simkin, December 2, 2006, EducationForum.com.

185: ""What do you think about this Vietnam thing?" Lyndon Johnson to Senator Richard Russell of Georgia. Conversation #WH6405. 10. #3519, #3520, #3521. Presidential Tapes of Lyndon B. Johnson, May 27, 1964. MillerCenter.org.

186: Walter Jenkins arrested: See for example, J. J. Duncan, "LBJ's Top Aide Caught in the YMCA Men's Room," ZIMBIO. Available online. And Mary K. Feeney, December 22, 1999. *Hartford Courant.* Available at tribunedigital—thecourant.

186: "I don't believe they're ever gonna quit": Lyndon Johnson in documentary *LBJ and Vietnam: In the Eye of the Storm.*

186: Clark Clifford warns Lyndon Johnson: Clifford warned Johnson at a July 25, 1965, meeting at Camp David. See John Acacia, *Clark Clifford: The Wise Man of Washington* (Lexington: University Press of Kentucky, 2009), p. 2.

187: "we concluded that maybe they hadn't fired at all": That the supposed firing on the *Maddox* was a false-flag operation has been universally acknowledged. See, for example, James P. Pfiffner, *The Character Factor: How We Judge America's Presidents* (College Station: Texas A & M Press, 2004), p. 52.

187: Operation Northwoods: See James Bamford, *Body of Secrets: Anatomy of the Ultra-Secret National Security Agency, from the Cold War Through the Dawn of a New Century* (New York: Doubleday, 2001), pp. 82–91.

188: "perfectly delicious eating": Some of the material on Lyndon Johnson and the Klebergs derives from my book, *The Great Game in Cuba: CIA and the Cuban Revolution* (New York: Skyhorse Publishing, 2013).

188: Lyndon Johnson investigates Bernard Fensterwald in 1966: Agency: LBJ. Record Number: 177-10002-10126. Records Series: Files of Mildred Stegall. Originator: DOJ: Title: Bernard Fensterwald, Jr. Date: 03/20/59. The date on this document is obviously in error.

188: Charles Luckman received an "unusual favor": "Link Luckman Gifts to LBJ with VA Job," *Chicago Tribune,* August 31, 1966, p. 1.

188–189: "fifty thousand acres around Santa Rosa and Clovis: Holland McCombs, Memo, July 10, 1964, to LIFE.

189–190: For Johnson's theft of gold from Victorio Peak, see Thomas G. Whittle, "L.B.J. and the Treasure of Victorio Peak," *The Investigator,* October 1981; Thomas G. Whittle, "Gold! The Mystery of the $30 Billion Treasure, Part I," *Freedom* 18, no. 10 (June 1986); Thomas G. Whittle, "Gold! The Mystery of the $30 Billion Treasure," *Freedom* (July 1986); John Clarence and Tom Whittle, *The Gold House: The Lies, The Thefts,* Book 2 (Las Cruces, NM: Soledad Publishing Company, 2012). Most of the second volume of *The Gold House* is comprised of the raw research conducted by Clarence and Whittle and consists of transcripts of their interviews with witnesses who observed Lyndon Johnson's efforts to extract gold from Victorio Peak as well as documents that have emerged, several initialed by LBJ when he was President. Whittle, a former Army intelligence officer, had served as a lieutenant for a top-secret unit of Army intelligence based at Fort Bliss. He began as an investigative reporter with Jack Anderson, who was the editor of *The Investigator* magazine. See also Bill Gulley and Mary Ellen Reese, *Breaking Cover* (New York: Simon & Schuster, 1980).

189: Co-author of *The Gold House* John Clarence has completed a book about Richard Nixon and his involvement in the Peak gold thefts which is forthcoming in 2016 as *Break-In: Nixon's $1.2 Billion Gold Heist.*

189: Tucker carries the fine Russian china to Lady Bird's car: Clarence and Whittle, *The Gold House,* Book 2, p. 429. Tucker and his "gold license": Ibid., p. 416. Tucker moving gold bullion legally: Ibid., p. 422.

190: funds for the "War on Poverty" shriveled: Hershman, *Power Beyond Reason*, p. 177.

190: Ralph Schoenman is the author of "The Hidden History of Zionism" (Veritas Press). He served 1960 to 1968 as Bertrand Russell's Executive Secretary.

190: "Who else but President Johnson?": Daniel Marvin, *Expendable Elite: One Soldier's Journey into Covert Warfare* (Walterville, OR: TrineDay, 2006), p. 263. One must hasten to add that Lyndon Johnson was not the first President to order the assassination of a foreign leader. President Eisenhower bears that distinction. John F. Kennedy acquiesced in the assassination attempts on Fidel Castro on at least one well-documented occasion.

191: Johnson's initiation of the bombing of Cambodia in 1965: See Operation Menu on google .com. See also Synopsis by John McCarthy, working title "American POW—in America," undated; and "An American P.O.W.—In America" by John McCarthy on From the Wilderness website. McCarthy does not acknowledge that he was the CIA officer who enlisted Dan Marvin. See also: Daniel Marvin, *Expendable Elite: One Soldier's Journey into Covert Warfare* (Trine Day: Walterville, Oregon, 2006).

191: "stashed" in this army hospital: Dr. Samuel Axelrad related this story to his patient Douglas Caddy and then to Joan Mellen on May 20, 2014: E-mail from Douglas Caddy to Joan Mellen, January 8, 2014.

191: "the meanest man I ever knew": E-mail from Mike Chesser to Joan Mellen, October 6, 2014.

192: "couldn't possibly live with himself": Drew Pearson Diary March 1, 1967. Pearson is interviewing Johnson at the White House. "Lyndon then gave a little more of his philosophy about the problem of bombing and said he couldn't possibly live with himself or the Congress if he stopped bombing North Vietnam."

192: "But we had to go ahead with it": Drew Pearson Diary, January 16, 1967. LBJ Library.

192: Otto Otepka attempts to deny Walt Rostow a security clearance: Joan Mellen, "Otto Otepka, Robert F. Kennedy, Walter Sheridan and Lee Harvey Oswald," in *A Farewell to Justice: Jim Garrison, JFK's Assassination, and the Case that Should Have Changed History* (New York: Skyhorse Publishing, 2013), pp. 428–55. Updated edition.

192: "one million students through college": Drew Pearson Diary for 1967, LBJ Library.

14: LYNDON JOHNSON AND THE USS *LIBERTY*: LYNDON JOHNSON AS PRESIDENT, PART II

193: "I don't care if the *Liberty* sinks": The source is Commander David Edwin Lewis, to whom Admiral Geis conveyed this information. Lewis was the chief intelligence officer aboard the USS *Liberty*. I spent three days in June 2014 with Commander Lewis in Colebrook, New Hampshire, and Leamington, Vermont, where he described his experiences on the *Liberty*.

193: I am indebted for the details of the attack on the USS *Liberty* to James Scott, *The Attack on the Liberty: The Untold Story of Israel's Deadly 1967 Assault on a U.S. Spy Ship* (New York: Simon & Schuster, 2009); and to James M. Ennes Jr., *Assault on the Liberty: The True Story of the Israeli Attack on an American Intelligence Ship* (Reintree Press: 2007). Originally published by Random House in 1980. See also Peter Hounam, *Operation Cyanide: Why the Bombing of the USS Liberty Nearly Caused World War III* (London: Vision, 2003). There has been no U.S. publisher. See also Ernest A. Gallo, *Liberty Injustices: A Survivor's Account of American Bigotry* (Palm Coast, FL: ClearView Press, 2013); and Phillip F. Tourney and Mark Glenn, *What I Saw That Day* (Careywood, ID: Liberty Publications, n.d.).

193: *Liberty*'s mandate was specifically not to spy on either the United Kingdom or Israel, but only on Egypt and the Soviet Union: The source is Lieutenant Commander David Edwin Lewis.

194: "the little respite that he wanted from Vietnam": Tavis Smiley with David Ritz, *Death of a King: The Real Story of Dr. Martin Luther King's Final Year* (New York: Little, Brown, 2014), p. 69.

194: unmarked American reconnaissance planes, bearing no insignia: The source for this is Joe Sorrels, a participant in the reconnaissance of the Egyptian air fields, who talked to Peter Hounam, author of *Operation Cyanide*. Hounam revealed the name of his source to me at his home in Scotland during the summer of 2014. Bryce Lockwood, who was one of the Marines who came aboard *Liberty* at Rota, Spain, recounted this information to me as well in June 2014 at the annual reunion of the survivors of the *Liberty*.

195: the argument that the presence of a Destroyer would have exposed *Liberty*: Author interview with Anthony Wells, Middleburg, Virginia, May 2014.

195: tracked by Soviet ships: E-mail from Lewis to Joan Mellen, May 10, 2014.

195: "brightness of his teeth": Hounam, *Operation Cyanide*, p. 23.

198: Allen Blue had worked on Lyndon Johnson's 1964 presidential campaign: Author interview with Pat Blue, Allen Blue's widow, June 9, 2014.

199: Jim Ennes exhibited an extraordinary act of moral courage by publishing his book, *Assault on the Liberty*, in defiance of the U.S. government stricture against the sailors writing about or talking about what had happened to them, even to each other.

199: waist-deep in swirling water: Ennes, *Assault on the Liberty*, p. 77.

200: "Leave them there to drown?": Author interview with Bryce Lockwood, June 8, 2014.

201: Automated Voice Network (Autovon): This was explained to me in an e-mail from Lewis, May 9, 2014.

201: "nuclear-tipped" weapons: Author interview with Phil Tourney, September 21, 2014.

202: Tony Hart hears the voice of Robert McNamara: E-mails from Dave Lewis to Joan Mellen, May 20, 2014; see also Ennes, *Assault on the Liberty*, p. 86.

203: "My flight did not launch": Brad Knickerbocker, "A Former Navy Pilot Recalls the Liberty Incident," *Christian Science Monitor*, June 4, 1982.

204: "We're on the way . . . Who is the enemy?" Scott, *Attack on the Liberty*, p. 85.

205: Lewis described for me the scene of Admiral Geis telling him of Lyndon Johnson's intervention in preventing the rescue of the sailors: Author interview with David Edwin Lewis, March 18, 2014.

205: Admiral Martin sits on Moe Shafer's bed and explains: Author interview with Moe Shafer, August 14, 2014.

205: the Israeli government summons the U.S. naval attaché, Ernest Castle, and apologizes: Ennes, *Assault on the Liberty*, p. 99.

206: White House diary: Lyndon Johnson's White House diaries are available online from the LBJ library.

206–7: the "happy few": A dedication used by French novelist Stendhal in *The Charterhouse of Parma*. The original source was in Shakespeare's *Henry V*.

207: repeatedly McNamara denied that he remembered anything about the USS *Liberty*: See, for example, the BBC documentary, *Dead in the Water*.

207: Souda Bay versus Malta: E-mail from Ron Kukal to Joan Mellen, June 13, 2014.

208: "mistaken identity": These details of the corrupting of Admiral Kidd's hasty investigation were outlined in Declaration of the late Ward Boston, Jr. Captain, JAGC, USN (ret). In June 1967, Captain Boston had served in the Judge Advocate General Corps of the Navy and had been assigned as senior legal counsel for the Navy Court of Inquiry into the attack on the

USS *Liberty*. His declaration is available in Gallo, *Liberty Injustices: A Survivor's Account of American Bigotry* (Palm Coast, Florida: Clear View Press, Inc., 2013).

208: "mistaken identity": Declaration of Ward Boston, Jr., Captain, JAGC, USN (Ret.) Counsel to the U.S. Navy Court of Inquiry's investigation into the Israeli attack on the USS *Liberty*. January 9, 2004. Coronado, California. Senior Counsel to the USS *Liberty* Court of Inquiry.

208: in an affidavit: Ibid.

208–209: Ward Boston reveals that Johnson and McNamara intervened in the Naval inquiry into the attack on the USS Liberty: See John Crewdson, "New Revelations in Attack on American Spy Ship," ChicagoTribune.com, October 2, 2007.

209: Each sailor was ordered never again to speak: I draw this conclusion from the interviews I conducted with twenty-three survivors of the attack. Every one said the same thing: They had been threatened with dire punishment should they talk about the attack.

209: for more than a decade no one talked: The silence was broken by the publication of Ennes's book, *Assault on the Liberty*, in 1979.

209: "The Israelis knew exactly what they were doing": Richard Helms, *A Look over My Shoulder: A Life in the Central Intelligence Agency* (New York: Random House, 2003), pp. 300–301. Helms spoke out against the official Israeli version of the attack in numerous places. He gave an interview to the *Marine Corps Times* on July 7, 2002, and was interviewed on the subject in the BBC documentary *Dead in the Water*.

210: "You Zionist dupe!": Scott, *Attack on the Liberty*, pp. 106–107.

210: "Keep my mouth shut!": Ibid., p. 221.

210: there was no press release: The White House. Memorandum for the President. May 15, 1968. From: Jim Cross. Courtesy of Dr. Robert Kamansky.

212: the principles of war crimes as defined at Nuremberg: See Gallo, *Liberty Injustices*, pp. 94–95.

212: Rear Admiral Merlin Staring says that Lyndon Johnson was guilty of a war crime: Author interview with Ron Kukal, whose home Admiral Staring visited in 2005; e-mail from Merlin Staring to Ernest Gallo, September 1, 2005; letter to the Secretary of the Army from Rear Admiral Merlin H. Staring, JAGC, April 20, 2006. See also "War Crimes Committed Against U.S. Military Personnel," June 8, 1967. Submitted to the Secretary of the Army in his capacity as executive agent for the Secretary of Defense, June 8, 2005. Available at http://www.ussliberty.org/report//report.htm.

213: "pure murder": Information Report. Central Intelligence Agency. November 9, 1967. References: 16835-46. Country: Israel. Subject: Prospects for Political Ambitions of Moshe Dayan/Attack on USS *Liberty* Ordered by Dayan. No. Pages: 1. Not everyone in authority in Israel endorsed the murder of the sailors on the USS *Liberty*.

213: Dayan had hesitated: See Stephen Green, *Taking Sides: America's Secret Relations with a Militant Israel* (Brattleboro, VT: Amana Books, 1988), p. 222: "Until this time [June 8], Dayan had opposed such an attack [on the Golan Heights], because, according to Gideon Raphael, 'he feared that it would create serious international complications.'" See also Gideon Raphael, *Destination Peace: Three Decades of Israeli Foreign Policy* (New York: Stein and Day, 1981), p. 162.

213: the Strategic Air Command is on alert in the early morning hours of June 8: Jim Nanjo, interviewed by Peter Hounam, October 16, 2002. I am grateful to Mr. Hounam for sharing this material with me. The entire SAC on alert: Author interview with Bryce Lockwood, October 9, 2014. Nanjo subsequently retracted his statements, indicating that he was not sure of the time he was called on alert or that he had decided not to remain on the record on so sensitive a subject.

214:   Lyndon Johnson writes that ten men died and one hundred were wounded, although by 1971
       accurate figures were available: *The Vantage Point: Perspectives of the Presidency, 1963–1969*
       (New York: Holt, Rinehart and Winston, 1971), pp. 300–301. Johnson falsified the figures of
       the dead and wounded on the USS *Liberty*.

15: DOWNWARD SPIRALS

215:   "I felt that I had used up most of my capital as President": Lyndon Johnson, *The Vantage
       Point: Perspectives of the Presidency, 1963–1969* (New York, Holt, Rinehart and Winston, 1971),
       p. 349. Johnson's statement "I am convinced that if I had run again I would have been
       re-elected" appears on the same page.

215:   "he knew he couldn't make it": Robert Dallek, *Flawed Giant: Lyndon Johnson and His Times,
       1961–1973* (New York: Oxford University Press, 1998), p. 569.

215:   he could contact Lyndon Johnson: Author telephone interview with Michael Wallace. Mac
       Wallace behaved as if he had nothing to hide about his relationship or history with Lyndon
       Johnson. There was no tension.

215:   "do what you have to do to get clean": Author interview with Virginia Princehouse, December
       10, 2012.

215:   he couldn't function any longer the way he once had: Author interview with Meredithe Nix.

216:   "John, why do they hate me so?": The Connally story is told in Paul Burka, "The Truth About
       John Connally," *Texas Monthly* (November 1979). Available online. For a detailed account of
       Johnson's activities during his final years, see Dallek, *Flawed Giant*.

216:   "the one man who could beat Robert Kennedy": Dallek, *Flawed Giant*, pp. 544–45.

216:   "a very mean, mean figure . . . an animal in many ways": Quoted in Edwin O. Guthman and
       Jeffrey Shulman, eds., *Robert Kennedy: In His Own Words* (New York: Bantam Books, 1988),
       pp. 411–12, 417. The relationship between Robert F. Kennedy and Lyndon Baines Johnson is
       described in considerable detail by Robert A. Caro in *The Years Of Lyndon Johnson: The
       Passage of Power* (New York: Alfred A. Knopf, 2012).

217:   "Raising his big right hand . . . I'll cut his throat": Caro, *Passage of Power*, pp. 139–40. Caro
       had multiple sources: Johnson lawyer Ed Clark; Posh Oltorf, the Brown & Root Washington,
       D.C., lobbyist; Charles Herring; and Evan Thomas, *Robert Kennedy: His Life* (Simon and
       Schuster: New York, 2000). At such moments, Johnson seems to be a man capable of
       anything.

217:   "open their hearts and work with a new sense of purpose": Dallek, *Flawed Giant*, p. 552.

217:   Johnson attempts to make Abe Fortas chief justice of the U.S. Supreme Court: Dallek,
       "Courtpacking: 'The Fortas Fiasco,'" in *Flawed Giant*, pp. 556–64.

217:   "kicks you in the face": Quoted in Dallek, *Flawed Giant*, pp. 570–71.

218:   Johnson refuses to expose the half-million-dollar contribution of the Greek colonels to the
       Nixon campaign: Conversations over many decades with the late Elias P. Demetrocopoulos;
       see also Dallek, *Flawed Giant*, pp. 579–80.

218:   Nor was he about to do anything to help Hubert Humphrey be elected: Ibid., pp. 570–92.

218:   animosity of easterners toward Texans: LBJ interview with Helen Thomas, November 22,
       1968, quoted by Dallek, *Flawed Giant*, p. 592.

218:   He talked often about Nora Ann: Author interview with Virginia Princehouse. Op. Cit.

218:   "You should respect them": Author interviews with Michael Wallace, November 27, 2012;
       December 6, 10, 12, 14, and 27, 2012; January 28 and 30, 2013; and March 9, 2013.

219: She heard the gospel and "was saved": Joan Mellen interview with Meredithe Nix, Dallas, November 22, 2013.

219: there was a hitchhiker in the car: Conversation with Michael Wallace, November 27, 2012.

219: Virginia filed for divorce: Cause #D-32250 was dated December 3, 1969, and was filed December 9, 1969, in the court of the Honorable H. Walter Steiner, Department #15, Superior Court of California, County of Orange. See also: Interlocutory Judgment of Dissolution of Marriage, D-32250. In re the marriage of Petitioners Virginia A. Wallace and Respondent, Malcolm E. Wallace. Filed February 16, 1970.

219: all Mac Wallace has is $300: Mary C. Bounds, "Accused Man's Relatives Dispute Estes' Story," *Dallas Morning News*, March 29, 1984, p. 1A.

219: "he was overqualified": Quoted in David Hanners, "Files on Wallace Missing, Officials Say," *Dallas Morning News*, May 13, 1984.

220: "mediocrity . . . a nondescript family member": Author interview with Nora Ann Carroll Stevenson, January 16, 2013.

220: "No Johnson has ever lived beyond the age of sixty": Drew Pearson Diary for January 16, 1967 — Addendum. LBJ library.

220: Mac Wallace writes out his will: Dallas County (Texas) Probate Court, File # 71–350.

220: He talked about having a medical workup: Joan Mellen conversation with Meredithe Nix, June 5, 2012.

221: Mac Wallace's car hits a bridge abutment near Pittsburg, Texas, and he is killed: There was a brief story about Wallace's accident with a photograph of the automobile in the *Pittsburg (Texas) Gazette*, January 14, 1971.

221: statement of Ronny Lough on Mac Wallace's car accident in Camp County: provided by genealogist Glenda Kinard, April 17, 2012.

221: suffering from narcolepsy: Mary C. Bounds, "Accused man's relatives dispute Estes' story," *Dallas Morning News*, March 29, 1984.

222: he must have taken his own life: Joan Mellen telephone conversation with Nora Ann Carroll Stevenson.

222: David Wallace tied the necktie ("one of mine since he did not own one"): E-mail from Dave Wallace to William E. Carroll, August 14, 2003.

222: "The body was easily recognizable": James Wallace to William E. Carroll. E-mail from Bill Carroll to Joan Mellen, January 9, 2013. Connie Perdue views Mac Wallace's body: Author interview with Connie Perdue, January 9, 2013.

222: Mac Wallace's death certificate: Texas death certificate #07899-71.
Living on into the millennium, David Wallace was vehement in his refusal to talk to the author. "Don't call again!" he snarled. He was the last surviving sibling of Mac Wallace.

223: Benny Binion, a cohort of Meyer Lansky: Larry Hancock, *Someone Would Have Talked* (Southlake, TX: JFK Lancer Productions, 2010), p. 253. Billie Sol Estes, in *Billie Sol Estes: A Texas Legend* (Granbury, TX: BS Productions, 2005), p. 41, refers to Binion and how Jack Ruby was a frequent customer of Binion's. William Reymond talks about Binion and the Horseshoe Casino in Las Vegas in an unfinished, untitled video about Estes.

223: Inventory and Appraisement. No. 71-350 P/2, in re: Estate of Malcolm Everett Wallace, deceased. In the Probate Court Number Two of Dallas County, Texas. December 15, 1971 and April 4, 1984.

223: "dangerous": Arthur M. Schlesinger Jr., *Robert Kennedy and His Times* (Houghton Mifflin: Boston, 1978), p. 282.

223: "Kill this man!" Holland McCombs notebook. Holland McCombs Papers, Box 149, File 16.

224: "whup Sonny Liston": Dorothy Tiffin to Holland McCombs, Holland to "DAY PRESS PAID." December 2, 1964. Holland McCombs Papers, Box 149, File 6.

224: "well-sealed off from reality," "manic-depressive cycle," and "private monster . . . public statesman": See Arthur M. Schlesinger Jr., *Journals: 1952–2000* (New York: Penguin, 2008), pp. 280, 306, 333.

224: W. Tom Johnson arranges a book party for Bill Moyers: Dallek, *Flawed Giant*, p. 606.

224: the LaRue Corporation: John Clarence and Tom Whittle, *The Gold House: The Lies, The Thefts*, Book 2 (Las Cruces, NM: Soledad Publishing Company, 2012), p. 252.

224–225: The source for these details of Johnson and the Victorio Peak gold is Chapter 18, Clarence and Whittle, "The Kennedy-Johnson Tour at White Sands, Mr. H and the CIA," in *Gold House*, pp. 185–201); in addition to Joan Mellen conversations with John Clarence; and tape of interview with Hugh James Huggins, who reported flying back and forth between Johnson properties in Chihuahua, Mexico. See Clarence, p. 261. Huggins was interviewed by Jack Staley (John Clarence) on July 2, 2006, in Waco, Texas.

225: "bitter and tormented": Letter from Jerome T. Ragsdale to Madeleine Brown, May 18, 1973.

225: "old, weary, and battered": Eric F. Goldman, *The Tragedy of Lyndon Johnson* (New York: Alfred A. Knopf, 1969), p. 512.

225: "smoked like a fiend . . . excessively fat": Dallek, *Flawed Giant*, pp. 602–603.

225: "the damn press always accused me of things I didn't do": Quoted in Leo Janos, "The Last Days of the President: LBJ in Retirement," *The Atlantic* (July 1973).

225: "wanted peace more than I." Ibid.

225: "a damned Murder Inc. in the Caribbean": Ibid.

225–226: Ramsey Clark would argue that Jim Garrison had been unfair in his prosecution of Clay Shaw: Joan Mellen interview with Ramsey Clark, February 21, 2000. New York City.

226: Bobby Baker visits Lyndon Johnson at his ranch in October 1972. This visit is described in Bobby Baker, *Wheeling and Dealing: Confessions of a Capitol Hill Operator* (New York: W. W Norton, 1978); and in Robert G, Baker, Oral History Interview II, Op. Cit., p. 15ff, LBJ Library.

226: "I wonder what it was he had to fear": Baker, *Wheeling and Dealing*, p. 275.

226: Baker asks Johnson to "put in a good word": Ibid., p. 281.

226: Baker says Rebozo had been "a real warm friend of mine": Bobby Baker, Oral History Interviews, April 27 to August 21, 1990, by Donald A. Ritchie, Senate Historical Office, Washington, D. C.

226: "big black headlines": *Wheeling and Dealing*, p. 196.

226: "sold out and gone sour": Ibid., p. 40.

227: "How about this damned Texas tycoon?" Baker, *Wheeling and Dealing*, p. 117.

227: "Christ-like character": Robert G. Baker, Oral History Interview I, October 23, 1974, p. 5, LBJ Library.

227: "intellectual superiority . . . a genius": Robert G. Baker, Oral History Interview III, pp. 1–3, LBJ Library.

227: Johnson listened repeatedly to "Bridge Over Troubled Water": Michael Beschloss, "LBJ Agonized over His Legacy," December 4, 2012.

227–228: The views of Dr. Martin Luther King Jr. just before his assassination are outlined in Tavis Smiley with David Ritz, *Death of a King: The Real Story of Dr. Martin Luther King's Final Year* (New York: Little, Brown, 2014), pp. 95, 183, 213.

228: "To be black in a white society": Dallek, *Flawed Giant*, pp. 621–22.

228: Details of Lyndon Johnson's last day and his funeral may be found in Dallek, *Flawed Giant*, pp. 622–23.

228: the Treasury Department holds gold bars for Lady Bird Johnson: Clarence and Whittle, *Gold House*, Book 2, p. 533.

16: Billie Sol Estes Creates an Urban Legend

229: "personal hit man": Roger Stone, *The Man Who Killed Kennedy: The Case Against LBJ* (New York: Skyhorse Publishing, 2013), p. 81. Madeleine Brown had Mac Wallace as a guest at the Murchison party, only later to remove his name. Roger Stone restores Mac Wallace to the Murchison guest list: Stone, p. 234.

230: "making deals and having fun": Billie Sol Estes, *Billie Sol Estes: A Texas Legend* (Granbury, TX: BS Productions, 2005), p. 130.

230: "regretfully, I have become a liar": Pam Estes, *Billie Sol: The Man Who Knows Who Shot JFK, King of Texas Wheeler-Dealers* (Pamelaco Productions, no city of publication, 2004), p. 173.

230: "lying and bragging": Billie Sol Estes, p. 135.

230: "the people who had the most to lose": James M. Day, *Captain Clint Peoples, Texas Ranger: Fifty Years a Lawman* (Waco: Texian Press, 1980), p. 135.

230: Shearn Moody: See James R. Norman, "Texas Gothic," *Forbes* 146, no. 9 (October 22, 1990). For a file of clippings on Shearn Moody, see Gus Russo Papers, Box 8, File 33, W. R. Poage Legislative Library, Baylor University.

231: Shearn Moody meets Jack Ruby: FBI. December 19, 1963. Special Agent Leo L. Robertson. CR 105. File #DL 44-1639.

231: Congressman Wright Patman's exposure of CIA involvement in foundations, including the Moody Foundation, is well documented. Patman exposed 534 foundations from 1951 through 1960: Louis M. Kohlmeier, "How President Uses a Family Foundation to Donate to Charity," *Wall Street Journal*, June 30, 1964, p. 1. See also "Heat on Foundations," *Business Week* (September 19, 1964), p. 39; "Panel Questions Foundations' Pay," *New York Times*, August 11, 1964; Felton West, "Foundations," Papers of Oveta Culp Hobby, Fondren Library, Rice University; E. W. Kenworthy, "Triple Pass: How C.I.A. Shifts Funds," *New York Times*, February 19, 1967, pp. 1, 26; Eileen Shanahan, "Limits on Foundations," *New York Times*, February 11, 1965; and "House of Glass," *Newsweek*, March 6, 1967.

231: "the sleaziest man in Texas:" Gary Cartwright, "The Sleaziest Man in Texas: A Story of Swindling, Scandal, and Sex," *Texas Monthly* (August 1987).

231: "blow the legs off": "In Galveston, Moody's Blues," *Newsweek* (February 2, 1987), p. 33.

231: a "history buff": Author interview with Douglas Caddy, December 18, 2013.

232: Estes poured out his tale to Moody: Joan Mellen interview with Douglas Caddy, December 18, 2013. Estes hoped Moody would fund a book devoted to telling his story.

232: how John Connally attempted to take over the Moody Foundation: E-mail from Douglas Caddy, March 16, 2006, posted on EducationForum.com.

232: Connally had been briefed by the IRS on Project Southwest: James R. Norman, "Texas Gothic," was a senior editor at *Forbes* magazine at the time. *Forbes*, 146, no. 9 (October 22, 1990). The Securities and Exchange Commission (SEC) was also enlisted in the harassment campaign, according to Watergate Committee documents. "In a separate investigation in 1972, the SEC closed down Moody's private bank on the grounds that its certificates of deposit were actually being sold as unregulated securities—the first time such action was taken against a private bank ... in 1988 Moody was convicted of improperly taking money from the Moody Foundation and was booted off the foundation's board of trustees." Moody contended that he was innocent. A federal appeals court eventually threw out two of the thirteen counts on which he had been convicted and sent the rest back for a retrial.

232: on guard against Connally's ambitions: Douglas Caddy, e-mail to Joan Mellen, March 16, 2006, EducationForum.com.

233: Douglas Caddy relates: "The Conservative Caucus, a national organization, was founded in the 1970s and headed by Howard Phillips. He was a founder of Young Americans for Freedom in 1960 when he was President of the Student Council at Harvard U., which was when I first met him. He died a few years ago. He was a close friend. When I was working in the Texas Secretary of State's office as Director of Elections in 1980, Howard contacted me and asked that I form the Texas Policy Institute as a 301(c)(3) tax exempt organization. The Moody Foundation could only give a grant to a Texas tax-exempt entity. I formed it and obtained the tax-exempt status and as a result it got a Moody Foundation grant in 1982. I resigned from the Secretary of State's office and became head of the Institute. The Institute, among other activities, sponsored a conference in Galveston in 1982 on the Star Wars concept, which President Reagan had not yet formally announced. Among the attendees of that conference was J. Evetts Haley. *The Dallas Morning News* carried an article on the conferences". E-mail from Douglas Caddy, April 11, 2016.

233: Douglas Caddy later defined himself as a "progressive liberal": E-mail from Douglas Caddy to John Simkin, January 18, 2006.

233: "I'm going to put Billie Sol Estes on the line": Author interview with Douglas Caddy.

233: "a secret financial empire": Douglas Caddy, "Shearn Moody Jr.," p. 2, March 16, 2006, EducationForum.com.

233: For the description of Billie Sol Estes in his prime: "thick-bodied, round-shouldered, bull-necked": See Evan Moore, "The Secrets of Billie Sol," *Houston Chronicle*, June 23, 1996.

233: Estes trusted Peoples: See "LBJ Accused," *Tyler (Texas) News*, March 23, 1984.

233: "one thing I want you to tell me": Charlotte-Anne Lucas, "Taking Care of Business: Lawman Solves Mystery After 23 Years of Trying," *Dallas Times Herald*, March 23, 1984.

234: "he wanted to get his life straight with the Lord": Quoted in Charlotte-Anne Lucas.

234: "killed because he was in the way of people": "LBJ Link Claimed in Official's Death," *Kilgore (Texas) News Herald*, March 29, 1984.

234: Estes would not testify about the other murders because he wasn't granted immunity for these: Billie Sol Estes, p. 138. Nor would he testify about whether Lyndon Johnson had had anything to do with the Kennedy assassination: William P. Barrett and Charlotte-Anne Lucas, "Sources: Estes Wouldn't Testify on JFK Assassination," *Dallas Times Herald*, March 25, 1984, p. 22A.

234: an investigator from Paschall's office tape records Billie Sol Estes' grand jury testimony: Joan Mellen interview with John Paschall, July 13, 2012.

234: Billie Sol Estes claims that Lyndon Johnson ordered the killing of Henry Marshall. This story made the papers all over Texas. See for example: David Hanners, "Billie Sol Links LBJ to Murder," *Dallas Morning News*, March 23, 1984; "Billie Sol Estes Says LBJ Ordered Official Killed," *Del Rio News-Herald*, March 23, 1984.

234: snow-covered: Busby exaggerated, stating that there was "six feet of snow" in the backyard: Horace Busby, Oral History Interview VIII, April 2, 1989, by Michael L. Gillette, LBJ Library.

235: Carter and Wallace meet with Estes at his Pecos home after Marshall is murdered: See Bill Adler, "The Killing of Henry Marshall," *Texas Observer* (November 7, 1986).

235: For the reactions of Mac Wallace's brothers and sister to the accusations of Billie Sol Estes, see William P. Barrett and Charlotte-Anne Lucas, "Family of Alleged 'Hit Man' Disputes Estes' Testimony," *Dallas Times Herald*, March 28, 1984.

235: Mac Wallace's brother provides an alibi for the day Henry Marshall was shot: Mary C. Bounds, "Accused Man's Relatives Dispute Estes' Story," *Dallas Morning News*, March 29, 1984, p. 1A; "Wallace's Brother Claims Alibi, Refutes Estes' Story," *Bryan (Texas) College Station Eagle*, March 30, 1984; Joan Mellen conversation with Michael Wallace.

236: "a portion of his application": "Was Billie Sol Estes Telling the Truth?" *Victoria (Texas) Advocate*, September 25, 1984.

236: "he and Johnson were in it together": Joan Mellen interview with John Paschall, July 13, 2012.

236: "Marshall had information that could link former President Johnson": David Hanners, "Files on Wallace Missing, Officials Say," *Dallas Morning News*, May 13, 1984. Many newspapers made this point: see also, for example, Deborah Wormser, "Estes Links LBJ to Murder," *Mid-Cities Daily News*, March 23, 1984.

236: "a multi-million-dollar political slush fund": See, for example, "Prison Doors Open For Billie Sol Estes," *San Antonio Express*, November 18, 1983; *The Sunday Express-News*, San Antonio, April 14, 1985.

236: Seventeen mysterious deaths: Ken Lanterman and Rebecca Pflugfelder, "Peoples: More Deaths May Be Tied to Estes," *Bryan (Texas) College Station Eagle*, March 24, 1984.

236: "just the word of an admitted con man": "Swindler Tells Jury LBJ Ordered '61 murder," *Galveston Daily News*, March 24, 1984. See also "Estes Worries For His Safety," *San Angelo Standard-Times*, March 24, 1984. The quotation appeared originally in the *Dallas Times Herald*.

236: "the first elected President accused of arranging a murder": Peter Hecht, "Footnote to History?" *Dallas Times Herald*, March 24, 1984.

236: "the believable hit man": There is a vivid description of Estes' scams in Bill Adler, "The Killing of Henry Marshall."

236: "I see no reason why he's not telling the truth": Wilson was quoted in newspapers all over Texas, including David Hanners, "Marshall Case: Federal Officials Uncooperative in Investigation," Bryan (Texas) *Eagle*, April 6, 1984; and "Believes Estes: Will Wilson, Texas Attorney General at the Time of Marshall's Death," *Dallas Times Herald*, April 6, 1984, pp. 15, 16A.

237: David Hanners searches for Mac Wallace files: David Hanners, "Files on Wallace Missing, Officials Say."

237: Ibid.

237: "inconceivable that Wallace could have held a management position on a missile contract and not have had a security clearance": According to Jim Crossland, the Vought spokesman. Ibid.

237: David Wallace reminded reporters: William F. Barrett and Charlotte-Anne Lucas, "Family of Alleged 'Hit Man' Disputes Estes' Testimony," *Dallas Times Herald*, March 28, 1994.

237: Estes never received the grant from Shearn Moody: e-mail to Joan Mellen from Douglas Caddy, February 20, 2015.

238: the death of George Krutilek is reopened by Sheriff Mike Davis: "Sheriff Reopens Probe into Death of Estes Associate," *Texas City Sun*, March 29, 1984.

238: the reply came back in the affirmative. Joan Mellen interview with Douglas Caddy. Op. Cit.

238: the deaths were ruled a murder-suicide: *El Paso Herald-Post*, February 28, 1964, p. 13.

239: Mac Wallace fired a shot from the grassy knoll that killed President Kennedy: Letter from Douglas Caddy to Stephen S. Trott, August 9, 1984.

239: Madeleine Brown claims that Mac Wallace killed the black nanny of her children: Madeleine

Brown interviewed in Lyle Sardie's film *LBJ: A Closer Look*. She makes this claim in her memoir, *Texas in the Morning: The Love Story of Madeleine Brown and President Lyndon Baines Johnson* (Baltimore: Conservatory Press, 1997) as well.

239–240: a pardon for the offenses for which he has been convicted: Stephen S. Trott, assistant attorney general, Criminal Division, U.S. Department of Justice. May 29, 1984.

240: "detailed debriefing": Letters from Stephen S. Trott to Douglas Caddy, September 13, 1984; Stephen S. Trott to Douglas Caddy, November 1, 1984. Irritated, Trott threatened that should Billie Sol Estes continue "to make allegations which he is unwilling or unable to support, it is a matter which we will report to his probation officer."

240: corroborative evidence is requested: Letter from Stephen S. Trott to Douglas Caddy, May 29, 1984. Caddy, Trott, and the litany of murders committed by Mac Wallace: see Stephen S. Trott to Douglas Caddy, September 13, 1984; and Stephen S. Trott to Douglas Caddy, November 1, 1984.

240: "completely, truthfully and without guile": Stephen S. Trott to Douglas Caddy, May 29, 1984. Available online under "The Estes Documents."

240: "false, misleading and materially incomplete": Stephen S. Trott to Douglas Caddy, September 13, 1984.

240: "my life would end": Billie Sol Estes, *Billie Sol Estes*, p. 162.

240: "You had your chance": Douglas Caddy, in conversation with Joan Mellen.

240: In a January 20, 2006, interview: Caddy was interviewed by John Simkin on EducationForum.com.

240: Kyle Brown calls Lyndon Johnson "a cold-blooded killer": Interview with Kyle Brown in *LBJ: A Closer Look*, directed by Lyle Sardie, 2003. Kyle Brown travels with Billie Sol Estes in 1984 on a "business matter": E-mail from Douglas Caddy to Lyle Sardie, July 10, 2012.

399: Estes changes the number of victims Mac Wallace has murdered to "more than eleven people, including President John Fitzgerald Kennedy": Billie Sol Estes, *Billie Sol Estes*, p. 54. The total went from eight to eleven to seventeen victims. "Lyndon should not have authorized Mac to kill the President," Estes writes piously on p. 143.

240: helped transfer cash: Kyle Brown asserts that he helped transfer cash to Lyndon Johnson and Cliff Carter on an untitled video directed by William Reymond in 2003.

241: Clint Peoples insists that Mac Wallace was both a homosexual and a Communist: Clint Peoples, Oral History Interview VII, November 21, 1984, p. 249, Dallas Public Library. Peoples elevates his own role in the Kinser investigation, presenting himself as having been in on the case from the first, which was not the truth. Peoples's views into 1984 remained benighted: "You see, homosexuality then was really frowned on. As far as I'm concerned, it ought to be frowned on now. I frown on it." Peoples then adds: "Homer Rainey and Mack [sic] Wallace were communistic friends" (pp. 251–52).

241: Wallace fit the composite drawing: Later Peoples changed his mind and expressed certainty that the composite depicted Mac Wallace.

241: "not be able to prove anything": Clint Peoples to James M. Day, 1980. Quoted in Day, *Captain Clint Peoples*, p. 135.

241: Clint Peoples wants the State of Texas to reopen its investigation into the death of Mac Wallace: "Marshall Wants Texas to Reopen Probe of Alleged Killer's Death," *Kerrville (Texas) Daily Times*, March 25, 1984. In fact, there never was an investigation in the first place. Barefoot Sanders, now a judge, chastised Clint Peoples: "Judges Chide Marshal over Estes' Testimony," *Mineral Wells (Texas) Index*, March 29, 1984; "U.S. Marshal Questioned About Estes," *Corsicana (Texas) Daily Sun*, March 29, 1984; Mary Ann Keps, "Flak Flies in Marshal Death Organization," *Waco Tribune-Herald*, April 13, 1984.

241: "Mack [sic] Wallace": Peoples' oral history, p. 247. "Mack Wallace and somebody else": Ibid., p. 254.

241: "faithful follower": Pam Estes, *Billie Sol*, p. 33.

241: Estes deleted passages from his ghostwritten memoir: E-mail from Tom Bowden to Treefrog, November 11, 2013. The late Ed Sherry's papers are housed at Baylor University in Waco, Texas.

241: "edited by him": Tom Bowden, conversation with Joan Mellen, 2012. Bowden spoke only briefly since he was working on his own book about Estes and Wallace. At this writing in mid-2016, the book has not yet appeared.

400: TK: Clint Peoples picked up Haley's inaccuracy, that Mac Wallace returned to Washington, D.C., and the Department of Agriculture after his conviction: Peoples, Oral History Interview VII, p. 253. So Peoples reveals his source.

400: See both Lyle Sardie's and William Reymond's videos for claims that Clint Peoples was murdered. Despite the assertions of a supposed eyewitness who has not come forward, the notion that Clint Peoples was murdered remains in the realm of speculation.

241: "Kyle Brown was not at the meeting with Cliff Carter": Billie Sol Estes, *Billie Sol Estes*, p. 163.

241–242: "I would speculate that Malcolm Wallace murdered George Krutilek": Ibid., p. 98.

242: "could be taken to implicate Lyndon Johnson as a murderer": EducationForum.com, January 13, 2005: William Reymond, author of *JFK: Le Dernier Témoin*.

242: it was the same voice: So Tom Bowden confided to researcher Alan Kent after he listened to a tape at the Johnson library. Alan Kent in conversation with Joan Mellen, November 11, 2012. Bowden told Kent that the voice he heard on the Estes tape was the same voice—Cliff Carter's—that he had matched to a tape of Carter's voice at the LBJ library.

242: Floyd Stephens comes forward: Stephens produced no documentary evidence of his father's involvement in the murder of Henry Marshall. He talked at length to historian Walt Brown, who says that Stephens produced nothing concrete, Stephens also talked with Austin lawyer Dawn Meredith and told her he had a "manuscript" and was planning to write a book. After Stephens's sudden death, his wife told Meredith that her lawyer had advised her to destroy the manuscript.

242: "Anything Lyndon wanted he got": Billie Sol Estes, interviewed by Joan Mellen, June 15, 2010. On another occasion, Estes insisted: "No one could explain LBJ" (April 8, 2000).

243: "You're going to do what I tell you": Billie Sol Estes, conversation with Joan Mellen, May 12, 2009.

243: "Mac Wallace would kill as easily as he would drink a Coke": Billie Sol Estes in conversation with Joan Mellen, June 15, 2010. Wallace's murderousness was as persistent a theme in our discussions as was Estes' fear and loathing of Lyndon Baines Johnson.

243: Mac Wallace knew Marina Oswald: Estes, p. 172.

243: George de Mohrenschildt: In my research into the life of de Mohrenschildt for *Our Man In Haiti: George de Mohrenschildt and the CIA in the Nightmare Republic* (Walterville, OR: TrineDay, 2012), I never came upon any evidence that de Mohrenschildt had met Mac Wallace.

243: "the assassin Mac Wallace": Stone made this assertion in a February 9, 2014, talk at Books & Books in Coral Gables, Florida, which was broadcast on C-Span's Book TV.

244: *Ask Not*: Max Allan Collins, *Ask Not* (New York: Tom Doherty Associates, 2013).

244: "Stop! This is not Billie Sol Estes": Stephen Pegues, "Texas Mafia," unpublished manuscript, p. 99. Pegues's videotapes of Billie Sol Estes have turned up in the hands of filmmaker Lyle Sardie: E-mail from Lyle Sardie to Joan Mellen, May 8, 2014. Other of Pegues's assertions are the following: "Lyndon sent Mac Wallace to Austin to deal with Kinser" (p. 31); Mac Wallace was "politically far to the left" (p. 41); Henry Wallace was Mac Wallace's uncle: "uncle was Secretary of Agriculture during the Franklin Roosevelt administration" (p. 29); Wallace killed

John Douglas Kinser with an "automatic pistol that he had borrowed from his college room-mate" (p. 37). Pegues adopts Madeleine Brown's story entirely (p. 176). His psychological analysis is equally questionable: "Killing Kinser fed Mac's narcissistic vulnerability" (p. 39). Pegues contends as well that Wallace had a "snake charming appeal" (p. 101). He does not place Mac Wallace at the backyard meeting (p. 98). A measure of his faulty research is how he characterizes Wallace's role in the protests against the firing of Homer Rainey. Wallace, Pegues asserts, was "inciting the students to riot against the governing order" (p. 34).

244: *The Men on the Sixth Floor:* The book was self-published in 2003.

244: Loy Factor required a legal guardian: This detail regarding Factor's incompetence comes to us from a book so riddled with errors that it offers diminished credibility, Vincent Bugliosi's *Reclaiming History: The Assassination of President John F. Kennedy* (New York: W. W. Norton, 2007), p. 919. Yet despite its flaws, Bugliosi's book does offer some facts, and this one about Factor appears to be one of them. The Loy Factor story is, indeed, as "silly" as Bugliosi suggests that it is. It's a comic-book version of the Kennedy assassination designed to blame Mac Wallace for the murder of President Kennedy.

245: "We make sausage meat out of people like him": Billie Sol Estes to researcher Ed Tatro.

245: Ed Clark didn't have the courage to be involved in the Kennedy assassination: Joan Mellen interview with his nephew, Guy Cade Fisher, January 10, 2013.

245: McClellan's depiction of the backyard meeting, where the murder of Henry Marshall was supposedly planned: See Barr McClellan, *Blood, Money & Power: How L.B.J. Killed J.F.K.* (New York: Hannover House, 2003). McClellan includes only three participants, Johnson, Estes, and Cliff Carter. In one of the few specific citations in the book, he cites the Clark Collection, Box 17, File 388, Southwestern University Library, Georgetown, Texas. There isn't a single reference to the meeting in Washington in the box and file that McClellan names. The locution makes it seem as if there were four people at the meeting, but the fourth was not Mac Wallace, but "one of Clark's former army buddies," which McClellan told the author was a reference to Cliff Carter.

The errors come fast and furious: Bill Carroll, a law student at the time, did not post bond for Mac Wallace. Carroll was not married to Mary Jo Carroll, a partner in the Clark law firm, where McClellan was employed until he came into conflict with Ed Clark. There is no evidence that the Office of Naval Intelligence was "oversee[ing] Wallace on behalf of Johnson." In fact, from 1957 on, the Navy opposed Wallace's security clearance and recommended that it be revoked and denied. Gus Lanier, the attorney who attended the Kinser trial for a few days, was not juror Deckerd Johnson's "uncle" but his first cousin. After the trial, Wallace went to work not for D. H. Byrd's TEMCO, but for Jonco Aircraft in Oklahoma, where his family lived for almost two years.

Mac Wallace did not marry a second time in California in 1961, but in Mexico in 1963. He did not "build up" property in California. When he returned to Texas in 1969, he owned no tangible assets. The 1984 Grand Jury in Robertson County did not "conclude that Johnson, Carter and Wallace were the co-conspirators in the murder of Henry Marshall." Billie Sol Estes asserted that claim. Nor did Estes ever produce any evidence that Wallace had murdered Josefa Johnson. Mac Wallace could not have driven back to California "to his waiting wife and daughter." In November 1963 he was separated from Virginia Ledgerwood and was living with his son, Michael. I have not even begun to chart the absurdities, among them this: "People of Johnson's, Clark's and Wallace's disposition tend to be grandiose and egocentric, having the so-called presidential gene."

The invented dialogue is equally embarrassing. "You still in the cause?" the fictional Wallace asks the fictional Oswald. "Oswald was also a Marxist," McClellan writes (p. 263), which was not the case. That Mac Wallace wanted to "make the world safe for extreme socialism" (p. 75) is preposterous.

Although I requested evidence from McClellan, he did not provide any corroboration for his statement that on the day of his death Mac Wallace, working for an Ed Clark crony, Harry Lewis, at L & G Oil had gone to blackmail Lewis (p. 242). Wallace supposedly was demanding a "bonus," hush money for his participation in the Kennedy assassination, nine years after the fact. That day the "exhaust" was "rigged for part of it to flow into his car." Mac Wallace was murdered, then, for his attempt to blackmail Lewis (and Ed Clark). In the source note for this description of the death of Wallace, McClellan writes only, "The medical report shows extensive physical injuries that are not consistent with the damages to the auto." There is nothing about L & G Oil, or supporting Mac Wallace's demand for hush money. McClellan mentions that an empty bottle of narcolepsy medicine was found in the car, again without a source.

I pressed McClellan only for him to write me that "Mac Wallace was killed by a man still living in Ft. Worth." E-mail from Barr McClellan to Joan Mellen, January 26, 2013.

In e-mail exchanges, I repeatedly asked Mr. McClellan for the sources of his description of the death of Mac Wallace. Promises of material forthcoming from his files in Gulfport, Mississippi, proved to be empty. When J Harrison read the manuscript, he begged McClellan to correct the errors. When he would not, J broke down and wept: Author interview with Walt Brown, September 1, 2012. E-mail from Walt Brown to Joan Mellen, June 20, 2013.

245: approval for the assassination occurred at a poker game at Brownie's restaurant in Dallas: Billie Sol Estes, p. 192. Michael Wallace remembers that his grandfather's office was in an adjacent building. His father took him for a haircut in a barbershop in the same group of buildings where Brownie's restaurant was located. Joan Mellen interview with Michael Wallace, December 11, 2012.

245–46: Lyndon Johnson and Jack Halfen: Stephen Pegues, "Texas Mafia," pp. 12–14:

246: Johnson as the perpetrator: Phillip F. Nelson, *LBJ: The Mastermind of JFK's Assassination* (New York: Skyhorse Publishing, 2013). See pp. 589–90. Nelson, among others, did not bother to reinvestigate and confirm that it was in fact Mac Wallace's fingerprint that had been discovered on the sixth floor of the Texas School Book Depository. In fact, as chapter seventeen of this book reveals, it was not.

246: "to help frame Oswald at the scene": Ibid., p. 311: See also pp. 271–98, 349, and 352. The fingerprint is discussed on p. 493.

246: Madeleine Brown and Billie Sol Estes gave interviews together on the subject of Lyndon Johnson and Mac Wallace: See Lyle Sardie, *LBJ: A Closer Look,* currently unavailable. See also the untitled and unpublished video by William Reymond. Brown continued to tell her story of a party on the night before the Kennedy assassination, varying her guest list, but usually including J. Edgar Hoover (although he was at his desk in Washington, D.C., the next morning), Mac Wallace, and Clint Peoples. Both Estes and Madeleine Brown supported the Loy Factor story. Factor would insist that he had done no shooting, although he was present at the sixth floor of the Texas School Book Depository. Pegues continued to insist that "Whatever this job was for, one thing was clear, Wallace was the boss of the project."

17: The Fingerprint

247: "You could go to the bank with the I.D. of that print": Walt Brown, conversation with Joan Mellen.

247: he insisted upon being addressed only by the letter "J": Malcolm Blunt, conversation with Joan Mellen, February 11, 2016.

248: after he turned his notebook over to the Dallas Police, Harrison never saw it again: E-mail from Walt Brown to Joan Mellen, June 6, 2012.

248: the security threat with which he was most concerned: Joan Mellen interview with Walt Brown, September 2014. Harrison designated Brown as the heir to his archives and Brown spent a great deal of time with him in the last years of his life.

248: I "creep around unknown": E-mail from J Harrison to Ed Sherry, April 2, 2004.

248: "more parts of the problem": Author interviews with Walt Brown, September 2012, and Dawn Meredith.

249: He spoke through implication: This portrait of Harrison was created with the help of his friends Ed Sherry, Malcolm Blunt, Walt Brown, Dawn Meredith, and Rachel Rendish.

249: "It was not John": William Reymond, untitled video, 2003.

250: "3 years ago in Lost Wages at Benny Binion's": E-mail from J Harrison to Ed Sherry, July 9, 2004.

250: Mac Wallace's FBI file: The author filed a Freedom of Information suit with the FBI on January 19, 2013, for a reprocessing of the Mac Wallace file in the hope that the redacted documents might be released in their original condition. The Bureau's first response was to deny on February 6, 2013, that a file even existed. When evidence was provided to them by Freedom of Information Act (FOIA) lawyer Daniel S. Alcorn that they had already released a file held for Malcolm Everett Wallace in the 1990s, the Bureau agreed to process Alcorn's appeal. The date was now June 10, 2013. Periodically, the Bureau sent follow-ups stating that they were "searching the FBI's indices for potentially responsive documents." Late in 2014, the FBI sent an unredacted, reprocessed FBI file for Mac Wallace to Mr. Alcorn.

251: "The party (if any took place) . . .": E-mail from J Harrison to Ed Sherry, April 2, 2004.

251: "Wallace survived the crash": Walt Brown recounted this information in an issue of *Deep Politics Quarterly* devoted to Mac Wallace. Brown also related this information to me in conversation.

252: a gun under his pillow: E-mail from Walt Brown to Joan Mellen, June 23, 2012.

252: Malcolm Blunt talked to Harrison right after his files were stolen from his car: E-mail from Malcolm Blunt to Joan Mellen, February 11, 2016.

252: old bread truck: Obituary, Harrison, John Fraser (J & Jay), by J Harrison. Courtesy of Dawn Meredith and Rachel Rendish. Self-published and circulated among friends.

252: "some people forget things . . . others remember things that never happened": E-mail from John Fraser Harrison to Ed Sherry (Treefrog), July 19, 2004.

252: J Harrison's investigative brainstorm: Harrison's efforts to obtain Mac Wallace's finger-prints: Ron M. Pigott to Mr. J. Harrison, March 29, 1996; J Harrison to Ben Kyser, March 22, 1996; Ron M. Pigott to Dan Morales, Attorney General of Texas, March 29, 1996, re: Public Information Request of J Harrison for the Criminal History Record Information of Malcolm Everett Wallace, Deceased; Ron M. Pigott to Mr. J. Harrison, July 26, 1996. Records of J Harrison. On the Texas Open Records Act, see J Harrison to Toni Chovanetz, Records Section, Austin Police Department, February 18, 1999. Files of J Harrison.

253: Mac Wallace's fingerprints taken when he entered the U.S. Marine Corps: U.S. military records were "reappraised" in 1999, ceasing to be the property of the agency that had created them, in this case the Navy. The process was finalized only in 2004 when military personnel files were transferred to the National Archives and Records Administration (NARA), thereby becoming permanent records of the United States. Previously only the subject himself or a designated next of kin or law enforcement could access military personnel files.

254: Nathan Darby writes to J Harrison: March 9, 1998. Files of J Harrison.

255: "Drop it! Leave it alone": Darby related this incident to J Harrison, who repeated it to Walt Brown.

255: "They match! They match!" Nathan Darby interviewed in the William Reymond video, 2003.

255: "Compare developed latent impressions with known impressions to establish identity": Contract of Employment, State of Texas, County of Travis. Dated April 15, 1998. Signed by E. H. Hoffmeister. Files of J Harrison.

256: "unknown generations of COPIES of the latent and NOT THE ORIGINAL": E. H. Hoffmeister to Mr. Barr McClellan, April 16, 1998. Records of J Harrison.

256: "untrackable": Joan Mellen interview with William P. Barrett, May 30, 2012.

257: "I would bet my paycheck . . . We had the first discussion on the night of the assassination": Joan Mellen interview with Michael Wallace, December 27, 2012.

257: "not at the top of the pyramid": Joan Mellen interview with Walt Brown, September 1, 2012, and Dawn Meredith. See also Dawn Meredith on EducationForum.com, May 26, 2005.

259: A "discrepancy," Garrett writes: Re: Evaluation and Comparison of Fingerprints. May 19, 2013. Including charts and illustrations and diagrams. Available in the Appendix to this book.

261: Richard Randolph Carr's statement: May 18, 1967. To: Jim Garrison. From: Penn Jones. Re: Investigation; February 3, 1964. Dallas, Texas. See also: handwritten Statement of R. R. Carr. 7 pages. The witness was Paul L. Scott, Special Agent, FBI, 2/3/64. The statement is signed both by Carr and Scott. It's a rare hand-written document released by the Dallas FBI from its "Oswald 100 Series Files."

261: on the matter of Nathan Darby's certification: Memo: Bob Garrett to Joan Mellen, August 11, 2014.

261: Garrett did further research: E-mail from Bob Garrett, July 1, 2013. Subject: FW: CLPE inquiry; Jamie Bush to Bob Garrett, July 1, 2013; Bob Garrett to Jamie Bush, June 28, 2013; Bob Garrett to Joan Mellen, July 2, 2013; Bob Garrett to Joan Mellen, July 1, 2013; Jamie Bush to Bob Garrett, July 1, 2013; Bob Garrett to Jamie Bush, June 28, 2013; Bob Garrett to Joan Mellen, July 3, 2013. Jamie Bush is the current Secretary of the International Association for Identification's Latent Print Certification Board, a post held previously by Garrett.

EPILOGUE

263: "The truth is so often that which we do not say": Holland McCombs to William Lambert, June 11, 1964. "SUGGESTIONS, IDEAS, AND UP-COMINGS FOR POSSIBLE INCLUSION IN SECOND DRAFT AND FOR INFO IN PRESENTING FIRST DRAFT." Holland McCombs Papers.

264: "Were they shooting at me?": Fletcher Prouty interviewed in John Barbour's 1992 film, *The Garrison Tapes.*

264: "hiding in the toilet": Select Committee of Assassinations. Mark Flanagan interview with Brigadier General Godfrey McHugh, May 11, 1978, Washington D.C. McHugh served as the Air Force Military Aide to the President. NARA.

264: J Harrison runs into Billie Sol Estes at a hospital: E-mail from Walt Brown to Joan Mellen, June 12, 2013.

265: "Texas group": William Reymond contends that a "Texas group" committed the Estes-connected murders. Education Forum, January 13, 2005.

265: "He used Mac Wallace's name as an alias for somebody else": EducationForum.com, January 13, 2005: William Reymond: *JFK Le Dernier Témoin.*

265: "We always used false names": Billie Sol Estes, *Billie Sol Estes: A Texas Legend.*

266: Nora Ann Carroll Stevenson's's dream: Nora Ann Carroll Stevenson, in conversation with Joan Mellen, June 10, 2013.

266: meeting at the Driskill Hotel: Billie Sol Estes, *Billie Sol Estes,* p. 138.

266: connecting Lyndon Johnson with Billie Sol Estes: Notes to Possum Kingdom Coon Creek Club, Box 149, File 11. Holland McCombs Papers.

267: Johnson made his money selling political influence: Holland McCombs, "Notes," Box 149, File 15. Holland McCombs Papers.

267: LBJ and Hoover telephone call of November 23, 1963: Transcript and Bradford article may be found on History-Matters.com. Courtesy of Rex Bradford.

Bibliography

Adler, Bill. "The Killing of Henry Marshall," *Texas Observer*, November 7, 1986.

Allen, Robert J., JD. *Beyond Treason: Reflections on the Cover-up of the June 1967 Israeli Attack on the USS Liberty an American Spy Ship*. Self-published, 2012.

Baker, Bobby. *Wheeling and Dealing: Confessions of a Capitol Hill Operator*. New York: W. W. Norton, 1978.

Bamford, James. *Body of Secrets: Anatomy of the Ultra-Secret National Security Agency, From the Cold War Through the Dawn of a New Century*. New York: Doubleday, 2001.

Beschloss, Michael. *Reaching for Glory: Lyndon Johnson's Secret White House Tapes, 1964–1965*. New York: Simon & Schuster, 2001.

Binkley, William C. *The Expansionist Movement in Texas, 1836–1850*. New York: Da Capo Press, 1970. Originally published in 1925.

Brown, Madeleine Duncan. *Texas in the Morning: The Love Story of Madeleine Brown and President Lyndon Baines Johnson*. Baltimore: Conservatory Press, 1997.

Bugliosi, Vincent. *Reclaiming History: The Assassination of President John F. Kennedy*. New York: W. W. Norton, 2007.

Byrd, David Harold "Dry Hole". *I'm An Endangered Species: The Autobiography of a Free Enterpriser*. Houston: Pacesetter Press, 1978.

Campbell, Randolph B. *Gone To Texas: A History of the Lone Star State*. New York: Oxford University Press, 2003.

———. *Sam Houston and the American Southwest*. New York: Longman, 2001.

Canning, Peter. *American Dreamers: The Wallaces and Reader's Digest: An Insider Story*. New York: Simon & Schuster, 1996.

Cantrell, Gregg. *Stephen F. Austin: Empresario of Texas*. New Haven, CT: Yale University Press, 1999.

Carleton, Don E. *Red Scare! Right-Wing Hysteria, Fifties Fanaticism and Their Legacy in Texas*. Austin: Texas Monthly Press, 1985.

Caro, Robert A. *The Years of Lyndon Johnson: The Passage of Power*. New York: Alfred A. Knopf, 2012. Although the time frame is appropriate, Caro does not mention either Billie Sol Estes or Mac Wallace in the text. Nor does he discuss the premature death of Josefa Johnson.

———. *The Years of Lyndon Johnson: Master of the Senate*. New York: Alfred A. Knopf, 2002.

———. *The Years of Lyndon Johnson: Means of Ascent*. New York: Alfred A. Knopf, 1990.

———. *The Years of Lyndon Johnson: The Path to Power*. New York: Alfred A. Knopf, 1982.

Chariton, Wallace O, Charlie Eckhardt, and Kevin R. Young. *Unsolved Texas Mysteries*. Plano, TX: Wordware, 1991.

Clark, John E. *The Fall of the Duke of Duval: A Prosecutor's Journal.* Austin: Eakin Press, 1999.

Collins, Max Allan. *Ask Not: A Nathan Heller Thriller.* New York: Tom Doherty Associates, 2013. Mac Wallace appears as a central character who is murdered by the hero in this shoddy potboiler.

Cowger, Thomas W., and Sherwin J. Markman, eds. *Lyndon Johnson Remembered: An Intimate Portrait of a Presidency.* Oxford, UK: Rowman & Littlefield, 2003.

Cristol, A. Jay. *The Liberty Incident Revealed: The Definitive Account of the 1967 Israeli Attack on the U.S. Navy Spy Ship.* Annapolis, MD: Naval Institute Press, 2013. This book is without scholarly value and seems part of a propaganda campaign by supporters of the cover-up of the assault on the USS *Liberty.* Cristol's book is unique in its unacknowledged embrace of the Israeli point of view.

Dallek, Robert. *Lyndon Johnson: Portrait of a President.* New York: Oxford University Press, 2004.

———. *Flawed Giant: Lyndon Johnson and His Times, 1961–1973.* New York: Oxford University Press, 1998.

———. *Lone Star Rising: Lyndon Johnson and His Times, 1908–1960.* New York: Oxford University Press, 1991.

Day, James M. *Captain Clint Peoples, Texas Ranger: Fifty Years a Lawman.* Waco: Texian Press, 1980. The case of Mac Wallace, with which Peoples was obsessed for a lifetime, occupies a scant three pages.

De Bruhl, Marshall. *Sword of San Jacinto: A Life of Sam Houston.* New York: Random House, 1993.

Dugger, Ronnie. *The Politician: The Life and Times of Lyndon Johnson.* New York: W. W. Norton, 1982.

———. *Our Invaded Universities: Form, Reform, and New Starts: A Nonfiction Play For Five Stages.* New York: W. W. Norton, 1974.

Ennes Jr., James M. *Assault on the Liberty: The True Story of the Israeli Attack on an American Intelligence Ship.* Reprint: Reintree Press, 2007. Originally published by Random House in 1979.

Estes, Billie Sol. *Billie Sol Estes: A Texas Legend.* Granbury, TX: BS Productions, 2005.

Estes, Pam. *Billie Sol: King of Texas Wheeler-Dealers.* Granbury, TX: Pamelaco Productions, 1983.

Fehrenbach, T. R. *Lone Star: A History of Texas and the Texans.* New York: American Legacy Press, 1983.

Gallo, Ernest A. *Liberty Injustices: A Survivor's Account of American Bigotry.* Palm Coast, FL: ClearView Press, 2013.

Gentry, Curt. *J. Edgar Hoover: The Man and the Secrets.* New York: W. W. Norton, 1991.

Goldman, Eric F. *The Tragedy of Lyndon Johnson.* New York: Alfred A. Knopf, 1969.

Goldstein, Gordon M. *Lessons in Disaster: McGeorge Bundy and the Path to War in Vietnam.* New York: Henry Holt, 2008.

Goodwin, Doris Kearns. *Lyndon Johnson and the American Dream.* New York: St. Martin's Press, 1991. There is no reference to either Mac Wallace or Billie Sol Estes in the index, and precious little on Josefa (here called "Josepha").

Guthman, Edwin O., and Jeffrey Shulman, eds. *Robert Kennedy: In His Own Words.* New York: Bantam Books, 1988.

Haley, J. Evetts. *A Texan Looks at Lyndon: A Study in Illegitimate Power.* Canyon, TX: Palo Duro Press, 1964.

———. "The University of Texas and the Issue," 1–31. N.d. Monograph available from the Dolph Briscoe Center for American History, University of Texas at Austin.

Hancock, Larry. *Someone Would Have Talked.* Southlake, TX: JFK Lancer Productions, 2010.

Hardin, Stephen L. *Texian Iliad: A Military History of the Texas Revolution, 1835–1836.* Austin: University of Texas Press, 1994.

Hersh, Burton. *Bobby and J. Edgar: The Historic Face-Off Between the Kennedys and J. Edgar Hoover that Transformed America.* New York: Basic Books, 2007.

Hershman, D. Jablow. *Power Beyond Reason: The Mental Collapse of Lyndon Johnson*. Fort Lee, NJ: Barricade, 2002.

Hounam, Peter. *Operation Cyanide: Why the Bombing of the USS Liberty Nearly Caused World War III*. London: Vision, 2003.

Jackson, H. Joaquin, and James L. Haley. *One Ranger Returns*. Bridwell Texas History Series. Austin: University of Texas Press, 2008.

James, Marquis. *The Raven: A Biography of Sam Houston*. New York: Paperback Library, 1996. Originally published in 1929.

Johnson, Lyndon Baines. *The Vantage Point: Perspectives of the Presidency, 1963–1969*. New York: Holt, Rinehart and Winston, 1971.

Jones, Anson. *Memoranda and Official Correspondence Relating to the Republic of Texas, Its History and Annexation*. Chicago: Rio Grande Press, 1966. Originally published in 1859.

Karalekas, Anne. *History of the Central Intelligence Agency*. Laguna Hills, CA: Aegean Park Press, 1977. Sponsored by CIA.

Karnow, Stanley. *Vietnam: A History*. New York: Penguin, 1984.

Lane, Mark. *Rush to Judgment*. New York: Holt, Rinehart & Winston, 1966.

Lasky, Victor. *It Didn't Start with Watergate*. New York: Dial Press, 1977.

McClellan, Barr. *Blood, Money, & Power: How L.B.J. Killed J.F.K.* New York: Hannover House, 2003.

McDonald, Hugh C. *Appointment in Dallas: The Final Solution to the Assassination of JFK*. New York: Hugh McDonald Publishing, 1975.

McGarvey, Patrick J. *C.I.A.: The Myth and the Madness*. New York: Penguin, 1972.

Nash Smith, Henry. "The Controversy at the University of Texas, 1939–1945." A Paper Read at the Request of the Student Committee for Academic Freedom, August 13, 1945. Published by the Student Committee for Academic Freedom, Students' Association, University of Texas.

Nelson, Phillip F. *LBJ: The Mastermind of JFK's Assassination*. Self-published by Xlibris Corporation, 2010. Reissued by Skyhorse Publishing, New York, 2013.

North, Mark. *Act of Treason: The Role of J. Edgar Hoover in the Assassination of President Kennedy*. New York: Skyhorse Publishing, 2011.

Oglesby, Carl. *The Yankee and Cowboy War*. New York: Berkley Medallion Books, 1977.

Paget, Karen M. *Patriotic Betrayal: The Inside Story of the CIA's Secret Campaign to Enroll American Students in the Crusade Against Communism*. New Haven, CT: Yale University Press, 2015.

Pearson, Anthony. *Conspiracy of Silence: The Attack on the U.S.S. Liberty*. London: Quartet Books, 1978.

Pegues, Stephen. "Texas Mafia." Unpublished manuscript.

Pratt, Joseph A., and Christopher J. Castaneda. *Builders: Herman and George R. Brown*. College Station: Texas A & M University Press, 1999.

Rainey, Homer P. *The Tower and the Dome*. Boulder, CO: Pruett Press, 1971.

Reedy, George. *Lyndon B. Johnson: A Memoir*. New York: Andrews McMeel, 1985.

Reymond, William, and Billie Sol Estes. *JFK: Le Dernier Témoin*. Paris: Flammarion, 2003.

Ross Sr., Robert Gaylon. *The Elite Serial Killers of Lincoln, JFK, RFK, and MLK*. RIE Publishers, 2001.

Sample, Glen, and Mark Collom. *The Men on the Sixth Floor*. Sample Graphics, 2003.

Schlesinger Jr., Arthur M. *Journals: 1952–2000*. New York: Penguin, 2008.

Schmitz, Joseph William. *Texas Culture in the Days of the Republic, 1836–1846*. San Antonio: Naylor Company, 1960.

Schrecker, Ellen W. *No Ivory Tower: McCarthyism and the Universities*. New York: Oxford University Press, 1986.

Schreiber, G. R. *The Bobby Baker Affair: How to Make Millions in Washington.* Chicago: Henry Regnery, 1964.

Scott, James. *The Attack on the Liberty: The Untold Story of Israel's Deadly 1967 Assault on A U.S. Spy Ship.* New York: Simon & Schuster, 2009.

Shultz Jr., Richard. *The Secret War Against Hanoi.* New York: Perennial, 1999.

Siegel, Stanley. *A Political History of the Texas Republic, 1836–1845.* Austin: University of Texas Press, 1956.

Sizer, Mona D. *Outrageous Texas: Tales of the Rich and Infamous.* Boulder, CO: Taylor Trade Publishing, 2008.

Sloan, Bill, with Jean Hill. *JFK: The Last Dissenting Witness.* Gretna, LA: Pelican Publishing, 2008.

Smiley, Tavis, with David Ritz. *Death of a King: The Real Story of Dr. Martin Luther King's Final Year.* New York: Little, Brown, 2014.

Stone, Roger. *The Man Who Killed Kennedy: The Case Against LBJ.* New York: Skyhorse Publishing, 2013.

Swike, Jack R. *The Missing Chapter: Lee Harvey Oswald in the Far East.* Self-published, 2008. Swike describes himself as an intelligence officer in the U.S. Marine Corps stationed at Atsugi, Japan, with the Marine Air Group 11.

Theoharis, Athan G., and John Stuart Cox. *The Boss: J. Edgar Hoover and the Great American Inquisition.* Philadelphia: Temple University Press, 1988.

Tourney, Phillip, and Mark Glenn. *What I Saw That Day: Israel's June 8, 1967 Holocaust of US Servicemen Aboard the USS Liberty and its Aftermath.* Careywood, ID: Liberty Publications, n.d.

Van Buren, Ernestine Orrick. *Clint: Clinton Williams Murchison: A Biography.* Austin: Eakin Press 1986.

Williams, Elgin. *The Animating Pursuits of Speculation: Land Traffic in the Annexation of Texas.* New York: Columbia University Press, 1949.

Wolfe, Jane. *The Murchisons: The Rise and Fall of a Texas Dynasty.* New York: St. Martin's Paperbacks, 1989.

Zelizer, Julian E. *The Fierce Urgency of Now: Lyndon Johnson, Congress, and the Battle for the Great Society.* New York: Penguin Books: 2015.

Zirbel, Craig I. *The Texas Connection: The Assassination of President John F. Kennedy.* Scottsdale, AZ: Texas Connection Company Publishers, 1991.

Index

A Note on the Author

Joan Mellen is the author of twenty-two books, ranging from history (*Our Man in Haiti, The Great Game in Cuba,* and *A Farewell to Justice*) to true crime (*Privilege*) and sports (*Bob Knight: His Own Man*). Her profile of then-Indiana basketball coach Bob Knight was a *New York Times* bestseller, and her joint biography of Dashiell Hammett and Lillian Hellman was a finalist for the *Los Angeles Times* biography prize. She has also written works of film history and criticism and won a prize to study Japanese film in Japan sponsored by the *Mainichi Shimbun* newspaper. She has written four books about Japanese cinema.

She is a professor of English and Creative Writing at Temple University in Philadelphia where in 2004 she won Temple's highest distinction to faculty, the Great Teacher Award. She resides in New Jersey.